Magicians of Manumanua

Magicians of Manumanua

Living Myth in Kalauna

MICHAEL W. YOUNG

UNIVERSITY OF CALIFORNIA PRESS
Berkeley   Los Angeles   London

University of California Press
Berkeley and Los Angeles, California

University of California Press, Ltd.
London, England

Library of Congress Cataloging in Publication Data

Young, Michael W., 1937-
    Manumanua : living myth in Kalauna.

    Bibliography: p. 303
    Includes index.
    1. Kalauna (Papua New Guinea people)   2. Kalauna
(Papua New Guinea people) — Folklore.   3. Mythology,
Melanesian — Papua New Guinea — Goodenough Island.
4. Goodenough Island (Papua New Guinea) — Social life
and customs.   5. Government, Primitive — Papua New
Guinea — Goodenough Island.   I. Title.
DU740.42.Y68   1983   306'.0899912   82-23835
ISBN 0-520-04972-1

Printed in the United States of America

1 2 3 4 5 6 7 8 9

To my father and mother

Contents

Acknowledgments   ix

Prologue   1

1   Of Myths and Men   9

2   The House of Lulauvile   42

3   Time's Serpent Honoyeta   61

4   The Blood of Malaveyoyo   92

5   The Jaw of Tobowa   110

6   The Head of Didiala   132

7   The Bones of Iyahalina   171

8   The Belly of Kimaola   206

9   Revelations   248

Epilogue   271

Appendix I   277

Appendix II   280

Notes   289

Glossary of Kalauna Terms   301

Bibliography   303

Index   311

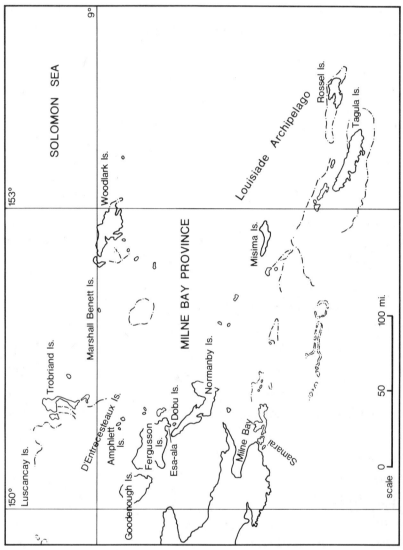

SOLOMON SEA

9°

153°

150°

Woodlark Is.

Marshall Benett Is.

Louisiade Archipelago

Rossel Is.

Tagula Is.

MILNE BAY PROVINCE

Misima Is.

Luscancay Is.

Trobriand Is.

D'Entrecesteaux Is.

Amphlett Is.

Goodenough Is.

Fergusson Is.

Esa-ala

Dobu Is.

Normanby Is.

Milne Bay

Samarai

scale

0   50   100 mi.

Nuamata Is.

Wataluma

Ibawanna • Iwabu

Waibula

Ulutuya

Vivigani

Oya Madawa'a · Wakonai

△ Galuwata
8000'

Eweli

Belebele

Wailolo

Bolubolu P.P.

NIDULA or
GOODENOUGH IS.

Kalauna

Awaiya

Navatutu

Barrier Is.

• Utalo

Mataita

• Diodio

Goiyala

Faiava

Bwaidoka

Wagifa Is.

Kilia

Abolu

0   5 mi.

approx. scale

Road

Eweli

Edu'Edu

Belebele

Wailolo

Bolubolu

Kalauna

△ Yauyaba

–N–

Kwabua

Awaiya

Nuatutu

Manua means "house" or "home"; hence, figuratively, "clan" and "village." Its reduplicated form, *manumanua,* can be glossed as "staying at home" or "remaining in the village." Sitting still was a ritual activity performed by Kalauna magicians when they conducted the ceremony called *manumanua.* This ceremony was designed to banish famine and anchor food in the community. In its broadest sense *manumanua* refers to any rite or myth concerned with creating or preserving communal prosperity.

Acknowledgments

Since its inception in 1976 this book has been written three times, each time by a slightly different person. Its metamorphoses no longer surprise me so I must be accountable for the result. To the extent that it is a collaborative ethnographic enterprise, however, the people of Kalauna must share some of the responsibility for refusing to stand still. But I owe them a profound apology for being unable, finally, to write the kind of bible they wanted: anthropologists make mediocre historians, diffident moralists, and hopeless prophets. Between the Kalauna people's innocent expectations and many readers' thoughtful advice, I have, alas, found myself unable to please everyone.

I am more grateful than I can say to the following persons: Adiyaleyale Iyahalina, Kawanaba Kaweya, and Manawadi Enowei, my friends and tireless assistants, who in 1966-68, 1973 and 1977, educated me in the ways of Kalauna and provided so many of the stories that appear in this book; Maribelle de Vera, who recorded and transcribed many of the myths and other texts I came to use; Mimi Kahn, who first encouraged me to pursue the unlikely project of collating myths and life histories; Larry Cromwell, who read the first version with exacting critical attention; Anthony Forge, Alfred Gell, Elizabeth Brouwer, Andrew Strathern, Rodney Needham, Jennie Scott, Judith Wilson, John Fallon, Bill Epstein, Martha Macintyre, Jimmy Weiner, Buck Schieffelin, Michael Jackson, and Donald Tuzin, all of whom read various drafts in part or whole and gave freely of their criticisms, advice and encouragement; not least, several anonymous publishers' readers, who punctured my pretensions and made me try harder. To Debbora Battaglia I owe special thanks for introducing me to the University of California Press, just when I had begun to suspect that the only place for the manuscript was the obscurity of a bottom drawer. To The Australian National University I owe a long-standing debt of gratitude for fieldwork funding, and also to Ann Buller, Ita Pead, and Ria van der Zandt for their indispensable typing services over the years.

Prologue

On my first exploratory visit to Kalauna, on a brooding day late in August of 1966, I was conducted around the village by several self-appointed guides, two of whom proved to be sons of Iyahalina. They showed me the sights of the village: the monolithic black rock at its center which (through the misunderstanding of an early resident magistrate) now gave its name to the village, the tumbling sources of water, the divisions between the hamlets, the stone sitting platforms of mute antiquity, the imposing house of the councillor, the row of pig mandibles strung outside the house of the village constable. There was not a great deal to see; little more than in any of the other twenty or so Nidula villages I had visited during previous weeks. But something about Kalauna excited me.

Its dwelling sites of hard-packed earth, its untidy crops of boulders, miniature ravines, and haphazard clumps of forest trees through which one could glimpse the mountain wall looming immediately west and the dark Solomon Sea miles to the east — all evoked in me a tremulous sense of the exotic, recalling those moments of an English suburban childhood when I visited the Welsh mountains and wondered at the existence of a Nature that was not put to ornamental and domestic use with fences and concrete. Kalauna seemed an unlikely place for anyone to dwell. Moving from hamlet to hamlet, sometimes even from house to house, was like those childhood games in which we invented obstacles to our passage: stretches of water for jumping across, rocks for clambering over, bushes for wriggling through. Here were people whose lives coped in actuality with what as a boy I had to imagine: a jungle of physical impedi-

1

ments outside one's very home into which one ventured, mildly heroic, exercising skill and muscle, with the promise of adventure at every step.

Professionally viewed, Kalauna seemed a most favorable place for me to set up house and begin my research (though I need not detail all the reasons here). Two factors assumed paramount importance for me. First, there was the compact and even congested settlement of the community (nearly 500 people on a site smaller than Trafalgar Square), and I was at once intrigued by the political accommodations that made this possible. Second, I was gratified by an immediate entrée into the field of investigation that interested me: leadership.

The morning after my arrival Iyahalina's two eldest sons came to talk with me in the rest house. Bunaleya was in his late twenties and Adiyaleyale a couple of years his junior. Both had reached standard five of primary school, and both had worked at a variety of jobs in Port Moresby and elsewhere. Their spoken English was as good as any I had yet heard on Nidula, and my ear was now attuned to the characteristically confused employment of prepositions and the oddly fractured syntax of "Samarai English." Bunaleya soon proved to be an inept informant. He was *towomomumu,* a "man of shame," shy and verbally unventuresome. When he failed to understand what I said he giggled or looked silently at the floor. Adiyaleyale had far fewer inhibitions. His voice was firmer, his intellectual curiosity bolder, and he was less inclined to be obsequious to whites. He enjoyed talking and was already something of a raconteur. I was wary of his turning out to be one of those people novice anthropologists are warned against: misfits in their own milieu who seek relationships with outsiders to raise their standing at home. But I was easily reassured by what I saw of Adiyaleyale's interactions with his elders and peers, for there were no obvious symptoms of antipathy. He did indeed prove to be remarkable in many ways, but his idiosyncrasies were not aberrations and although I did not know it then, Adiyaleyale was a big-man in the making. Over the years he proved to be one of my most articulate, reliable, and valued assistants. Through Adiyaleyale, too, I had more frequent and informal access to his father than might otherwise have been the case, and to some

2

extent my own view of Iyahalina was colored by his son's attitude toward him.

Iyahalina joined his sons that morning in the rest house, and at this first meeting I was impressed by his willingness to answer questions on leadership and tell me "stories." After an hour or two I had intriguing notes on Kalauna's history, fragments of mythology, and a sketch of what appeared to be an attenuated form of chieftainship —so exciting after the dispiritingly pat responses I had been offered in other villages. My notes on the last topic, in the basic English of Adiyaleyale's translation, condensed to something like the following:

> The chiefs of Kalauna are chiefs because they know how to look after the food. They know how to put taboos on food. They walk around the gardens and inspect the crops. They can tell people when to plant and when to harvest. Their food magic is their power: we call it *manu-manua*. They tell people how to eat. Everyone respects them because they know these secrets. Their work is to look after the land and the people.

It took me months of further work, of course, to put this summary statement into perspective and to add the appropriate qualifications. But pondering those initial notes many years later, I was amazed at the blunt, factual accuracy of the picture of the ritual leadership of Kalauna's "guardians." However, I could now also discern an ethnographic fact of the second order: Iyahalina had deliberately sought me out to offer me his credentials. This was a ploy to establish his legitimacy and that of his line before others pronounced contradictory versions. It was remiss of him, for instance, not to mention that there were two other living "guardians" besides himself: Didiala and Kimaola.

The genesis of this book lay in my attempt to fathom Iyahalina's response to my subsequent request for his life history. For instead of telling me tales from his childhood, recounting the circumstances of his marriage, or enumerating his mature achievements, he narrated a sequence of myths and legends that described the activities of his

3

ancestors. He concluded with a passionate peroration on the ritual duties they had bequeathed him, the central task of which was to "sit still" in order to anchor the community in prosperity.

While puzzling over Iyahalina's use of the myths of his lineage to construct his social identity, I began to understand why men of his society were so jealous of their myths, why they resented it so deeply when others tried to narrate them, and why they were so sensitive concerning the truth or falsity of different versions. Coming as I did from a civilization that has debased myths by defining them as falsehoods, and professing an academic discipline that tends to leach them of moral and emotional content, it took me some time to respect the solemnity and high seriousness with which Kalauna men regarded their myths.

There were at least two good reasons why they displayed such proprietorial attitudes to them: first, the social uses of mythology in providing validations or charters for magical knowledge and ritual, and second, the more subjective and imponderable uses of mythology in providing meanings for personal identity and biography. Much anthropological wisdom has been applied to the investigation of the first of these uses of myth but very little to the second, perhaps because the realm of "lived experience" is so refractory to the kind of objective analyses that anthropologists normally pursue. For much the same reason, one suspects, biographical anthropology or the study of life histories is a relatively neglected genre, one badly in need of reinvention. But unless anthropologists address themselves to the problems of biography in preliterate societies it is doubtful if others will. Anthropology, after all, lies precisely in the delineation of those social and cultural "givens" which individuals make over to themselves in the business of living; and this is surely a privileged starting point for understanding the experiential realities of particular lives.

By the time I had written Iyahalina's biography it was a second- or thirdhand "fiction," in the original sense of "something made or fashioned." As an exercise in biography it pointed two ways: inward to his conception of selfhood, and outward to his lineage and the mythological heritage with which he identified. Placing these, too, in their context, Iyahalina's lineage was one among several in the

4

clan of Lulauvile, while his priestly office of "guardian" was but one
of three. The directions for me to pursue here, then, were yet other
lives: those of his peers and rivals, and those who preceded him in
legend and myth. A sequence if not a cycle of lives seemed necessary
to explicate more fully the one biography. And once these had been
assembled in outline, Iyahalina's had to concede centrality, for the
other lives had mass too and pulled at one another like planets in a
gravitational field. Each life, then, emanated power and idiosyncratic purpose; yet there was a unity of overall theme, a pattern
motivated by something like political endeavor. In the last analysis
it was the political arena of Kalauna with its conflicting ideologies
which gave coherence to these life histories, for they were all Lulauvile lives, and they were all concerned to assert the ritual hegemony
of their own clan over the rest of the village.

My collation of biographies could then be viewed as something
else also: an "inside" study of political process in a Melanesian community. Moreover, once I had defined the moving spirit of the life
histories as political, it followed that these men's autobiographical
statements, no less than the uses to which they put their myths,
could be viewed as ideologically motivated. To see through the eyes
of these men, actors in a system of political relationships, is to see
their political universe severally. While this enriches it for an ob-
server accustomed only to seeing such things from without, not the
whole of this universe is shown with equal fidelity; I have given the
sharpest focus to the Lulauvile leaders' view. These men represent a
minority party of which Iyahalina was the chief ideologue. But
other viewpoints have been presented throughout the book, and
indeed, they are essential for an understanding of Lulauvile's struggle to maintain its status in Kalauna.

The plan of the book is as follows. Chapter 1 presents mythological and biographical issues that have attended the study, my aim
being to state in general terms the social and cultural conditions
under which myth can be said to be "lived" and how it might inform
biography. I introduce the concept of the person and the components of identity in Kalauna, and also the key notions of "victimage"

and resentment, which are so salient in the community's view of its own history. Readers more interested in the "stories" than in the hows and whys of their social construction may wish to skip the theoretical excursions of this chapter.

Chapter 2 is an ethnographic introduction to the society of Kalauna and the place of the "ranked" clan of Lulauvile within it. I outline the ritual roles of the leaders of Lulauvile and those contradictory principles of egalitarianism and hierarchy, the contention of which provides the main political dynamic of Kalauna. The chapter concludes with an account of the constitutive ceremony of *manumanua,* which "banishes" famine and "anchors" food in the community. The myths of *manumanua* appear later in the book in the biographical contexts of their owners.

Chapter 3 presents and analyzes the paradigmatic myth of Honoyeta, a snake-man and deity of the sun who seeks death following the destruction of his disguise but then punishes men for their attempt to kill and eat him. This myth illuminates major concerns of Kalauna: the fear of greed and famine, the magical control of regeneration, the relations between fathers and sons, leaders and followers, and not least, the tragic consequences of heroic resentment.

In chapter 4 I present the legend of Malaveyoyo, a cannibal warrior and despot whose story has been subtly assimilated with the Honoyeta myth. His disastrous assertion of the hierarchy principle brings famine and the cannibalism of children, though his "sacrificial" death marks the beginning of the colonial era in which competitive food exchange domesticates vengeance and provides an alternative to violence.

Chapter 5 offers fragmentary biographical materials on the first modern leader of Kalauna, a strong-man, master sorcerer, and crypto-cannibal, who nevertheless won government favor as a progressive village constable in the 1950s. His attempts to modernize Kalauna met with failure, and he died after resentfully dispersing his magical inheritance.

The following three chapters form the core of the book. They deal in turn with the lives and the myths of three "guardians" of the 1960s, men whom I knew personally and whose autobiographical

6

accounts I had attempted to record. They are presented in chrono-
logical order — eldest first — which also happens to have been the
order of their demise. Chapter 6 is devoted to Didiala, who died in
1969. He was a "great provider" and officiant of *manumanua* who
nevertheless suffered the recriminations of the villagers for his sorcery of the sun. Chapter 7 essays the biography of Iyahalina, a descendant of Malaveyoyo and brother-in-law of Didiala, whose death
(like theirs) had tragic and sacrificial overtones. Chapter 8 traces
the career of Kimaola, a much feared and devious sorcerer who by
1977 was the only surviving big-man of Lulauvile; his political style
as a Melanesian Machiavelli is shown in terms of the politics of
feasting.

The concluding chapter brings together the threads of lives and
historical movements; it describes recent cargo cults based on the
myth of Honoyeta and the idea of the "return of the heroes," and it
examines the local identification of Honoyeta with Jesus Christ. The
fall of the House of Lulauvile is accounted for and the cyclical pattern of community aggregation and dispersal is aligned to Kalauna's
own view of its "serpentine" history, underlying which is the dominant victimage theme of the mythology. An epilogue brings the
story of Lulauvile up to date with a brief account of Kimaola's persecution in 1979.

In sum, the book presents a sequence of overlapping portraits of
heroes and leaders from the mythological to the contemporary. It
moves from the past to the present, from the primordial time of the
sun god Honoyeta through the legendary era of the tyrant Malaveyoyo to the historically recent times of Tobowa, Didiala, Iyahalina,
and Kimaola.

Since so much of the book has been constructed from narratives,
many of them tape-recorded, it would have been desirable to present all such texts in the vernacular with translations in double-
column or interlinear form. Besides daunting the general reader,
however, this would have added considerably to the length of the
work and probably rendered it unpublishable. As a small concession
to scholarly expectations in this matter, I give two sample texts in
the appendices to illustrate both the deployment of language by
Kalauna narrators and my own handling of problems of transla-

7

tion. A glossary of essential Kalauna terms is also appended. The language of Kalauna belongs to the far-flung Austronesian family. As a simple aid to the pronunciation of names and vernacular terms, it is helpful to remember that the vowels have the "pure" value of Italian and Spanish, and that the stress or accent always falls on the penultimate syllable. For example: Kalauna (Kal-*ow*-na); Lulauvile (Lool-ow-*vee*-lay); Manumanua (Man-oo-man-*oo*-wa); Didiala (Di-di-*ya*-la); Iyahalina (Ee-ya-ha-*lee*-na); Kimaola (Ki-ma-*ow*-la).

A concluding word on the name of the island. Since 1976 there has been some dissatisfaction among educated islanders with the colonial name Goodenough, though it is still in current use. Nidula is claimed by many to have been the traditional name for the island, although perhaps just as many claim ignorance of the word and offer others in its stead. In the dialect of Kalauna *nidula* appears simply to mean strand or foreshore, the margin of beach covered and uncovered by the tide. My own decision to use Nidula as a synonym for Goodenough (both nominally for the island and adjectivally for the culture) was happily authorized by the printing in 1979 of a 1:100,000 map series that gives the label Nidula to the sheet featuring Goodenough Island. In time Nidula will probably prevail and I have anticipated its general acceptance in this book, retaining Goodenough Island whenever the geographical, historical, or administrative contexts demand its use.

1
Of Myths and Men

Myth and person are so closely inter-
woven that we see them support each
other, proceed from each other, stabilize
each other, explain each other and justify
each other.

— Maurice Leenhardt, *Do Kamo*

∧∧∧∧∧

My aim in this book is twofold: to enlarge the anthropological
understanding of the uses of myth, and to expand the genre of
anthropological biography. As a compilation of stories about a
clan's aspirations to leadership in a Papuan village this work is neither a theoretical treatise nor an ethnography in the conventional
sense. It is self-consciously experimental. My starting point is the
fact that the most powerful myths in Kalauna are heritable property. This fact suggested the basic biographical design of the book,
since owned myths confer collective identity and influence personal
destiny. From this salient fact, too, flows much of the book's ethnographic color and all of its political argument.

Anthropological studies of myth generally accord it a privileged
status as a cultural product, a form of "objectified thought" which
transcends the subjective worlds of its narrators. In the overture to

9

his monumental *Mythologiques,* Lévi-Strauss even claims that "myths operate in men's minds without their being aware of the fact" (1970:12), though in the finale of the same work he concedes that "utterance is a function confined to subjects, and every myth . . . must have its origin in an individual act of creation" (1981:626). Even so, Lévi-Strauss rightly insists that in order to enter a collective tradition as myth, a narrative must cease to be individual and relinquish those subjective elements or "probabilist levels" that derive from the narrator's "temperament, talent, imagination and personal experiences" (ibid.). While there are some problems with this formulation in a community like Kalauna, I accept the general point that although all individual narrations are potential myths, only if they are adopted by a community or a group within that community do they achieve mythic status. My analyses of myths in this book have proceeded accordingly, though I have been alert to subjective elements or probabilist levels, not in order to neutralize them, but to examine them as autobiographical revelations of their narrators. For Lévi-Strauss, the elimination of the subject or mythologer is a "methodological need" of structural analysis: "it corresponds to the scrupulous desire to explain no part of the myth except by the myth" (ibid.:628). For my own needs in the present work, which is phenomenological and hermeneutical in character, I have restored myth to the mythologers, thereby allowing them to demonstrate how myth can be deployed as a political instrument as well as a symbolic resource for the construction of biography. Since the lives of the mythologers are central to my project, insofar as I "explain" certain myths, I do so by recourse to the cultural context and social milieu that shape both myths and men.

Recent full-scale studies of mythology in Melanesia, notably Burridge's *Tangu Traditions* (1969) and Wagner's *Lethal Speech* (1978), also situate them firmly in their ethnographic contexts. They nonetheless remain primarily concerned with myth as "objectified thought," as crystalizations of cultural themes and social experiences. Both Burridge and Wagner establish a dialectic between myth and culture, and both authors (albeit in quite different ways) work toward an understanding of myth-in-cultural-context through an exploration of collective experiential realms. Now while my own

10

analysis of Kalauna myths follows the same trend (I also use a modi-
fied structuralist approach in decomposing them), the thrust of this
book is in the opposite direction: toward, that is, an exploration of
individual or subjective experiential realms.

If it were indeed true that myths operated in men's minds without
their being aware of the fact, there might be little for me to say; but
even "objectified" thought has its locus in the consciousness of individuals, so that myth is forever being reinterpreted, reinvented, or
— as Wagner would have it — "obviated" anew. Processes of oral
transmission indicate that the "meaning" of a myth is not intrinsic
to it, but is rather the result of a negotiated relationship between the
narrator or mythologer and the tale he or she is telling. Studies of
the dynamics of literary response suggest that what a reader reads in
a given text is not necessarily what the author wrote; the reader's
appropriation of a text, therefore, is as complex a psychological
enterprise as the writer's authorship of it and "meanings" emerge
from the relationship between them (Holland 1968, 1975). Hence
the truism that one can never read the same story twice, just as a
narrator can only tell the same myth once.[1]

$$\wedge\!\wedge\!\wedge\!\wedge\!\wedge$$

The ever-renewed and inexhaustible corpus of Kalauna oral literature comprises myths, legends, folktales, spells, songs, chants, sermons, jokes, and anecdotes. It has been greatly enriched since European contact by the addition of Bible stories — many of them apoc-
ryphal — and tales from other villages and other islands. There are
four traditional genres of relatively stable form to which new or non-
traditional items are assimilated. *Kweli* are spells, songs, and
chants. *Laumamala* are orations, sermons, and other rhetorical
public speeches which are avowedly political or proselytizing in
intent. *Neineya* are heritable, owned, magic-bearing myths which
tell of the exploits of ancestors, heroes, demigods or *dema* (see
Schwimmer 1973:62). Finally, *ifufu* are stories of any other kind:
profane or unowned myths, legends, folktales, anecdotes, jokes, etc.[2]

The six or seven myths I will analyze in this book are of the *nei-*

11

neya class, and all belong to Lulauvile clan. There are perhaps a couple of dozen more in the village as a whole, for each lineage claims at least one *neineya* myth (without necessarily being willing or able to tell it to the ethnographer). *Neineya* give title to and provide narrative vehicles for systems of magic concerned with weather control, crop fertility, gardening prowess, and the suppression of hunger. These magical systems are still deployed, but there are a few others—concerned with war-making and warrior prowess—that are nowadays defunct (though the *neineya* are still carefully guarded by their owners). *Neineya* should only be narrated—with discretion as to time and place—by their rightful owners, whereas the general class of "stories" can be told at almost any time by almost any person before any audience. Although *neineya* have restricted audiences most nonowners have a general idea of what they are about. On the rare occasions when a narrator tells his *neineya* to an audience of nonowners he will carefully censor it by omitting secret names, spells, and any other clues to its magical significance. So consequential are such myths that even truncated narrations are believed to evoke a cosmic response (*towava*) of thunder, lightning, and rain. Such portents also accompany the performances of magicians using the spells that are encapsulated in this genre of myth.

Neineya are the myths that matter most, both to the people of Kalauna and to the argument of this book. Honoyeta's myth, analyzed in chapter 3, is a *neineya,* as are the *manumanua* myths presented in chapters 6 and 7 and Kimaola's myth of Kawafolafola given in chapter 8. All the other stories are *ifufu*. Thus, although I work progressively from myths of origin through legend and folktale to anecdote and reminiscence, all are undifferentiated "stories" in the Kalauna view. Nor is there a separate genre for what we call biography and autobiography; a person verbally recalling his own or another's life is simply "telling stories," a point I shall return to in a later section. Strictly speaking, of course, the *neineya* I present in this book are reduced to *ifufu* status by the omission of their secret magical formulas. By withholding these I have tried to keep faith with their owners. The magical charge of *neineya* is an esoteric category, and one not essential to an understanding of such myths *for us*. Hence, the fragments of spells I offer are illustrative only, and

rendered into English they are robbed of their supposed power to
work upon the world.

$$\wedge\wedge\wedge\wedge\wedge$$

Writing of the Trobriand Islands (Kalauna's "Muyuwa") over half a
century ago, Bronislaw Malinowski tried to convey to a myth-bereft
Western audience what it might mean to dwell in a society where
myth is not merely a story told but a "reality lived." His comments
are still pertinent to Kalauna attitudes to their *neineya*.

> It is not of the nature of fiction, such as we read today in a novel, but
> it is a living reality, believed to have once happened in primeval times,
> and continuing ever since to influence the world and human destinies.
> [1954:100]

As well as the practical social uses of mythology in providing religious, moral, political, and quasi-legal charters, Malinowski was
also sensibly impressed by the affective properties of Trobriand
myth. He tells us, for example, how narrators bragged and boasted
(1935:464), and how "the manner of telling a story and the way in
which it was received . . . were quite as important as the text itself"
(1936:10). He recognized that oral narratives were not merely oral
but involved an orchestration of the senses: they could be sung,
danced, enacted. He also alluded to a more profound "mythological
rapproachment . . . made between the primeval past and the immediate destiny of each man," but he pursued this no further than a
rather trite illustration of myth's opiate in reconciling men to death
by screening "the vast emotional void gaping beyond them" (1954:
126, 138). In short, Malinowski did not demonstrate convincingly
the living reality of Trobriand myth by showing how it might be a
reality lived.

For Maurice Leenhardt, that other great pioneer of Melanesian
ethnography, myths were not merely charters for action but the very
forms of thought that explained such action. His remarkable essay
in sociomythic phenomenology, *Do Kamo*, was the summation of a

lifetime's study of the *Canaques* of New Caledonia, where he had spent 24 years as a missionary.[3] He quietly challenged the work of his celebrated mentor, Lévy-Bruhl, who had characterized primitive mentality as "fluid" and "mystical," typified by its products of myths and folktales. Leenhardt proposed "mythic" as a more accurate characterization of such thought, arguing that myth was a "mode of knowledge" complementary to (and not exclusive of) rational knowledge. The two modes of thought coexist, although "we do not know where mythic reality ends and empirical reality begins for Melanesians" (1979:19). Adapting Van der Leeuw's minimal definition of myth ("a word which circumscribes an event"), Leenhardt sought to purify its meaning; to "word" he gave the force and fullness of the *Canaque* term *no*, which aptly translates the biblical sense of "word." Myth, in this view, is constitutive of certain inner states: "a particular kind of engagement with a world of concrete presences, intersubjective relations, and emotional participations" (Clifford 1982:7). These formulations could be used to describe the experience of men like Didiala and Iyahalina, heroes of this book, whose lives were rooted in a "socio-mythic landscape" such as Leenhardt depicts for his Caledonians. Mythic knowledge is not narrated but "lived" in aesthetically patterned events that otherwise elude comprehension. Mythic thought does not classify images, it juxtaposes them. It is affective rather than intellectual, a matter of moods rather than ideas. In a word, mythic thought and knowledge are *embodied,* both literally and figuratively. As we shall see, an illuminating example of mythic thought is embodied in the Kalauna myth of Honoyeta, with its powerful mood of resentment and vengeance. In this, Kalauna's principal myth in a cognitive, structural sense, we find also a *mythe vécu* in Leenhardt's sense, with its sociomythic embodiment of an emotional reality.

In trying to convey an understanding of lived myth to the reader, the ethnographer must violate its canon: discursive language separates what mythic participation experiences as unity. Ethnography, of course, must privilege intellect over feeling as its mode of knowledge, writing over gesture as its medium of expression; and it is, after all, the rational mind that isolates the category of myth and subjects it to scrutiny. *Do Kamo* is not entirely successful in surmounting these difficulties. Leenhardt slips into mystified identifications of his own in his attempts to explicate the inexplicable: those participatory modes of being that are paralinguistic, if not prelogical. He also lacked a modern appreciation of metaphor, seeming to confound *Canaque* descriptions *of* experience with evidence *for* experience; and he sometimes confused myth as a *Canaque* mode of knowledge with myth as an ineffable, intuitive construct of his own. James Clifford, Leenhardt's biographer, concedes that his "rather mystical *Canaque* is an exaggeration" (just as Malinowski's Trobriander is an improbably rational empiricist), and he suggestively notes that whereas prescience stands behind Malinowski's "magic," it is prereligion that stands behind Leenhardt's "myth" (ibid.:137). These positions are not easily reconciled.

From his own perspective of the immanence of *mythe vécu,* Leenhardt chided Malinoᵀ ki for granting priority to magic, a priority that "suppressed the ᵢ ᵢythic" and allowed "his intuition about lived myth to escape" (1079:188). If he meant that by dwelling on the observable performances of magic Malinowski's empiricism occluded any deeper understanding of the myths that charged them, then he certainly had a point. Yet Leenhardt's matured definition of myth renders it more a metaphysical than an anthropological category, more profound but less serviceable than Malinowski's.

> Myth — All manner of gesture or speech which, by circumscribing a reality that cannot be realized in rational language, imposes on man a comportment in relation with that reality. [Cited by Clifford ibid.: 222]

Ethnography must begin with observation and proceed by interpretation true to it. Leenhardt's insistence that myth is lived before it is formulated, that it is an affective mode of knowledge before becoming a cognitive one, that it is "the word, the figure, the action which circumscribes the event in the heart of man . . . before becoming a fixed story" (1979:190) surely inhibits open-minded investigation. If Malinowski allowed the mythic to slip through his fingers he did remain true to his observations, and he recorded them in a manner which, if not always compelling belief, permits us to revise his interpretations. This is largely because—unlike Leenhardt's—his texts were always presented with reference to the social contexts in which they occurred. In this respect, as Vincent Crapanzano has noted, *Do Kamo* "is closed to further interpretation" (1979:xx).

In taking a more Malinowskian point of departure, my project in this book provides firmer ground for Leenhardt's brilliant insights. My approach to the myths of Kalauna is through narrative and the contexts in which narrative is constructed and construed; perhaps this is the only way—short of dwelling among a people for as long as Leenhardt did—that lived myth can become accessible to the ethnographer. Again, although it will be evident from my portraits of Kalauna men that "myth" overflows its modern Western meaning, I have not sought to enlarge the conventional definition by incorporating Leenhardt's phenomenology of the "mythic." Being equally concerned with observable behavior and practical activity, with affective perception and experience, all of them situated within a landscape of lived myth, the present work attempts to mediate Malinowski and Leenhardt.

Mircea Eliade is another scholar who has written extensively about lived myth. He might be said to have adapted Malinowski's theory of myth to the cosmological scale of the history of religions. I mention his views on "archaic" and "primitive" man's relationship to his mythology in order to state a more extreme position of "lived myth." Eliade pictures human life under the domination of mythical paradigms—"divinely established and periodically re-enacted"—as a kind of consecrated imitation. The meaning and value of human acts, he writes,

> are not connected with their crude physical datum but with their property of reproducing a primordial act, or repeating a mythical example. . . . In the particulars of conscious behaviour, the "primitive," the archaic man, acknowledges no act which has not been previously posited and lived by someone else, some other being who was not a

man. What he does has been done before. His life is the ceaseless repetition of gestures initiated by others. [1959:4-5]

In such a milieu, Eliade contends, "the only profane activities are those which have no mythical meanings, that is, those which lack exemplary models" (ibid.:28). Now it strains credibility to view human consciousness, with its critical capacity for making choices, succumbing in such thralldom to the products of its imagination. This is a brainwashing view of myth reminiscent of the earlier, more dubious conjectures of Lévy-Bruhl, and it surely exaggerates the imitative propensity of humanity, whether "primitive" or otherwise.

Having said this, we must allow that the "impersonations" Eliade mentions most certainly occur, principally in ritual contexts. I confine myself to a few Papuan examples. The Trobriand magician identifies with a mythical personage to the extent of uttering his name in the first person when reciting spells (Malinowski 1922:412). Likewise, in what F. E. Williams called "the magic of impersonation," the Elema magician does not simply invoke the aid of deities or heroes, but actively imitates them, thereby "seeking to re-enact the successes which those mythical characters had achieved" (1932-33:166). Quite generally in Papua, perhaps, magic is a "product" of myth as it is for the Elema: "it relies on mythical precedents, reenacts mythical episodes, and impersonates mythical characters" (Williams 1940:342). As a final example, Schwimmer writes of Orokaiva demigods and culture heroes: "Not only are *dema* commemorated in myth, but collective ceremonies are held in their honour. Man celebrates them by identifying, during these ceremonies, with the *dema* of original time" (1973:63). During feasting and dancing the celebrants "imitate what they believe to have been the ways of their primal ancestors" (ibid.). Schwimmer implies that this kind of enactment is important for reaffirming the charter—what he calls the starting mechanism—for social exchange among the Orokaiva.

Such identifications and imitations do not gainsay the everyday identity of an individual; nor, we may presume, do they abrogate his sense of himself as distinct from the hero or ancestor with whom (aided by imagination and the mild dissociation induced by areca nut narcosis) he seeks a temporary identification. To propose that

17

the identification was more than self-directed and evanescent, however, would be to suggest that such a man was deluded if not mad.

The asylums of the West are full of people who claim, in all good faith, to be other than they are and to wear the "skins" of their given identities. "Skin" is a pervasive image in Kalauna mythology, and as we shall see, it has reverberations in political life too, which is beset with prevarication and dissimulation. But these maskings are self-conscious, strategic, and governed by choice, save in the relatively rare event of possession. When possession occurs, however, Kalauna people clearly recognize it as such. The very fact that they explain it by the act of a sorcerer who inflicts the possession from without is ample evidence (if any were needed) of the normative view that people are free and responsible actors in society—in short, that they are *self*-possessed. There is no mass delusion in Kalauna that would make a conspiracy of society by viewing its members as mythical incarnations, eternally enacting their given destinies through the bodies of the living. This is as far as the "impersonation" or "mythical mimesis" view can be taken, and it patently slides into absurdity. One may presume that no human society has ever adopted the literal assumption that all or most of its members "are" other than they seem.

All this is to state what is perhaps obvious. Yet I wish to steer a clear course between the quasi-mystical positions of Leenhardt, Eliade, Jung, Kerēnyi, and others for whom "primitive" man lived in some kind of thrall to his myths, and the demeaning, secular view that myths are mere stories, fictions, or fables with no more "living reality" than the disenchanted Western mind finds in the myths of its own heritage. Our own relationship to myths (however we define them) is arbitrary, contingent, and greatly complicated by literacy.

In the Kalauna view, a hard and fast distinction between fact and fiction is difficult to maintain: *ifufu*, as we have seen, does not prejudge a story's truth or falsity and canons of plausibility are greatly different from our own. The appropriation of myths, especially when they are personal possessions and a part of one's inalienable heritage, means taking them to heart as consequential statements about one's life. A man's relationship to his myths in Kalauna is neither arbitrary nor contingent, and it is colored by the fact of inherited ownership.[4] They are things he carries around within himself as a singer carries a song or, more aptly, a magician his spells. A tendency to exclusive ownership reflexively confers a kind of immortality upon the owner, insofar as his thought mediates the lives of his ancestors or heroes dwelling within him. The individual notionally becomes the vehicle for their lives: they live through his thinking and telling them. In this view, such myths are more than practical charters for ritual acts, property rights, or mundane privileges; they are constituents of selfhood, which affect a person's psychological stance and thereby his social behavior.

If we deny myths as having "living reality" in this sense, then it becomes impossible to understand Iyahalina's apostrophizing. Iyahalina presents us with a case as close to Eliade's model as one might hope to find in reality. He affected to live in quotation marks, as it were, and projected himself as a synecdoche of his ancestors and his lineage. One might even fancy that he saw himself as a kind of divine king, a cosmic corporation sole (Kantorowicz 1957). But, as I argue in chapter 7, Iyahalina's sense of irony was so developed that the quotation marks he put around his actions were done with the knowing wink of one in complete self-possession. And we can infer from this, too, that Iyahalina was attempting to make *himself* exemplary for those who succeeded him.

In the last analysis, however, it is invalid to contrast unique biography (lived experience) with impersonated myth (exemplary experience), for biography in Kalauna is shaped, even contaminated, by myth in its very construction. Here again, we can escape any unwonted suggestion of determinism by invoking a mutual process, a dynamic interaction. Men such as Iyahalina, who internalize their myths to a marked extent, such that they perceive their lives in terms of the idioms and ideals that the myths promote, appear to submit to them while yet exerting their own purposes through them. They thereby unwittingly modify their myths quite subtly in the process.[5] Moreover, myths are not as fixed as Kalauna people like to believe; they permit explorations of "alternity," and they challenge the intellect as puzzles as readily as they comfort it by proferring solutions. They yield, in short, as many meanings and as much ambiguity as the interrogating mind is disposed to find in them; it can select one interpretation or another according to mood or circumstance. Thus, in appropriating their myths, Kalauna men construct of them secondary myths, reshaping them to conform to subjective needs. This creative scope offers release from the stultification of reenactment. "Bad faith" occurs only if the individual blames his myth for being the way he is, if he uses it to excuse his actions or to stereotype himself in its image. Didiala, Iyahalina, and Kimaola, whose entwined biographies I present in the second half of this book, manipulated their myths (each in his own idiosyncratic way) to suit ends extrinsic to the myths while using them to explain to others what they were up to. This is not thralldom. "We are not lumps of clay," wrote Sartre with the stigmatized Jean Genet in mind, "and what is important is not what people make of us but what we ourselves make of what they have made us" (1963:49). Likewise the figures in this book, "mythologized" as they are to a degree by their heritages and by the way their stereotypes cast them, reciprocally recreate their heroes in their own images. Here, then, is the use of mythology for biography. We inspect the myth as mirror and therein discern the reflection of the person in the image of the hero.[6]

∧∨∧∨∧

Something must be said at this point, however briefly, about concepts of the person and the constitution of self in Kalauna. No abstract terms exist for "person" or "individual" as distinct from "this man" or "that woman"; and "self" can only be expressed as a reflexive pronoun: *Iya tauku,* "I myself." Body, spirit, soul, and speech confer essential human identity (*kalivamoena,* "real man"), while basic social identity is given by gender, age, and marital status. Then there are the connative givens, so to speak, of filiation and descent group membership: personal name, totems and taboos, and many other *dewa* (customs, habits), such that a large part of a person's social identity is determined by and made representative of his or her group identity. Behavioral characteristics are sometimes also associated with particular clan or lineage membership; sobriquets such as *tonuakoyo* (angry man) and *tohumahuma* (humble man),

20

while appearing to give a clue to personality, may really be stereo-typing it by invoking group *dewa* (see Young 1971:68). A Mulina subclan, for example, is said to have been "spoiled" by its heritage of war magic which, in Lamarckian fashion, endows members of this line with an unusual propensity to violence. There is a degree of group "speciation," therefore, that critically influences personhood by the fact of birth into a particular descent group. This is a "genetic" theory of personal identity according to which the "genes" (*dewa*) are — as we would say — cultural rather than natural items of heredity. And insofar as this kind of formula of personhood is underwritten by mythological charters, then *neineya* myths too are particularizing influences in the construction of self: myth maketh man.

Individuation proceeds by other means too. For example, nicknames frequently supersede given names. They usually seize upon some bodily peculiarity as a metonym for the person: "Lame-leg," "Bad-nose," "Skinny," "Bad-head," "Bent-arm," "Crook-back," "Sores," "Bad-eyes," "Double-skin" (a sufferer of tinea). These names carry less stigma than our Western sensitivity might suppose. (I have played my own variations on this individuating process in the metaphorical conceits of my chapter titles.) "Name" in the sense of reputation, however, is a summary of personhood that can only be achieved. As in English, it is metaphorically equivalent to "fame" which, as Nancy Munn has put it, is "the social circulation of the self in the form of one's name" (1977:50). "Name" in Kalauna is associated with wealth (pigs, bountiful gardens, and shell valuables), but to understand the relationship between self and possessions we must make a linguistic digression.

In common with many other Austronesian languages in the area (Lithgow 1976), Kalauna's pronominal and possessive forms encode three degrees of relatedness: intimate, intermediate, and distant. Notionally inalienable components of the person (body parts, kinship and affinal relationships) are denoted by a suffix: *nima-ku,* "my hand"; *tama-ku,* "my father"; *vavine-ku,* "my wife." Detachable or detached possessions are denoted by two classes of prefix, although the phonemic distinction between them is slight and not always evident. Thus, *aku-eyana,* "my name," and *aku-la'ila'i,* "my

21

OF MYTHS AND MEN

armshell," fall into the intermediate class of detachable possessions, while *yaku-manua,* "my house," and *yaku violili,* "my divorced spouse," fall into the distant class of detached possessions. Some subtle distinctions are possible. For example: *nua-ku,* "my mind, my heart"; *nuanua-ku,* "my desire" ("I want"); *yaku-nuanua,* "my thought, my idea." My thought is a less intimate part of myself than my mind or my desire, though I distance most feelings to objectify them as a cause of my behavior: *yaku-nuakoyo faina ya-nau,* literally, "my anger because-of-it I went."

There is a special form of the intimate possessive for staple foods: *akuya,* "my food"; *anaya,* "his food." Crucially, this form denotes that the food referred to is to be eaten by the possessor or his close kin. In referring to a person's food that he is intending to give away, the form is *yana-au'a;* that is to say, it is already classified as distant. Consider also the following: *aku-nila,* "my coconut," *aku-bawe,* "my pig," both of which I am going to eat; but *yaku-nila,* "my coconut," *yaku-bawe,* "my pig," both of which are destined to be eaten by others. In short, these possessives encode information about gifts and about the relatedness of one's possessions to others.

The word for "give" in Kalauna is rarely used intransitively, so the recipient is usually present in a suffix. For example: *yaku-bawe ya-vele-na,* "my pig I gave him" (i.e., "I gave my pig to him"); *aku-bawe hi-vele-ku,* "my pig he gave me" (i.e., "he gave his pig to me"). Marcel Mauss pointed out long ago that the gift is a part of oneself; equally, oneself is part of the gift—the *aku* within the *yaku,* as it were. Seemingly, there is a less radical disjunction between person and property than we know in the West; indeed, property relations can be fruitfully regarded as metaphors of social relations (see Strathern 1981). At issue here, however, is the Kalauna notion that personhood can in part be constructed and construed by material objects or "possessions," though to grasp this notion we must soften the obdurate Western distinctions between subject and object, spirit and matter, and allow that in the Melanesian view they interpenetrate.

An anecdote will serve to make my point in another way. Once, while trying to understand the elusive Kalauna concept of *kubama* (which defies translation but which might be glossed as "the state of

being without something one normally possesses"), my helper Manawadi drew a picture of a stick figure to represent a man, bounded by
a triangle to represent his house and other possessions. He then
sliced off a corner of the triangle: *kubama* was this kind of loss. It
could be a bushknife left behind in the garden, or some other mis-
laid tool; it could be a pot borrowed by a neighbor and not returned, or even a dependent of the household who stayed away over-
night. Whatever the cause of *kubama,* the man suffered a temporary diminishment, such that any crops he planted while in this
state would refuse to grow. Until the missing possession was restored
to the house, the remedy was to arise before dawn and detach oneself from the house before going to plant. Why? Manawadi was ada-
mant that *kubama* was not some kind of spirit that "protected"
property and punished careless householders; rather it was an
absence, a depletion which had nullifying effects. If this was the
case then the only way to make sense of *kubama* was to postulate a
double metaphorical identification, between house and person on
the one hand, and between person and crops on the other. The
house/person was depleted by the loss of something, and unless the
person disengaged himself from the house (by the rite of early rising
and evacuation), he transferred the depletion to the crops in his garden, which registered their own insufficiency by withering.

Intrigued by the cut corner of the triangle, I asked Manawadi if it
could also represent what occurred when a man voluntarily gave
something away rather than inadvertently lost it. Manawadi pon-
dered for a moment, then drew a second stick figure enclosed by another triangle; it was adjacent to the first but intersected it, overlapping one of the base angles so that they shared a third, smaller triangle. We stared at his two figures. They were separate yet joined by
their mutual "possessions" in one corner. "When we give something," said Manawadi, "it is like that. Maybe we don't keep it, but
we don't lose it either."

It is a premise of most if not all Melanesian societies that no one is
born into them with wealth. Wealth must be acquired, usually in
competitive circumstances, only to be given away again—for one of
the paradoxes of the gift is that it is not a diminution of the donor's
self but an enlargement of it. Wealth objects such as pigs, large

23

yams, and shell valuables aptly symbolize, therefore, those components of personhood that have to be achieved. Up to a point, the very elusiveness of wealth and the demanding struggle to attain it mean that constructions of self based upon it are precarious; men are sensitive to slight and to real or imagined delicts against them, and they respond with demands for compensation (*fata*, "equivalent return, balance, repayment" [cf. Young 1974:55]). This should be seen as restitution for damage to selfhood rather than as payment for damage or loss of possessions.

The disbursement of wealth generates "name," and beyond a certain threshold (which few men reach) name itself becomes a resource for attracting further wealth, the distribution of which further enhances name. Fame is then synonymous with the social circulation of one's name. The facilitating means of this process is magic, or what we might call the persuasiveness of a powerful personality. All of the subjects in this book achieved their commanding personalities through others' belief in their magic, by which they managed their identities and manipulated their social relationships.

There are obvious difficulties in essaying biographies of persons who do not themselves claim individuality, character, or personality as we claim to understand them in the West. By its very nature, biography "delivers a self."[7] But this book could not have been written if I had been unwilling to transcend the "emic" view or if I had believed that stable definitions of personal identity in Kalauna were impossible. At the very least, one can accept Hallowell's (1955) dictum that a sense of "self-continuity" is a generic human trait, from which it follows that moral responsibility in society presupposes a self-conscious self, which others respond to and interact with. Beyond this the anthropological biographer must venture where psychologists fear to tread, and in this section I bare my own presuppositions and indicate how I have constructed the three main life histories of this book.

The most valuable starting point for any biography is what the

24

subject has to say about himself. Whether or not we dignify self-accounts by the term "autobiography" in a culture where this genre does not exist, they can be elicited and they can be scrutinized as texts to yield information about a person and his culture. Pursuing for a moment a metaphor of the biographical process, I borrow Korzybski's notion of the metacommunicative relationship of map to territory (1941). One might then conceive of the autobiographical enterprise (or self-explanation in a historical mode) in the following way.

The territory of a man's life as it exists in his memory is at the very least coordinated with the tangible circumstances of his present: a wife, a child, a house, a cleared patch of bush, a grove of fruit trees —anything in fact which from his viewpoint is an index of his present personal identity. In giving a verbal account of these things, of how they came to be in relation to himself and how the thread of remembered experience encompasses them, the author of the life creates a verbal representation—a map. The mapmaking proceeds by labeling according to conventional criteria: by entitlement, by summary, by omission, by invention too, perhaps, to fabricate links that memory has lost. The map, we may be sure, will never be exactly the same on two occasions. It will be redrawn to highlight this contour or that, for whatever immediate purpose or prevailing whim. Only writing gives a modicum of fixity, an extra dimension of reality-definition, to such biographical maps. But for those who recount their lives orally there will be a ceaseless trekking to and fro across the remembered terrain, not unlike the characters in Iyahalina's myths. The truth status of the map, the degree to which it accurately represents the territory, may be wholly questionable; but the important point is that the map, however distorted or ill-drawn, tells us much about the person who made it.

In one of his short fables, Jorge Luis Borges conceived of an ambitious College of Cartographers which "evolved a Map of the Empire that was of the same scale as the Empire and that coincided with it point for point" (1975:131). Such a degree of exactitude in science, implies Borges, is futile; the absolute fidelity of map to territory, model to reality, tells us nothing about territory—or reality. Who would devote a life (and to what purpose) to recording (or even reading) a biography that matched the life with such exactitude? The biographer, however, is at one further remove from the crude maps provided by his subject; documents, texts, events all have to be sorted, collated, and synthesized to produce a map of the maps. There can be no question of making this coincide "point for point" with the territory of the subject's life or memory. The data the biographer selects to fashion a life story come from other sources as well as from the subject; the biographer can by these means test the veracity or validity of the subject's view of himself. One of the principal devices used by the biographer to synthesize various sources is the organizing image or "metaphor of the self."[8] Like projection and scale on a map, these orient the reader in the unfamiliar territory of another's life. Through such images or metaphors the fragments of the map fit together with some semblance of consistency, and the reader "understands" the subject. The biographer's map is not a point-for-point representation (of the fabulous Empire in which even Borges's cartographers lost themselves), but a miniature. The metaphors that accomplish this transformation of refractory and of itself meaningless information are ideally provided by the biographer's subject. They should be concepts resonant in his own culture which also translate effectively into English. They are the biographer's means to meaning. The most fertile source of such idioms for my Kalauna subjects are the myths that live in and through them.

In approaching each life history I have been aware that no single view of it is adequate. Biography itself becomes absurd from a fixed viewpoint, and quite unprofitable unless hagiography or caricature is intended. In looking at each of my three main subjects I took three principal standpoints: one from a formal distance of their place in the community, one from the middle ground of my own interaction with them and my observation of their interactions with others, and one from as close as their self-expressions, their myths, and my own empathetic insights would allow. Each of these standpoints interpenetrate and influence one another; it would have been a spurious exercise to manage the information so that it appeared to fall neatly into categories according to its source. For similar reasons I have avoided subheadings in my text, apologetically aware that this imposes an extra burden on the reader's concentration.

Intruding as far as I have been able into the lives of my subjects, I have entered territory normally avoided by the anthropologist. "In the case of extant life histories," wrote Langness in 1965, "the lack of analysis and interpretation is ubiquitous." While a number of notable interpretative attempts have been made since then (e.g., Read 1965, Wilson 1974, Crapanzano 1980), the scope for innovation within the genre remains enormous. But there is still a widespread assumption that "a life history speaks for itself" (Frank 1979: 71). Two other recent studies, Keesing's 'Elota's Story (1978) and Strathern's Ongka (1979), present the autobiographies of Melanesian leaders in the classic manner of Radin's Crashing Thunder and Simmon's Sun Chief, that is, as self-evident cultural documents rather than as textual materials to be analyzed and interpreted.[9]

Bold interpretation seemed essential to my own purposes of examining personal political style in Kalauna and testing myth's isomorphic relationship to life history. My main objective has been to portray unique individuals in terms of their representative culture, rather than to present a unique culture in terms of representative individuals. I have not been concerned, for instance, to establish how "typical" or "deviant" my subjects were by measuring them against some hypothetical modal personality. What I have tried to identify, discursively rather than definitively in each case, is a personal style constructed from biographical idioms and the bits and pieces of information at my disposal. These fragments, like the scattered leaves of a dateless diary, I have sorted and assembled to make an interpretation based on the simple supposition that there is something patterned and hence characteristic about a person's behavior through time. The interpretations I offer are, so far as my understanding of Kalauna culture goes, largely within the idioms and ethos of that culture. But to effect translation I have sometimes resorted to idioms that are not indigenous: anthropology would otherwise be impossible. The phenomenological perspective of "lived experience" does not preclude reference to Western models in seeking to understand alien categories; it insists only that the former

27

maintain the status of analogies and not be used subversively to explain the latter. In other words, when I allude to our own interpretative models (from the discourse of psychoanalysis or literary criticism, for example) I do not invoke them to explain Kalauna thought, but to explicate or unfold it. Freud's Oedipal myth is a profound symbolic resource in our own culture, analogous to the symbolic resource of the Honoyeta myth in Kalauna's culture: both focus on the tragic conflict between fathers and sons. I do not thereby intend a psychoanalytical interpretation of paternal and filial ambivalence, but rather to effect a translation of meaning for them into meaning for us.[10]

In situating the lives of my subjects firmly in their social setting, in ascribing them cultural goals and political motivations, I have adopted a "dramatistic" perspective.[11] I do not offer this as a theory of society, but as a gross metaphor, a way of speaking about it. The nature of one's materials predisposes to particular perspectives; here, my predominantly textual data incline me to view Kalauna society "as narrative" rather than as a species of "big animal" or a type of "big machine" (Peacock 1969). The dramatistic perspective also enjoins consideration of the actor's view of his roles: it serves to remind us that, as Duncan puts it: "The actor is always bound to his audience, just as the audience is always bound to the actor, to discover what roles mean" (1962:79). This is particularly relevant to the situation of Iyahalina and the other ritual guardians, for their roles were scrutinized most critically by their Kalauna audience.

The actor's perception of his political role involves at least three things: its task or competence, its legitimacy, and its valuation by others. Most political scenarios in Kalauna involve the assertion, denial, or renegotiation of these aspects of role; hence they are integral to Kalauna's political dramas. Such dramas, insofar as they are repetitive, can be examined to elucidate political processes (Turner 1957). By political processes I mean the ways (devices, strategies) in which people (leaders, groups) achieve ends in a public arena (that is, exposed to the conflicting ends sought by others). These ends have to be adjusted continually to meet goals that are normatively valued; and this is where the rhetorical manipulation of ideology flourishes.

Tasks, in this simple scheme, may refer to any kind of work or role-competence that men perform to gain status, and having gained it, to maintain or enhance it. Generally speaking, men seek fame for their names to be remembered after they are dead. They strive to accomplish tasks heroically with finesse and aplomb. For all ambitious men in Kalauna it involves a never-ending round of garden work, of negotiation, challenge, and confrontation; and for those who are leaders, it entails greater exertions and risks, which, measured in the public eye, are cumulative indices of status and achievement. Tasks, then, are both subjectively motivated and objectively elicited, subjectively monitored and objectively evaluated.

Legitimacy involves the rights and credentials associated with a role: the right to perform a task and the right to exclude others from participation in it. The quest for legitimacy is coterminous with the contest for control of resources, whether these be land, labor, crops, or magical knowledge. Legitimacy, therefore, has also to do with the right to exercise authority. It often entails the rhetorical appeal to myths as charters and statements of precedent.

Under the rubric of evaluation can be found varieties of attitudes and behavior to do with redressive action. Here I am mainly concerned with a pattern or paradigm of singular importance in Kalauna, one which motivates a type of drama that provides, as it were, the plot of the book. I have deliberately employed a weighty substantive as a cover term for this action pattern: *victimage,* Kenneth Burke's coinage for the scapegoat motive or function in human society.[12] Victimage in Kalauna is institutionalized in two principal modes: a projective system of vengeance, homicide, and sorcery, and an introjective system of self-castigation. Although these types of victimage may sometimes appear in pure form as vicarious sacrifice and self-sacrifice respectively, they are often found in combination. The mythology is replete with heroic victims, and Kalauna people seem to read their own history in terms of the complex interplay of these themes of victimage.

A sense of fateful drama attends the working of victimage. One could speak of "emplotment," or simply of plot with its dramatistic connotations, its hint of conspiracy, and its aptness as a translation of Aristotle's *mythos*. Turner writes of "social dramas" (1957, 1974), and Schieffelin of "cultural scenarios" (1976), though I believe we are describing similar things. In Turner's usage "social dramas" having "processual form" are generated by conflicting "root paradigms," which are "cultural models in the heads of the main actors" (1974:17, 33, 64). Victimage would seem to be a "root paradigm" in Turner's sense:

> Paradigms of this fundamental sort reach down to irreducible life-stances of individuals, passing beneath conscious prehension to a fiduciary hold on what they sense to be axiomatic values, matters literally of life or death. [Ibid.:64]

For Schieffelin, a "cultural scenario" is a "typical event sequence," "embodied in everyday, informal courses of action." "It is empirically recognizable in the general procedure by which a people repeatedly approach and interpret diverse situations and carry them through to similar types of resolution" (1976:3).

The working out of victimage through drama has the force of a collective representation, an ineluctable and destined consequence within a closed yet divisive political structure. The dynamic aspects of role, which I have labeled tasks and legitimacy, run headlong into victimage time and again. There are innocent victims and guilty victims; there are victims who accept their sacrificial role and there are victims who avenge themselves by recourse to mortification. The latter can assume a heroic magnitude, dramatically expressed in destructive gestures of profound resentment. To the extent that this becomes damaging of self also, victimage describes a feedback loop. To a Westerner such resentment and spiteful kicks against fate might seem futile, empty gestures; but, accommodating ourselves to the scale of Kalauna's world view, they can also be seen as tragic in the best Aristotelian tradition.

To die, however, is not necessarily the worst thing. Physically or morally incapacitated "rubbish men" are emasculated by victimage —sacrificed, vicariously, by fitter men to flatter their own worth.

And victimage is virtually predicated by the fierce egalitarianism that would cut down to size all extraordinary achievements, especially those in the field of competitive gardening. Kalauna men fully understand this. But enmeshed as they are in their system, they view sorcery as a *reality* of victimage, and not simply as an enduring idiom consequent upon their striving to accomplish tasks and fulfill legitimate roles. In Kalauna's rhetorical idiom the three terms are typically (though not invariably) related as follows. A middle-aged man says to his growing son: "When I die you will take my place [legitimacy]. I will work hard to leave you with no debts [tasks]. But not too hard lest others try to kill me with sorcery [victimage]."

What Kalauna people do not see so clearly, perhaps, is that the consequences ("sorcery") also feed back by virtue of the very idiom to produce fresh grounds for renewed tasks and claims to legitimacy. In many instances, indeed, sorcery may itself become a heroic task of vengeance, one sanctioned by myth. This is true of the bereaved, suffering the death of a kinsman and conspiring to punish in their turn. It is particularly true of leaders, who handle victimage in a manner commensurate with their greater powers. Flagrant abuse of sorcery power may lead to despotism, a political genre in which many of the normative relations of reciprocity and negotiated opposition are suspended for a time. Despotism might be seen as a form of sustained and collective victimage in the name of legitimate tasks. In the figures of Malaveyoyo and Tobowa I shall illustrate these strategies and temptations of the basic drama, and I shall conclude, in my study of Kimaola, with a potential despotism that was thwarted by popular action.

∧∧∧∧∧

The fact that all my biographical studies in this book are of leaders —and Lulauvile leaders at that—disposes the account to illustrate a particular mode of "heroic" victimage. Because they assume relatively weightier roles with correspondingly greater tasks and more powerful rhetorical legitimations than ordinary men in Kalauna, their victimage resounds with greater clamor and wider conse-

31

quence. Moreover, as leaders of Lulauvile, the clan that claims pre-eminent status in the community, they bear the brunt of concerted victimage. I defer discussion of the clash of the covert principle of hierarchy (as represented by these men) with the overt principle of egalitarianism (as represented by the majority), but here it is pertinent to remark that the interplay of myth and life finds its most perfect closure in such figures of stature. From a dramatistic point of view, the victimage of "order figures" promotes the greater catharsis of pity and fear in the audience.[13]

Whether the relatively closed sphere of Kalauna thought could articulate conceptions of tragedy is a moot point (I know of no term for it), but I would claim that the affective dispositions are incontestably present. I observed, for example, that Kalauna men sometimes wept "for pity" (*nuavita*), not when they narrated myths, but when I played back their tape-recorded narrations for them to hear. They apprehended tragedy in the mirrored form of the playback. Such, in essence, is theater.

The consciousness of plot in Kalauna, undergirded as it is by the experience of social symbols as compelling and almost omnipotent, bespeaks a dramatistic ambience difficult to grasp by those of us who dwell in amorphous cities and experience social life as fragmented and discontinuous. But let us pause to consider the general specifications of life in a small, preliterate, self-sufficient, and relatively isolated community like Kalauna. Its members live in face-to-face communication for the whole of their lives; they are interrelated in numerous ways, so that the many-stranded relationships require some dramatic or ceremonial emphasis to demarcate role-assumption and role-separation. The scope for the irony of the mask is enhanced under these conditions. Further, the system of verbal communication tightens the dramatic unities. It is restricted rather than elaborate and hence loaded with presupposition; it is standardized with respect to role-adjustments; it conveys information rather than knowledge; it is developed in metaphor in respect of manipulative political rhetoric, and also in respect of performative magical commands; finally, verbal communication in Kalauna is subtly dissimulative.

Moreover, the world view is parochial and sociocentric; it is characterized by analogical or "magical" thinking such that schema of meanings conflate subjective experience and objective event; given, too, a "sorcery theory of man" (Barth 1975:132), according to which members of the society are held to blame for one another's misfortunes, then a dramatistic ambience — at the heart of which lies the enticement of victimage — seems not only plausible but virtually assured. On this tiny stage, with its restricted cast of actors adopting different roles and expressing the gamut of human emotions centered on birth, copulation, and death, there are only finite trajectories, limited possibilities for destiny. Small wonder then, that dramas recur, that characters are histrionic, and that myths provide the actors with shadow scripts that cue their improvisations.

In the course of this book I have tried to convey some of the ethos in which there is convergence between myth and life, and in which the past is always present in the future, engendering thereby a sense of fatedness. If some of my allusions to this fatedness seem contrived, the contrivance was not of my own invention: the clues came from the actors. There remains an unsolved conundrum here, for what I took to be coincidence they assumed to be motivated. Where I scented synchronicity (what Jung dignified by calling "an acausal connecting principle"), they seemed unperturbed by any threat to their epistemology.[14] Within the causal mold of my own thought I could only attribute such coincidence to statistical improbabilities being rendered somewhat less improbable by the close-knit and involuted currents of life in a population as small as Kalauna's. I sometimes thought of their lives as tangled strands in a large ball of yarn. More fancifully, I imagined their psyches prodding one another with cues, so that they might act in anticipated ways in order to confirm, in self-fulfilling fashion, an overdetermined world view in which chance and contingency played almost no part.

The dramatistic ambience is not necessarily dispelled by the intrusion of the outside world, for the villagers are selective as to what shall penetrate. While the conditions outlined above remain in force, extrinsic influences can be accommodated and absorbed. New ideas derived from the experience of wage labor abroad, and the contents (if not the form) of a radically different world view introduced by Christian missionaries, are molded to match the old

33

premises. Wage labor itself becomes a youthful rite of passage saturated with drama, while the curse of sorcery comes to be explained as mankind's punishment for victimizing Jesus Christ. Thus the parameters of the sociocentric and synchronistic modes of thought are not profoundly altered. The outside world does not represent an open door to radical changes in thought, but rather a source of more of the same kind: hence the notion, for example, that returning workers import virulent foreign sorcery which they purchase abroad with cash. Under such conditions of restricted contact, the community stage is simply widened a little to accommodate a few extra props and a handful of new roles. But the essential plots remain, enlivened by some innovative themes and alternative resolutions. The basic myths, too, retain their vitality and speak through the recurrent dramas.

/\/\/\/\

To illustrate some of the abstract themes of this chapter I conclude with an exemplary story. It is a story about the vicissitudes of recording a *neineya* myth in Kalauna; it thereby provides a context for a text. Since the story involves myself, actor as well as narrator, I am entitled to draw several lessons from it. The first is that one cannot enjoin a "conversation" between a myth and its culture (as Burridge proposed) without acknowledging one's own part in initiating and sustaining it. The tacit role of the anthropologist in stage-managing a dialogue, however, is preceded by a more direct intervention: that of eliciting the narration. The anthropologist may then be responsible for generating an event that obliges the actors to revalue their myth. From this follows another lesson. The event that provides the context of elicitation can be read for its social and political significance just as one reads a myth for its cultural significance. Such events may reveal the extent to which a myth lives and remains vital in political debate. A third lesson underscores a point I have made already, that the ownership of myths is a crucial factor in the negotiation of their meanings and in the way they may be unfolded for interpretation. This is my point of departure from studies of myth

34

that treat it as "objectified thought" or narrative folklore. Myth is reconstructed through lived experience which mediates culture; and culture is reconstructed through lived experience which mediates myth. A final lesson concerns the embedding of text within text. The advent of the tape recorder has enormously facilitated ethnography while making anthropology considerably more difficult. If my story shows how mythology is not as innocent as we were once inclined to believe (even full brothers can quarrel about their myth's import), it also shows that ethnography too can no longer be innocent.

It is the fifth of May, 1977. I am seated on the floor of Wasikeni's large house in Edu'edu, a hamlet on the edge of Kalauna territory. Outside the rain has stopped and a late afternoon sun draws a pungent scent from the sodden ground. Wasikeni stares at me intently as I explain—yet again—why I want to record his *neineya* story, the myth of Vatako. He ruminates on a quid of betel and slowly shreds the tobacco I had given him when I arrived. Two of his grown sons squat in a corner playing cards. Adiyaleyale, one of my companions from the village, sleeps on the mat with his head resting on a bent forearm. Another companion, Kawanaba, restates my argument and reminds Wasikeni that my wife had already recorded the story of Vatako in 1973, but that I had since been told it was incorrect. Wasikeni chews and nods. He is a big-man of Iwaoyana clan, a descendant of Vatako himself, and therefore one of the owners of his ancestor's magic. (This magic is of the class called *yaleyale*, its purpose to promote tireless strength in gardening; Iwaoyana men value it as the secret of their prowess.) It would be unthinkable for Wasikeni to recite the *neineya* in the presence of Adiyaleyale and Kawanaba, for they belong to Lulauvile clan, Iwaoyana's traditional enemy; but Wasikeni understands that it is the story I want and not the magic. He nods again, and recalls how John Tomoadikuyau had told my wife the story of Vatako, and how it was he himself who had put the word about that John's version was incorrect. John belonged to a different lineage, though whether it was senior to Wasikeni's could be a matter of dispute and Kawanaba and I tactfully avoid the subject. John had died in 1975, while still a comparatively young man, leaving a widow and five children, the eldest of whom was named Vatako.

Wasikeni says he will tell me the story providing his elder brother, Nadeweya, agrees; we must wait until he returns from his garden. I hopefully unpack my cassette recorder, and to amuse my hosts I play some songs recorded the previous evening. The plaintive voices and the moist warm smell of drying earth make me drowsy and I sink against the soft pandanus leaf wall. I open my eyes to see Nadeweya climb into the house. He lays his bushknife aside and squats by his brother, then proceeds to roll some tobacco in a scrap of newspaper. Wasikeni tells him the purpose of our visit. Nadeweya nods and grants him permission to recite their myth. In anticipation I start the machine to record. Nadeweya gestures to me to stop it. He wants first, he says, to go through the story with his brother to make sure he has got it right. Very rapidly, he begins to relate the story himself. And after a few moments I surreptitiously switch on the machine, thereby recording the second half of the myth as told by Nadeweya to remind his younger brother.

NADEWEYA: . . . I go down and pluck betel nut and mustard leaf and put my net by my side. I put my lime and limestick by me and I chew and chew until daybreak. When I can just see my body, I roast some taro and yam. When they are cooked I take the leaf lid of my wife's pot and wrap my food in it. I place it inside my basket. I put my stone axehead underneath the food. Then I put my armshells, boar's tusk pendant, and shell necklace inside. Finally, my black palm shuttle too; but not the one my wife cooked. I sleep and before dawn [sic] I start to go down the hill. I go to Oya'oya but they do not know me. I come to Wa'ilaka but they do not know me . . . [list of other places omitted]. I come to Miyavalatana and from Yabala-vefouna I get it—my yaleyale secret. So I come home to Uyalibebe [the original stone sitting platform of Ukevakeva hamlet]. I look around at my brothers' houses. They untie their doors, and I tell them: "I was suicidal so I left. But now I return. Tomorrow morning I will disappear again and you will not see me. You can catch my fish now. See how I have taken the twine off my foot!"

36

And he, that man Vatako, took off the twine and gave up fishing. In the morning he went to make gardens. He planted every morning, planted, planted, and planted. And his wife ate taro tops every day, she ate and ate and ate. That's all. How he died you can tell them later.

WASIKENI: [recapitulates some points] . . . He went to Oya'oya but they didn't give him *yaleyale*? He came to Wa'ilaka and they also refused him? There was no quarreling but they refused him. Then he came to Awaiya and they gave it to him. These men: Kaibutuna, Wa'ila, Mataboye, Maleledi . . . they gave him *yaleyale*.

NADEWEYA: You see our son [John Tomoadikuyau] made a mistake and didn't begin with Yaloyaloya [where Vatako clears his first big garden]. So when you tell the story you can mention that land.

WASIKENI: Good. Like you, I will identify myself [literally, "put-together"] with Vatako. [He signals me to turn on the recorder, and I make a pretense of doing so. He clears his throat, thinks for a moment, then begins his recitation in a resonant voice.][15]

I am Vatako, and this story is about my custom. I will talk about my wife's resentment [*veumaiyiyi*]. I am "Fishnet Weaver" and she is resentful. I weave fishnets all the time because it is my custom. And all the time my wife and children are hungry. So she is resentful toward me and cuts up black palm [the shuttles he uses for weaving], and she cooks it in a big pot. Then she goes down to sweep the hamlet. I am weaving as usual. My wife's back hurts and she says: "Vatako, watch the food on the fire while I go to wash my hands. Go up and check the food." She goes to wash the pots and dishes and I go up into my house. I go up and uncover the pot, I take the leaf lid off and see only black palm, the black palm my wife is cooking. I do not speak. I go down and pick up my shuttle and I thread more of my fishnet. I weave. My wife comes back from the river. She says: "Have you been up to look already?" I do not answer because of her fury. She lifts the pot and throws it down to the ground. It smashes into pieces and the black palm spills out. I am very resentful [*unuwewe*]. I climb onto the stone sitting platform and I weave for two days and two nights. I want to die. I remain thus, weaving. And my inside is cold with anger—

[At this point in his narration, Wasikeni is interrupted by a loud voice from beneath the house. It is Todaiyana, his younger brother.]

TODAIYANA: What story are you telling? What do I hear? Do you think

you get ideas from a stone, or learning from a tree? Your son Yawalele, has he learned it yet? Where is he? Has he learned it already?

YAWALELE: [Wasikeni's eldest son and heir] I'm here. I questioned
Tony [Kawanaba] but he said it's all right, and I could not stop
them.

WASIKENI: [angrily] Answer back! I won't give it to him. I'll forbid it
forever and it can stay, but I won't give it to Yawalele.

YAWALELE: Our custom, our story, but I myself made my father wait,
and he didn't give it to me.

WASIKENI: We "close" it forever, and Yawalele will never know it.

TODAIYANA: Our custom killed him. That man [John Tomoadikuyau]
was a small boy, not even your age, let alone Nadeweya's. He died
because of custom. You said so yourself: "Custom killed him."

WASIKENI: He started the story in the middle. It's a weighty matter so
we cannot speak about it. There are two support posts, and we cannot talk about them. But everyone knows the story of "Lazy Gardener." But that other story about the support posts is our law, and
we do not tell that one. Only this one about "Lazy Gardener."
Enough, Michael. . . .

I turn off the machine but the argument continues. The mutual
resentment of the brothers escalates into genuine anger and the
father's contempt for his son threatens the latter once more with dis-
inheritance. Nadeweya and Todaiyana swear at one another and
end up calling each other lazy gardeners like Vatako. The youngest
brother's objections to my being told the story prove to be fourfold.
He had not been consulted. The "custom" had not yet passed to its
rightful heirs, so if I wanted to hear it I should pay handsomely for
it. John Tomoadikuyau had told the story — and then died, so Wasikeni should be warned. Finally, my Lulauvile companions might
learn the story "for nothing" while helping me to transcribe it. Each
one of these is a sensitive issue which could take all night to air. Adiyaleyale speaks to me loudly in English, with evident exasperation,
saying that we should forget about Kalauna stories and go to some
other village where they will be only too pleased to have their
customs recorded for posterity. Kawanaba declares that he is
"ashamed" of the quarrel we have inadvertently caused. Their

resentment is contagious and I find myself adopting a similar tone, saying that if I believed anyone would die by telling me their stories then I would leave the island, go back to Australia, and look for another kind of job. By now it is quite dark and Todaiyana (who had remained beneath the house throughout the argument) marches off to his own house. We take our leave of the elder brothers, who make vague conciliatory promises to complete the story some other time. Each of us knows they will not.

Let me summarize Vatako's simple tale. Nicknamed "Fishnet Weaver," he is one of many resentful heroes in Nidula mythology (Young 1982b). Stung by the insults of his wife ("you never plant, we eat only fish"), whose own resentment culminates in her cooking her husband's weaving shuttles, Vatako wanders "suicidally" in search of gardening magic. For the exchange of valuables he acquires powerful *yaleyale* formulas. He returns home and declares he will never fish again. Then he plunges into gardening activity (Tomoadikuyau's version mentions four garden sites he miraculously cultivates), until his poor wife complains of taro, nothing but taro.

As a *neineya* the myth is a vehicle for two magical systems (the weighty "support posts" that Wasikeni cannot talk about): *yaleyale* for tireless gardening effort, and *sisikwana* for the suppression of hunger and preservation of food. It is this productive aspect of the "custom" that "killed" John Tomoadikuyau, for his own conspicuous success in growing large yams and plump taro attracted the envy of his peers. He died by their sorcery. This is particularly ironic in view of an implicit moral of the tale, which Nadeweya took pains to make sure I understood. Vatako, he explained on a later occasion, is not simply a lazy gardener who becomes a miraculous provider; he is also known as *natufayafaya,* one who looks after orphans and others in want of care and protection. Likewise, Nadeweya insisted, it is Iwaoyana's clan custom to succour the needy by feeding them generously.

As an *ifufu,* the tale is about the conversion of an indigent fisherman into an industrious gardener, a transformation brought about

39

by the hero's acquisition of magic; but the means to this, the motivation of his quest, is his answering resentment of his wife's resentment. This motivation is crucial in the Kalauna view, and as we shall see, self-punishing or suicidal resentment (*unuwewe*) is the basis of an indigenous theory of social action. Vatako will be encountered in several guises throughout this book, but his motivating resentment will be strikingly similar in every case.[16]

Another story, an anecdote this time, came my way a few weeks after the event in Wasikeni's house. I was told about M., a truly lazy gardener of Ukevakeva hamlet and Vatako's line, a man who enjoyed eating but who could scarcely provide for his wife and children. Weary of gossip and of having to accept the sympathetic gifts of her brothers, M.'s wife gathered some stones from the river one day, put them in a pot, covered them with water, and set the pot upon the fire. Then she told her husband to mind the cooking while she went down to sweep the hamlet. On checking the boiling pot, M. saw the stones. "O sorry Ewelia, I never plant for you!" he wept. (Ewelia, we may note, was the name not of his own wife but of Vatako's.) He kicked the pot over, spilling the stones. Then, mortified, he fled to his garden hut, where he spent the night alone.

"And did his gardening improve after that?" I asked.

"Yes! He worked so hard that people asked his wife what had happened. 'Ah, you taught him a lesson!' they said."

Another lesson. In this negative instance of mythical enactment an identification with the hero was forced upon M. by his resentful wife. Hers was the creative appropriation of the myth, which cast her hapless husband in the role of Vatako, thereby shaming him into an attempt to emulate the hero's conversion. But we may be sure that the device would have failed if M. had not been of Vatako's line. Had he belonged to any other clan he could have dismissed his wife's pointed action and even plausibly feigned ignorance of the story for the same good reason: it was not his "custom." The force of the sanction lay in his socially inherited disposition to identify or be identified with Vatako. Indeed, if any woman in Kalauna other than one married to an Iwaoyana man had used the myth in this fashion, Iwaoyana clansmen would have been quick to demand compensation for the theft of their story.

In these mundane examples, we begin to see dimly what it might mean to own a myth, and not only to come under its influence, but to be enticed, tempted, or enjoined to live it. Kalauna men can no more shake off their myths than they can shed their skins.

2
The House of Lulauvile

The senators of Rome are this good belly,
And you the mutinous members. For
   examine
Their counsels and their cares, digest
   things rightly
Touching the weal o' th' common, you
   shall find
No public benefit which you receive
But it proceeds or comes from them to
   you,
And no way from yourselves.

                  — *Coriolanus,* I, i

/\/\/\/\

Kalauna is a compact village of some 470 people that sits on a cramped and rocky shelf about a thousand feet up the mountain slope of eastern Goodenough Island.[1] It faces the rising sun and a broad sweep of sea, beyond which lies the area called Muyuwa, the islands of the northern Massim. Behind the village the forested mountains rise precipitously to join the island's spine. For a few hundred feet the more accessible slopes are dotted with taro gardens, while the gentler, grassy slopes below the village are planted with yam, sweet potato, sugar cane, manioc, and other crops. On the

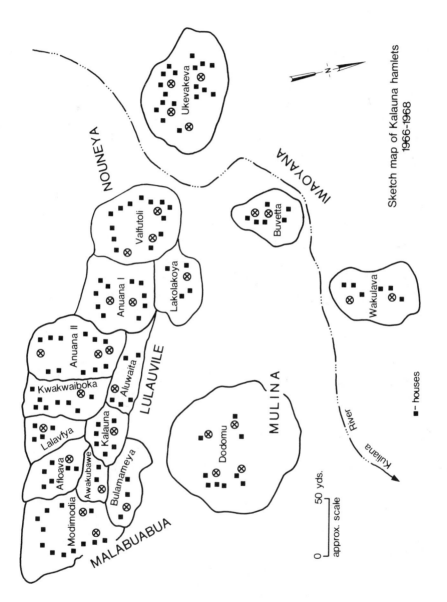

Sketch map of Kalauna hamlets
1966-1968

NOUNEYA

IWAOYANA

Ukevakeva

Valfutoli

Buvetta

Lakolakoya

Anuana I

Wakulava

Anuana II

Kwakwaiboka

Aluwaita

LULAUVILE

Lalavfya

Kalauna

Afioava

Awakubawe

Dodomu

Modimodia

Bulamameya

MULINA

MALABUABUA

Kuliana River

0   50 yds.

approx. scale

■ – houses

flatter ground toward the coast there are banana groves and small plantations of coconuts. Despite their ready access to the sea, Kalauna people regard themselves, and are regarded by others, as "people of the mountain"; they neither build nor own canoes. Men enjoy fishing in the sea or in the swift rivers, as they enjoy hunting in the bush or on the grasslands, but they always subordinate such activities to the greater demands of gardening.

Traditionally, Kalauna was an independent and autonomous political unit, which fought with neighboring villages and celebrated its own festival cycle based on the island-wide ceremonial moiety division into Modawa (Drum) and Fakili (Comb). Since 1964 Kalauna has formed a ward of the Goodenough Island local government council and is represented by its own elected councillor. Internally, the political organization of the village is based upon a conglomeration of clans (*yabu*), which are in turn composed of subclans or lineages (*unuma*). One or more *unuma* occupy a single hamlet, of which there were seventeen in 1968. The hamlet is effectively the minimal political unit, a group of agnatic kinsmen who acknowledge the leadership of one man. Ideally, though not always in practice, this man is the "firstborn of the firstborn," the senior member of the hamlet's genealogically senior lineage. With the exception of Lulauvile, clans—and therefore hamlets too—are exogamous, and the rule of residence after marriage is patrivirilocal (wives join their husbands to reside in the husband's father's hamlet). Households are based on the nuclear family, which is also the principal unit of production and consumption. Each subclan or lineage possesses a sitting platform (*atuaha*) constructed of stone slabs, beneath which the founding ancestors laid anchoring magic (*bakibaki*), and around which their descendants' houses cluster. These sitting circles are the most enduring human constructions in Kalauna; to their owners they are lithic symbols of the continuity of their lines.

The majority of marriages in Kalauna (86 percent in 1967) are between natal members of the community; there is thus a strong preference for in-marriage, which promotes cohesion through ties of matrifiliation. Other sources of integration are the permanent pairings of clans and hamlets in food-exchanging partnerships (*fofofo*), and a countervailing set of enmities (*nibai*) based on the blood-debt of past enemy relationships. *Fofofo* partnerships (which exist between clans, lineages, and individuals) are colloquially defined as "those who eat our *niune*," that is, formal, political prestations of food. *Nibai,* or enemies, are colloquially "those who killed and ate our grandfathers." Hence, there is sanctioned enmity within Kalauna as well as an ideal comity, and the political balance between the clans is normally a delicate one.

The subsistence economy is based on the cultivation of yam, taro, banana, and sweet potato (in that order of prestige ranking). Pigs are important tokens in a complex exchange system that embraces marriage, mortuary ceremonies, and the various kinds of feasting. Cash circulates readily nowadays, of course, and its main source is the wage labor of young men who go abroad to work for a year or two at a time. Some men regularly make copra from their coconuts, but the cash from this source is hardly equal to that obtained by women who sell food at the weekly market at the patrol post of Bolubolu, an hour's walk away. Most crop surpluses, however, are absorbed by feasting and competitive exchange, for vegetable food provides the principal idiom of political assertion. Political relations within and between Kalauna and other villages are expressed in sumptuary food-giving contests (*abutu*), and in year-long festivals, which the clans sponsor in approximate rotation. For the duration of its festival, a sponsoring clan enjoys a dominant position in the community and its leading men affect the chiefly title of *kaiwabu*.

Leadership in Kalauna is complicated by the existence of a number of ritual experts or "guardians" (*toitavealata*) belonging to the largest and structurally anomalous clan of Lulauvile. By virtue of its founder myths, this superclan claims preeminent status in the village, but under the prevailing ideology of egalitarianism these claims are seldom overtly acknowledged by the rest of the community. Since there is no real economic basis for Lulauvile supremacy, and only the sketchiest of formal appurtenances of hierarchy, I describe Lulauvile as having "submerged" rank. At the level of quotidian political process, however, the tension between Lulauvile's view of itself and the other six clans' view of Lulauvile provides the most interesting dynamic in the community. Because the five leading figures under scrutiny in this book were all Lulauvile men, this dynamic will be explored tangentially throughout. I shall also have much to say about Lulauvile itself, for the life histories of these leaders were to a great extent shaped and inspired by the venerable traditions they were heir to.

∧∧∨∧∧

Despite some seventy years of European contact (including sixty of intermittent mission influence), Kalauna has obdurately retained a semipagan identity as it continues to celebrate its own *dewa* (customs, way of life). Compared to many other Nidula communities, Kalauna's ethos has a charged Dionysian quality which is almost anachronistic in such an exposed area of seaboard Melanesia. Save briefly in 1959, the community has had little to do with cargo cults, though the millenarian flame occasionally flickers. I have argued elsewhere that Kalauna's response to pacification involved an intensification of its competitive exchange institutions as a surrogate for fighting (Young 1971). Probably, with its larger population, its efflorescent feasting activities, and its broader contact with the world outside, Kalauna culture is richer in its collective life-style than it was at the turn of the century. In many ways, too, it must be a more agreeable society in which to live.

Nevertheless, the fostering of a relentlessly competitive spirit (the price of equality being eternal competition) makes for a "driven" consciousness familiar to the industrial societies of the West. An obsession with status battles breeds a sensitivity to slight, a developed sense of shame, and an elaboration of devices for its infliction. The grounds for attributing misfortune to the malice of others remain intact, and sorcery beliefs flourish as vigorously as they ever did in the past. There is a common defense to pervasive sorcery fears: a syndrome of surface geniality, tact, modesty, dissimulation, and an unwillingness to criticize or condemn. Such attitudes, however, as Fredrik Barth has pointed out (1975:134), are strategical means for the exercise of relationships rather than the expression of any positive morality of social relations. Not everyone cultivates

46

these manners, of course, and it would be unbecoming for leaders and big-men to appear too ingratiating. But when normal defenses break down persecution theories proliferate, and men may even run amok, though it is more common for the anxiety-ridden to escape the community for a time by working abroad or taking refuge in their gardens. Resentment and self-pity are institutionalized: *veumaiyiyi* (ibid.:262-3) and *unuwewe* (of which I shall have much to say later) are species of revenge by recourse to self-injury. I have borrowed Kenneth Burke's rubric "victimage" for these aspects of Kalauna's ethos. This is not an analytical concept but rather, like "eidos" or "ethos" itself, a bit of Batesonesque shorthand for identifying a cluster of attitudes and affects in a social milieu.

The most striking theme in Kalauna culture (for the sorcery complex, after all, is largely hidden) is the symbolic idiom of that mundane but vital substance, food. At some point all other value configurations and symbolic idioms lock into a concern with food-getting, food-keeping, and food-giving. There are few semantic domains one can enter without tripping over lexemes that connote food or are food-flavored by association. I have already given some account of the narrower domain of food symbolism and its value configurations in *Fighting with Food;* here, I want to pose one or two bolder questions.

While food provides a master symbol for the articulation of the main areas of Kalauna social experience, and while at the level of cognition Kalauna people themselves grasp the iconic uses of food in standing for a variety of things and relationships that are not-food, what can be said about the unconscious significations of food? Put another way, why have Kalauna people found food (as Lévi-Strauss might say) so "good to think" with? Some rational explanations suggest themselves but none are entirely satisfactory, if only for the reason that neighboring cultures of the same genetic stock do not go to quite the same lengths in making food the measure of all things. The ecological nudge provided by periodic drought (experienced as the threat of famine) is a necessary, perhaps, but not sufficient reason for the richness of the complex. As a response to the possibility of drought it seems incommensurate with the level of actual threat, especially so since European contact, which brought a variety of additional food crops plus an administrative guarantee to safeguard the population against starvation.

Yet the overadaptation remains something of a strain for those subject to its customary compulsions, and the logic of the value system that gives food such emphasis greatly exacerbates sorcery fears. Even if these are discounted as a symptom of some collective malaise —of something rotten in the state of Kalauna—there are other, more direct, maladaptations which flow as a consequence from the inordinate valuation of food. I mention here only two: the destruction of the nutritive properties of the best yams by hoarding them until they are scarcely edible; and the resentment against young offspring with an unsocialized tendency to eat too much.

These illustrations point beyond rational explanations, toward, that is, the unconscious foundations of the culture. At this level, food provides simply one expression (albeit the most symbolically weighted) of the culture's concern with orality: ingestion as the center of experience. Other modes, less developed by comparison but thematically obtrusive nonetheless, are betel-chewing and cannibalism. The former is in fact a euphemism for courtship, and is thus heavily loaded with sexual connotations of marriage and procreation; the latter, although now suppressed in practice, lives on in the ideology of traditional *nibai* enmities and its idiom of oral vengeance. One might say that if betel-chewing is redolent of eros in Kalauna culture, then cannibalism was redolent of thanatos. Both are rooted in orality, but as mythology testifies this is profoundly ambivalent. For at the level of culture it seems that as much ingenuity has gone into obviating and denying orality (yet without giving compensatory rein to sexuality) as into its celebration and gratification. I shall forbear from further speculation, and I simply note that a partial answer to the question why Kalauna finds food so "good to think" lies in its ambivalence about the proposition that food is "good to eat."

∧∧∧∧

Kalauna groups are differentiated by their myths and their magic and, hence, by their rights to plant and grow crops in certain ways.

The elaboration of what they call "food customs" is, as might be expected, particularly marked in Lulauvile, the clan that not only claims to be the founding core of Kalauna, its *owola* or center post, but also the "bringer of food." The six other clans possess comparatively impoverished mythologies, less grand magical systems for food, more cursory gardening practices, and fewer burdensome food taboos. Lulauvile sees its historic role as that of guardian and exemplar: it provisions, prospers, and protects the community's food supply. Lulauvile also provides the only coherent historical tradition of Kalauna as a collectivity.

Structurally, Lulauvile is composed of two sections which are *fofofo* partners to one another. There is no absolute consensus as to which of these sections is the senior, for the myths are at variance on this point.[2] For convenience, however, I shall follow the usage of majority opinion and call the larger section Lulauvile Number One (I) and its smaller partner Number Two (II). Lulauvile I comprises seven *unuma,* which occupy the three hamlets of Anuana, Aluwaita, and Kalauna (or Heloava II). Lulauvile II comprises six *unuma,* which are unevenly distributed between two hamlets: Heloava and Anuana II. These five hamlets form a cluster in the center of the village along with the three hamlets of two smaller clans, Ainaona and Mifoloyai. If it were not for the low stone walls that separate one hamlet from another and for the disposition of the stone sitting platforms that govern the orientation of houses, the visitor might imagine that Lulauvile and its two small neighbors occupied one large hamlet. Table 1 summarizes Lulauvile's composition. The two sections are exogamous but can and do intermarry with one another, often seeking to reinforce a *fofofo* partnership by means of alliance. The hamlets are paired in *fofofo* partnerships as follows:

Lulauvile I		*Lulauvile II*
Anuana I	⟵⟶	Heloava I
Aluwaita	⟵⟶	Anuana II (senior *unuma*)
Kalauna (Heloava II)	⟵⟶	Anuana II (junior *unuma*)

This arrangement has the sanction of an origin myth, which tells how the Lulauvile ancestors emerged from the ground in pairs:

49

TABLE 1

Hamlet	Leader (1967)	Population (1967)	
LULAUVILE I			
Anuana I	Didiala	34	
Aluwaita	Siboboya	19	
Kalauna (Heloava II)	Kimaola	25	
			78
LULAUVILE II			
Heloava I	Iyahalina	28	
Anuana II	Malawidiya	29	
			57
		Total:	135

Didiala and Matalaukonina of Lulauvile I and Kedeya and Uyavai-yava of Lulauvile II. These men brought as their *dewa* ("customs") coconut, yam, taro, and pig respectively, plus a variety of lesser foods. In another version Didiala and Kedeya alone appeared and carried the food between them. (In still other myths, even those that belong to Lulauvile, all of these foods have alternative origins; but mutual consistency is not an issue when it is the same group that owns the contradictory stories.) All versions seem to agree, however, that it was Didiala who initiated the *fofofo* system of food-exchanging partnerships. He is said to have torn a spray of betel nuts and given half to Kedeya, telling him that henceforth they must "help" one another, by accepting and eating food on each other's behalf whenever it was presented to them. He paired off all later arrivals from the world underground so that the ancestors of all the clans had their own *fofofo* partners.

To disentangle the origin myths and legendary lore of Lulauvile would require a small book in itself. I have given elsewhere a brief account of Kalauna's folk history (1971:29-30; 186-187), and I shall occasionally refer to it in the chapters to follow. It is only necessary here to outline this oral tradition to establish the tenet that Lulauvile was indeed the ruling house (*manua u'una*) of ancestral Nibita.

Having emerged from the hole at the summit of the sacred hill of Yauyaba (ibid.:12-13), the people of Goodenough spread over the island. They lived contentedly until the depredations of a giant sea eagle called Manubutu caused them to scatter and hide. Nibita people went back to the hole of Yauyaba, where they lived underground again until Manubutu was killed. With a keen sense of persecution and exile, Nibita people likened themselves to the freshwater crab, *kauka nibinibita,* which burrows in sand to seek temporary shelter from predators; hence the folk etymology of the name Nibita connotes "the homeless ones."

When they emerged from Yauyaba again, their leader Adikunuwala took them to the ridgetop site of Kwabua ("you sit") where they settled for a while. Later they moved to a more congenial hillside and founded a settlement called Kwamalauta ("child embraced"), where a pregnant woman gave birth the day they arrived. By this time Nibita people had begun to reclaim all their food crops (having lost them during the sojourn underground), and when a second child was born they named him Ulaiya (the Nibita word for taro but used more generally for plump tubers of any kind). Two other hamlets were established at Kwamalauta: the first was Aukamonakuya ("stomach replete with food"), which celebrated the good times, and the second was Bakiyava ("anchor safely"), which the leader declared would "hold the people together" so they would never need to wander.

Alas, it was not to be. Kedeya quarreled with his "brothers" because they spied lasciviously on his young wife while she was bathing. The groups fought with coconut husks instead of spears, but a major dispersal ensued. Three groups migrated: one went south to the Mataita area, another to Awaiya on the coast near Bolubolu, and the third traversed the mountain northward to Eweli district. The rump that remained was Lulauvile (which is said to mean "to

[make] turn around and come back"). Lulauvile promised to provide yams and taro in exchange for various commodities from the dispersed groups. When Adikunuwala died four "sons" took his place: Kedeya, Uyavaiyava, Didiala, and Matalaukonina, who are the ancestors of the principal Lulauvile lines. It was these men who came down to the present site of Kalauna, having been invited to occupy it by Belebele clans which had fought following the murder of their leader's son. The Lulauvile groups anchored themselves in their present hamlets, and all lived well until the terrible times of Malaveyoyo, whose saga I shall tell in chapter 4.

This story of migrations and settlements, dispersals and regroupings, with its play on names that fondly evoke the most cherished values of Nibita people, is known in detail only to the elders of Lulauvile. Yet the other clans of present-day Kalauna (Ainaona, Mifoloyai, Malabuabua, Nouneya, Iwaoyana, and Mulina) all claim to have been there too, at Kwabua and Kwamalauta and then at various other sites before converging upon Kalauna. But the paucity of detail in their own versions of the story and their weak grasp of its narrative thread are puzzling; when they can tell any of it at all, it is only to dot an *i* or two of the Lulauvile version. A likely explanation is that these other clans were numerically weak compared to Lulauvile, and that it dominated them by sheer weight of numbers as well as by assertion of ritual hegemony. The evidence from genealogies suggests that Lulauvile comprised as much as half the total population of Nibita/Kalauna about a century ago. In 1967 Lulauvile represented just under 30 percent of the community. Thus its membership may have declined in relative strength over the past three or four generations from as much as a half to less than a third of the village. Two other clans appear to have grown rapidly during the same period: Iwaoyana, Lulauvile's closest rival, which represented 28 percent of the village in 1967, and Malabuabua, which comprised 14 percent. These two burgeoning clans have gained an assertive voice in Kalauna affairs which they probably lacked before, and when backed by some of the other clans they are now able to challenge Lulauvile's view of its own historic role. Certainly, some Lulauvile leaders interpret their querulous assertions as threats to their self-esteem, and as we shall see, they tend to view their eroded authority with the nostalgia of a declining aristocracy. Hence, perhaps, their autumnal preoccupation with the past.

In the Lulauvile stories of division and dispersal there is evidence that its power was also divided, symbolizing a surrender of at least part of its supremacy. They speak of "sharing out" some of their "food secrets" before they descended to Kalauna, a story given to explain how the magical systems of banana, betel nut, sugar cane, pitpit (inflorescence of *Saccharum edule*), and even sweet potato came to be in the hands of leading lineages of other clans. A suggestion of coercion underlies this granting of ritual concessions to others, for one version of the story tells how the Lulauvile ancestors were given a friendly warning that they would all die by sorcery unless they relinquished some of their magical knowledge. But Lulauvile has somehow retained control of the more important crops (yam, taro, coconut), as well as the magic of prosperity (*manumanua*) and the various weather sorceries of wind, rain, and sun. These ritual controls provide their continuing claim to legitimate community leadership.

/\/\/\/\

At the time of my first stay in Kalauna there were three Lulauvile leaders who everyone agreed were the community's "fathers" and "guardians": *toitavealata ana melala,* "men who look after the village." These men were known by name over much of the island, thanks largely to their hereditary ritual competences. These, as we shall see abundantly in the chapters to follow, were a power for prosperity and also a power for deprivation. The conservative ideology that favors their authority is implicit in the following statement by a Mulina man: "If they did not look after us we would have to search in the bush for our food. If we make them angry they can banish the food to punish us for our pride." "Pride" here refers to the arrogance, the hubris, of those dissident individualists who would challenge the ritual hegemony of Lulauvile and deny these men any extraordinary status.

To take a balanced view, it is undeniable that the *toitavealata*

53

perform for the whole community the kind of tasks a hamlet leader performs for his small group. Just as hamlet leaders are "food managers" for their kinsmen, so are the *toitavealata* food managers for the whole of Kalauna. They receive no tribute or renumeration for their standard ritual services (only when they are specially solicited), and they perform them with only the intangible rewards of esteem and a measure of political authority. They have no insignia of office, nor any claims to privileges save those that preserve their dignity: the right to be offered the choicest tubers and cuts of pork at a distribution; the right to be listened to respectfully and without interruption; the right to eat in seclusion when away from their houses, and so forth. All such behavior toward them, from the subtle and covert to the contextually ostentatious, are indicators of their rank and expressions of protocol rather than extraordinary rights or privileges in themselves. Such behavior also expresses the notion that the *toitavealata* possess more than the usual degree of authority, and consequently are charged with more than the usual amount of responsibility.

The tasks of the *toitavealata* are of two broad kinds. There are the magical rites, which they perform to accompany the normal rhythm of the annual gardening cycle; these can be regarded as regular, calendrical duties. Then there are the special magical rites, which two or three of the experts perform in collaboration in order to counter the threat of famine. This ceremony, called *manumanua,* was traditionally performed every year during the "hungry period" of the northwest monsoon. A few decades after European contact *manumanua* was performed only contingently, probably because the diversification of crops obviated its need. One may surmise that the introduction of the sweet potato and the despised manioc (*tapioca*) has done as much as anything else to weaken Lulauvile's authority. In the past, reliance upon a seasonal crop like yam and a rain-thirsty one like taro meant a far greater vulnerability to drought. Today there is something anachronistic about the *toitavealata* claim that Kalauna relies ultimately upon their good offices in safeguarding the food supply. By the 1920s, probably, *manumanua* had become a contingent instead of a calendrical rite, and nowadays it is not performed at all. The last occasion of the full-scale ceremony was reportedly 1958. I was told that Didiala and Iyahalina were about to perform it in 1965 but that they refrained in pique when there was lack of community consensus as to whether it was really necessary. That was perhaps the occasion of the anti-Lulauvile faction's greatest victory, for with *manumanua* a defunct ceremony, moribund beyond revival, Lulauvile would lose its greatest single justification for asserting its right to ritual leadership in Kalauna.

The *toitavealata* still perform their calendrical duties, however, and I shall examine them more closely in the biographical studies of Didiala, Iyahalina, and Kimaola. These men also spoke of *manumanua* as if it were alive and well; indeed, many others also seemed to believe that it would be performed again, and in 1968 heirs were being carefully schooled in its myths and magic. *Manumanua* survives in traditional thought. I shall refer to it frequently in later chapters, for its mythical validations, its rich symbolism, and its paradigmatic expression of Kalauna values are essential to an understanding of the lives of those Lulauvile men who performed it. To sketch biographies of Didiala or Iyahalina without referring to *manumanua* would be like writing the lives of saints without mentioning the Church. For these men, *manumanua* represented a dedicated way of life, a veritable cult of which they were the priests. In what follows, therefore, I shall give a concise account of *manumanua* that will serve to orient my future references to the ceremony.

/\/\/\/\/\

Manumanua, literally glossed, means "stay(ing) at home" (*manua,* "house"; though here it also connotes "village" in the sense of dwelling place or home). The reduplication of the word intensifies it to the point of insistence, for *manumanua* enjoins a set of prohibitions. It is mandatory for everyone to remain at home on the day of the ceremony, and for a whole day and night no one (with the two or three exceptions mentioned below) may enter or leave the village. This is ritually quarantined by closing the paths with bespelled vines and leaves anchored with stones. Silence and general inactivity should prevail. Villagers may not chop firewood nor scrape coconuts; they should neither laugh nor play. These injunctions provide the ceremonial background for the actual performances of *manumanua* by the *toitavealata*. They create the necessary solemnity and stillness, which the magicians intensify by their own rites.

At dawn on the assigned day the two (or three) *toitavealata* commence chanting their respective magical spells in the seclusion of their own houses. Later they descend slowly and meet in Anuana, the center of Lulauvile. There they begin the construction of an edifice of sticks, twigs, and vines, which had been gathered from the bush the previous day. They plant a center post and encircle it with sticks from various trees, binding them together with vines before enclosing the whole with a fence of woven coconut leaves. All the while they softly sing the magical formulas bequeathed by the heroes of the myths of Hudiboyaboyaleta, Kuyakwokula, Kiwiwiole, and Tomoudi. When they have finished the construction, they sit down side by side on a mat for the remainder of the day, telling their myths to one another and singing the spells associated with them. They sit as motionless as possible and they can neither eat nor drink until after dark.

While the magicians are engaged in their interminable chanting, two or three of their heirs leave the village and go to the strategic sites of ancestral coconut trees. There they perform the rites of coconut-prospering magic, beating the trees with a stone to punctuate the spells that bid the fruits to flourish. Meanwhile, the other men and women of Heloava and Anuana are cooking in their hamlets. They prepare two pots of yam and taro, which they boil on their respective stone *atuaha*. When they are ready the pots are set down by the magicians, who continue to sing their spells, which now infuse the cooked food. Heloava then exchanges its two pots with Anuana, its *fofofo* partner, and the people of both hamlets dip into them and nibble sparing mouthfuls. Later, other members of the community may come along if they wish and take pinches of food from the same pots, sharing the "bitter" bespelled food that will deaden their appetites.

Some clue to the meaning of *manumanua* for the performers is given by the symbolism of the various plants used in the construction

56

of the edifice of sticks and vines. I will not enumerate them here, but in general they stand for desirable qualities such as size, strength, endurance, tautness, drought-resistance, redness, and bitterness. The edifice becomes a self-contained and charmed "house," built of icons of concentrated powers and quintessential values. Some of the symbolic associations of the plants are recondite, such as the one that links the tiny white flower of *matakibo* with an undesiring eye, able to resist the oretic temptation of a luxuriant garden. Others are more obvious since they occur in other ritual contexts. The creeper called *baniyala,* for example, which the magicians wind around the circle of sticks, is also used by mourners following a burial. They tie it around their wrists and ankles to counteract (they say) the withering influence of the corpse with its slack, sagging skin. In the context of *manumanua,* the use of this taut, glossy-leafed vine (which grows vigorously even in drought) to bind together some of the other ritual symbols evokes its power as a countermeasure against the withering of death. I might add that none of the plants are believed to be efficacious in themselves; what power resides in them must be activated by a distinctly human operation, namely, the singing of a spell.[3]

Other clues to the meaning of *manumanua,* therefore, are contained in the imagery of the spells. I cannot present these incantations for analysis here since they are too lengthy, but one or two fragments will appear in their mythological contexts when I recount these myths in later chapters. In the meantime, the following is a sample verse in free translation. It is one of the spells sung while the magician is tying a vine around the ring of sticks.

> Stay still, I stay still
> Younger brothers, elder brothers
> You wander weakly, starving
> You will stay
> You search vainly, losing your way
> You wander with crooked fingers
> You will stay
> Stay still, I stay still
> Your hearts trembling
> Your hearts sad

57

You search vainly, losing your way
You wander weakly, starving
Stay still, I stay still

The incantation summons the imagery of desperate, aimless wandering in search of food, but it does so in order to submit it to the control of the refrain, which offers the soothing remedy of stillness.

On the day following the ceremony the people can leave the village to gather food or to fish. But they should not plant, and they should make no unnecessary journeys or gratuitous noise. On the third day life can return to normal and people may plant in their gardens. A few weeks later, to conclude the ceremony, the *toitavea-lata* walk slowly around all the gardens. They carry nothing but their baskets of betel-chewing equipment. They sing their spells continuously and spit impregnated betel juice in each garden area. Through eyes doctored with *matakibo* leaves, they inspect the crops. They also symbolically tidy each garden by picking up a piece of twig or root and laying it on a rubbish heap. The women who normally weed the gardens should then, by these exemplary magical actions, be induced to tidy their gardens likewise, their eyes "nondesiring," their bellies "small and contented," so that, like good housewives, they will not be tempted to gather more food than the minimum needed for the family meal that evening.

The aim of *manumanua*, then, is almost paradoxical: to banish famine by making food notionally inedible. In the words of Adiyale-yale of Heloava:

> So when *manumanua* is done the people can stay, calmly. They stay, and they do not finish more than a morsel of their food. They stay, and their food will ripen and rot. They stay, and its smell will become sickly. Fruitflies will gather and sit upon it. *Manumanua* makes us ashamed to take food from our gardens.

While this is surely a masochistic solution to the problems posed by food shortage, it is the most direct. By addressing itself to the human consumer *manumanua* advocates a kind of quietism, nostalgically recalling, perhaps, the golden age when men licked only stones and did not need to eat at all.

Although it focuses ultimately on the human belly as the source of man's most grievous misfortunes, *manumanua* also subsumes other magical concerns. Its incantations address the crops, the wind, and the climatic circumstances of prosperity. But these are subordinate spells, digressions as it were, and the burden of the main chants is carried by the persistent imagery of disdainful eyes, reluctant hands, and rotting food. The idioms of collective benefit in *manumanua,* then, are at least threefold: crop prosperity, favorable weather, and curtailed appetite. These conditions are interdependent and together describe the most positive value of collective well-being: *malia,* which I translate as prosperity, plenty, or abundance. Traditionally, so Lulauvile men claim, *malia* was wholly within their leaders' beneficence.

It is also within the competence of Lulauvile leaders to revoke the condition of *malia,* and this was clearly their most potent punitive sanction. Corresponding to the threefold beneficial idioms of *manumanua* there are three idioms of collective misfortune. The first and second are those sorceries of scourge that bring crop pests and excessive rain, wind, or sun. Magic of the weather is known only to Lulauvile, but a few other descent lines in Kalauna know how to "spoil the crops" by conjuring various bird or insect pests. Once again, though, it is Lulauvile that has the greatest monopoly on these baneful techniques. The cruelest idiom of all, however, is the reciprocal of *manumanua*'s tender ritual tutelage of the belly: it is the sorcery of gluttony and insatiable hunger. This magic, a triumph of sadomasochistic invention, is the ultimate weapon in a culture profoundly anxious about human greed. *Tufo'a,* as this sorcery of gluttony is called, belongs exclusively to Heloava of Lulauvile II, and it lends a strong argument to the Heloava men's case that their line provided the original chiefs of Nibita.

Within the magical realm of *manumanua,* then, Lulauvile could invert the signs to produce the antithetical state of *loka,* which is a doomsday concept of famine. The concerted sorceries of crop pests, drought, and induced greed signify all that *manumanua* seeks to ally in banishing hunger. Whereas the rites of *manumanua,* predicated on the acts of mythical heroes, invoke the still harmony and contented bellies of prosperity, the sorceries of scourge and gluttony invoke the restless wandering and hungry bellies of famine. As we shall see, these vengeful or punitive acts are also modeled upon the fateful behavior of mythical heroes.

In terse summary I quote Tabuona, a superb narrator, who was dying of tuberculosis in 1967 and who, as a man of Mulina clan, held no particular brief for Lulauvile.

When people first came out of the ground they did not know how to garden. They just licked stones for food. Then Ninialawata [a mythical first woman] gave food to Lulauvile. She gave them taro and yam first, then all the other food as well. Later famine came and chased all the food away. It was because Honoyeta wanted to punish our ancestors.

3
Time's Serpent Honoyeta

Your words are clear
at last, O Heraclitus. God and man die
each other's life, live each other's death.

— W. B. Yeats, *The Resurrection*

∧∧∧∧∧

Nidula myths are distorting mirrors. In many of them the hero is a
bent or broken body image, grotesque and stigmatized, but reflecting some vision of an ideal selfhood. Honoyeta, probably the most
widely known myth of the island's corpus, is the name of such a
hero: a snake-man who eludes social definition by evading all obligations; a sun-spirit and father-figure who is ageless, aloof, and
vengeful. To explore in full all the facets of this myth would require
a volume in itself, since they are reflective of the very ethos of Kalauna. My more limited aim here is to locate the myth in Kalauna
consciousness, to show some of what I perceive to be its local refrac-
tions. Subsequent chapters bear the proof, the extent to which the
themes I identify in the myth are exemplified and illuminated by
historical figures and living men of Kalauna. I present the myth,
therefore, as a prelude to the chapters that follow; these variously
improvise upon its themes. This is a device to reveal the mutual
interplay between myth as form and lived experience as content: the
"epic fabric of which myth is the warp and reality the woof" (Leenhardt 1979:192).

61

The following version of Honoyeta, the hero whose most singular characteristic is his duplicity, was recorded in Kalauna in 1968. The narrator was Kafataudi, leader of Valeutoli hamlet and Kimaola's brother-in-law. His credentials for telling the myth were not impeccable, for it is acknowledged to belong to Lulauvile. But I have chosen to present Kafataudi's version for its balance and lucid narrative style, and also for his peroration, which identifies Honoyeta as a god (*yiduwa*) of the sun. Most versions I possess do so only implicitly by means of allusion, or briefly in a throwaway line. The association of Honoyeta with the sun, however, especially in its destructive aspect, is crucial to Kalauna thinking; and it is for this reason that none of the Lulauvile "owners" (notably Kimaola, Kiyodi, and Ewahaluna) would record it for me, in case drought ensued and their irresponsible narrations be held to blame. Kafataudi was less scrupulous; he did not know the magic (though he indicates in his narrative where he thinks it should be recited). Another dramatic feature of his version is noteworthy. Whereas most narrators reveal the precise nature of the hero's human disguise early in the story, Kafataudi delays this revelation to the last possible moment: the listener's (or reader's) discovery coincides with that of the hero's wife. The original text of this version of the myth is given in appendix II.

Honoyeta and his two wives lived at Yauyaba. He used to deceive them in the following way. First he told them: "Go and fill our saltwater bottles at the beach. I am an old man, so I'll stay here and sleep." Then he curled up in the ashes by the hearth and slept while his wives put bottles in their baskets and set off for the sea. When they had gone Honoyeta got up to eat, then went inside his back room to decorate himself: he put on his headdress, armshells, and feathers. Taking his fishing spear from beneath the house, he then went down to the sea at Laue'e. He fished and followed the beach around until he was in sight of his two wives. They eyed him shyly: "That handsome man is coming. Let's talk to him." He approached along the beach, still spearing fish. "Where are you going?" they asked. "Nowhere, I'm fishing," he replied. "Ah, brother, what about some fish?" "I'd give you some but what about your husband? He might come and catch me." But he gave his fish to the women, and while they were stooping to fill their bottles with seawater he left them and returned home. There he took off his valuables and hid them inside the house, sat down in the ashes and rubbed himself with them. Then he went to sleep. His wives returned and started to roast the fish he had given them himself. He would ask: "Is this our fish?" And they would explain: "We caught them at low tide." Then they would eat. Things went on in this manner for a long time.

One day one of Honoyeta's wives entered the back room and saw an armshell with fresh coconut oil on it, and she recognized it as the one worn by the young man at the beach. She thought: "Oh, perhaps our husband is deceiving us, chewing betel with us and courting us as if he were some other man. We go down to the sea first and then he follows." And indeed, Honoyeta deceived his own wives like this many times, tricking them like a cowboy* and courting them as if he were a stranger. But now his first wife had discovered his armshell and found him out. She said to her cowife: "Friend, you spy on him next time. We can leave together but when we are in the forest you can return and hide and keep an eye on him." At eight o'clock next morning the two of them put bottles in their baskets and set off while their husband watched them go. The second wife secretly returned and hid herself and waited. The first wife went on to the sea. Honoyeta took out his valuables, washed and decorated himself, then took his fish spear and went down to the beach in order to deceive his wives again. He fished and followed the beach. This time he saw only one of his wives there. But he went down and washed, and took off his skin and folded it and placed it on the shriveled fiber of an Alocasia plant. He shed his skin like a snake and hung it on the Alocasia. He decorated himself again and then continued fishing and following the beach until he found his first wife. His second wife was hiding like a cowboy in the forest watching him. And while Honoyeta was giving fish to his first wife, his second wife took his skin from the Alocasia plant and tore it up. She tore it up and threw it away, then returned home to wait. When Honoyeta returned she greeted him. "Thank you, my wife," he said bitterly. "You found my skin. It was my disguise as a man. But now you have destroyed my skin, how can I be a man?" And he was angry. His first wife arrived but he stayed outside and didn't go into the house. His wives cooked food but he refused it. He climbed a betel palm tree and plucked some nuts, and he picked mustard leaves to chew with them.

*"Cowboy" was common usage in Kalauna in the late sixties. Imported from Port Moresby by returning workers who had enjoyed Westerns at the cinema, it was synonymous with trickery and cool cheek.

He stayed on his sitting platform until evening, then he descended and decorated himself.

He began to wander from village to village because he wanted someone to kill him. At each village he got angry and swore at people to provoke them. But people were afraid to kill him; they suspected he was a god and that if they killed him they would all die themselves. So he wandered from one village to another until he had visited them all.

Finally he came to Iwabu. He climbed on top of the sitting platform called "You Wrong Me." The villagers were making gardens, all except one man who was minding his young son. Honoyeta said to him: "You are minding your younger brother." The man replied: "No, it is my son!" They argued back and forth until the man grew angry. He took down a spear and speared Honoyeta. The spear went up into his body. He speared him many times but Honoyeta did not die. He climbed down and said: "No, I am Honoyeta. It is not easy for me to die. But I'll tell you my taboo. Go and cut a branch of the *ilumwadaleta* tree, and if you hit my throat with it you will kill me. My name is Honoyeta. I am a god, not a man." The Iwabu man went to find an *ilumwadaleta* tree. He chopped off a branch and brought it back to the village. Then he hit Honoyeta across the throat. He sat down on the ground, then crawled onto the sitting platform. People came forward and began to cut off his limbs, though he was still talking. They filled up one pot with his pieces, and then another until they had a line of pots. They began to cook him, though his mouth was still speaking, whispering weakly. They stirred the pots but he wouldn't cook; the earth beneath the pots became scorched but still he didn't cook. "Oh, this isn't a man," people said. "This is a god. It was a mistake to kill him, for his flesh remains raw. If it would cook we could eat it. What are we to make of this? He must be a god."

The people cut coconut leaves and wove baskets into which they put the remains of Honoyeta. To the sound of a conch shell they carried the baskets, and waved coconut branches and spears. They yelled riotously as they carried Honoyeta over the mountain. They crossed the ridge and brought him to Galuwata, halfway up Mt. Tuwaka. They took him inside a rock shelter called Mouth of Kaliyata, and there they dug a grave. They put his bones and his limbs in their baskets in a pile in the tomb, then they fetched big flat stones to seal it. They finished by covering it with earth. But Honoyeta spoke to them from inside, as if he were still alive. Although his body was in pieces he could speak from his head. He said: "You did not see this hole, but I can still see

64

through it. You must close my eyes properly." And from inside the earth he directed them how to seal the tomb.

Then he said: "Oh now you have completed it and buried me properly. My name is Honoyeta. If you speak thus [i.e., sing spells] you can awaken me in the ground and I will turn myself over. Then a big sun will burn and there will be no food. Or if you speak thus [i.e., sing spells] all my bones will sleep well in the earth. Then food and wealth will be plentiful and you will plant and harvest many things. Everyone will eat well. Or you can speak thus and I will turn myself over once more and there will be dearth again. My name is Honoyeta; I am a god. You killed me and it was your mistake."

That night his killers ate and slept. Children and adults, dogs and pigs, all slept forever, they all died. So the god sleeps inside the earth. Those villagers put him in baskets and entombed him in the mountain at Galuwata, and there he remains. The man called Honoyeta was really a god. They killed him on top of the sitting platform called "You Wrong Me" in the hamlet of Yabiliva in the village of Iwabu. They killed Honoyeta who was not a man, but more like God or a spirit. His story ends thus.

∧∧∧∧∧

The myth of Honoyeta is unique in the Nidula corpus in that it is known all over the island and is narrated everywhere with remarkable fidelity to a single form. Twelve recorded versions, gathered from every corner of the island, show such an uncommon degree of consistency, such a tidy isomorphism, that one must assume the myth has evolved into a fully satisfying form. Although the dozen narrators varied in their elaboration of details, all cleaved faithfully to an identical plot and developed it by means of the same sequences. Honoyeta (Honogeta, Onogeta, Wanogeta in other dialects) may be located in different dwelling places when the story opens, but he is invariably butchered at Yabiliva and invariably buried at Galuwata. It is always two wives that he deceives in precisely the same manner and with identical consequences. Where the versions do appear to differ most (that is, where idiosyncratic interpretations of the narrators are afforded most scope), is in a concluding commentary upon the significance of the hero's fate. Such addenda provide cosmological insights into the myth, but they are not essential to it. As we shall see, there is disagreement between some narrators at this point, reflecting the ambiguity of Honoyeta himself and the mystery of his intervention in the world.

In what follows I promote a "conversation" (that device of Burridge's) between the Honoyeta myth and Kalauna culture. The stable form of the myth through its variants warrants confidence in treating it as a free text, relatively independent of its individual narrators. Honoyeta's universality on the one hand, and his story's immutability on the other, allow more general reflections than so many of the other myths related in this book, jealously wed as they are to particular social groups. To begin the conversation I shall retell the myth, bringing to light its dialectic and calling to the aid of interpretation its numerous versions.[1] It will be simplest to proceed by guidance of the plot, which is structured by a temporal sequence of episodes. Most versions of the tale acknowledge six of these, each of which can be defined by the dramatic unities of time, place, and action. Since the hero's transformations dictate the plot, each episode is centered upon his location or his movement:

1. Initial domestic situation.
2. Courtship of his wives at the beach.
3. Destruction of his (dis)guise.
4. Wanderings in search of death.
5. Butchery in Yabiliva.
6. Burial at Galuwata.

Such is the perfect balance of the plot that, viewed as drama, these six scenes pair accommodatingly into three acts.

Episode 1

Not one of the narrators tells how Honoyeta came to acquire his wives, and only two bother to name them. (All the narrators were men; women do not tell the story.) The wives are clearly exploited by their husband. While he affects a passive and dependent senility

66

they plant and cook for him. Their attitude toward him varies according to the narrator. Adiyaleyale of Kalauna stressed their contempt: "They put his food in a coconut shell and spat in it, saying, 'Ugh! You ugly old man.'" In his view, Honoyeta's motive in transforming himself was a response to this contempt: "They didn't respect him, but he wanted them to love him." (Adiyaleyale was, incidentally, an insecure polygynist, struggling to handle his own two spirited wives.) Tomohuva of Ibawana, on the other hand, speaks of the wives' solicitousness: "They brought water for him, their hearts aching with anxiety in case he died while they were away." Honoyeta's childlessness is taken for granted, though one version (as we shall see) attributes him with a son for a seemingly ideological purpose. In his guise as an old man, then, Honoyeta is senile, nonproductive, asocial, asexual, and utterly dependent for sustenance upon his anonymous wives.

Episode 2

But we quickly learn that these domestic circumstances are illusory, and that the "real" Honoyeta is the antithesis of what his wives take him to be. At intervals the old man sends his wives to the sea for salt water and shellfish, then he transforms himself into a handsome young stranger and courts them. All versions agree on the manner in which he accomplishes this: he doffs his aged skin and hangs it on a *vilaya* plant. This act of rejuvenation is worth examining in more detail for what it reveals about Honoyeta's nature. Most narrators refer to his "skin" as *nuyana,* which is the term used for the slough of a snake. According to Adiyaleyale: "He took off his bad skin like a snake and there was a white one underneath." Others liken his skin to a "covering," while a published version (McElhanon 1974:111) goes too far in its concession to common sense: "He wore a complete set of clothes which were a disguise and looked just like a skin." The notion, then, is clearly that Honoyeta's "real" self is represented by his beauteous and youthful appearance, while the slough, "ugly and ridden with sores," is his disguise. Tomohuva speaks lyrically of his beauty as seen by the wife who spies him shedding his slough: "He rose like the sun, his body shining pink, burning bright like a flame."

67

Honoyeta's association with the sun is established in every version by the symbol of the *vilaya* plant upon which he hangs his discarded skin. *Vilaya* is the tarolike *Alocasia macrorhiza,* an exceedingly durable plant, which Goodenough people reserve for use in times of drought. The tuber is bitter and burns the mouth unless it is given prolonged cooking. The inflorescence of the plant is a spadix: a fleshy white spike enclosed in a skinlike spathe (see Massal and Barrau 1956:7). During regeneration the plant appears to slough its old skin. The perceptible properties of the *vilaya,* then, startlingly resemble the mythical attributes of Honoyeta. The *vilaya,* moreover, has a direct mythological kinship with the sun. Ninialawata (the creatrix) was peeling a *vilaya* tuber one day. She split it in two, and when her back was turned one half leaped into the sky and became the sun; then the other half followed and became the moon.[2] One might even see in this brief tale the kernel of Honoyeta's saga, but there is no further need to labor the point that there is a symbolic equation between Honoyeta and the sun, mediated by the emblematic *vilaya* plant.

Having transformed himself, Honoyeta seeks his wives on the shore. A few versions stress his supernatural powers at this juncture, for they have him traveling rapidly underground. All narrators mention his effortless spear fishing before he meets the women, and all refer to the essential transaction in which they accept his gift of fish. Some narrators allude coyly to the spiciness of the encounters, for they have the flavor of adulterous assignations. But no version states explicitly that Honoyeta sleeps with the women; they "court" or "flirt," terms synonymous with the sharing of betel nut between unmarried couples. Tomohuva, for example, develops the notion of the women's fidelity despite their amorous disposition toward the handsome stranger:

> He spoke in a different dialect: "Women, can I chew betel nut with you?" They thought, "We should ask him if he is Wagifan or not." "O friend," they said, "that would be nice, but we are thinking of our old man at home, so we cannot." He gave them the fish he had speared, and they said: "We must go now." But they liked him and wondered about him. They wanted him to court them. They were still thinking

about him on the way home. "O friend, let me ask you . . ." "No, let me ask *you!* Perhaps we can get him to court us . . ." "O friend, stop it! But if he comes once more we can invite him to chew betel with us."

Although it may appear as if Honoyeta is testing his wives' virtue by this ruse, none of the versions explicitly says so; nor does Honoyeta betray disquiet at what he knows to be the love of his wives for the "young man." Whatever motivates him, it is not jealousy. The gift of fish to his wives has sexual overtones in Nidula culture, and in all versions of the tale the wives lie to their husband concerning the source of the fish (a transparent deception which he probably relishes, dictated as it is by his own deception of them). Thus, in this inversion of his domestic situation, Honoyeta not only enjoys his own wives vicariously as an ardent suitor, but also provides himself with fish through them. Both gratifications are mediated by deception.

The entire marital edifice of Honoyeta with its two compartments defined by his guises (passive domesticity and active courtship) is built upon short-circuited and illusory reciprocities, which benefit only Honoyeta. His wives are doubly exploited and doubly deceived.

Episode 3

The women come to suspect their husband's duplicity. In Kafataudi's version their suspicion is aroused by an armshell. In another version they glimpse his "real" body through a hole in his armpit, while in another they trace his footsteps back to their own house. In the majority of versions, however, the wives observe that the betel nut the stranger on the shore gives them is identical to their own. And indeed, this proves to be another of Honoyeta's economical deceptions, for just as he contrives to give himself fish, so he also presents his wives with their own betel nut, taken from their trees outside the house. Like the fish, the betel is notionally a gift for sexual favors, but by his deception Honoyeta inverts — and perverts — the normal signification of both. Ironically, by yet another deceptive appearance in the myth, it is the skin of his wives' betel nut that leads to his undoing. The suspicious wives scratch marks on the

69

shells of their betel nuts on the tree, and when the stranger unwittingly presents them with the marked nuts their suspicions are confirmed. All that remains is to spy on the old man; they use deceit to catch him in his deception. Many of the narrators dwell on the poignant moment when one of the women witnesses her husband transform; she is indignant, fearful, yet jubilant.

One of the wives destroys Honoyeta's skin, though none of the versions examine her motives. Perhaps the best clue is offered by those who say how pleased the women are to have the beautiful man for a husband: "In their minds they loved him greatly." In two versions the wife burns the skin, but in all others she tears it up, shreds it to pieces, and casts it into the stream. This foreshadows the fate of his flesh; for in Kalauna at least, the image of shredded skin floating downstream evokes the rite of lustration after a burial, and also the destiny of discarded food peelings (see chapter 7). Tomohuva quotes the wife: "I tore up our husband's skin and gave it to the prawns, the black forest spiders, and the snakes." To her it is merely a useless, repulsive slough.

Alas for Honoyeta, it is his "human" identity and the basis of a *modus vivendi*. What was a naive and well-intentioned act by the wives to gain their hearts' desire proves to be a tragic error. For Honoyeta's response reveals it to be the critical juncture or peripeteia of the mythical drama. The more literary narrators make a great deal of this turning point. While the wives are marveling at their good fortune in discovering the "real" identity of their husband ("That handsome man who flirted with us is really our own husband after all!"), Honoyeta is brooding over the destruction of his "normal" identity. He returns home and sits on the stone platform outside his house. He is said, variously, to be angry (*nuakoyo*, "so angry he could hit himself"), suicidal (*ulo*), sad and sorry for himself (*nuavita*), but above all resentful (*unuwewe*). In some versions he challenges his wives accusingly: "Why did you tear up my skin? Why did you spoil me?" In others, he is reproachfully silent. They call him to eat, but he refuses: "He would not be appeased. He told them: 'My skin is spoiled, so I cannot eat. Eat the fish yourselves.'" He spends all night chewing betel on the cold stones. Leholeho's version plays upon Honoyeta's chiefly abstinence, his *kai-*

wabu-like restraint. His wives return to find him revealed, their shining suitor: "Friend or stranger?" they jest. They cook, and in the same ironical vein call out:

"Old man, come and we can eat." But he did not want to because his chiefliness forbade it and he was angry. So he sat with his hunger and chewed betel and lime. His wives slept but he remained like that until dawn.

Tomohuva examines the wives' attempt to form a new relationship with him, based on the pattern of the old:

He saw them coming along the path. They too saw him. "Look, friend: that man on our stone platform. His skin shines like fire. Our husband's appearance is magnificent." And in their minds they loved him greatly. They arrived and saw him watching them out of the corner of his eye, so they hurried to cook. One cooked tubers, the other fish, blowing the fires constantly. When it was ready they called out to him: "Husband, you should eat now. It is afternoon and you have not eaten for a long while. You are sitting there chewing betel but this broth will warm your stomach." Both of them spoke to him thus. But it was not easy for him to reply. He could not speak because of his resentment at their tearing of his skin. He was sad and sorry for himself and he kept his hunger. He sat there for a long time. His wives could not persuade him to come down. But they would not eat so long as he refused, so they stayed hungry into the night. One woman came to sit at his side and the other came and sat close to him on his other side. They remained like that through the long night. The man chewed betel and the women talked softly to him. But he would not answer. They sat there in vain until their eyes closed and they slept. But he stayed awake and heard the magpie call the other birds of the dawn. He looked down at his lightening body. "O my wives, you have seen my true appearance. You tore up my skin. I will go."

In the only version which attributes a child to Honoyeta, Iyeya of Galuwata (the hero's birthplace as well as burial place) has him deliver a speech of self-justification and bitter prophecy to his young son.

71

At dawn he told his child he was leaving. "If your mothers had not spoiled my skin I would stay. But they destroyed it so you must listen. I will wander and provoke those villages. I will talk of war and challenge them. They can kill me. No matter! Henceforth fire will burn you, sweat will pour from your body, you will fell trees, you will plant food and spear fish. You will work hard to stay alive. So I shall go now and take everything away."

In this version, Honoyeta's *unuwewe* or resentment is a terrible event for the whole of mankind. As we shall see, Iyeya's version (and others from the same area) have the flavor of cargo cult.[3] Honoyeta is the cause of poverty and deprivation, and even the origin of death. Such momentous consequences of his *unuwewe* appear grossly out of proportion to the wrong done to him. What can this hyperbole mean?

A digression is necessary here to examine more closely such colossal resentment. *Unuwewe* is a negative, highly charged motive force, held by Kalauna people to be one of the most powerful agencies in their theory of social action. It is a starting mechanism, one which can occur in many contexts and for a variety of reasons. Although *unuwewe* may be activated in the form of a response (typically to false accusation, unjust insult, maligned identity), it swells grotesquely into a vengeful cause of its own. No longer a mere response morally tied to the idea of reciprocal counteraction, it edges beyond the reach of ethics.

The etymology of *unuwewe* is doubtful, though one inspired informant suggested *uwe* as its root: the term for the wild lawyer cane that tangles, coils, and ensnares with its vicious thorns. Powerful resentment does fancifully resemble the grip of lawyer cane, the lacerations of which are inflicted by the squirming victim upon himself; the word *unuwewe* has an onomatopoeic insinuation of writhing resentment. The emotion is largely self-generated, the wounds self-inflicted. While the wrong or injustice that provoke it may be real, the resentful self, brooding upon and "resensing" (*resentire*) the injury, takes a further plunge into misery by means of self-punishment and willing victimage. In its hyperbolic form, *unuwewe* exceeds masochistic extortion and becomes perversely and spitefully satisfying—a form of revenge.

I have described elsewhere an almost synonymous category of emotion for Kalauna: *veumaiyiyi,* "a mixture of anger, shame, self-pity and resentment" (Young 1971:262-263; 1974:54). The distinction between *veumaiyiyi* and *unuwewe* is elusive (people would often use them interchangeably), though I suspect *unuwewe* to be a stronger, more extreme and morally unprincipled form of *veumaiyiyi.* The latter has connotations of redress: one punishes oneself only to "get even" with those whose behavior has diminished one. Repaying *veumaiyiyi* is a way of regaining equivalence, of restoring balance in an egalitarian milieu with its pervasive principle of exchange. *Unuwewe* seems to go further: self-castigation becomes an indulgence adrift from the moral ends of redress and restoration. It connotes intransigent and willful destructiveness—the destruction of others by means of self-destruction.

It is for precisely these reasons, I suspect, that the term *veumaiyiyi* is not used to describe Honoyeta's response (nor those of other heroes provoked to abandon or destroy). *Unuwewe* alone is fitting, for Honoyeta transcends the social order and cannot be controlled by exchange. Supremely self-contained, asocial and amoral, he is the antithesis of social man who bargains, negotiates, and exchanges in his mundane relations with others. Honoyeta is literally above all this; he deceives, dominates, deprives, and destroys. He cannot be defined by the social exchanges that are necessary for normal human identity. He is singular. His duplicity is a disguise for dwelling in the world of men, a condition of his being an imitation human. Just as his self-involved exchanges with his wives are illusory, so too are his abortive transactions with others in the second half of the myth. He gives nothing and receives nothing save in pretense. So when his wives discover his singularity, his true appearance, he must begin to abandon the world.

Honoyeta's *unuwewe,* then, brings about the turning point of the tale. It is the emotive force that propels him from the oscillating and infinitely repeatable domestic charade into the world beyond, which he would destroy along with himself. *Honoyeta unuwewe hi-nana*

73

("Honoyeta resentment he-will-go") is a form of curse belonging to those groups who claim him as their hero and his story as their own. If they utter this formula to those with whom they quarrel, all social relations are severed: exchanges cease, communications are suspended. The breach is in principle absolute and irrevocable. *Unuwewe* is the motive of all the myths discussed in this book, from Vatako to Oyatabu, and, as we shall see, it provides men with license to stage and participate in the most irresistible dramas in the culture.

Episode 4

To return now to the consequences of Honoyeta's *unuwewe*. Most versions of the myth pass over the episode of his wanderings rather briefly. Adiyaleyale reduces it to a few sentences:

> In the night he left. He went to Belebele and said: "Kill me!" But they said, "We cannot kill you, we know you are our ancestor, and if we kill you we shall die also." He went on to Eweli, Afufuya, and Wakonai and insulted them, but they refused to kill him.

Iyeya tells how Honoyeta challenged one village after another:

> They tied up pigs for him, they built food platforms to present to him, they caught chickens and stunned dogs for him, they plucked betel nut and pepper leaf. . . . He took only the betel nut and pepper leaf and moved on.

Other versions present detailed itineraries within and beyond Nidula: Fergusson Island, the Amphletts, Boyowa (the Trobriands), and even the mainland, before the journey ends at Yabiliva. Involving such distances, his quest takes on the appearance of a *manua-madumadu* expedition. This is a traditional institution of delayed gift exchange in which the visiting party solicits gifts of food wealth with a new canoe or some other resplendent object (Young 1982a). The gifts received are called *niune* (a cognate of *kune*, which is the southern D'Entrecasteaux term for the more famous Trobriand *kula*) and they must be passed on to exchange partners. But the significance of Honoyeta's *manuamadumadu* journey is that while his shining "new" appearance challenges, solicits, and in local idiom "asks for" massive gifts of food, he then spurns them. With supreme arrogance he condescends to accept only betel nut, the "food" of *kaiwabu*. Tomohuva makes it perfectly clear that Honoyeta is transcending the normative political order of Nidula, for although he rejects gifts his refusal of them does not diminish his stature.

> He entered another village and dogs barked and pigs grunted. He climbed onto the sitting circle and stood there, fierce and terrifying. His body shone like fire. Men gazed at him, then they searched for pigs to tie up and food to present to him. . . . But he told them: "Men, cook your food and roast your meat. I am going to another village." He stood up, and taking only betel nut, he left them.

After his long and fruitless journey, resisting all attempts to engage him in exchange, Honoyeta finally arrives at Yabiliva. Tomohuva explains why he chose to "die" there:

> At Kulumeta men tried again to force food upon him. But he looked inland and saw the pass of Ididiya over the northern flank of Mt. Madawa'a. "I know that road. It is my mountain that I see. My village lies behind it. I can prepare myself here. . . ." And he went down to the river Yaweli and bathed and transformed himself with magic on his body. . . . Then he climbed up to the village called Yabiliva.

Episode 5

Notwithstanding the destruction of his earlier disguise, Honoyeta is still the arch-deceiver. He "turns his tongue," as Tomohuva puts it, and somehow contrives to present himself as a man. It is clear from all versions that the men of Yabiliva attempt to kill him on this assumption. As in previous villages, he climbs onto an *atuaha* and arrogantly sits there chewing betel nut. Stone sitting platforms in Goodenough villages are private emblems of descent-group continuity; they symbolize stability and permanence. It is a truculent and disdainful act for a stranger to mount one, as Honoyeta does, without invitation.

Yabiliva is empty, however, save for one man and his child. A remarkable consistency in all twelve versions of the myth is the precise nature of the insult by which Honoyeta incites the man's anger. He addresses him ("a mature man whose appearance was youthful") and asks if the child he is carrying is his younger brother. Despite the man's increasingly vehement denials, Honoyeta insists that he is. The essence of the calumny (like an inverted riddle of the Sphinx) is the conflated generations; in effect, Honoyeta is denying the man his fatherhood and calling him a child. In Memeuna's version Honoyeta intensifies the insult by threatening to steal the man's wife; and later, when all the villagers have been summoned from the gardens, Honoyeta repeats the insult, telling them they are "mere children" and that he will take their wives from them.

Tomohuva describes how they try to kill him:

> They took their spears; not ordinary ones but very large ones. They sharpened them and began to spear him. They thrust and threw; they speared him as if he was about to flee into the bush. But he sat on the sitting circle as if he would stay there forever.[4] They tried hard to kill him, and they sweated with the effort for they wanted his flesh to eat. They threw their spears for a long time in vain. He said: "I will not run away, so you can get as angry as you wish and spear me unhurriedly. You need not tire yourselves, for I am he-who-looks-for-death."

Finally, he tells them his secret vulnerability. If they fashion a club from a branch of the *ilumwadaleta* tree and strike him on the neck, he will die. (The sap of this tree, it might be noted, is used as a fish poison; it stuns and immobilizes the fish so that they can be caught by hand. As far as I know it is not drunk by would-be suicides, unlike the more potent fish poison extracted from derris root. *Ilumwadaleta* is symbolically apt, perhaps, because when the bark is peeled off the glistening white wood of the interior oxidizes into a brilliant red.)

Tomohuva inserts lugubrious comedy into the scene that follows:

They went and cut a tree down. They carried it back and shaped it. First they speared him with it, but he didn't move. Then they hit him with it like a club, but still he didn't die. He was like a rock. He remained invincible and unhurt, and he neither shivered nor struggled. "That is the wrong tree," he said. . . . A man went to the forest again and brought back a branch. "Is this the one?" "Yes, that's it." So they hit the *giduwa* with it and he fell. Many men guarded him and then others arrived. "Have you killed him yet?" they asked. "Yes, and he's our meat."

All versions stress the futility of the attempt to cook Honoyeta. He has been dismembered and disembowelled, and his "pieces" placed in one or more pots and covered with special leaves. As Tomohuva puts it (echoing the futile cooking *for* him which Honoyeta's wives did just before he left them):

The women cooked and cooked and cooked in vain. The blood remained in the pots. They cooked on until dawn. Then they cooked until evening again, and on until dawn once more.

At this point they decide this is no ordinary human flesh. ("Our mistake," they cried. "We have killed a *giduwa*!") Again we are confronted with Honoyeta's peculiarly distanced relationship to his body. He is a spirit, but his flesh (*vido*) refused to die. Even after dismemberment, according to Memeuna, his flesh "talked and moved by itself." *Vidoita* or *vidoyawa* — literally, "living flesh" — is a very materialistic and literal conception of immortality. As we shall see, it is also one of Honoyeta's more grisly "secrets."

Iyeya's version depicts the disgruntled butchers munching on Honoyeta's raw flesh, but most narrators have them reject it altogether, revolted, terrified, or simply dissuaded by the talking head which, Orpheus-like, addresses them in peremptory tones. According to Memeuna:

He talked and talked from the pot. "I cannot die," he said. "I am immortal like the sun. My flesh lives like the sun." Inside the pot he talked on and on. His teeth blackened and his pieces spoke one by one.

77

He orders the men to fell huge trees for firewood ("to make them work hard"), parodying by the futility of the task the daily chore of cooking. In Lalaoya's version, Honoyeta's flesh partially cooks, but on his own instruction the people pour his broth away into a banana grove:

> The next day at dawn, the people saw the sun rise and Honoyeta's broth turn into the sun. And the bananas, too, went up and became the sun. The people called: "Friends! We cooked this man in vain yesterday. We emptied him out of the pot and now we can see him rising with the dawn. He is turning into the sun!"

Episode 6

Honoyeta's loquacious head, flesh, or (in some versions) his very bones, convey urgent instructions as to how his remains are to be disposed of. All versions agree that he tells people to make baskets of yellow coconut leaves and place the pieces of his body inside them. Then they must carry them over the mountain to Galuwata. A few versions say that he sends messengers for his "own people" to come from Galuwata to bear him thither; but most say that he tells Yabiliva people to do so — perhaps the better to castigate them. According to Adiyaleyale:

> They carried him in a basket which they slung on a pole like a pig. Men, women, and children beat drums and blew conches on the way. . . . Every time they stopped to rest he urged them on: "Come on, come on!"

A sense of ceremony informs the journey, but its mood is uncertain for there are hints of both mourning and jubilation. Honoyeta's bizarre voice nags the bearers, telling them when and where to rest and sleep, when to yodel and when to be silent, when and where to find water.

At Galuwata he issues instructions for his burial. These vary slightly according to the narrator, but the detail that most of them stress (some obsessively so) is that every crack and cranny of his tomb be sealed, so that he cannot "see." "You must not put me in the soil," he tells his buriers in Adiyaleyale's narrative, "but beneath a rock, and cover me with stones; then fill all the gaps with pieces of banana plant stem." In northern Goodenough it was indeed the practice until fairly recently to bury the dead in caves, under rocks or in natural stone tombs. In some places (Ibawana and Iwabu among them, in the district where Honoyeta was killed) only the washed bones were buried thus after being placed in sepulchral pots, a tradition of long antiquity in this locality (see Egloff 1972; Young and de Vera 1980).

According to Iyeya, who claimed that Honoyeta was born in his own village of Galuwata, Honoyeta was buried beneath his stone sitting platform. In 1973 I was conducted there by Iyeya. The site was a stone's throw from the almost abandoned village, which occupies a grassy plateau beneath the looming heights of Madawa'a. The "grave" was inside a tangled grove of forest trees. I was not permitted to approach it closely, and all I could discern was a tumbled pile of stones. "Honoyeta's bones are inside," my guide whispered. As we gazed at the stones a thin rain began to fall out of a seemingly cloudless sky, and a small rainbow floated above the nearby gorge. We crept away. Before, I was told, when people used this path they took the baskets off their heads or the yams off their shoulders and stooped to crawl past the grave; if they were wearing good clothes, they took them off and concealed them. Such exaggerated gestures of deference are appropriate to chiefs beyond the rank of any who live on Nidula. For several weeks after our visit to the unquiet grave, my Kalauna companions were apprehensive lest portents ensue: hot sun, sickness, or spoiled crops. They attributed the heavy rain which fell the following day to our impertinent visit.

∧∧∧∧∧

It remains for me to amplify the scope of this conversation between the narratives by comparing what my narrators say about the consequences of Honoyeta's chosen death and burial. Not everyone who told the myth was inclined to state conclusions; but among those

79

who did was a consensus that Honoyeta's fate was a disaster for mankind. Their various commentaries amount to a theory of human suffering, almost a theodicy. They agree on one important point: that despite the curse laid upon mankind by the vengeful god, man himself is ultimately responsible for his own condition. The wrong done to Honoyeta burdens mankind forever, and the proof of man's guilt is the necessity of toil, the ubiquity of suffering, and the existence of death.

We may recall that Kafataudi's version of the myth (with which I began) concludes with a somber speech delivered by the entombed head of Honoyeta. It speaks of magic by which the movement of his bones might be controlled; if they are awakened by invocation "then a big sun will burn, and there will be no food." I failed to learn any details of this magic other than that it involves the manipulation of a special stone, red ochre paint, and a sharpened spear of *yabalava* wood, accompanied by incantations addressed to Honoyeta. As is customary when performing destructive magic, the sorcerer abstains from food and coitus and secludes himself in his house — unless he has already left the community in a pointed display of *unuwewe*. Such beliefs and practices are not unique to Kalauna, though few other narrators of the myth made explicit reference to its significance as a charter for sun magic. But this aspect of the myth is the one most likely to be omitted or dissembled in public recitations.

There is some small solace in the notion that the magical regulation of drought and famine lies in the hands of men; for even the most intransigent sorcerer is vulnerable to pity and the cajolery of gifts. Honoyeta, on the other hand, is beyond the reach of reciprocity; as we have seen, his story can be read as a cruel parody of social exchange. Nidula people do not overtly sacrifice to their gods and spirits: gifts neither coerce nor propitiate them. Hence, there is logic — and hope — in the attribution of *magical* control to men of knowledge who presume to conjure the supernatural by verbal means.

For those narrators who denied or disguised Honoyeta's legacy of magic, the sentence of punishment is beyond appeal and mitigation. As in other versions, Leholeho of Imuleya declared that his own Yabiliva ancestors (those who had killed and buried Honoyeta) all died before they reached home:

Men, women, children, youths and maidens, all of them died. Now, whenever Honoyeta cracks his finger joints, all the people of Goodenough fall sick and many die.

Navakwaya of Wakonai (which lies at the mouth of Galuwata gorge) claimed that Honoyeta's bones were scattered throughout different villages:

> Anyone who cuts down trees, plants, gardens, or walks over a place where one of his bones is buried becomes very ill and dies. Once, such an area was cleared as a firebreak. The sun baked the ground and the bones lying beneath it, and as a result there was a big famine. [McElhanon 1974:114]

Such arbitrary afflictions point to a palpable guilt: the "wrong" or "mistake" of which Kafataudi and others speak. Consider now how Muigeya of Utalo generalized this original sin to account for the felt disparities of wealth between Papuans and whites, thereby deriving a rudimentary cargoist doctrine from the myth. After the people had buried Honoyeta,

> He said: "Oh, now I must go, I cannot stay." So he went and did not return. He went forever and his blood still makes men angry. "If you had done things properly," he said, "I could have stayed and you would be wealthy. I would have transformed, and some of you would have lived forever. But you spoiled me, that is why I must go, and that is why you will be destitute. You tore up my skin. The snake and the prawn renew their skins and live; but you will not renew yours. You tried to eat my body, so the wealth will disappear with me." He went and the whites became wealthy, but we became poor. He went, and they became knowledgeable, but we remain stupid. It is because we spoiled him ourselves that our grandfathers became poor.

Muigeya develops this funeral oration into an indictment of the colonial regime, under which Papuans labor for a pittance while Europeans retain their wealth and knowledge by refusing to share them. But he declares the Papuan to be guilty, ultimately to blame for his own subordination and the loss of his birthright of wealth and immortality.

It is but a short step from this quasi-Biblical view of original sin to identifying Honoyeta with Jesus Christ. This particular narrator does not do so, but the idea of their identity is prevalent in some parts of Nidula, notably in the villages of the north with which Honoyeta's destiny is most closely associated. In the minds of the faithful, "Honoyeta Lives" through the material testimonies of the sitting platforms on which he sat, the red stones of the stream bed at Ala'alawana where he bathed, the crimson soil where his blood stained the ground in Yabiliva, the scars that pucker the mouths of Iwabu people, descendants of those who had sipped his broth. . . . Like fragments of a nascent cult, such daily confirmations of belief lie scattered evidentially—and some quite literally—on the ground. In my final chapter I mention how, in 1976, these fragments cohered and vitalized a cargo cult based upon the myth of Honoyeta.

Let us follow Muigeya's point that men lost their immortality through the destruction of Honoyeta's slough, and forfeited their wealth through the attempt to eat his body. The only etymology I was offered for Honoyeta's name was *wa-na-vagata*: literally, "you (pl.)-go-forever." This is more or less phonemically plausible, depending upon the dialect, and it is consistent with Honoyeta's nicknames: Vidoyawa ("Living Flesh") and Lulutuwa ("Hard/tough/undecaying Bones"). His very names, then, connote immortality. One of his secrets, distilled in magical formulas and known to certain sorcerers, animates the flesh after ostensible death has occurred and the spirit has departed. I came across two well-attested cases of premature burial in Kalauna, when by all accounts the bodies were still alive, though according to their buriers' conviction they were deceased. The gruesome imitation of life that these "corpses" displayed was believed to be the result of *vidoyawa*: the magic used by Honoyeta when he bathed and rubbed his flesh with doctored stones at Ala'alawana. The response to these pathetic claims to immortality is interesting, for it shows that most Kalauna people had a squeamish, if not wholly skeptical, resistance to them.

Honoyeta's mythical attributes of skin-shedding and tenacity of life are natural attributes of snakes; and even if our narrators were not explicit on the matter, the spectrum of local mythology would provide many reasons for viewing Honoyeta as a snake-man. The most infamous serpent in Nidula mythology is Matabawe (Matabikwa in some areas) who is born of a woman, secluded in a cave, and fed daily in exchange for one of its "tusks." These "tusks" were fashioned into neck pendants which men used as wealth.[5] One day, the woman's human child sees the gigantic snake and screams in terror, spilling broth over its head. The snake is offended and abandons his home in resentment. Bwaidokans can show the sinuous path Matabawe took through the reef on his way to Muyuwa or the Louisiades, whence he took all Goodenough's wealth.

It will be fairly obvious that this myth is a simple permutation of the first half of the Honoyeta tale (or vice versa). Consider the homologies of plot:

1. Women feed a stay-at-home creature who is their husband/son.
2. He rewards them (or pretends to) with gifts of fish/tusks.
3. The wives/sibling discover the creature's real identity and fatefully damage its body-image.
4. The creature abandons them in resentment, taking away immortality/wealth.

Tomohuva provided a striking confirmation of the structural identity between manlike snake Matabawe and snakelike man Honoyeta. He prefaced his version of Honoyeta's myth with the full Matabawe story, joining them seamlessly by stating that Matabawe "turned into an old man" when he left his cave. Thus, whether or not other Nidula peoples are inclined to make the same conscious identification (and for reasons I consider elsewhere, Kalauna men deplore the promiscuous coupling of discrete myths), the Matabawe tale, with its theme of wealth deprivation due to some casual human offense, carries its symbolic thrust into Honoyeta's story. The miseries of mankind are unequivocally held to be a form of punishment.

83

∧∧∨∧

An unraveling of the Honoyeta myth could take us almost anywhere (a singular property of myth being its sinuosity and willingness to travel). We could trace Honoyeta's genealogy to his close cousins in neighboring societies, Tokosikuna and Kasabwaybwayreta, those skin-shedding culture-heroes of the Kula ring (see Malinowski 1922: 306-311; 322-326; also Young 1982*b*); or to more distant Papuan kinsmen from the Central Highlands to Torres Strait, snake-men with long penises who are variously shamed by women, then abandon them and curse mankind (see Wagner 1972:19-24). We could seek Honoyeta's distant relatives in the serpent myths of northern Australia, or among the head-hunting heroes of Borneo, and speculatively nominate his putative ancestors in the dismembered fertility gods of the ancient world, such as Osiris and Dionysus. The recitation of such a lengthy lineage, however, would tell us little more about Honoyeta than that he belongs to a universal genus of sacrificial heroes. At this rarefied level Sir James Frazer in *The Golden Bough* had identified the species long before Honoyeta was reported from Goodenough Island; and it is perhaps not too fanciful to see in him a vegetation god, a tuber who is peeled, chopped up, and cooked, but who takes a leisurely revenge by denying man sustenance and seasonal security, his tortuous lesson being to warn men of their own greed.

Another, more modest, interpretative exercise might trace the permutations and transformations of figures and themes through the total corpus of Nidula mythology. This, too, would take us well beyond Kalauna and the concerns of this book, and into epistemological categories ("nature" and "culture," for example) which have no demonstrable foundation in local systems of thought. Since my task in essence is one of translation, I must forego some of these heady privileges of an ethnographer with extrinsic knowledge, and be guided by the touchstone of what has felt significance for Kalauna people. Having said that, it still remains for the ethnographer to exercise his privilege in selecting among those matters that have "felt significance" for the purpose of focusing his enquiry. I therefore plead for the suspension of disbelief during the remainder of this chapter, while I select a number of themes that recur throughout the book, namely, the oral preoccupations of Nidula culture, the genealogical imperative of the relationship between fathers and sons, competitive yam growing, and the victimage scenario of *unu-wewe*. This bundle of themes unexpectedly coheres if, instead of pointedly ignoring the psychoanalytical implications of a myth as anthropologists usually do, we yield to the temptation to attend to them.

Honoyeta is ostensibly fatherless and childless,[6] and therefore of indeterminate generation; but it is apparent that he undergoes symbolic death a number of times while affirming his immortality throughout. A Jungian interpretation of the myth would presumably view Honoyeta's search for death as a quest for transcendence. This he certainly achieves in those versions that grant him divine ascension to the sun. His death and dismemberment is a rite of passage; his duplicity is serpentine wisdom in encompassing his own rebirth through the agency of others. But such an interpretation merely restates the myth without illuminating the level at which its symbolisms exercise their fascination. Here, a Freudian-inspired interpretation seems to provide a more profound understanding.

Honoyeta, in this view, is father to himself. He is a composite figure incorporating aspects of both the dominant, punishing father and the rebellious, sinful son. The myth begins with him playing the role of an old man, childlike in his dependency upon his nurturant, mothering wives. Periodically shedding this guise, he transforms into a virile lover, offering his wives/mothers gifts of fish (symbols of his potency and, incidentally, the very stuff of Nidula marriage gifts to wives' and mothers' brothers). Once his deception is discovered and his skin has been destroyed, he abandons the cosy, quasi-incestuous haven provided by his womenfolk. In the outer world he matures by rejecting the surrogate nurture it offers; he is bent on domination through resentful self-castigation.

At Yabiliva he exposes the "Oedipal" foundation of the society, though his riddle provokes angry denial of the obvious: that men carry their sons "as if" they were their younger brothers. The men are incensed by this denial of their fatherhood (and further infuri-

85

ated by the threat to steal their wives). For stating an intolerable truth (with its corollary that men deflect hostility for fathers onto brothers) they proceed to kill him: an act which is also ordained by the Oedipal plot.

At this point, then, Honoyeta assumes the role of the "primal father" killed and eaten by his "sons," as in Freud's own myth of *Totem and Taboo*. As a "good father" he invites and even welcomes their aggression; in telling them the secret of his vulnerability, he consents to their emasculating him (the deathless phallus stunned and immobilized by fish poison). The father/phallus is dismembered and chopped into pieces.[7] But the "sons" discover that they have been deceived: they are unable finally to kill him or to cook him. His body remains inedible and cannot be incorporated. He commands them to observe the last rites, which ensure his domination over them as a sun deity. His "curse" is at bottom a trick played on Time; as one who is forever father to himself he denies the genealogical promise of generational succession.

The tragedy of the myth according to this reading is its failure to offer any religious consolation of atonement. Honoyeta only pretends to give himself to be eaten; the "good father" is revealed to be "bad," rejecting and capricious. There can be no consolatory cult of "eucharist" or transubstantiation, for if the "sons" cannot eat him (yet are still damned for trying) there are only the bitter ashes of failed communion and withheld sacrament. Honoyeta's pitiless bones speak only of fear and deprivation.

This interpretation can be pushed even further, for Honoyeta the serpent is not only the image of the dominant, resentful, punishing father, but also of his phallus. As such Honoyeta could stand for potent masculinity (if not the genealogical principle). But clearly this reading will not suffice, for the burden of the tale seems to contradict this value; or rather, it appears to enjoin the renunciation of masculine sexuality in favor of something else. Honoyeta's initial guise as a childishly dependent old man with a wrinkled skin is a detumescent version of his vigorously youthful self as his wives' secret lover. Yet it is the former state he mourns when his wives conspire to keep him shiningly tumescent, and he responds to the destruction of his skin as if they had castrated him. During his wanderings, he rejects the food presentations that challenge him to match by performance his appearance of manhood, for he has repudiated sexuality and with it the surrogate masculine games of aggressive food-giving. Paradoxically, by another twist of serpentine duplicity, he offers himself to be eaten, but then denies himself to those who would eat him. His uncookable body is a corollary of his snakelike deathlessness. In Nidula idiom a corpse is said to "cook" after burial, but Honoyeta remains forever "raw." As phallus, however, he has been chopped up and destroyed utterly as a sexual threat to his "sons," though his buried remains retain their fructifying power. So the hero undergoes progressive reduction by various symbolic castrations until he is "reborn" as a deity of the sun—a fructifier and a destroyer.

One of his lessons for mankind, then, particularly the "sons" who were agents in his transformation, is that sexuality must be restrained for the sake of crop fertility. As every Kalauna adolescent knows, an active sex life is inimical to the cultivation of good gardens. Honoyeta's lesson can also be extrapolated to reinforce the values of *lokona* (the deliberate abstention from food in order to preserve it), for his progressive denudation is accompanied by a rejection of food. He does not eat, and—perverse vegetation god that he is—denies himself as food to others. The values of food denial as well as sex denial are thus obliquely affirmed. Man pays for his livelihood by restrained libido (a perfectly orthodox Freudian conclusion), but Honoyeta's hapless tribe is burdened with the additional repression that it is necessary to deny orality also in order to ensure an abundance of food. This is a fact of Kalauna life which, with some justice and ecological perspicacity, can be blamed on the vagaries of the sun.

∧∨∧∨∧

If it were my purpose to parade them, Nidula mythology could yield any number of man-eating or man-rejecting monsters. Matabawe, as we have seen, is a demi-human serpent who punishes by with-drawal. Another giant serpent, Matalolobikwa, pursues two sisters with an eye to marrying (eating) them, but he is chopped into pieces by their grandfather-protector, and his buried remains yield sugar cane. Yet another serpent, Kelukeketa, also born of a human mother, cannibalizes whole villages until he is speared through the naval and hacked to pieces by a brother and sister who celebrate their victory by incestuous union.

Such villains are like faces of the father, just as their stories seem to be refashioned fragments of the Honoyeta myth. The boldest ren-dition of the monster-killing theme, however, occurs in Manubutu, a myth that rivals Honoyeta in its blatantly Oedipal import. This is the widely known story mentioned in chapter 2 where it was cited in the Lulauvile cycle of legends. The man-eating bird Manubutu is slain by two "fatherless" small boys, who thereby reunite their sun-dered parents, restore tranquility to the island, and become its chief. Small wonder that this romance is more popular than the cheerless tale of Honoyeta.

It would take me too far afield to present details of Kalauna fam-ily organization, but to justify this speculative digression into the experiential underpinnings of these myths I must refer to some objective grounds for father-son hostility.

The idiom of nuclear kinship is cast in terms of nurture through "feeding," while the growth toward and eventual achievement of manhood is likewise conceived as the result of food-provisioning or fostering by fathers, whether real or classificatory (Young 1971:40-43). This realm of symbolism is so basic, so close to infantile oral concerns that it almost certainly generates expressions of ambiva-lence. Rather than deflecting or disguising oral discontents the idiom sharply focuses them: it puts the child's ambitions and anxie-ties where his stomach lies.

Let us consider briefly the passionate emotional investment that men make in their yams. Yam cultivation provides a man with the competitive means of achieving individual distinction, a personal renown that can long outlive him if his name is appended to those lists of illustrious yam growers chanted in gardening spells. Thus,

88

fame and the assurance of nominal immortality are the rewards of the successful; but for all men, the quest conduces an identification between themselves and the objects of their endeavors. In Kalauna, as among the Ilahita Arapesh (see Tuzin 1972), there can be little doubt that yams are not only conscious symbols of male pride and preconscious symbols of the bodies of their growers, but also unconscious symbols of the phallus. Hence the notion that debilitating sexual activity has adverse effects upon a man's competence as a yam grower. Conversely, successful yam cultivation is held to be evidence of sexual restraint, if not prolonged celibacy. The rationale of *abutu ana hoyalana,* competitive food exchange over adultery or "woman-trouble," is predicated entirely upon the supposed incompatibility of yam-growing and sexual concupiscence (see Young 1971:212-213; and 1977 *b*).

Having been taught from infancy that his father's biggest and best yams are not to be eaten, that they are "poisoned" by magic and hoarded against the day of their aggressively competitive exchange, a son later learns the rudiments of yam-growing from his father, from whom he also receives his own seeds. Yams are thought to be quasi-human with their own lines of descent, so an inheritance of yams lost or squandered (by eating the seed yams, for example) is not easily replaced. As a young man intensifies his gardening activities, he strives to produce the large yams (*kuvi*) that will ineluctably draw him into the political arena.

As he does so, however, his father's efforts are likely to be waning. The rise of the son who wishes to succeed, and the decline of the father who resents being superseded, inevitably creates friction between them. (During public food distributions, a vindictive device for stirring family discord is to call the name of the son to receive his father's share: "You have already replaced your father.... We rely on you to repay.") The father may withhold the transmission of his yam magic, suspecting that only this now stands between his son's deference and his negligence. Old men without magic are often pathetic and solitary, neglected shamelessly by their grown sons. In such cases recriminations rebound, charged by the hurtful, basic idiom of "feeding": the aged father accuses the son of neglect, to which the son retorts that he is paying back for being poorly fed as a child.[8] It does not always come to this, but the values encourage the rationalization of grievances in this way.

Another story expresses this double bind of the father-son relationship.

A sad little orphan is gathering shellfish at the beach when a giant bird snatches him up and carries him to its nest. "O grandfather, perhaps you are going to eat me!" cries the boy. "No, grandson," replies the bird, "I'm going to feed you." And he flies hither and thither catching fish and fetching food for the boy. The child grows up, and one day he sees from the nest some children playing in the distance. When the bird has gone in search of food for him, the boy climbs down the tree and joins the children in their play. He does this day after day, sending the bird further and further afield for more and more exotic foods, until eventually he goes with the children to their village and does not return to the nest. The bird laments his loss. One day the boy is playing on the beach and the bird swoops down to him. He reproaches the boy bitterly for his ingratitude in tricking and abandoning him. He tells the boy to build a pile of sticks and set fire to it. When he has done so, the bird leaps into the flames and immolates himself. "I am *unuwewe!*" he cries. "You did not love me after all I did for you, and you ran away." The bird dies and the youth mourns him.

In this tale there is little attempt to disguise the provider as a father-figure. But whereas in the Manubutu myth (of which it is thematically an inversion) the "sons" vengefully slay the "bad father," in the above story the "good father" resentfully kills himself to punish the "son" with guilty remorse. The two acts are facets of the same father-killing fantasy, however, and they would seem to articulate the hostilities and anxieties of sons and fathers. By implication, since sons grow up to become fathers themselves, the latter are ultimately successful in imposing their control by guilt and (as in the paradigmatic case of Honoyeta) by religious fear projected onto the capricious sun.

Father-son hostility, then, is more or less pervasive in Nidula society and more or less consciously acknowledged. Fraternal strife is also endemic, and brothers quarrel frequently over their patrimonial inheritance: land, fruit trees, house sites, seed yams and, not least, magic.[9] As for the villagewide authority figures, it is one of the principal burdens of leadership—particularly those guardians whose biographies I shall be examining—to have to bear the animosities of their followers. Such leaders are called "fathers" too, and they are frequent scapegoats for any misfortunes that befall the community. Their response to victimage is typically that of the mythical heroes: they abandon their village "sons" in resentment, and punish them with crop or weather sorcery. The community is brought to its knees in real or imagined hunger and begs the forgiveness of the "fathers," who then attempt to make things right.

The choice of idioms is thoroughly consistent in its oral mode. The most terrible punishment of the "fathers" is to inflict *tufo'a*: the insatiable mass appetite and unrestrained greed that makes the community consume its food reserves until famine forces it to exchange and cannibalize its progeny. A chilling metaphor indeed of social suicide. The ultimate punishment is therefore a dialectical complement of the original sin. If the Honoyeta myth expresses this primal sin as eating the father, then the ultimate punishment is being condemned to eat the children. The genealogical imperative is negated and Time itself is stilled.

4
The Blood of Malaveyoyo

Therefore, O Jerusalem, fathers will eat
their children and children their fathers
in your midst; I will execute judgments
on you, and any who are left in you I will
scatter to the winds.

—Ezek. 5:10

/\/\/\/\

At the time of Malaveyoyo's birth in Kalauna, New Guinea was on
the threshold of European intervention. In 1848 the Dutch East
Indies government laid claim to West New Guinea in the name of
the Sultan of Tidore, and in 1849 Captain Owen Stanley surveyed
the southern coast of Papua in the *Rattlesnake*. At this period Goodenough Island was represented by a teasing, discontinuous line on
the map drawn by Bruni d'Entrecasteaux in 1782 while conducting
his desultory search for the missing explorer La Pérouse. The island
was still nameless, unless Nidula, Dauila, or Morata had more than
local currency among a few village clusters. More likely, the geographical bond of insularity was of lesser moment to the folk on
opposite sides of the precipitous island (one of the highest in the
world) than was the fact that they faced in different directions. The
easterners looked toward Fergusson, the Amphletts, and the Trobri-

ands; the westerners looked toward the mainland. It was from these places that Nidula's parochial horizons were enlarged by canoe-borne trade.

The charting of the island by Captain John Moresby in 1874 went unremarked by Malaveyoyo's generation. It was only in the last decade of the century, with the advent of gold prospectors, intrepid British administrators, and Wesleyan missionaries, that Good-enough Islanders could begin to suspect that something revolutionary was afoot. But it was to be another decade before they would learn that they had been absorbed, without consultation, into an alien people's imperial history.

In their own representations of the past, Kalauna people depict at least four epochs. There was the primordial and timeless era of life underground, when people neither ate, procreated, nor died. Then followed the discovery of the world above, the emergence from the sacred hill of Yauyaba, the division into clans and villages, the discovery of food, sex, and death, and the dispersal of people over the island. The next epoch is a tumultuous one of famine and warfare, cannibalism and social disintegration. This was Malaveyoyo's era. Finally, just after his death, Europeans appeared, bringing with them a new dispensation.[1] Whatever reading one gives to Kalauna folk-history, Malaveyoyo cannot be ignored. His epoch (which, in his people's view, he created) mediates the idealized golden age and the mundane present of sundry discontents.

He was probably born about 1850, for he died in vigorous maturity before 1900, the latest date by which Kalauna could have ignored the spread of government control over the island. I was introduced to Malaveyoyo's legend early in my fieldwork, and I sensed its importance by the way people told it and the conclusions they drew from it. Sometimes they even seemed to claim that he had invented cannibalism as well as the food exchanging contest called *abutu*. By far the most detailed versions of his legend were given me by Adiyaleyale, son of Iyahalina who was Malaveyoyo's collateral descendant (brother's son's son). Adiyaleyale was ambitious; but living in the shadow of this notorious ancestor, he was as troubled as his father by the spiritual patrimony of Malaveyoyo. Both would have been happy to assume his mantle provided it could be cleansed of blood; but no matter how many times Adiyaleyale told me the tale he was unable to avoid the conclusion that Malaveyoyo was an incorrigible monster. He would not tell it in the presence of others, for like his father he feared the enmity of the descendants of Malaveyoyo's numerous victims. Yet his involvement with the story was so intense that he felt compelled to tell it to me again and again, arresting me like the Ancient Mariner, promising to reward my attention with yet another significant detail previously withheld, a rendering more truthful than the last. He sought the catharsis of confession. One evening in Bwaidoka, free from his fears of Kalauna eavesdroppers, he told me the tale for the fifth time. This is the version I reproduce below.

∧∧∧∧∧

Malaveyoyo's father was Kedeya of Heloava and his mother Amauli of Awakubawe, Malabuabua clan. He was born in good times, when plenty of food was growing and trees bore well. His name promised further prosperity [*mala,* "weather/wind"; *veyoyo,* "to cluster thickly"], and Nibita people were happy and lived in peace. When Malaveyoyo was old enough he asked his father to teach him his magic, his good and bad secrets. He grew to be a tall strong man with powerful muscles, a firm jaw, and gardener's hands. Kedeya, his father, taught him all his knowledge; then he died. As the firstborn, Malaveyoyo took his place as leader of Heloava and Lulauvile, even though he was still a young man. People said of him, "Ah, Malaveyoyo is going to be a good man, strong enough to protect the people well." But they did not know him. They did not know that one day he would become an evil man.

   In Nouneya there was a man called Tomonauyama. He spoke to his clan Iwaoyana and declared that he would become chief of Nibita. "That boy Malaveyoyo is too young to know how to be chief." Malaveyoyo heard this and was incensed. He sat in his house and brooded. "I have no wife yet and no children. I am invulnerable. I can try all the magic Kedeya gave me." He started by banishing the coconuts. People climbed the trees and found only shrivelled husks. Then he banished the breadfruit and chestnuts. There was no fruit. People complained, but they did not leave the village. Malaveyoyo then

94

began to send away the food from the gardens. The taro, yams, and bananas died or failed to grow well. People began to feel hungry, but they still did not move away.

Malaveyoyo went up the mountain to the hamlet of Miyawala to see an old woman called Wamanudake, the only survivor of her line. "Why do you visit me, my son? Now is a bad time, for there is no food to offer you." "My mother, I want you to tell me your secret about the wind, *bolimana.*" "Ah, my son, if I give you that magic perhaps you will disperse the people." "Yes, my mother, that is what I want. Tomonauyama is too arrogant. I have to show that I am stronger and teach him a lesson. I alone will stay in Nibita." She was alarmed by his hardheartedness but taught him the magic to summon the southeast wind. It blew like a hurricane and many trees and houses fell. Some of the people left the village and slept in caves or between the roots of trees. But still some stayed.

Malaveyoyo summoned his followers, tough men like Yaluwaiyeya, Kayevau, and Kabudaiyaya of Lulauvile and Aditomonuwana of Mulina, and he told them: "You must terrorize the people who remain. You are hungry. Go and kill some children and eat them." Malaveyoyo also sent them to demand children from families hiding in the bush and gardens. The people became very frightened of him. They even killed themselves, or exchanged their own children to eat. "If we don't, Malaveyoyo will surely kill us!" So the people scattered. They fled to the bush or the beach and lived in caves or between the roots of trees. Soon only Tomonauyama and Malaveyoyo with their kinsmen remained in Kalauna.

Tomonauyama called a challenge to Malaveyoyo one day. "You cannot chase me away as you chased the others. You cannot kill me until my bananas and my *vilaya* [*Alocasia*] are finished. I am strong with my *lokona.*" "Don't praise yourself, my friend," said Malaveyoyo. "One day you will finish your crops and I will kill you at Falayaleya where you keep your bananas and your *vilaya.*" Tomonauyama replied, "I also have one yam called *kwaiyana* which is my pillow. As long as that stays too, you cannot kill me."

But Tomonauyama was a kind man, and when hungry women brought him firewood or betel nut he gave them a banana or some other piece of food he had been hoarding. Then Malaveyoyo sent his henchmen to steal Tomonauyama's pillow. When he awoke and found the big yam gone he wept. He spoke to his brother-in-law, "Come, we have to leave the village now and look for more food." They went to the beach and fished with their wives and children. At sunset Tomo-nauyama said, "We should go to Falayaleya where we can cook, eat, and sleep." So they went to this garden site on the slopes below Kalauna, and they dug up the last of the *vilaya*. They cooked and ate it with their fish, then they lay down to sleep.

In Kalauna, Malaveyoyo sent his men to Belebele to search for coconuts. Walking back up the path in the dark they saw Tomonauyama's fire at Falayaleya. "That is the fire of the man our brother must kill if the famine is to end," one said. They returned and told Malaveyoyo. He took down his war club from the roof of his house. It was decorated with a single cowrie shell at the end of the blade. He went down the path to Falayaleya with his men and they surrounded the sleeping Tomonauyama and his group. Malaveyoyo said, "If his wife and her brother try to escape you must stop them, but do not spear them." Then he approached quietly, moving twigs and dried leaves from his path. When he reached Tomonauyama he raised the club above his head and swung it down upon the sleeping man's throat. "I am Malaveyoyo!" he cried in triumph. "You boasted about your food and your leadership. Now you are lying in the dirt with your neck broken. You finished all your bananas and *vilaya,* and your last yam is gone. So I killed you as I promised. Now I am going to eat you and plant your bones."

The dead man's wife and her brother Lolo tried to flee but Malaveyoyo's men easily caught them. Some wanted to kill them too, but Malaveyoyo said, "No, I will marry her and keep Lolo as my servant, to fetch firewood and climb coconut trees for me." Then he summoned Tomoyalina of Iwaoyana, whose *lokona* magic was strong. "You know how to conserve yams," he said. "You can help me to cook a large potful and we will eat Tomonauyama. Then I will bury his bones and the people will come back to the village."

They carried Tomonauyama's body up to Kamoyeta in Kalauna, and there they roasted and ate him. Malaveyoyo buried his bones in the earth with his *sisikwana* magic of prosperity. He stilled the bones and the famine turned. He sent his men to the beach and into the bush to invite the people to return, for he intended to hold a Modawa festival.[2] People came in ones and twos to beat drums and dance and Malaveyoyo gave them betel nut and told them to stay in the village. At the climax of the festival he distributed food and pigs among all Kalauna people, and they lived together as before.

To hold them firmly, Malaveyoyo carved a wooden food bowl and made *manumanua* magic in it to anchor the food. He also planted an *idaidala* tree [*Ficus* sp.] in Heloava—the great tree you can see there today surrounded by the stone sitting circle which was Malaveyoyo's *atuaha*. He set a taboo on that tree, and no one may climb it or burn its branches for firewood, for it is used in the ceremony of *manumanua*. Because of these deeds and because of the bones of Tomonauyama the food returned to the gardens and people soon harvested plump tubers.

Before presenting the sequel to this legend of the destruction and reconstruction of Kalauna, I should mention some points of difference it has with other versions. It will come as no surprise that men of Iwaoyana (clansmen of Tomonauyama) vary the telling in order to put Malaveyoyo firmly in the wrong regarding the instigation of the sorcery battle that devastated the village. In Adiyaleyale's version Malaveyoyo is affronted by the "arrogant" upstart Tomonauyama. But the non-Lulauvile versions I recorded attest that Malaveyoyo was already the leader of Nibita, and it was to challenge his vicious despotism that Tomonauyama asserted himself. These versions present Malaveyoyo as a wanton killer and cannibal even before famine reduced everyone to the fearful choice of eating others or being eaten by them. For example, one version has it that Malaveyoyo was in the act of seizing Tomonauyama's son as a victim when his father speared Malaveyoyo's right arm. Too proud to retaliate in kind, Malaveyoyo there and then challenged Tomonauyama to a do-your-worst sorcery battle. In another version, Adiyaleyale mentioned that Tomonauyama was not himself a cannibal; he rejected the gifts of human flesh that Malaveyoyo mockingly sent him during their contest. Obliged to repay each gift, however, Tomonauyama would return a single banana; in this way did Malaveyoyo cunningly deplete his rival's resources. As for his last yam, other versions say that it was one of Tomonauyama's own hungry kinsmen (and not Malaveyoyo) who stole it. So it would not be correct to assume that while the Iwaoyana versions attempt to paint Malaveyoyo as black as possible, Adiyaleyale's (Lulauvile) versions attempt to exculpate him.

With regard to the nature of their contest, I have pointed out elsewhere that it is a kind of inverted *abutu*: instead of doing their best to outgive each other, they do their worst to outdeprive one another (1971:188). The range of crop-scourging sorcery they employ varies from version to version, and it is not always clear whether Tomonauyama is thought to use any at all. Malaveyoyo is variously mentioned as bringing sun and wind, and invoking that terrible Heloava specialty, *tufo'a*, the sorcery of gluttony. In one version he is also said to make *aba vealiya,* the sorcery of dispersal, which involves countermanding the anchoring magic of the sitting circles and "pushing" people out of the village and into the wilderness.

Can we fathom these excesses? What is the meaning of this passion that would disintegrate society and even risk its abolition in a holocaust of cannibalism? Why must everyone suffer so calamitously for the rivalry of a couple of men? While none of the versions explicitly mentions Malaveyoyo's *unuwewe* as motivating him to destroy Kalauna, I believe it to be understood. But if this is so, what is the justification for his towering resentment? Can it be only a matter of power, of demanding recognition for supremacy (as those kings of Benin and Dahomey slaughtered their subjects for no better reason than to demonstrate their omnipotence)? So many of the myths and "real" events that I deal with in this book provoke this kind of question. The affect that is the "cause" of critical and disruptive social action seems to be a response quite disproportionate to its stimulus. It is exorbitant, extravagant, extreme, and it results in victimage on a potlatching scale.

The sequel to the legend concerns the death of Malaveyoyo. I recorded it several times and in varying detail from Adiyaleyale and his father, and on one occasion from a gathering of Iwaoyana and Mulina men. The ideological slants of their respective renderings are less evident than in the main part of the legend; for insofar as the sequel has any purpose as a charter it serves Heloava as a rationale for their enduring enemy relationships with Malaveyoyo's killers. That is to say, the descendants of Malaveyoyo's victims, although also regarding themselves as enemies of Heloava, have less interest in promoting their own versions of Malaveyoyo's death than they do their versions of his depredations. Accordingly, I offer a composite account in what follows, though its substance is based on one of Adiyaleyale's narrations.

After some years had passed Tomonauyama's sister decided to seek revenge [*miwa* is specifically blood vengeance]. She cooked a pot of taro pudding and concealed shell valuables inside it. She carried it on her head to Moiye, a big-man of the village of Utalo [several miles to the north, beyond Eweli].[3] She presented him with the pot and he asked her what she wanted. "I want *miwa* for my brother," she said. She returned to Kalauna and told Malaveyoyo that Moiye had sent a message: he had pigs which he would exchange for shells if Malaveyoyo would go to fetch them. Tempted by the offer, Malaveyoyo and a group of Heloava men went to Utalo.

Moiye waited for him inside his house. Malaveyoyo sat down on the *atuaha* and asked to see the pigs. A woman beat a drum to call them from the bush, but it was really the signal to attack. Moiye sprang from his house as a lame man hurled the first spear from behind a tree. Malaveyoyo dodged, and it rattled off the stones of the sitting circle. "War!" he cried, and as the Utalo men closed in the Heloava visitors tried to flee. Malaveyoyo's son Tomotaubolo was struck unconscious by a club and left with an old woman to guard him. They chased Malaveyoyo down to the river at Dududu. There he paused and heard his pursuers' jeers. "We have caught your son and we will eat him," they cried. (He did not know that the boy had already revived and that the old woman, feeling sorry for him, had let him escape and even advised him on a safe route to take.)

Malaveyoyo was *unuwewe*. "So you have caught my son! Why am I running away? We should die together, for he is my firstborn!" And he allowed his enemies to surround him. They raised their spears but he said: "Wait, let me weep, then you can kill me." The warriors paused. But Malaveyoyo tricked them. As he wept he spat on his body and whispered a spell to poison his flesh. Then he let them approach to spear him, and he died. They carried him home and cooked and ate him near the creek of Yewamanala. (Blood seeps from the stones there, and if people bathe at this spot their bodies ache.) All who ate his flesh died from the sorcery with which he spoiled his body. These people were of the Lalauneya clan of Utalo, and today, when Heloava men name a pig Kwanamilalauneya [Man of Lalauneya clan] they can eat it themselves in memory of Malaveyoyo.

Another sequel tells how Malaveyoyo's son reached Kalauna safely, but how his brother Bunaleya died from loss of blood after being carried to Belebele. Later, the Heloava men induce their Belebele friends (with a pot of taro pudding containing armshells) to avenge Malaveyoyo's death. The plot of Tomonauyama's sister's *miwa* is repeated. The Belebele leader calls the Utalo men to receive a pig and when they arrive he is hiding in his house; the treacherous ambush is successful, and the slayers of Malaveyoyo are killed and eaten.

Yet another short sequel explains how Malaveyoyo's bones are brought back to Kalauna by men of Afufuya, a neighboring village of Utalo. They also bring a sprouting coconut, and Heloava men plant it over the bones, which they bury near the creek at Falike-waiyana. They name the tree Kwanamilalauneya in memory of Malaveyoyo's murder, and this same tree (or its offspring) is used by Heloava magicians in the *manumanua* rites for coconut prosperity. Thus has Malaveyoyo been assimilated to the mythically patterned fate of Tomoudi, the hero from whose headless body the first coconuts grew (see chapter 6).

◇◇◇◇◇

Such is the core legend of Malaveyoyo. It is not a myth (*neineya*), for it provides warranties neither to magic nor anything else; it is a story (*ifufu*) of admittedly secular character. Yet it is easy to discern an emergent mythical structure as it conforms, in the telling, to the familiar shape of Kalauna myths. The compelling pattern is provided by Honoyeta: Malaveyoyo, a man of known pedigree and historical verisimilitude, is in the process of being transmuted through the alchemy of narrative into an incarnation of Honoyeta the world-destroyer. But let us first examine more closely the status of the legend and its "uses" in the Kalauna people's thinking about themselves and their history.

It is clearly necessary to distinguish between Malaveyoyo's significance for his Heloava descendants (and to a lesser extent the rest of Lulauvile, which is also tainted by his ancestry), and his significance

100

for the community as a whole. The fact that the most infamous tyrant in Nibita/Kalauna history was a Heloava man has immense consequences for Heloava's view of itself three or four generations after his death. This tiny group—of six male householders in 1967 —still lives in his shadow even as their houses crouch in the shadow of the towering tree he planted. His relics lie in the smoke-blackened roof of Kawanaba's house: a bundle of black-palm spears, a broken club, a handful of stones he clutched to strengthen his fighting fists, and a couple of cracked wooden bowls, larger than the arms can encompass, whose very names are renowned in Kalauna.

But these material legacies are as nothing compared to the social and spiritual ones Heloava inherited. His cannibal victims were countless. (Iyahalina could not or would not enumerate them all for me; when I pressed beyond the twentieth name he grew angry and sank into a harrowing silence.) A map drawn of the *nibai* ties of perpetual enmity created by Malaveyoyo's killings would link Heloava to almost every clan in Kalauna and practically every village in the region. This uniquely comprehensive vengeance network is a burdensome legacy indeed. Not only are Heloava men uncomfortable during casual visits to villages where such *nibai* live, but whenever there is a festival or an *abutu* they can nervously anticipate shaming gifts from their enemies.

Again, Malaveyoyo's deeds may be invoked to justify an *abutu* contest. "All Kalauna are your enemies because your grandfather ate so many people!" yelled an Ukevakeva man at Adiyaleyale in October, 1966, when the latter's affair with another Ukevakeva man's wife suddenly came to light. It was on this occasion of the first *abutu* I ever witnessed, when I was bewildered by the angry flurry of prancing men laying out their yams, that Adiyaleyale tried to clarify the event for me by telling how Malaveyoyo had decreed the custom:

When he had buried Tomonauyama's bones and brought all the food back for his Modawa festival, he orated to the people. "I give these pigs and this food to Iwaoyana. They need not pay back because I killed their leader. We cannot fight each other any more. Whenever there is trouble between our groups you must put hornbill feathers in your hair and carry baskets of food to exchange in *abutu*."

101

Thus did Adiyaleyale, in turn, invoke Malaveyoyo's deeds to explain the mode of nonviolent resolution of the "trouble" between himself and Iwaoyana.

The following year I heard Malaveyoyo being pressed into service again, this time as a political strategy to avert a shaming gift. The occasion was a *lauhiwaiya,* an exchange of cooked food during Ukevakeva's Fakili festival (Young 1971:235-238). One of the sponsors made it known that he intended to give a shaming proportion of several large pots to Adiyaleyale for his adulterous liaison the previous year. His father Iyahalina began a diplomatic offensive to deflect the gift. The winning argument was to the effect that Kawanaba, not Adiyaleyale, was the true lineal descendant of Malaveyoyo and hence the Ukevakeva sponsor's "real" traditional enemy. The man was convinced, and when the time came he called Kawanaba to receive the pots. Appropriately, too, Kawanaba's *fofofo* partner Kiyodi (who had to accept the food on Kawanaba's behalf) was also implicated in Malaveyoyo's crime through his ancestral namesake. Iyahalina explained the story.

> During the famine of his own making Malaveyoyo went to Vatako of Ukevakeva and demanded his daughter Nekilele to eat. Vatako refused to surrender her, pleading that she was nubile and "soon to marry." Malaveyoyo threatened Vatako with sorcery. Vatako stood his ground and declared that if he wanted his daughter he would have to find her and kill her himself. Nekilele overheard the conversation and fled to her mother's hamlet, which happened to be Awakubawe, "Malaveyoyo's own mother's place." She hid inside the house of her mother's brother. Malaveyoyo soon traced her there and, ignoring all appeals to the bond of maternal kinship between them, he entered the house and tried to drag her out. He pulled her by the ankles but she clung to the housepost ("until her knuckles turned white"). Unable to dislodge her Malaveyoyo called to Kiyodi of Anuana for assistance. Kiyodi rushed forward and yanked at the girl's legs while Malaveyoyo cracked her fingers until she let go. Once outside, they clubbed her to death, butchered her and ate her.[4]

On yet another occasion this same story was told by Kimaola, who claims connection with Kiyodi (though the line is not clear). In his

mischievous manner (see chapter 8) Kimaola was attempting to provoke Heloava men into making an *abutu* challenge to Ukevakeva.
He said to them:

> Do you remember how your grandfather Malaveyoyo tried to pull
> Nekilele from Ewalueya's house in Awakubawe? He could not do it.
> Well, my grandfather [Kiyodi] came up and asked what he was doing.
> "I want to kill and eat this girl, but she is resisting," said Malaveyoyo.
> "Let me help you," said Kiyodi, and he grasped her legs. When she
> was down on the ground and Malaveyoyo was about to raise his club,
> Kiyodi said, "Ah, you wait! I will kill her and give her to you to eat."
> [That is, he was invoking their *fofofo* relationship; by doing the dirty
> work for his exchange partner he was denying himself any right to eat
> the girl.] So Kiyodi raised his own club and killed her, and Malave-
> yoyo and his group ate her body. That is why we [Kiyodi's descen-
> dants] are also enemies of Ukevakeva today.

Malaveyoyo's crimes then, are by no means fastened exclusively to
a single, culpable line. Indeed, they are negotiable to the degree
that partisan memory allows; and other Lulauvile groups may wish,
strategically, to avail themselves of the legacy of enmities that Malaveyoyo bestowed on Heloava. The ideological flexibility of such tales
can be illustrated in counterpoint by one that documents Malaveyoyo's breach with Kimaola's forbears. I heard it mentioned when
Kimaola's sister wanted cause to distance herself (and her brother)
from Iyahalina.

> Three children of Heloava II [Kimaola's hamlet, otherwise known as
> Kalauna] were hunting for food in the time of famine. They came by
> Malaveyoyo's garden and found some yams which he had dug out and
> left on a bed of soil. They stole them and crept away to a cave where
> they roasted and ate them. Malaveyoyo returned to his garden and
> saw their footprints. He tracked the children to the cave, and trapping
> them there, clubbed them all to death. Returning to the village, he
> told their hapless fathers to fetch their bodies and bury them. They
> were too afraid to speak out but conspired to seek revenge. They
> planted sorcery in the bushes where Heloava folk used to excrete, and
> soon several of them died. Surmising the reason, Heloava broke off
> their *fofofo* relations with Heloava II.

103

/\/\/\/\

These and other tales of Malaveyoyo's atrocities cluster around the central legends; they are detachable, lacking any sequential or structural relationship to it. They can be told, as I have shown, as anecdotes with charter potential for different sets of relationships. Thus, Malaveyoyo still overflows the mythologizing mold by which his core legend would contain him.

Looking beyond Lulauvile's ambivalent identification with him we find in the rest of Kalauna a trace of pride with regard to his warrior prowess: his violent excesses in the service of Kalauna's aggrandizement as a community. Again, these are celebrated in tales not directly connected to the central legend. They may refer to the period of "his" famine or they may antedate or postdate it; tradition is vague on this matter. The so-called wars with Eweli, Kalauna's neighbor to the north, over a couple of low grassy ridges, are said to have been provoked by famine, but whether this was Malaveyoyo's famine of the core legend is difficult to decide. In whatever phase of Malaveyoyo's life they took place, however, these wars made him Kalauna's champion, a fearless leader of raid and battle.

I will not relate any of these war stories, for they are tedious to anyone not acquainted with the locations, the terrain, and the named fighting groups involved. I shall simply remark upon Malaveyoyo's reputation as an innovative war leader. This was brought home to me one day as I was toiling up the path to Kalauna from Eweli. My Heloava companion halted and excitedly pointed out a black, flat-topped rock, which jutted above the rank grass and commanded a fine view of the path we had taken from the thin line of houses on a spur a couple of miles distant. We clambered up the rock, called Kabinamatu; and there was a solitary backrest wedged into the top, an almost vertical slab of stone pitted with pale green lichen. This was Malaveyoyo's *atuaha* for war, explained my companion. It was here that he and his war party came after raids into Eweli territory, dragging their stunned victims with them. Under Malaveyoyo's instructions his warriors would slaughter the captives, sever their heads and limbs, and toss them from hand to hand. They

104

would tear out the hearts, which were eaten warm by Malaveyoyo himself or given to other daring warriors. This orgiastic display could be seen from the ridges of Eweli, and in case their enemies were in any doubt as to what they were witnessing, Malaveyoyo's men would blow conch shells and chant:

> Hey! Hey!
> Your skulls will break!
> You will eat our shit!
> Come and fetch your brother's bones!

Stung into paroxysms of rage, the Eweli men would hastily prepare a retaliatory war party, which on at least one occasion was successfully ambushed by Malaveyoyo's warriors.

It is not as an eminent strategist that Malaveyoyo is remembered, nor as a skillful warrior renowned (as were some Kalauna men) for the ability to spear or dodge ably, nor yet as a war magician, for the secrets of war were owned by the Giyo (Spear) people of Mulina and Mifoloyai clans. Rather, Malaveyoyo is glorified for his *meadoba,* "tongue-fury," which may better be glossed as fighting frenzy. *Meadoba* was a state of near-amok desired by all warriors. It was induced by war magic that "dazed their senses" (Jenness and Ballantyne 1920:85), and by chewing red crotons of *Cordyline* and bitter young betel nut without lime, which is said to "make your head go round like whisky." Under these influences a warrior went berserk: his eyes rolled, he salivated, his limbs trembled and his body perspired profusely. He was said to look *kwava*—crazy, deranged—and terrified all who beheld him. In this state he could ingest other concoctions to enhance his rage: ginger root and pig's excrement mixed with blood. Incensed beyond reason, reckless and foul-mouthed, such warriors would then attack the enemy with, quite literally, bloodthirsty abandon, risking their own lives without fear.

It is claimed to have been Malaveyoyo's discovery that eating the raw flesh of captives induced or renewed the frenzy of *meadoba.* Uncooked human flesh was not a gustatory preference, and Malaveyoyo had to order his followers to eat it—until, that is, they appreciated its stimulus to *meadoba*'s blood lust. So the black stone of

105

Kabinamatu commemorates Malaveyoyo's proclivity for berserk behavior in war and his ability to induce it also in his warriors. On this stone, too, there used to be a croton planted by Malaveyoyo, a plant he had journeyed to Bwaidoka to obtain from the owners of the coral sitting circle of Wifala, whose potent war magic was famous throughout the island.[5] If these are the things for which Malaveyoyo is still remembered and admired by all Kalauna (including the descendants of his victims), then they testify to a covert cult of violence not yet renounced by modern generations. Malaveyoyo, therefore, remains an exemplar.

I draw attention to his ferocity in war as a further example of his extravagance of affect, his demonic extremism; and I suggest that the fact that this evokes a responsive chord of awed admiration in Kalauna people even today (softened as they are by seventy years of Christian teaching) is evidence of their fundamentally catastrophic world view. Beneath the controlled and dissimulative surface of their society there is the sense of imminent collapse, of a people conditioned to anticipate, if not welcome, calamity. But it is a man-willed and man-made calamity that Kalauna people read in Malaveyoyo's legends; it is human agency and not any impersonal force (environment, history, fortune) that makes their society seem precarious to them. Hence, the magical world view of exaggerated human control and the profound belief in the role of human agency in world maintenance (and world destruction) is fully conducive to apocalyptic expectations — for what can be more unpredictable than human passion? It follows too, perhaps, that this "religion" celebrates human power even when (*especially* when) it is monstrous and ultimately self-destructive.

∧∧∧∧∧

Let us develop this insight into Malaveyoyo's appeal to Kalauna's ethos by viewing him as a spiritual successor to Honoyeta. The parallels between these death-infatuated heroes are unlikely to be coincidental; they are surely motivated. Fundamentally, of course, the Honoyeta myth and the Malaveyoyo legend share the same con-

106

cerns: power, food, death, and vengeance. (In Freudian idiom they are about oral aggression and oral guilt.) But there are also direct homologies and apparent inversions of plot that suggest some strain toward the assimilation of Malaveyoyo to the Honoyeta model. Let us take the Kalauna view and suppose the heroes to be motivated by *unuwewe*. Following the destruction of his skin, Honoyeta abandons a well-fed domestic life and wanders in search of death. In the first part of the Malaveyoyo legend, the hero forces *others* to abandon domestic life and wander in search of food. In the second part of each tale the heroes allow themselves to be killed (one provokes his killers by insulting their fatherhood, the other is provoked by his killers who insult *his* fatherhood); and in both tales those who taste the heroes' flesh also die. Finally, the burial of the heroes' bones is magically efficacious, though they must be "stilled" to remain so.

The Malaveyoyo legend also permutes the Oedipal theme of the Honoyeta myth, its dialectic of love and hatred. The rebellious young Malaveyoyo pits himself against an authority figure (a "good provider"), slays him, and marries his widow. His victim's sister arranges his talion death, which Malaveyoyo embraces in the belief that his own son has been slain. (I cannot resist the observation that my narrator allowed Malaveyoyo, inhuman ogre though he was, an intimation of pure tragedy when he gave him the Homeric line, "Let me weep, then you can kill me.")

Pursuing the interpretation in this vein, it will be recalled that at the end of the last chapter I observed that if Honoyeta's myth expresses the "primal sin" as "eating the father," then the consequent punishment is being forced to eat the children. Malaveyoyo's legend expounds this in a dialectically inverted manner. Malaveyoyo cold-bloodedly eats children; then, having killed and eaten the father-figure Tomonauyama, his own death is accomplished by the threat to eat his son.

We must also recall that Malaveyoyo is credited with having invented *abutu*, the competitive exchange of food as a surrogate for killing and eating one's enemies. In terms of the simple model I sketched in the previous chapter, Malaveyoyo's innovation implies a redirection of hostility from the "fathers" to the "brothers" and a displacement of the objects of oral incorporation from the flesh of

107

one's enemies to the food they have grown and the pigs they have reared.

Abutu, therefore, retains the idiom of oral aggression, though what was ontogenetically a familial and domestic issue is extended and politicized. Fostering thereby becomes a community matter, colored by the more forthright antagonism of nonkinsmen. In the family domain fostering engenders affective bonds and moral obligations, but it also generates hostility and resentment through the child's experience of the "bad" parents who hoard and withhold food. Food-giving in *abutu* (which has some resemblance to force-feeding) is a politicized form of fostering no less ridden with ambivalence, for the publicly grateful but privately resentful recipients are aware that the gifts of food make them subordinate to the donors. Massive *abutu* prestations, of course, are made precisely to this end; they are fully intended to shame and to evoke in those who receive them a sense of inferiority, dependence, and lowered self-esteem.

Thus, in both domains, fostering or food-giving is the expression of presumptive authority relations. And in both domains there is acute ambivalence toward the authority figures who dispense food. Malaveyoyo's *abutu* is a displacement activity that pits the food-givers and the would-be authority figures against one another in contest. The familial fostering bond, which culminates in the father's gift of yam seeds to his son—the transmission of a patrimonial political potency—is ceremonially endorsed in *abutu* by the son's aggressive yam-giving to his "brothers" and peers. That is, he redirects his filial hostility toward men of his own generation, thereby demonstrating his independence of paternal authority and his achievement of manhood.

I have ventured far beyond any Kalauna person's interpretation of Malaveyoyo's significance for his society, though I should add that there is a ready recognition of his similarity to Honoyeta. Adiyaleyale, for instance, was the first to point out to me that Malaveyoyo, "like Honoyeta," terrorized people with his vengeful *unuwewe,* and finally doctored his body so that those who feasted on his flesh would die. But Adiyaleyale also went beyond such particulars in saying: "He could not change his skin like Honoyeta. He had to die like a man, and so he decided to make his name immortal. He achieved this by his wickedness."

Malaveyoyo realizes Honoyeta, brings the mythical hero's aloof and protean character within the compass of human possibility, captures him in human genealogy and situates him in local history. Through Malaveyoyo, Kalauna people can better appropriate Honoyeta and his terrible lessons, reflexively tightening the grip of his fascination for them. Malaveyoyo's rampant evil is an epiphany of the sufferings promised by the sun god. Malaveyoyo exploited Honoyeta's potential for ultimate evil, and explored to the full the dire possibilities of Honoyeta's curse on mankind. Hence his salience in Kalauna's folk-history, signalizing as he does the culmination of the pagan ages and the nadir of savagery.

He also marks a transition between the traditional world and the modern, and he is held to have been not merely harbinger but also instigator of the new era, as if it were in direct response to his violent excesses that missionaries and colonial government officers intervened to "save" whatever enfeebled society remained.[6] There is some psychological — if little historical — truth in this view. For just as the anthropomorphizing vision of Kalauna has created the legend of a man born to expose the flaws in its social system and epitomize the negative traits of its culture, so it has also created personifications of the new regimes. Misibibi (Mr. Vivian), the first white patrol officer, is one such historical figure; Doctor Blomlo (Bromilow), the pioneer missionary, is another.[7] And within Kalauna itself a modern successor to Malaveyoyo emerged in Tobowa, the despotic village policeman.

5
The Jaw of Tobowa

So the Platonic year
Whirls out new right and wrong,
Whirls in the old instead;
All men are dancers and their tread
Goes to the barbarous clangour of a gong.

—W. B. Yeats
"Nineteen Hundred and Nineteen"

∧∧∧∧∧

Separated by less than a generation from the insensate cruelties of
Malaveyoyo's era, Tobowa's life spanned five decades, from approx-
imately 1914 to 1964. He had died only a year or so before my
arrival in Kalauna, recently enough for his absence to be palpable,
probed by reminiscent tongues like the cavity of an extracted tooth.
Strange as I was to everything, it took me some time to weigh the
import of this name, Tobo'wa, dropped in conversations and
alluded to in speeches with the hint of a glottal catch mournfully
extending the vowel. The feeling-tone of Tobowa's memory impressed me; for except by his sons and one or two others, that memory was generally reviled. Most agreed that he had been, in that
blandly damning term, *kaliva koyona,* a bad man. I was led to believe that, far from mourning him, the community had heaved a

110

collective sigh of relief when he died. Here, then, was another fearsome figure in the mold of Malaveyoyo, though the lineaments of his personality were far less stark and grotesque in the "remembrance" (a noun synonymous with "love" in Kalauna). Tobowa had his redeeming features: openhanded generosity, sympathy for the underdog, an enterprising spirit, and a distaste for disorder. These made him a formidably conscientious village constable, an office suffused by the mystique of colonial omnipotence. But for the most part, Kalauna seems to have feared Tobowa as one tempted by the despotism that had been the bane of Malaveyoyo's Nibita.

Tobowa's pedigree was simple and uncomplicated by any competitive clamor of brothers or close cousins. His line, one of the senior *unuma* of Anuana II, is impeccable Lulauvile and carries entitlement to one of the three most important magical systems of *manumanua*, the ritual of prosperity. Had he been moved by no other ambition, he could have been assured of the esteem that Kalauna extends to the Lulauvile *toitavealata*. As it was, he sullied the role of guardian by his aspiration to be a master sorcerer.

Never having met Tobowa myself, I rely entirely upon hearsay accounts given by informants, some of whom were his kinsmen and others his victims. No one had been indifferent to him, no group immune to his influence; hence no testimony was without its particular bias. The following sketch has the black and white contrasts of a caricature, and lacks the shadings of full biography. Clearly, a reputation reconstructed in a language deficient in fine adjectival discriminations presents the bearer larger than life, with gross features and opaque motivations. And while the tales I shall tell of Tobowa are still too fresh to be legends (they are reminiscences merely), myth is always nascent and narratives feel for its form.

Consider, as a clue, the statement that Tobowa ate dog. Kalauna people do not eat dogs, though a number of other villages on the island (including neighbouring Eweli) customarily do so. They are occasionally exchanged between groups, and debts of dogs may be accounted for as scrupulously as debts of yams or pigs. In Eweli dogs are clubbed, singed, butchered, distributed, cooked, and eaten in much the same manner as pigs. But there is an edge of contempt to the Kalauna people's voices when they discuss this alien practice, which they hold to pollute the pots the flesh is cooked in. Yet Tobowa ate dog with unconcerned relish. Anyone else but he, I was told, would have been the object of derision, and his contaminated pot ostentatiously avoided. "But we could not laugh at Tobowa because we were afraid of him." Tobowa, then, was an autonomous man, one who put himself beyond the common decency of good taste by eating the inedible and defying censure. So potent a sign of individuality is oral eccentricity in Kalauna that this single quirk of Tobowa's behavior illuminates his character.

But while dog-eating can be overlooked as an imported affectation, another eating habit attributed to Tobowa provoked moral outrage. It was widely supposed that he ate human corpses: he was a *kwahala,* or "witch." *Kwahala* are agents of mystical attack: bird- or batlike creatures with long talons and cruel beaks, whose axillae flicker at night, whose excrement is luminous like fireflies, and whose sinister presence is betrayed by the stench of putrefaction. They can be conjured out of round stones, which sorcerers keep on the shelves of their houses, and they are directed to attack sleeping victims whose vital organs they tear out and feast upon. The victim awakens as if from a nightmare, perhaps ignorant of the damage done to his insides; he may even live for a day or two. But in a sense he is already dead, a zombie at the mercy of the sorcerer's *coup de grace* involving an incantation, a burned leaf, or his frail voice captured in a tin. *Kwahala,* then, are not autonomous beings but agents under the control of sorcerers with whom they are phenomenally identified. It is held that if a *kwahala* can be struck (and I have seen frantic men flail the empty darkness with bushknives), then its owner will sustain an identical wound while ostensibly lying on his bed. So too, it is argued, these creatures who gorge on the innards of their victims simultaneously feed their masters. The conception, then, is of a kind of were-bird, appropriate in a culture whose mythology exploits the diverse avian fauna of the island. Tobowa was such, not only sending *kwahala* to seek out live victims, but also directing them to violate the graves of the recently dead for their remains.[1]

There can be no kind of proof for these imagined deeds of Tobowa, though one man claimed to have seen and smelled "an Eweli man's arm" poking obscenely above the rim of Tobowa's pot one day. But the fact remains that Tobowa's reputation and social personality were frequently depicted in the idiom of oral excess. One more example will suffice.

Tobowa's first wife was a woman of Kwakwaiboka, who bore him four children (two of whom died in infancy). Tobowa complained to his wife that he was tired of the way she always ate her brother's gifts of food without giving him any. In the words of the maternal kinsman of Tobowa who related the story to me:

> Tobowa said to himself: "I'll get my pig!" And that night he took the flesh out of his wife's arm as she slept. He did it by sorcery—just the spirit of her arm, so that when she awoke she didn't notice the difference. He sent her to the gardens and told her, "I'm going to Belebele to get pork." When she had gone he cooked her arm and ate a piece with vegetables, and when she returned he offered her the pot. "You eat some pork. My stomach is full." She ate it, then he said, "You have eaten yourself," and told her what he had done. She died soon afterwards, for the sorcery killed her.

Whether or not Tobowa rejoiced in his reputation as a cannibal I do not know; but he almost certainly helped to foster it. Moral stigma notwithstanding, it gave him evidence of his power. At a time when genuine cannibalism was but a fading memory for a handful of old men, Tobowa perpetuated the pagan tradition in phantom guise.

ᐱᐯᐱᐯᐱᐯ

Tobowa was physically imposing. Manawadi of Mulina, one of the kinsmen who buried him, described him thus:

> He was a very big strong man, tall and muscled. While catching crabs in the mangroves, if one pinched his arm with its claw he would offer it the other arm to nip, then carry it ashore and flick it off. His skin was so tough it did not tear. Once he punched an areca palm and his

113

fist went right through the trunk. He didn't say anything but waited for my father to cut him free. His hand wasn't even scratched. He had tattoos like snakes on his arms which ran over his shoulders, down his chest and crossed above his stomach. No one else would dare to wear such a fine tattoo; it meant that he was strong and could fight anyone.

Once he was playing football at Eweli when a Dobuan teacher from Wailagi Mission got angry with him. Tobowa ignored him and continued playing. After the game the Dobuan wanted to fight him, so Tobowa said, "All right, yourself!" And he let the teacher hit him three times. Then he said, "Now it's my turn." He swung his fist, just once from the waist, and the Dobuan jerked into the air like a football. Tobowa leaned over him as he lay on the ground and shouted: "You see! I wasn't even angry with you, but maybe I'll kill you now!" Eweli men tried to hold him but he shrugged them off, and some fled to their houses in fear. The Methodist missionary stood in front of him with his Bible and said: "You've knocked him down, he can't fight any more," and he made Tobowa touch the Bible. Tobowa was shaking with anger and would have killed the man.

Another testimony to Tobowa's fighting prowess comes from Tabwaika, Lalaveya's hamlet leader, who grew up with Tobowa, having been fostered by the latter's father.

Men were afraid of him because he was so very strong. He gave no second warning; he spoke only once, then took hold of the man and hit him. . . .

He went to work at Mogubu plantation [on the south coast of Papua] where there was a big group of Mailu men. But they were no match for him. He beat them all by himself. His name still lives in Mailu, for they became afraid of him. When Kalauna men go to Mogubu today people there still ask about him, but our men do not admit they were his friends. They lie and say, "Oh, Tobowa came from some other village," in case the Mailu men are sorcerers and want to avenge their brothers or fathers.

Another time he worked at Nuatutu [a plantation on eastern Goodenough] and there was a Kukuya man [from western Fergusson] with whom he quarreled. Tobowa hit him too hard, and the man died. They buried him. Tobowa was a fierce man and people were very afraid to offend him. In this way his fame spread from place to place.

114

If Tobowa ever killed anyone by physical violence it escaped official notice. While this was certainly a possibility during the years of government neglect that followed the Japanese war, these tales can simply be read as evidence of Tobowa's willingness to assert himself by brute strength. This seems to have been as intimidating to Kalauna people as were his threats of sorcery. He is said to have beaten his wives regularly, struck his kinsmen periodically, and to have had no qualms about hitting other men's children, an act as provocatively insulting as any in the culture. In short, he could be an incomparable (and perhaps sadistic) bully whom no one dared stand up to.

The dismal catalogue of Tobowa's alleged sorcery attacks need not be detailed in full. I recorded more than a dozen in some detail, which amounted to 14 percent of a total of ninety-one cases I elicited in 1966-68.[2] Here I shall mention only two cases, both of which illustrate Tobowa's ambiguous admissions of culpability.

During an *abutu* contest with Wailolo in 1960, Heloava received a very large pig. As Iyahalina's chief *fofofo*, Didiala had the right to decide how it was to be butchered and distributed. Out of deference to Tobowa (who made up the third *toitavealata* of Lulauvile at that time), both men invited him to offer his opinion. Some disagreement arose during the discussion and Tobowa stalked away saying, "Do it your own way; I'm not your *fofofo*." He took umbrage and sent back the piece of pork that Didiala gave him as his rightful share. Some weeks later Iyahalina's youngest son, Awadava, aged about six, fell sick. His mouth clamped shut and he could neither eat nor speak. As he lay writhing on the floor, Iyahalina sent Adiyaleyale to Kimaola with a pound note, asking him to come and cure the child. Kimaola doctored his own eyes and "saw" Tobowa. He told Iyahalina: "It is Tobowa who made him sick for he is still angry about that pig." Kimaola forced some bespelled leaves between Awadava's teeth and the child's mouth relaxed. Then he advised Iyahalina to send for Tobowa, though not to tell him who had said so, but to say that Awadava himself had dreamed of him during his delirium. When Tobowa came to see the child he laughed. "Perhaps he fell sick himself, or perhaps it was me," he said. "But I wouldn't have killed him. I was only a little bit angry." Then he rubbed Awadava with leaves and the boy soon recovered. Iyahalina gave Tobowa a shell necklace and there the matter ended.

The second case, from another source, also shows how Tobowa colluded with his accusers. A widow of Nouneya clan neglected to give Tobowa some fish he believed he was entitled to receive. She fell ill with *vedouva*, a sickness that prostrated her with putrid sores. She lay motionless in her house for many months while her kinsmen waited for her to die. Towakaita, Nouneya's leader, suspected Tobowa because the woman kept her arms crossed over her chest in the gestural sign of a fishtail. He called Tobowa and protested: "This woman is dying because of fish. Either cure her or help her to die quickly." Tobowa spoke to her with sorcery in his mouth: "O Nekwaluwela, you can die now!" And she did, it is said, that same day.

∧∧∧∧

So far I have testified to Tobowa's blameworthy and antisocial traits, the things which in the weight of Kalauna opinion condemned him as a Bad Man whose death they could not mourn. It is now time to present whatever evidence exists for his kinsmen's claim that he was also a Good Man, however short his virtues might fall of redeeming him. Nikuya, Tobowa's eldest son, was a man I met for the first time in 1977—so long had he lived abroad to evade the possible consequences of his father's heritage of hate in the community. When I asked him to talk about his father his eulogy was predictably pious, and it centered on the notion that, for the community, Tobowa's despotism was ultimately beneficient. Things had never been the same since his death.

> He was Kalauna's real boss, the only one. He looked after the people. If any trouble occurred he stopped it. If the gardens yielded badly he did *manumanua*. When he died the village fell too. Everything declined; there was no food. And since he died there has been no strong man in Kalauna.

116

Tabwaika, probably Tobowa's closest companion throughout his life, gave a testimony ridden with ambivalence.

> He was really a good man. He didn't hoard meat, fish, or tobacco for himself but gave them away generously. He treated people kindly. But he was a fierce man, sharp and tough, and people were afraid of him. That's why his name went high in fame. . . .
>
> Tobowa was a good man—for what evil is there in all of us? But he was also bad, with bad ways; though he did not hit those of us who were well behaved, and he made good friends of us. . . . But I told him once, "Sometimes you are not good; sometimes you get angry for nothing."

Such relatively favorable testimonies, however, focus their most genuine admiration on Tobowa's achievements as a village constable. It is to his official career that I now turn.

Village constables had been appointed on the island as part of the colonial pacification policy since just before the turn of the century. The first appointment in the Kalauna area was in 1910, when a Wailolo man was given jurisdiction over Eweli, Belebele, and Kalauna, as well as his own village. His influence in Kalauna seems to have been negligible. This arrangement persisted for thirty years. Then, sometime in 1940, a visiting patrol officer nominated Tobowa as Kalauna's first village constable or *folisiman*. He gave him a dark serge *laplap* and a heavy leather belt, with a promise to remunerate him one pound for every year of service. But why Tobowa? His son Nikuya maintained that the officer had actually sought him out: "The government found him and knew he was a strong man and would look after the village well." It was an appointment that probably suited everybody. From the government's point of view the sturdiest-looking figure had been selected; from the community's point of view their strongest man had been chosen to intercede with the intimidating white men who threw their weight around from time to time. And from Tobowa's point of view, of course, the office legitimated the exercise of his "natural" authority.

A few years later, in 1943, the Second World War brushed Goodenough Island, though it must have seemed to those islanders whose lives were dislocated that the war had engulfed them. Along with the populations of other villages of eastern Goodenough, the military administration evacuated Kalauna people to Deba on Fergusson Island. At Deba, poor water supplies, unfamiliar soils, fractious neighbors, and whatever other hardships one might imagine of a refugee community wrenched from its home, led to a spate of deaths among the very old and the very young. But many of the young men, including Tobowa, had fared very differently. The allied garrison and airbase at Vivigani, the large, flat, strategically important plain that can be seen from Kalauna's spurs, had mushroomed into a vast complex of military installations where local men were employed as casual labor. The effect upon Tobowa of this ephemeral canvas city of some 10,000 white men, with its awesome technology and prodigal commisariat, can only be surmised. It is enough to say that he was there, working alongside many of his fellow islanders, speculating with them on the sudden disappearance of yesterday's world, and perhaps celebrating with them the emergence of a somewhat skewed millennium. "Tobowa learned many new ideas at Vivigani," remarked one of his contemporaries, with a hint that he had acquired a taste for cargo cult doctrines.

What these "ideas" were has become a matter of local legend. There were those that engaged him in the economic "development" of Kalauna, and those that he applied to keeping "law and order" in the community. Soon after the war, it is told, Tobowa went to the government officer at Esa'ala (the subdistrict headquarters on Normanby Island) and asked to be allowed to form a *komiti*. Tabwaika explained:

> "Yes, that's what you need," the government said, and told him to go back and make a *komiti*. He came home, and we were still sleeping early in the morning when he blew his conch shell. People gathered in Anuana. "People," he said, "I have searched; I went here and there, and now I have found a way. Let us make a *komiti*." He made Didiala chairman and Enobwau his deputy, with other men as *komiti* too.

Didiala was *toitavealata* and ritual guardian of the yams; Enobwau of Anuana II—Tobowa's own hamlet—had the traditional ritual

118

task of inaugurating the yam gardening cycle. Most of the other members of the "committee" were also Lulauvile men with ritual expertise in crop growing. The first task of the committee, it seems, was to plant what it called a "general garden" to grow crops for market (there being a vague idea that the produce could be shipped to Esa'ala, for there were no markets on Goodenough). After lengthy disputes about what land to use, the committee organized the villagers to plant a communal garden of pumpkins, tomatoes, and pineapples. It was a total failure. According to Kawanaba:

> You know Kalauna's custom — there was jealousy and people talked. Someone spoiled the trees with *wala* [disease-inflicting "protective" magic], and someone else did *imamaiyaudi* magic to make people lazy and disinclined to work [this sorcery is the obverse of *yaleyale,* the magic of fortitude used by industrious gardeners]. So grass choked the plants, and no one cared. Tobowa was resentful and said, "Oh, enough! Let it go."

Some time later Tobowa inspired the community with another of his ideas. This was to raise a general subscription and open a village store. Tabwaika said:

> He told us to bring our money together, and when men came back from working for whites he asked money of them. It grew to a hundred pounds. Tobowa took it to Esa'ala and the government said, "Go back and get another ten or twenty, then you can start a store." But Kalauna people didn't want to put any more money down, and that's why the store didn't work. The government let Tobowa put the money in a bank and gave him the passbook. He went to Esa'ala often with prisoners for court, so he took out the money and used it himself. When only half remained he asked us: "Should I buy a 'general' shotgun?" We said yes, so he went to Samarai and bought a gun. Then he went out shooting all the time. He shot many pigs and wallabies, but he wouldn't let anyone else use the gun. The trigger broke finally. It was his own fault for he used it too often. He took the gun to the patrol office and left it there; so it disappeared forever.

Another sort of testimony to Tobowa's enterprising activities can be gleaned from patrol reports. There is normally no place in these terse documents for the names of local personalities, but during his twenty years as policeman Tobowa was mentioned in dispatches no fewer than five times. The first, recorded in September 1940, just a few months after his appointment, notes that Tobowa, as instructed, had built two new resthouses on the edge of Kalauna, and that he had "a large amount of native food for sale," which the patrol officer obligingly purchased and shipped to Esa'ala (Champion 1940).

The following year Tobowa made another attempt to impress the government. Patrol Officer Timperley noted, on 11 May 1941, that "VC Tobowa provided much more cooked food than the patrol could eat," and his inspection of Kalauna prompted the approving comment that "the village was extremely clean and well-kept." (Some thirty years later, Kalauna men recalled their bemused obedience to Tobowa's insistence that everyone should plant flowering shrubs around their houses — a "*dimdim* custom" he had admired in Esa'ala.) The officer found fault with Kalauna's roads, however, and declared that "in this respect the people need a shaking up" (Timperley 1941).

The next report to mention Tobowa, some eight years later, records another rebuke:

> The VC of Kalauna claimed he had made much money by buying goods from the tradestore and selling them again in his own and nearby districts. He was told that this must cease as trading without a licence is illegal. He wants to apply for a licence. [Tolhurst 1949]

To which the district officer in Samarai appended a crushingly paternalistic comment: "It is not considered desirable that any VC (particularly the VC of Kalauna with a population of 362) should engage in any large-scale native trading activities" (ibid.). It was presumably to buy the necessary license that Tobowa canvassed his villagers' savings, with the result we have seen. A year later, however, another patrol officer implicitly commends Tobowa's progressive ideas: "Tobowa VC keeps on producing copra in conjunction with Belebele people, who have a smoke house in Maladomea. Tobowa is interested in the idea of co-operatives" (Woodhill 1950).

Tobowa earned these passing references because, unlike the great majority of islanders of the time, he was showing a spirit of enterprise which the visiting whites thought worth remarking. It must have seemed to these exasperated officers of the postwar years (who frequently complained of the apathy of the people) that here at last was a man worthy of his V.C.'s cloth, a man who took to heart their incessant pleas for more coconut plantings, more copra production, more backs-to-the-wheel cooperation to help make Papua a more self-sufficient colony. But poor Tobowa! In the flush of his enthusiasm for middleman trading (though one shudders to think of his potential for extortion) he is restrained by officials who put the letter of the law above the spirit of laissez-faire. His progressive interest in 1950 in the idea of cooperatives, moreover, was to be as frustrated as his plan for "general" gardens to supply a distant and perhaps imaginary market. Almost another twenty years were to pass before the first cooperative association was formed in a Goodenough Island village.

In addition to his willingness to try copra production (though we may be sure he did not do all the hard work of breaking and bagging himself), he showed himself receptive to almost any new enterprise. Kawanaba recalls how Tobowa recruited him to assist in planting rice, peanuts, and English potatoes.

> The government gave him seeds and said, "Try these." He brought them back and got young men like me to help him. We made a large garden at Ulolona. We harvested the rice, but we had no machine to husk it, so we used sticks to beat it instead. Then his wife cooked some and we tasted it. The tough skin scratched Tobowa's mouth and it bled. I couldn't chew it either. "Oh, sorry," he said, "we haven't done it right."

Nor, apparently, were the peanuts and English potatoes any more successful.

So much for Tobowa's precocious enterprises, most of which foundered through ignorance. It is only fair to add that, in the twenty-five years since his disillusionment, no other Kalauna man has tried quite so earnestly or been notably more successful in stimulating economic "development" in the community. At the very least, Tobowa achieved some recognition for his attempts, and Tabwaika described him (in an English phrase) as the government's "Good Boy." Used as a sort of model village constable and spearhead of native enterprise by the administration, he was sent around the island with a patrol to address village meetings on the importance of agricultural projects and to explain the new systems of taxation and village councillors. As his son Nikuya said, with mild irony: "He hadn't been to school, but he learned the ideas of the government very quickly and the government thought he was a good man."

Among his own people Tobowa gained a reciprocal reputation of being knowledgeable in the ways of Europeans. His illiteracy was no handicap. He spoke Police Motu, a little English, and was believed to keep a finger on the pulse of local administrative developments, such as they were in the relatively stagnant fifties. Whenever he returned from Esa'ala or from a patrol of the island on official business, he would summon a village meeting (itself an important political innovation). He would harangue the people, giving them scarce information from abroad, urging them to pursue his latest idea and castigating them for their collective shortcomings in neglecting his previous one. It was a role which, after his death, the local government councillor was to assume and (I was told) perform in an almost identical manner.[3] On these occasions Tobowa gave his prophetic imagination free rein, and Kalauna people continue to be astonished at his prescience. Nikuya, for example, remembered that:

In 1950 he told everyone a local government council would come, that's why people had to work harder in their gardens and making copra. He also told us about self-government and the independence of Papuans from whites.

These political developments occurred in 1964, 1973, and 1975 respectively, and Tobowa barely lived to see the first of them. Kawanaba suggested that he might have heard about these things from the government, or "dreamed" about them. But the first possibility is scarcely more credible than the second. More likely he listened to some anticolonial — and equally prescient — soldiers during the war. "After he died all these things came," Nikuya continued. "He did not lie. And people remember and say, 'O, truly, Tobowa was right.'"

The other side of the praiseworthy coin of enterprise Tobowa displayed to the administration, and an adjunct to his predictions of colonial change, was a thrilling millenarian speculation. When Obedi, a Bwaidoka man, was arrested on Samarai for creating a disturbance at the wharf where a ship unloaded cargo stenciled with what he thought was his name, Tobowa was the one to announce the event in Kalauna and ruminate publicly upon its possible significance. In 1959, when a Wagifa cult leader made prophecies which spoke of the coming of a woman called Elizabeth who would right all wrongs and deliver cargo by the returning ancestors, Tobowa was among those Kalauna men who were enraptured and expectant (see Young 1971a:50). Though when the district commissioner made an investigatory patrol following the suppression of the cult, Tobowa was among the first to condemn its foolishness and berate its gullible adherents. It sometimes seemed more important to him to remain on good terms with the government than with his fellow villagers.

∧∨∨∧∧

There remains another, perhaps the most important, aspect of Tobowa's exercise of the office of policeman: his coercive power in the name of a foreign concept of law and order. He was obviously quick to seize the opportunities his position gave to enhance and legitimate his personal power, but there is no evidence that he used it to persecute rivals or establish a nepotic regime. He appears to have been so singularly unmoved by family faction or clan rivalry that of all the things said against him favoritism is not among them. His eye seems to have been fixed upon a much wider horizon of public good than that enjoined by the obligations of kinship, a fact that might partly be explained by his lack of close agnates.

He was not invariably a bully, and his threats of violence were often used to prevent its use by others. I liked the story of how he protected Leoleo, an indigent "rubbish man" who was being pursued naked through the village by an enraged kinsman and a derisive crowd. Tobowa sat him between his own legs, covered his loins with a piece of calico, and dared anyone to approach. Or the story of the missionary teacher who took his young charges into the bush in search of lawyer cane, got lost, and returned long after dark to find the anxious parents in a lynching mood. Tobowa stepped in to cool their anger and forbid retaliation.

These were acts of a responsible village constable, as perhaps also were some of his "ideas" for punishing people. According to Kawanaba, "He would make men plant fifty coconuts each. Or he would make women sweep clean the watering places, and plant crotons and hibiscus to improve the village." That he took quite seriously his formal duty of keeping the peace is the most reasonable interpretation of the determined efforts he made in taking adulterous couples and brawling brothers on the tedious journey to court at Esa'ala. Even more suggestive of a public morality that transcended local factions was Tobowa's arrest, on one occasion, of a number of Kalauna men (his Lulauvile clansmen among them) who had violently attacked some Belebele villagers. Despite their protest that village loyalty should come first, he took them to the magistrate knowing that they would be imprisoned. On another occasion, he was shown to be sufficiently feared by Belebele men to be able to round up several and take them to court for stealing crops from Kalauna gardens.

I cannot read into these or other accounts of Tobowa's career as a village constable evidence of a heavy-handed strategy to subjugate his domain by means of the power of his office. I have argued elsewhere that Tobowa did not appear to abuse unduly the sanctions available to him as a V.C.; and in the two decades of his reign as the most feared man in Kalauna, Tobowa did not create a coterie of henchmen nor did he exact "tribute" from his subject villagers (Young 1971:141-142). The prerogatives he did assume—such as assistance in his gardens, the best cuts of pork, an unfailing supply of betel nut—were essentially no different from those granted to other *toitavealata* and big-men. He was merely able to insist upon them more vigorously. Kalauna people remember him as a sorcerer first and a *folisiman* second, which is to suggest that he would have been the same kind of strong-armed leader whatever his official role. In short, Tobowa was no more a satrap than he was a stooge. When asked by the government to nominate a successor, he made no attempt to perpetuate his influence through nepotism. The young man he selected was of good standing and modest education, but he was neither kinsman, clansman, nor special friend to Tobowa.

The history of Tobowa's infamy, then, is softened by patches of redeeming light. There were other illuminations, shed by men who had no particular reason to feel any sympathy for him. I heard of two occasions when, approached with customary gifts by men who wanted him to ensorcell their enemies, Tobowa bluntly refused to act as their assassin. Nor was he insensitive to the traditional sanction of shaming by *ketowai* gifts and formal public insult. There is a story that reveals him humbled in this way.

Tobowa happened upon a wounded pig in the bush one day. He killed it just as a group of Eweli hunters appeared and protested that it was their own game. Tobowa stood with his foot on the beast, silently claiming possession. Afraid of him, the Eweli men backed away and went home. Tobowa called some Lulauvile men to carry the pig to Kalauna, where he boasted that he had tracked and killed it himself. At the climax of an Eweli festival a few months later, the sponsors called Tobowa to receive a *ketowai* pig — a punitive, shaming gift. Taking full advantage of the customary license to insult recipients on such occasions, the Eweli orator publicly embarrassed Tobowa by explaining in detail what the gift was for. "You stole our game and told your people you had caught it yourself." "People were too afraid to laugh loudly," commented my informant, "but he was very ashamed!"

Surprisingly, perhaps, for one who sought and achieved local fame, Tobowa never sponsored a festival of his own, nor even initiated an *abutu* contest. These are the two orthodox ways of inviting recognition as a big-man. *Abutu* is an appropriate means to launch a career of leadership, while festival sponsorship is an appropriate means to cap or consolidate it. Tobowa was not a gardener of the first rank (a *tofaha*) and his support system of agnates was neither extensive nor strong. His *fofofo* partner (Awakili of Kwakwaiboka) was a rather weak man, and only seems to have been recruited because Tobowa had married his sister. (Tobowa's group's traditional *fofofo* was a Heloava II subclan, but this had died out and it was in casting around for a substitute that Tobowa paired with his brother-in-law, a solution not unprecedented in Kalauna.) Still, had he wished to make *abutu* or hold a Fakili festival, Tobowa could undoubtedly have found willing support elsewhere in Lulauvile, or even from his mother's clan, Mulina, itself a numerically powerful group in the fifties.

A number of villagers nonetheless saw in Tobowa a paragon of the traditional leader, one who could intimidate by the fierceness of his demeanor and compel by the force of his rhetoric. Some recalled his spontaneous *manuamadumadu* expedition to Mataita in 1957 when he had climbed a forbidden *atuaha,* and, with the ferocious visage of Honoyeta, had taunted the startled Mataita men into giving him six pigs. To have extracted two pigs from reluctant hosts would have been regarded a success; to have won four would have been a distinctive achievement; but to have extorted six against an empty promise of their immediate return seemed the act of a mythical hero. Impressionably youthful at the time, my informants still murmured with admiration at the manner in which Tobowa conducted this adventure. So terrifying was his presence that the hosts were beyond provocation and gave up their pigs, not shamingly in a spirit of *veumaiyiyi,* but fearfully in a placatory gesture of submission. Unlike the inconsolable Honoyeta, however, Tobowa did not spurn their prestations but had them carried back triumphantly to Kalauna. It was a year later before Mataita men reciprocated the visit (no less unexpected than Tobowa's had been), and he contrived to meet his debt by somehow persuading the visitors to accept only two pigs plus a measured equivalence of yams for the remaining four.

〰〰〰

Tobowa's painful decline must have commenced about this time. It is difficult to say how long he had suffered from tuberculosis, but by late 1959 the disease was sufficiently advanced for him to decide, quite voluntarily, to resign his position as village constable. Everyone I asked knew the source of Tobowa's sickness, for tuberculosis is held to be the result of sorcery called *yobiyobi,* which was known only to certain men of Nouneya clan. Assuming the source to be Nouneya, people were prepared to assert the cause. This was an incident in which Tobowa quarreled with (and struck) Nouneya's leader, Towakaita. A sorcerer of no mean repute himself, Towakaita exacted revenge by afflicting Tobowa with tuberculosis. In turn, Tobowa resorted to vengeance sorcery and although he failed to kill Towakaita, he eliminated some of the treacherous Lulauvile conspirators who had assisted him.[4]

During the last few years of his life Tobowa's irascibility increased. As he grew weaker people's fear of his physical violence waned, but as if to compensate for this, their fear of his rampant and random sorcery mounted. For those who suffered misfortune it was easy to surmise that the sick Tobowa was venting his pain, vindictiveness, and *unuwewe.* No further provocation seemed necessary: "We do not know why else he might have killed those children," people said. It was also the time when those who wished to gain from his inheritance gave him succor, bringing green coconuts, fresh fish, and betel nut, and sitting with him through the feverish heat of the day.

It remains to tell of his death. According to most versions it all began with a preemptive strike Tobowa made against Kimaola, whom he had begun to fear (some say Tobowa suspected him of complicity in Towakaita's plot). Kimaola was stricken with a sickness that lasted for months, but he recovered and planned his own revenge. First he lamed Tobowa with *kasiwala* (cassowary), a sorcery technique designed to induce paralysis of the legs, so that he became housebound. In his own good time Kimaola persecuted him next with a brace of *kwahala.* They perched menacingly outside Tobowa's house for several nights, until he cried out in terror, "They are going to eat me!" Kimaola then decided to put an end to him. He hid near the house, and when Tobowa yelled again he trapped his voice inside a bespelled tobacco tin. Tobowa died that night, just as Kimaola had warned Lulauvile he would.

Tobowa was buried by his own sons, by two other Lulauvile men, and by the two sons of Enowei, his mother's brother's son. The event was without incident save for the scandalous conduct of Tobowa's

127

widow, a considerably younger woman whom he had enticed away from her first husband. Kalauna's moral sensibilities were more offended by the age discrepancy between them than by the fact that Tobowa had stolen a clansman's wife. The marriage was fertile; the young wife bore Tobowa three children and his occasional blows with equanimity—though she was to declare him a "bad" husband after his death. It was as an extravagant expression of her feelings for him that she defied custom in refusing to lie prostrate at his graveside, and, even more pointedly, walked away from it unaided instead of allowing herself to be carried on the back of a brother. Nor were these mere token gestures of disrespect, for what she did next demonstrated her total repudiation of the role of widow. It was as if she had annulled the marriage at the moment of Tobowa's death.

A widow should be carried to a brother's house, where she is placed inside a fenced enclosure beneath it and made to sleep on the ground, covered at night by thin mats of coconut leaves. Tobowa's widow walked to the house of her "brother" Towakaita, where she slept within on a comfortable pandanus mat, covered at night by a blanket. A widow should eat only the coarsest and most despised foods to signalize her poverty and remind her of her loss. Tobowa's widow denied herself nothing, not even the richest of dishes creamed with coconut oil. A widow should dress only in the tattered remains of a leaf underskirt, and her unwashed body should bear no decoration or any other sign of self-regard. On the day following his burial, Tobowa's widow bathed, teased her hair and dressed it with hibiscus flowers, donned a fine colored skirt, smoothed her skin with coconut oil, and reddened her mouth with betel juice.

In this brave woman's gestures of defiance the community must have seen some reflection of its own sentiments, for expressions of relief at Tobowa's death were scarcely disguised. But there were to be consequences, for Tobowa's son Siusiu was deeply chagrined. Virtually despised by his father, this albino son proved to be his most fiercely loyal heir. The insult to his father's memory provoked him to make *bolimana* magic "to punish the people for their disrespect." A tearing wind toppled trees, lifted roofs, and stirred fears of worse to come. But after three days Siusiu calmed it, apparently mollified. The matter of avenging his stepmother's contempt demanded a less gross solution, but it is said that Siusiu fixed the blame for her behavior on her protector Towakaita, the man who had also (as everyone knew) inflicted the consumptive disease on his father. Within the year Towakaita was dead, his insides consumed by a *yafuna* spirit sent by Siusiu.[5] Thus ended a prolonged sorcery feud which is believed to have cost the lives of at least five men. Centered around Tobowa, it was finished by his avenging son, the first but not the last to use the inheritance of evil magic Tobowa disseminated so widely.

$$\wedge\wedge\wedge\wedge\wedge\wedge$$

"Tell me," said Iyahalina to Siusiu a few months after Tobowa's death, "did a man from Lalaveya come to listen to stories in your father's house when he could no longer walk about?" "Yes," Siusiu innocently replied, "Tabwaika did."

Thus were Iyahalina's suspicions confirmed that Tobowa had, with willful mischief, taught Tabwaika the *manumanua* magic called Auyoke, which was the prerogative of Lulauvile II. Iyahalina's rage over the alienation of this magic brought him into bitter conflict with Tabwaika during the sixties.[6] In 1977 Tabwaika admitted Tobowa had taught him: "It is true what they say — Auyoke *sisikwana* is inside me." But he protested that he had never used it and would not pass it on to his children. "I only listened to him, and the story will stay in my mind and die with me."[7] Ten years previously, however, Iyahalina was convinced that Tobowa's treachery was a calculated plot to undermine Lulauvile influence by weakening its ritual hegemony in the village. His reasoning went more or less as follows.

Tobowa planned to eliminate Heloava's leadership to enhance the prestige of his own line by ensuring that it held exclusive possession of the Auyoke magic. To this end he killed Kedeya (Heloava's leader in the fifties) and made an attempt on Iyahalina's life. But the plan was a double failure: not only did Iyahalina survive, but Tobowa's direct heirs were a disappointment to him. His eldest son, Nikuya,

129

already in his twenties, had at first refused to learn any of his father's magical arts. He claimed a Christian conscience and a determination to live by it. (When Tobowa begged him to learn from his sickbed Nikuya had even struck him, flushed with the shame of rumors that his father had caused this or that death.) There is still some doubt in Kalauna as to whether Nikuya relented, though he insists that he remains ignorant of any magic. Tobowa's second son, Siusiu, had learned willingly enough, but as an albino he is physically handicapped for leadership and it is doubtful that he will ever marry. Frustrated in this ambition, then, Tobowa took the recourse of *unuwewe*-inspired subversion. He decided to sow havoc by the selective distribution of his magic, both good and bad, knowing that it would be the last political act of his fast-fading life.

In this manner did Iyahalina interpret Tobowa's deployment of his legacy: as a scheme to create political upheaval in the years to come. For not only did Tobowa weaken Lulauvile's hegemony by teaching Auyoke magic to Tabwaika, a known iconoclast, dissenter and outspoken opponent of Lulauvile,[8] but he also furnished Tabwaika's son with lethal sorcery in the expectation that he would inherit the Auyoke secrets from his father. Members of other clans, too, not all of them leaders, were Tobowa's unexpected beneficiaries. Finally, by bestowing some knowledge of sorcery upon an attentive adolescent son of Iyahalina, Tobowa seems to have prepared the ground for future discord within Heloava. Nothing is so divisive in Kalauna hamlets as the rupture of the bonds between full brothers, and few things are more conducive to rupture than rivalry over magic, especially when juniors might be accused of appropriating the authority conventionally accorded to their seniors.

In all of this (and I do not follow the full trajectory of articulated fears) one can discern the outline of an outrageous master plan. Whether or not one agrees with Iyahalina that Tobowa's intention was to destroy Heloava and subvert Lulauvile by the threatening disposition of his magical legacy, there does seem to be a case for suspecting Tobowa of promoting mayhem from his deathbed and willing anarchy to succeed him. It would be too charitable to surmise that this was his means of demolishing the old order to usher in the new—the fickle millenium that had eluded him in his search for better things for Kalauna. More likely, in the mold of other heroes, his *unuwewe* took the guise of a death wish, a barbarous exultation in imagined social destruction as solace for his own suffering. The new era whirled in by Tobowa was little different from the old.

6
The Head of Didiala

> Where are you going?
>> Come & eat some roots & drink some
>> water.
> Thy crown is bald old man;
>> the sun will dry thy brains away.

> —William Blake, *Tiriel*, 7

/\/\/\/\

It must have been a disconcerting experience for the people of Kala-una to have a white anthropologist set up house, with his wife and baby son, in the heart of their secluded community. Why had I come? To learn their language and customs, yes, but why and to what end? An immediate effect of our presence was a stiffening of their self-awareness, a kind of collective preening. (I heard of a clan caucus at which the men resolved never to quarrel in my presence and instructed the women and children to be always on their best behavior.) Feeling our strangers' gaze upon them they began to compose and define themselves by recourse to mythology, stories that purported to explain and legitimate their collective and personal identities. Until the novelty of our presence faded they fed us sweet potatoes and stories, and watched me from the corners of their eyes as if I were a new conscience.

An urgent exercise for them was to explain our racial differences; this was done principally in terms of why Papuans are poor and *dimdim* (whites) are rich. Later they obligingly expounded the differences among themselves not evident to the eye: why Kalauna is superior to other villages, and how its clans, subclans, and moieties are radically distinguished by customs. Their attention to stories was reinforced by my own obvious interest in recording them. In their eagerness to tell me, they sometimes trespassed upon one another's domains of knowledge, causing recriminations and pained attempts to set the record straight. Our presence, then, encouraged them to ponder not only their status in relation to whites but also the grounds of their relationships to one another.

The venerable elder Didiala exemplified the attitudes and responses of many other Kalauna men toward me. At first he avoided me, knowing that his brother-in-law, Iyahalina, had sought me out to present some version of the "facts" about Lulauvile's supremacy. Then one day he came to visit me with a gift of pumpkin, and offered tokens of his identity in the tidbits of stories he told. It later proved that our first encounter was beset by a misunderstanding, which took me months to fathom. I was told that he took me to be a reincarnation of a younger kinsman, a man named Wakiluma who had been savaged by a crocodile and died of gangrene more than ten years before. To say that he "believed" this might be to overstate the case, though it was put to me in this form when I investigated a faint cargo rumor a few months after my arrival.

Among others in the village, Didiala entertained (shall we say) the possibility that I was not a *dimdim* but a returned ancestor, sent to check upon the fortunes of Kalauna. I wore a European's skin but that was simply my disguise; and (like Honoyeta, too) I affected a different dialect. There was evidential support for this conspiracy theory of my role in many aspects of my behavior: my insatiable curiosity about village affairs, my absorption with genealogies and attention to the minutest census, my proposal to measure gardens, count pigs, and assess the contents of houses. Then there was my generosity with tobacco, my solicitous engagements, man to man, with people whose usual experience of Europeans defined them as disdainful, aloof, and ungiving. All these things pointed to a nefarious purpose behind my visit. For those persuaded that I was a "spy" for the ancestors, a counterdeception had to be played with me in order to avoid some millenarian disadvantage.

I do not think Didiala ever went this far; perhaps he was too old or had been too successful to care deeply about the kind of "luck" that a few others sought in disguising themselves from me. I learned to value him as a trustworthy informant, discomforted by direct questions but marvelously enlightening in his rambling discourses on traditional life. He became a familiar figure on the large boulder that served as an *atuaha* in front of my house, his thin legs crossed, his spine straight as a palm, and on his round head an old straw boater to protect his bald pate from the elements. I spent many hours in his house, too, a mere booth on stilts with scarcely room to stretch my legs, listening to any only half-understanding his voice, gravelly and indistinct as it was from a lifetime's mastication of betel nut. I doubt if he ever saw me clearly; his red-rimmed eyes were almost opaque with the cataracts that were blinding him. When I judged I knew him well enough I thought to ask him one day, with trepidation for my alienated identity, why he had thought I was his kinsman Wakiluma. My courage failed, and I said instead that I had heard some people believed I was an "ancestor." He laughed, and told me to ask his brother-in-law Iyahalina. I did so, and Iyahalina piously mimed a parable by covering his eyes, ears, and mouth. Then he grinned and the matter was left at that.

∧∧∧∧

Didiala was born in Kalauna in the early years of the century and died, within a few yards of his birthplace, in January, 1970. His life spanned the three generations of white colonial rule on Goodenough. No more than two or three Europeans had visited his village by the time of his birth, and within a few years of his death Europeans had ceased to hold positions of authority in the local administration. An event of some historical moment for Kalauna occurred in 1921, when the first tax and census patrol visited the village and counted 392 souls. The patrol was conducted by a Mr. Vivian, who has entered local legend as Misibibi, the perpetrator of a number of astonishing feats. In his autobiographical reminiscences, Didiala tells how he was making his first trip to Misima to work in the gold mines at the time of Misibibi's visit, so he would have been in his late teens in 1921. A few years later he married a woman of Heloava, his *fofofo*'s hamlet, and soon afterwards took up residence in Anuana I, his natal hamlet. Since early childhood he had dwelt in Anuana II, whence he had accompanied his mother when she returned to her brothers after the death of her husband. Didiala's first wife bore him four children, two of whom died quite young.

While he was working in Misima for the third and last time in 1942, the Japanese invasion of New Guinea began, and most Australians fled the region, including Didiala's employers. Abandoned in Samarai, Didiala found his way back to Goodenough. Shortly afterwards Kalauna people and neighboring communities on eastern Goodenough were evacuated to Fergusson Island, and during this year of exile Didiala married a second wife, Kwahihi, also of Heloava and a "sister" (father's brother's daughter) of Iyahalina.[1] Kwahihi bore him three children, all of whom survived. With the deaths of several older men in Lulauvile, Didiala gradually came into prominence as the inheritor of some of the most important crop and weather magic. By the late fifties he had apparently acquired, by legitimate or devious means, all the principal Lulauvile magical systems, and much other magic besides, though he never sought the kind of infamy as a sorcerer that Tobowa relished. He built instead a solid reputation as a wise and responsible leader through his conduct and supervision of food exchanges, festivals, and the prosperity rituals of *manumanua*.

It was as a veritable pillar of the community—center post (*owola*) in local idiom—that I came to know him in 1966. His first wife had died and he was living alone with Kwahihi and a couple of grandchildren, his tiny house flanked by those of his sons and their growing families. He became increasingly blind and immobilized during these last years of his life; but such was his mental vigor and personal vitality that people presumed him to have been killed by sorcery rather than to have died from anything so banal as old age. Sixteen of his young kinsfolk dug his grave, the largest group of buriers I ever heard of in Kalauna. And unlike the forgotten graves of most men, Didiala's is still conspicuous with its red stones and colorful crotons.

135

THE HEAD OF DIDIALA

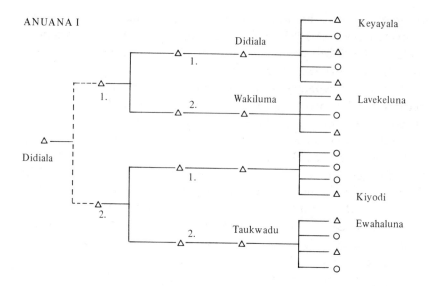

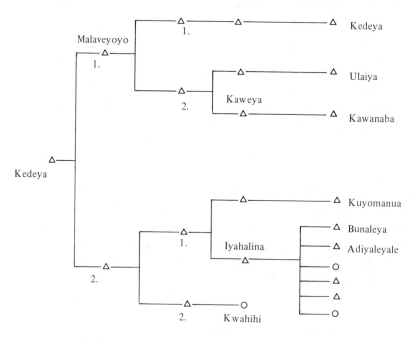

Skeleton Genealogies of Two Lulauvile *Unuma*

Seven years after his death I recorded a number of testimonials and reminiscences by his wife Kwahihi, his eldest son Keyayala, and several other kinsmen and peers. They were unanimous in recalling Didiala's ritual importance as a *toitavealata,* a performer of the *manumanua* ceremony for banishing hunger and ensuring prosperity, and they eulogized his guardianship of the various crops. Keyayala, for example, said:

> During his life there were good and bad times, but all lived well because he ensured there was enough of everything—food, meat, fish. If famine threatened he went with his brother-in-law [Iyahalina] to inspect the gardens. If they saw people going to the bush in search of edible roots and vines, if they saw them destitute, hunting for wild yams, then they would plan to make things better. They would increase the food and increase the pigs. They would pull back the orphans, the widows, and the destitute who scoured the bush; they would pull them back to the village where they could live well again. If it was the time of the flowering *hiyu* [the period of scarcity between December and March] they made sure we still lived well. They inspected the gardens carefully and sometimes they decided to make *manumanua* so that everyone could eat and be happy.

Tabwaika, who had frequently quarreled with Didiala and Iyahalina in previous years, also praised their providential partnership.

> They were good men, with gentle ways. When times were bad they investigated. If famine loomed they discussed it. If they saw people going to the bush and noticed their poverty, they discussed it and laid down rules. Iyahalina would stand up and say, "Today you must prepare. Collect your food, coconuts, and firewood, and be ready for tomorrow. For we must stay in the village and make this thing good." We would prepare everything and stay at home. They made a small pot of food and sang their spells over it. All day long we stayed in the village, and they turned the famine away. Then we had food in abundance. Our taro increased, our coconuts multiplied. People were happy and thanked them. "*Siule* Didiala! *Siule* Iyahalina!"

∿∿∿∿

To the descriptive outline of *manumanua* which I gave in chapter 2 I must now add two of the four myths that validate the ceremony.

137

These are Didiala's myths; Iyahalina's will be given in the next chapter. It will be recalled that Malaveyoyo performed *manumanua* to restore Kalauna's prosperity following his catastrophic attempt to banish it. I suggested that his legend, itself a motivated transformation of the Honoyeta myth, constituted a paradigm of magical vengeance and retribution. We glimpsed an outline of this pattern of social action in Tobowa's life, but we shall see it emerge in bolder relief in Didiala's biography. The coils of resentment, of *unuwewe*, which entangled Didiala at various times will be unraveled below. Here it is enough to note that he was believed to have caused, on a number of occasions, the famines that he later helped to "set right" by *manumanua*.

During the long day of the ceremony the two magicians sit motionless on a coconut leaf mat in Anuana. They recite their myths to one another and sing the spells that punctuate events in the stories. Didiala tells the myths of Manukubuku (or Kuyakwokula) and Tomoudi. Iyahalina tells the myths of Hudiboyaboyaleta and Kiwiwiole. They chew betel nut and smoke tobacco but they cannot eat nor leave the mat until darkness has fallen.

Manukubuku had three grandsons: the firstborn was Kulefifiku, the secondborn was Makiolelena, and the lastborn was his namesake Manukubuku. They prepared a canoe to sail to the Amphlett Islands and loaded it with taro, sugarcane, betel nut, green coconuts and pork. They set off and arrived at Maliawa'awana. "Ah, Grandfather, let us eat now," the young men said. "Wait," he replied, "when we reach Maliuna you can eat and drink." They paddled on until they reached Maliuna. "Ah, Grandfather, let us chew some sugarcane now and drink green coconuts." "Wait," he replied, "when we reach Kwatauta you can chew sugarcane and drink green coconuts." They paddled on until they reached Kwatauta. "Ah, Grandfather," they said, "we are so tired and hungry we can hardly speak. Give us some food and drink now." "Wait," he replied, "when we reach our own place again you can eat and drink your fill." Exhausted, they paddled homeward.

They beached at Bolubolu, and the youngest spoke to his brothers. "Soon we'll be home and he hasn't given us any food. He brought us all this way and he's worn us to a shadow! Look how thin we are. I'll

kill our grandfather!" His brothers replied, "He's a bad man indeed!"
The youngest retorted: "If you say that, then I'll cut off your heads
too." The others were silent. They were frightened of him because he
was headstrong and violent. They watched as Manukubuku took his
axe, crept up to their grandfather and cut his head off. At once the
weather changed. The three of them stood, unable to move, as it
thundered and lightning flashed. Kulefifiku, the eldest, understood
the portent, and he picked up his grandfather's head and ran to a *laiyava* tree. He climbed it and ran along the branch so that he was over
the sea. Then he sang a spell and three the head into the sea. It sank
and settled on the sand. The weather calmed immediately.

Kulefifiku then spoke to Makiolelena: "Our younger brother is enraged. Perhaps he'll try to kill us too." They were afraid of him. They
all walked on to Bilobiloloya in the hills behind Bolubolu. They
spotted a site for a village and said to Manukubuku, "See that place?
Go and dance in a circle and flatten the grass, then we'll see. Perhaps
we can live there." "Ai! I will howl in triumph and make war cries," he
replied. Meanwhile his brothers fled and hid from him. He returned
and called out: "My brothers! Come and see, I have cleaned our village!" But he called in vain, for they had fled. He called out again:
"Split your arse, break your skull! If you were here I'd kill you like I
killed our grandfather! You are afraid of me!" And Manukubuku went
to Bilobiloloya and lived there by himself.

Manukubuku was the ancestor of Ulodidi and Ulaiya [of modern
Awaiya village], and Hardheaded Manukubuku is their story. The
first- and secondborn settled in Nibita and they are ancestors of [Anu-
ana] Lulauvile men Lavekeluna and Didiala, so it is their story also.
Their grandfather Manukubuku was unkind to them with food.
That's why his name is also Kuyakwokula, because he hoarded his
food as if he were a stone.[2]

In offering an interpretation of this myth, the names of the characters should first be translated. Manukubuku (*manu*, "bird,"
kubuku, "my grandparent/child," in Bwaidoka dialect) is said to be
an "important" bird. Its most notable characteristic is a wide beak
which it clamps shut with a loud clap. It has been appropriated as a
symbol of *lokona*, the practice of food abstention. Moreover, it is
believed that the bird appears as an omen whenever famine is nigh:
"You can hear it shutting its mouth so that no food can enter." It is

139

fitting, therefore, that the *lokona*-obsessed grandfather of the tale is called Manukubuku. His other name is Kuyakwokula, a hard, heavy (probably basaltic) stone of the type used for so many magical purposes, especially those in some way connected with the control of food. As we shall see in the following chapter, stone is also an apt symbol for the principles of retention and containment on the one hand and abstention on the other.

The firstborn brother's name, Kulefifiku (or Ulefifiyo, which is a wagtail), means one whose bottom waggles, and suggests incontinence, the very antithesis of *lokona*. But an alternative name for Didiala's other mythical hero, Tomoudi, is Ulefifiku, for reasons I shall suggest below. I have no folk etymology for Makiolelena, the second brother's name (all I can offer is that *lelena* means "seek it/him"), but it is said to be another secret name for the sun. There are no hints in the story that this hero might provide a charter for Didiala's sun magic, however, and I recorded no other myths featuring a character by this name. In a pedigree of mythical heroes given me by Adiyaleyale of Heloava, Makiolelena is the father of Tomoudi and Adikunuwala.

Let us now consider an interpretation of the Kuyakwokula myth on a level not far removed from the manifest meanings of the symbols it employs.

The voyage the men embark upon is a curious inversion of the inaugural, long-distance trip any new canoe might make. According to this coastal custom the owner of a new canoe takes a crew of young men to visit a number of foreign villages, where they make requests for food, pigs, and shell valuables. Gifts are made to the canoe, which are subsequently repaid when the donors make return visits. This is an almost Massim-wide institution for the solicitation of gifts (cf. *kula, kune, une,* or on Goodenough *niune*). It initiates delayed gift exchange, and thereby extends the network of trade partnerships. On Goodenough, it is a seaborne counterpart of the inland custom of the *manuamadumadu* expedition, such as Honoyeta parodied.

The heroes of the story take their own food with them, and when they visit distant places they neither request nor receive food nor any other form of *niune*. The voyage is a closed circuit, self-contained and seemingly purposeless, for the men initiate no new contacts and engage in no exchanges—a practical negation of the customary institution. But as the voyage comes to an end a purpose does emerge, for it proves to have been a lesson in restraint. In denying his paddling grandsons the food they had so carefully prepared for the trip, the grandfather was teaching them the virtue of *lokona*. Parenthetically, this highlights the authentic institution, for in soliciting food from a strange village one denies oneself the food from one's own; such voyagers should go "hungry" and "empty-handed," it is said, the better to ask for gifts. Moreover, like any other *kaiwabu* (Young 1971:248-253), the canoe owner should not be seen to eat during the voyage; nor can he eat any of the food he receives, but must pass it on to his exchange partner. Such gifts are his *niune* (ibid.:69-70; Young 1982*a*).

The grandsons do not appreciate this exhausting lesson in abstention and they complain bitterly. The youngest (namesake of his hard-hearted, tight-mouthed grandfather), is himself strongheaded (*tayakulo*, literally "ear-deaf") and the complementary opposite to his grandfather in his wild, unrestrained violence. He terrifies his brothers and cuts off his grandfather's head. The portentous signs that follow indicate that this is the moment when cosmic energies are unleashed. There are homologous acts in the other *manumanua* myths—acts of severing or bursting asunder—when the food dammed up in *lokona* is released in abundance. Simultaneously, it is the moment when a successor takes control of these powers. In this instance it is Kulefifiku, who calms the elements by tossing the severed head into the sea. The *laiyava* tree he climbs is a recurrent symbol in local mythology: a tree that takes root precisely at the intersection of land and sea, and hence mediates four domains. From this ritual act Kulefifiku derives a second name, Lavaikeluna ("to balance on the *laiyava* tree"), a name exclusive to Didiala's lineage.

The rest of the story concerns the abandonment of the violent youngest brother by his elders, and the establishment of their respective identities as ancestors of existing subclans of Lulauvile people. But note the plot inversion of the first half of the myth, which is again mediated by trickery. Whereas the grandfather led the brothers on a fruitless sea voyage to teach them restraint, his namesake is led by the two brothers to found a settlement on land to escape his lack of restraint.

Let us now move to another level of abstraction, simplifying the main sequences of the story into allegorical form.

1. On Sea: Restraint/Retention controls Hunger, or: Elder (Manukubuku I) controls Juniors (the brothers).
2. On Beach: Greed/Violence kills Restraint/Retention, or: Junior (Manukubuku II) kills Elder (Manukubuku I).
3. On Beach: Incontinence restrains Elements, or: Elder's heir (Kulefifiku) controls Abundance.
4. On Land: Greed/Violence threatens Restraint, or: Junior (Manukubuku II) threatens Elders (the brothers).
5. On Land: Restraint abandons or exiles Greed/Violence, or: Elders (the brothers) abandon or exile Junior (Manukubuku II).

These values and their negations illuminate the quintessential moral concern o the ceremony of *manumanua*: to banish greed (and hence the threat of violence) by instilling restraint. This allegorical reading of one of the charter myths for *manumanua* also establishes the right of elders (and their legitimate heirs) to prevail over unruly juniors. But the implicit struggle between good and evil (prosperity and famine, restraint and greed, elders and juniors) is not unambiguous in its outcome. Indeed, the myth also illuminates some critical contradictions. These can be seen most clearly if we recombine what the myth separates, and allow that Manukubuku the grandfather and Manukubuku the grandson are Janus-faces of a single identity. The composite figure (Everyman?) then embodies conflicts arising from hoarding versus hunger, restraint versus greed, passivity versus violence, or, at their most inclusive and abstract, retention (or failure to ingest) versus expulsion (or failure to be restrained). The resolution of these conflicting principles, impulses, and values is hardly a happy one, for Manukubuku destroys himself! Like Honoyeta, he is trapped in duplicity; moved by the coiled spring of his *unuwewe,* he seeks release from self-contradiction by "suicide."

142

∧∧∧∧

Didiala's second *manumanua* myth provides a charter for the ritual control of coconuts. I present it in abbreviated form here, for when Didiala narrated it he took over an hour in the telling, embellishing details and making frequent exegetical comments upon its relevance to the planting and prospering of coconut trees.

Tomoudi and his wife Ninialawata had two sons. He kept large gardens of taro and he asked his wife to cook him some so that he could take it to the beach and spend the day fishing. He left his Oyaoya home [in the hills behind Bwaidoka] before dawn next day and walked down to the sea at Wailagi. There he hung his basket of food on a tree and also his square fishing net. Then he waded into the sea and stood on the reef. Singing a spell, he took off his head and placed it beside him. Then he turned himself upside down in the water and waited. Fishes smelled his blood and swam through his neck into his stomach —fishes as large and fat as a man's thigh or a banana trunk. He grew heavy with them, and he said: "I'm already full of fish." So he righted himself, picked up his head and carried it under his arm to the beach. There he emptied himself. The big fish wriggled out and he killed them. He filled his basket with them. Then he hung it on the tree again and took his fishing net down. He scooped it in the water a few times and many small fish swam into it. There were so many that he could scarcely lift the net back onto the beach. He made a leaf basket and emptied the small fish into it. When he had eaten his cold taro he set off for home, carrying the basket of big fish hanging over his chest. The load was so heavy that his buttocks waggled from side to side. When he reached home he gave the large fish to his brothers and sisters and his mothers and fathers. He kept the small fish for himself and his wife roasted some in leaves, boiled others in broth, and left most of them to smoke on a shelf above the fire.

Time passed and all the fish were used up. Tomoudi told his wife, "Fetch taro and cook some for me. The shelf is empty of fish." The next morning he went fishing in the same manner as before. This happened three times until one day his brothers and sisters spoke to Ninialawata. "We were well, but every time we eat Tomoudi's fish we become sick and vomit in the night. And how is it that he always catches so many?" His wife couldn't answer their questions but she said she would find out. Accordingly, when Tomoudi went to Wailagi she remembered that she needed some salt water for cooking, so she took her gourds and secretly followed him. She saw him hang his food and net on the tree. She saw him wade into the water and stand on the reef. She saw him take off his head and turn himself upside down in the water. "So this is how he makes our stomachs ache!" she exclaimed. "We eat the fish that has been inside his stomach." She took off her skirt and swam out to the reef. She found her husband's head lying there and she kicked it off the reef and the waves carried it away. She came back to the beach.

After a while Tomoudi became heavy with fish and righted himself. He searched for his head in vain. "Oh, you have killed me!" he cried to his wife. He turned himself upside down and emptied out the fish; then he tried to find his head, but it had been carried away. "Why do you want to kill me?" he asked. "No," she said, "your brothers wanted to know why they always fall sick after eating your fish. Now I know, because they enter your stomach and you regurgitate them." "O my wife, your thoughts were bad. You spied on me. My name is Tomoudi! Why are you angry and why do you want me to die?" She started to run away. "No, do not flee! My breath is failing so you must listen to what I say." He stumbled up the beach and lay down under an *idaka-fulifuli* tree and a *mimwaitula* tree. "Tell my sons they must not bury me," he said to his wife. "They must simply leave me here and cut branches from these trees and cover me with them. Then they must only visit me again at new moon." Tomoudi died, and his mourning wife went back to the village. She explained to her brothers-in-law: "I killed him myself and his head was carried away."

Tomoudi's sons went down to Wailagi next day and saw his footprints in the sand. They were very sad, but did exactly what he had said. Then they went away until the new moon appeared. Now they found that the leaves they had covered him with had turned red and white. Next moon they saw that they had turned black. Many new moons later they saw that several young coconut trees were sprouting from the body of their father. The younger brother wanted to uproot them to play with, but the elder forbade it. The trees grew fast and in a few months they were very tall. The boys' mother taught them the spells their father had told her. So they went to the trees and tied leaf-taboos around them, and hit the trunks with a special stone and sang the spells. Then they cleared all the leaves away from the base of the trees, all the dead leaves which had covered their father. When they returned the following month they saw that the trees had grown fruit, like undescended testicles in the encasing leaves of the crown. Another month and the nuts ripened. These were the first coconuts. "Mother, some of our trees have red fruit and others have yellow fruit." They returned next month to find that some of the ripe nuts had fallen. They remembered the rule of the magic, that they must not touch them with their hands but roll them with their feet to the base of the trees. They made two mounds, one at Tomoudi's head and one at his feet. Their mother forbade them to eat any. Later the seeds broke through the husks and took root. The boys told their mother and she said, "This is your food, your inheritance, you must look after it."

They waited another month, then they told their kinsmen. "Come and see what grows from our father's chest." They came and saw the young trees. They wanted to taste the fruits, but the mother had said they must use the ripe ones for seeds. "If you taste them they will not grow, they will all run away." So the boys climbed to the top of the trees for the green nuts. The eldest took the husk off one and pierced a hole in it and drank the milk. Then he ate the soft flesh. "Truly, this is our food and it is good."

The news spread and Mibodala people from Fergusson Island came in their canoes and exchanged shell valuables for coconuts. They took them home and planted them. Other people came: from Muyuwa, from Kiriwina, from Amphletts and from the mainland. They came with their goods and valuables to buy them. The boys said to all those who came, "Our mother told us that this is our food. She killed our father, so we had no one to plant for us. We covered his body with leaves and these trees grew from it. We looked after them, and now we can exchange the nuts for your yams and valuables. We open the nuts and our father's urine is inside. We drink it to quench our thirst, and we scrape the flesh and squeeze the oil of the nut to pour over our food."

The level of interpretation in Didiala's exegesis was a purely practical one: he read the myth as a set of coded instructions. With regard to planting coconuts, for example:

First you take the seeds and cover them with leaves and sing a spell. You cut the leaves from those trees the boys used to cover their father's body. You must not uncover the leaves then. Tomoudi will look after the seeds and they will grow up through the leaves. . . .

Didiala also saw the myth as a warrant for his group's possession of the magic. Notwithstanding his home in the hills behind Bwaidoka, Tomoudi is claimed as a Lulauvile ancestor. His severed head floated up the river mouth near Bolubolu, on the coast below Kalauna. Some of the spells used in the magical system suggest a somewhat different interpretation, however, for they give the names of a sequence of places whence the coconuts are "called" to Kalauna. Part of this magic involves bringing winds to drive the coconuts to the river, then calming them once the nuts are there. Iyahalina also has a claim on the coconut magic for the very reason that one of his myths, Kiwiwiole, gives him control of *bolimana,* the southeast wind. One day, it is told, his ancestor Kedeya was bathing in Tuabeda River when Didiala's namesake was invoking winds to bring the coconuts to Kalauna. Kedeya grew annoyed and calmed the wind, so Didiala taught him the coconut magic on the understanding that they would never again work at cross purposes. This tale legitimates the ritual collaboration of the Anuana and Heloava *fofofo* partners whenever coconut magic is performed. As we have seen, there is yet another, perhaps slightly different, magical system called Auyoke, which belonged to Tobowa. In the past all three ritual experts coordinated their powers during the coconut-prospering phase of *manumanua.*

Over and above the spells and ritual acts that the myth encodes and the warrants it provides for the right to use them, there is another level of meaning to which Didiala seemed to respond in his telling. In such phrases as, "You can rub the oil on your body so it shines like the sun," or, "The coconut has a face and the sons thought of their father when they looked at it," Didiala betrayed an emotional involvement with the myth, for in a lifetime's embellishment he had richly personalized it. Having incorporated its messages he participated in Tomoudi's fate as in his own; or, rather, used one to illuminate the other. Didiala seems to have looked beyond the grotesque manner of Tomoudi's provisioning and felt, as in his own experience, some of the awe and envy with which ordinary mortals respond to men of great achievements. This, at any rate, is a dominant theme in his autobiographical narrative. So too is the theme of legitimate succession which pervades the second half of the Tomoudi myth. And finally, when the hero is victimized for his equivocal achievements, *unuwewe* rears its head.

While this last theme is underplayed in the Tomoudi story, there is an almost identical tale concerning a resentful hero called Ulefifiku. Like Tomoudi, he fishes using his body as a net, but instead of removing his head and inverting himself, Ulefifiku removes his buttocks and squats in the water. His family sicken in the same fashion, and his wife (having complained of eating fish, nothing but fish) exposes him in the same way. But at this point the stories diverge. For Tomoudi it is death and transformation into coconuts and an inheritance of "good body contents" for his sons; for Ulefifiku it is *unuwewe* and a resentful declaration that he will never fish again, though before long his wife and family are complaining of a fishless diet of vegetable staples.[3]

This story also belonged to Didiala. Indeed, he frequently referred to Tomoudi as Ulefifiku, as if he sought deprecatingly to disguise the noble hero behind a more profane persona. But the tale of the buttocks-removing hero provides no magical charter. I suspect that Didiala valued it for the way it isolates and focuses upon the *unuwewe* predicament of the hero, inconsequential though the myth may be for the magical systems that anchor Lulauvile's power.

How did Didiala view his own achievements? He spoke of them in a general way, unstinting of self-praise, in an autobiographical narrative I recorded in 1967. A notable feature of his narrative is the way he counterpoints his wealth, industry, and renown in the past with what he asserts to be his present circumstances of poverty, inactivity, and obscurity. He has retired and his sons have taken over from him, or so he claims. As we shall see, this was far from being the truth.

147

When I was young I stood up and made *abutu*. I orated powerfully and my *abutu* were amazing. People made huge prestations to me. I went down and killed pigs and repaid them and people were happy. I would call out to inspire them and we would go to other villages to demand food. I, Didiala, was like that. But today I am old as you see, and I have passed these ways to my children. They have taken my place and rule the hamlet, for now I am quiet and stay still. I withdraw and stay around, useless. My house is small like a child's. I have no valuables. I feed no pigs. I plant no yams. You cannot see any good things in my house for I have already given them all to my children. I live only to tell stories. Yes, that is the truth. Only the stories remain with me; all else I have given away.

My gardens were amazing. Men tapped the comb and gourd to make a festival and they needed big gardens. I told them: "We shall clear a big yam garden." And men dug until dusk and planted until dusk. I, Didiala, worked thus. I completed everything. Now my children have replaced me. I gave them seeds and knowledge. They work as I used to. They dig large yams as I did. They plant bananas to rot in abundance. They feed their pigs well as I did. Their coconuts, betel, and sugarcane flourish as mine did. Their taro grows huge in the streams and I see them and say, "Yes, I planted like this myself."

I used to wear croton leaves and hornbill feathers for *abutu* challenges. I filled my big wooden dish with food so heavy that women tried to lift it in vain. They fingered the big yam which rested inside and said, "Oh, feel the size of this!" There was nothing I did not do. I tried and accomplished everything. Tongues wagged about me. People saw my hands, my gardener's hands, and the many gardens they made. All the big-men knew of me and my capability and they said, "Each man is different, but you have excelled." They swore at me because of my gardens and my wicked strength; they cursed my *lokona*. But now I am old and have put aside many things. Some of them my children have taken up, others they have neglected.

Some of my children are weak, their work incomplete, their authority feeble. No matter; they can try. But now I am retired. I am short of energy and empty-handed. My face is the face of no-one-in-particular. Only my mouth is important, for it was born to live forever [a reference to his magic]. For a long time I fed pigs with curling tusks which people feared. I hunted in the bush, and despite the size of the pig or wallaby I would kill it. No matter the size of the banana garden, I would tend all the plants and cover their fruits. No matter the size of

148

the forest tree, I would chop it down. And of my gardens they would say: "Whose big plot is that?" "That is Didiala's." "Ah!"

All these were my accomplishments, my secrets. Now I am a bald man. I am retired and my skills remain unused. I say now, "If you children are strong you will compete with one another." They may yet grow strong, but not as strong as I was. I was just one man, but my hands were too much for the others. . . .

Didiala had no doubts about his own importance during his virile years. He spoke for much longer about the industry he had applied to his gardens and the reputation it had earned him. Such boastful pride is uncommon in Kalauna and would be viewed as unseemly, as well as dangerous, in anyone younger than he. But his boasts were not the empty ravings of an old man, for many of his juniors testified to his extraordinary capacities and organizational skills. Two of his enterprises are particularly well remembered.

The first of these occurred during a time of acute scarcity in 1958. Didiala was visiting Wailagi in Bwaidoka to place a special taboo on the coconuts at the site where Tomoudi died and his magic originated. A Bwaidoka leader, Lauwafa, approached Didiala and offered him a public compliment. "Your bald head is like a *kwavi-kwavi* yam," he said, "and we are tired of eating tapioca." This was tantamount to a request for a massive prestation of food, since it was cast in the formula of requests made for *abutu* or *manuamadu-madu*. Didiala returned to Kalauna and consulted his *fofofo* partner Kedeya and other Lulauvile leaders. A few weeks later they sent an invitation to the Bwaidokans to fish for them and they would be given the yams they desired. They built several temporary houses on the beach at Bolubolu, and a large group of Bwaidoka men and their families came to live there for several weeks. They fished daily in their canoes off the rich reefs of the Barrier Islands in Moresby Strait, and they smoked the fish each night to preserve them. Kalauna people kept them in vegetable staples for the season, receiving fish in exchange. This practical partnership culminated in a massive exchange in Kalauna when the visitors made a final effort and brought dozens of baskets of fish for their hosts. They were greeted with huge platforms of yams, bananas, and taro. "There was so much they could not carry it all away," members of Didiala's group proudly recall. There was some attempt to organize a similar exchange in 1967 (while I was living in Bwaidoka) but it failed through lack of interest on Didiala's part. Also (and perhaps more pertinent), a festival was under way in Kalauna at the time and, for the foreseeable future, the community's surplus resources were already earmarked.

Even better remembered, though apparently less successful, was Didiala's *manuamadumadu* of 1959. Such enterprises are usually rationalized in terms of the inauguration of a new object, custom, or gimmick, which is said to "ask for food" (Young 1982a). In Didiala's case it was new drums and several dances. Some Lulauvile men had purchased a drum called Kitolo, which they had admired while working in Port Moresby. It was a drum "with a new sound" and had many songs to accompany it. They had also bought another drum, which originated in Mekeo, and a new headdress of many unfamiliar feathers. With these prizes Didiala proposed to "dance round the island," as he put it, and solicit prestations for them. The journey lasted several weeks and was undertaken by a few dozen men, many with their families. It was vividly remembered by those of my informants who were youngsters, for it was their first trip to such distant villages as Utalo on the west coast, from where the mainland and the setting sun can be seen. Few villages were as generous as Didiala had hoped, and the party was given only a few pigs, pots, mats and enough food to keep it on the move. They visited affines and distant kinsfolk and, of course, *solama,* traditional trade partners who are obliged to offer shelter and hospitality. Didiala's celebratory jaunt was also vitiated by the sickness of many members of the party. Several returned before it was over, and Didiala himself fainted at Utalo. Most suspected Kimaola of sabotaging the enterprise with sorcery, which emanated from the hornbill feather bobbing on his head. Didiala confronted him at last. "Wash your hands!" he demanded. Kimaola protested his innocence, but they returned to Kalauna with rancor between them.

One aspect of Didiala's achievement, which others do not mention but which had immense personal significance for him, was his repayment of obligations. In his narrative he dwells obsessively upon

150

the means he took to establish his legitimate status in society. As so many mythical heroes, he is riven by some early experience of rejection; and it may be that *unuwewe* starts uncoiling here, prompting an impulse to achieve.

> Those big-men of Anuana sent me away unwanted from my own place. They said, "Now you are fatherless, alone, and without brothers." So my mother took me across to her hamlet and there I grew up. They had dismissed me because I was born without support. But I built up my custom, my body, my hands, my yam store, and my garden plot. And I paid back for my mother and for my fostering in her hamlet. I brought down big pigs and wallabies. I went to the sea and pulled in big fish. I paid them all back with ease. They had tested me, insulted me and called me "stranger." They had said I was alone with no one to help. But you see me now, already retired. I step aside and my children come up behind me. I see Keyayala, my firstborn, and I smile at him. And I see Taniyaula, my lastborn, and I smile at him too. But those big-men who chased me away from my own place— they lost, for they did not leave any children!

There is a clear note of vindication in this recital of accomplishments: the sense of unjust opposition roundly defeated, of triumph in the struggle against an early handicap. What pleasure it must have given him to recall his "expulsion" from his natal hamlet, his return to it at maturity and his subsequent assumption of its leadership. For the present he can boast; although retired from the struggle he has left his sons favorably situated to carry on. Indeed, he who was alone and almost a "stranger" in his own place has lived to see his children and their children grow to constitute the largest subgroup in Anuana.[4] We must not underestimate this demographic view of achievement in precariously small populations. To have supported two wives and raised five children to reproduce themselves is indeed a success, and Didiala was fully aware of the consequences for the future of his line. Well might he smile at his sons with self-satisfaction.

He is also at pains to remark the scrupulous attention he paid to meeting the obligations that customary law laid upon him, and with what consummate ease he managed it. He "pushed back the grass" for his mother, he says, referring to a belated bridewealth pig which travels in the opposite direction to the journey a woman makes when she joins her husband, "flattening the grass" as she goes. Few sons, perhaps, would be zealous or conscientious enough to make such a payment on behalf of their dead father and his kin. But Didiala was also fostered by his mother's group, and before he could leave them and take his rightful place among his agnates, he had to repay them for bringing him to maturity.

> I paid back my mother's brothers. I hunted for pig and wallaby and brought them bananas and taro. When they died they had eaten my food. The last of them was Kwalaiwaka, and I buried him because he had looked after me. I had eaten their pork and their yams and grown well, so I paid them back. They who looked after me, I looked after them in turn. I caught game and told them: "Here is your meat. Before you planted food for me to eat. You fed me when my father died, so now I am paying you back for your care."

In an early part of his narrative he recalls his first experience of wage labor, and he characteristically exploits the account to demonstrate his generosity and sense of obligation.

> I was small when I went to Misima for the first time. Kainana [of Mulina clan] and Mwailu [a mother's brother of Anuana II hamlet] took me there. I worked for eighteen months as a cook-boy, boiling water. My father's brothers all died while I was there. The news reached us in Misima and I said: "Oh, sorry! First my own father died, then I came here and my other fathers die." Afterwards we prepared to come home. I went to Bwagoia to get my wages from Mr. Evans. The pay was paper, and there seemed so much of it that Mwailu said, "See, you have dropped some in the grass." Full of pound notes we went to the store and bought many things which we tied up like white man's cargo. But I hid twenty notes in my pocket for I wanted to bring them home.[5] Mwailu said to me, "Let's take our money out and count it. Your father is dead and I'm looking after you." We all counted our money. I had most. They argued about their debts, but I had none, so they said, "Ah, Didiala's money grew bigger than ours." They quarrelled again about their debts. Then they said to me: "Our fathers are

all dead, but yours was born first, so you should share your money. We want five pounds or ten." I bowed my head and listened. Then I said, "All right!" and dealt out my money like playing cards. I gave them ten and brought home only ten for myself.

Here he explains how he allowed his elder "brothers" to persuade him to share his own hard-earned wages with the specious argument that his own father was born "first," so that he too is "senior" and must therefore act with open-handed generosity. He expresses pride and disdain by throwing his money down "like playing cards."

A singular feature of Didiala's autobiographical narrative, then, is its sustained boast. In loose rhetorical style he extolls his own virtues as a master gardener, an incomparable hunter, a feeder of the young, the old, the widowed, the orphaned and the hungry—in brief, as a great provider. This was no vain boast; others testify to his achievements in producing and mobilizing food resources, in magically ensuring prosperity, and in bestowing a benevolent inheritance upon his children. Truly, no one could have been more energetically inspired by his own myth than was Didiala by the miraculous provider, Tomoudi. Didiala reads his life's story as a sequence of successful provisioning exercises: sharing his first wages with his brothers, paying back those who fostered him, providing Kalauna with yams and coconuts by his magic, initiating *abutu* and lavish festivals to the glory of Anuana and Lulauvile. Understanding his tape-recorded narrative to be a bequeathment of his word to posterity, Didiala insists most of all upon his renown as a master gardener. In a long peroration he asks, who is the greatest gardener now active in Kalauna? He nominates Yaneku, his own sister's son; and in a majestic claim he takes full credit for Yaneku's powers of *lokona* and husbandry, and declares that the mantle of the great provider has passed to him, his own protégé.[6]

~~~~~~

It is time to investigate the darker side of Didiala's reputation: his notoriety as a sorcerer of the sun and the rain. The full secret of Didiala's sun magic (Matakunuwa, another secret name for the sun) died with him, or so his sons claim. All I was able to glean was a general description of the rites and a few fragments of spells which, nonetheless, convey some idea of the symbolism of the magic.

The sorcerer rises before dawn and walks to Kabunene, a ridge behind Kalauna which commands an extensive view of the plain of northeastern Goodenough, the sea, and the massive bulk of northern Fergusson Island above which the sun will rise. He carries with him a large round stone: Matakunuwa's stone. On the way he plucks the roots of a small plant called *matadiudiu* which he chews while awaiting the first rays of the sun. As they appear he shows the stone to the sun and spits the juice of the root toward it. Then he begins his slow incantation:

> Firestones
> Everywhere
> In the bush and in the house
> You gaze upon everything
> You gaze hotly
> You look redly like hibiscus
> You look redly like croton
> You climb up
> You come.

When the sun is fully risen and the stone has absorbed its rays, the sorcerer returns to his house. He places the charmed stone in the rafters, where the sun can warm it through a hole in the roof; he places the chewed *matadiudiu* root above the fireplace. (*Matadiudiu,* it might be noted, is also chewed as a contraceptive; it is believed to have properties that inhibit fertility.)

This, in brief, is the rite that "clears" the sun and induces it to shine hotly, scorching the earth for as long as the sorcerer remains unmoved in his determination to make mankind suffer. When he is prevailed upon to relent, the spell is removed in the following way. He throws the piece of root into a river or submerges it in a coconut shell of water, and he takes the sun stone from his roof and washes it carefully—"like a baby"—before hiding it in the dark inner recess of his house. As he performs these acts he chants:

Firestones
Everywhere
In the bush and in the house
You gaze upon everything
You gaze coolly
You look greenly fresh
You look making-bitter
You look making-unpalatable.

The magic calls upon the sun to assist in making food less appealing to the human appetite as well as bidding it to "gaze coolly" instead of "hotly" upon the crops. This antidote "closes" the sun by dimming its power with mist and cloud. It is not thought to bring rain by itself. For that another magical system has to be used, one that involves bathing in a pool and dousing quite different stones.

By such means, it was believed, Didiala controlled the sun for malign ends. People spoke of this magic as "making the sun hot," but it should be noted that it was complementary to his yam magic, which also invoked the sun. In this ritual the sun has to be "made right." It must be "slowed" or "hurried" to the point where there is an auspicious concordance between the planting of the first yams, their harvesting some eight months later, and the respective places where the sun rises over Fergusson Island. Didiala (and other Lulauvile leaders with yam magic) are said to "talk to the sun"; though here their intention is to keep it benign.

Several times during Didiala's life the community held him responsible for the suffering caused by drought. On at least three occasions he appears to have accepted responsibility, but clearly felt himself justified in his actions. We can only assume that he performed his sun magic (or pretended that he had) with the intention of causing the community to suffer; or, as a somewhat more charitable Kalauna view would have it, with the intention of "teaching people a lesson." This formulation suggests some sympathetic accord with his motives, and hence with the grounds of vengeance for his actions. While deploring the vengeful sorcery which makes them suffer, Kalauna people understand its motivation and they deflect ultimate blame onto the one who provoked the sorcerer.

155

This, presumably, is one of the sorcerer's principal intentions.

In 1942 Didiala was stricken by the death of Vivita, his firstborn and much-loved daughter. He was reticent about the incident in his autobiographical narrative:

> My first child died and I was very angry. I prepared to leave, and I went back to Misima. While I was there the whites announced there was war. They heard it on the radio and said they must flee. And all the whites and their ladies and the half-castes fled. Only one master remained, and he radioed for a boat from Samarai. I was still angry about my dead child. At Samarai all the whites fled, just one government man remained. The boat brought me to Nuatutu [the largest coconut plantation on Goodenough]. I disembarked and looked around. The Europeans had fled, but a few coconuts remained. I looked toward Kalauna and Eweli and I could see their plight: their trees were bare.

In her own account of the event, Didiala's second wife Kwahihi explained more fully.

> We were living well. Then Kwaimatu [of Mulina] challenged Tabwaika to make *abutu*. They were harvesting yams at Kuwalafa, and old Nawasekula was carrying them down on her head. And because she was an Anuana woman and Tabwaika's stepmother, Didiala decided to help her and her son. It was one of his immense yams which he gave in the *abutu,* one which Kwaimatu could not repay. Because of that big yam Didiala's daughter died. Kwaimatu spat his sorcery and she died very quickly. Didiala was angry and went to Misima. War came and he returned. But the people had searched for food in vain.

Kwahihi pins the ultimate blame for Didiala's drought on Kwaimatu, the man who had been defeated in *abutu* by Didiala's yams. Iyahalina confirmed this interpretation in an account of the event he gave his son Adiyaleyale:

> Before the war came Kwaimatu made sorcery to Vivita. She met him one day on the path and he gave her a coconut, and that night she

died. "Why did you kill my daughter?" Didiala cried. "If you were jealous of my yams you should have killed me instead." So he made the sun hot, then he went away to Misima. There was a sun which burned the land, not only Goodenough but all the islands.

"People cursed my *lokona,*" Didiala had said proudly. Perhaps it amused him to think how his hero Tomoudi had similarly "poisoned" others with his gifts; and perhaps it did not surprise him that his *lokona* yams provoked envy and spite, as did those huge fish of Tomoudi. But his myth had not prepared Didiala for the tragedy of surrogate victimage. "Why did you kill my daughter?" he lamented. "You should have killed me instead."

Some suspected Didiala of making sun magic in 1958 when a severe drought occurred (Young 1971:171, 174), but he always denied it. In 1960, however, he seems to have acknowledged responsibility for a damaging spell of hot sun. His reason, again, was a death he wished to avenge. This time it concerned the neighboring village of Wailolo. The rain-making clan of Kwabu was one of the Nibita sections, which, instead of cleaving to Kalauna when Nibita people came down from the misty ridges, descended even further to a site that came to be known as Wailolo. Kwabu comprises two subclans, each of which possesses a different rain magic. While still a young man, Didiala cultivated the friendship of Wawaneya of Kwabu, taking him gifts of pork and fish until Wawaneya protested: "I cannot repay all these things. Why are you so good to me? What can I give you?" Didiala asked to be taught the secret of his rain magic. During the drought of 1958, the other Kwabu subclan tried repeatedly to bring rain. For reasons of internal political rivalry they blamed their failure on Wawaneya, Didiala's patron. A year later Wawaneya died, and it was widely supposed that he had been killed by the sorcery of his rivalrous clansmen. Didiala was incensed, and he renewed the drought in 1960 to punish them.

In 1965 a classificatory son of Didiala's died and the old man was believed to have made sun magic yet again. For reasons that are still unclear to me, the ultimate scapegoat was Tabwaika, the disrespectful political rival who had scoffed at the powers of the Lulauvile magicians. I have reported this event in detail elsewhere (1971:82-86).

In late 1966 I observed the gestation of a quarrel which induced fears that Didiala would make sun magic yet again; and I participated in some of the forebodings my friends experienced. Didiala's second son and his youngest daughter were parties to an exchange marriage with another sibling pair of Malabuabua clan. The son's marriage broke up violently, and within days the linked marriage was also in jeopardy. Following his son's divorce, Didiala ordered his daughter to leave her husband. She obeyed, bringing her skirts and dishes to store in Didiala's house, but leaving her baby son in the care of her husband. A few days later, having decided that her brother's divorce need not have such a detrimental effect upon her own marriage, she returned to her husband and baby. (Privately, she derogated her father and his exacting demands for the full brideprice which her husband now owed. As long as both marriages remained harmonious, of course, questions of brideprice had been tacitly ignored by both sides.) Didiala was infuriated by his daughter's blatant disobedience, and a rumor flew around the village that he would make the sun hot to express his displeasure. I suspected a deep disapproval of his son, too, whose own child he now bounced upon his knee, keening a song he had composed to shame its fickle parents.

New as I was to Kalauna, I could read the signs of communal dismay. Early on the morning of November 11, Didiala called at my house. He answered my greeting unsmilingly and sat for a while amid a cluster of grave men. When he asked me for a stick of tobacco he explained carefully that he was going to "walk about," to Belebele, Eweli, or Bwaidoka. This was an ominous indication that he had already performed sun magic. I stuffed some tobacco into his basket and a moment later he got to his feet and left, his straw hat set on his bald head, his stiff spindly legs almost vigorous. His eldest grandson led the way, carrying his basket and a bundle of taro. Adiyaleyale watched him go and turned to me. "We are very frightened," he said.

> Everyone I have talked to takes the threat of Didiala's sun magic very seriously [I wrote in my diary for that day]. At 10:30 am it was 88 degrees [F.] and at 1 pm 90 degrees, the hottest day I can remember. Others remarked on the oppressive heat. "You see . . . ?" said Manawadi.

158

The months between yam-planting (July-August) and November had been dry, and good rains were needed to soak the soils and ensure a reasonable crop. For a week the village sweated. Didiala had returned after four days but no one was willing to surmise his intention or interpret his mood. On the night of 19 November an inch of rain fell, the first for many weeks. The remainder of the month saw more than three inches, so fears of Didiala's sorcery of the sun were dispelled.

∧∧∧∧

Despite his persistent claim to have passed on his inheritance to his sons and to be living only to tell stories, in fact Didiala was far from having made peace with the world. He could not or would not retire gracefully from the arena of village politics. Like his wagtailed bird-hero, Kulefifiku, he could not sit still. At village meetings he was on his feet, arguing longer and louder than anyone else. At food distributions he was among the first to shout advice from the sidelines. He simply could not let go in the way that other men his age had done: Adianamatana, Kumaibuwa, Kivina, Ailofu, Yawaidiya. Admittedly, none of them had been so active in their prime, and none had the reputation for gardening skill that clung to Didiala's name. When Kimaola initiated his Fakili festival in late 1967, Didiala was peeping over his shoulder, plotting, planning, proffering strategies. It was his right to do so, certainly, as a member of the Lulauvile sponsoring group; but his active role was far in excess of that of an old man who was alleged to have retired. Although his gardening efforts were cursory during these final years, he minced no words when exhorting others to greater efforts. Some resented his interminable urging.

Didiala's sons were humbly unassertive men, still in their father's shadow when it came to public demonstrations of leadership. Keyayala, the eldest, seemed unfitted for the task of succeeding Didiala as Anuana's leader, as I intimated earlier (1971:96). A decade later, in 1977, Keyayala was the only man of the lineage to remain in the village; the others had founded a new hamlet on the grassy slopes

159

below Kalauna. In that year Keyayala lacked even a yam garden, for a series of unfortunate harvests had depleted his seed stocks. He was a rather pathetic figure, prematurely stooped and balding, wistful, bitter in the belief that others had shriveled his yams by sorcery; and he continually bemoaned the bad times that had overtaken the village since his father's death. While not alone in this opinion, it was in his case perfectly consistent with the knowledge that he would never match his father's achievements. Consequently he seemed unable to succeed him, as if he could not accept the fact of his death. His reason for staying in the virtually abandoned hamlet of Anuana was pure piety. "My father is buried here," he said, "and here I shall be buried." But this was the carrion comfort of self-pity. Keyayala's inability to succeed his father was symbolized by the attention he gave to the grave at his doorstep, when a more appropriate memorial would have been a lavish festival or an *ebanuadu'u,* a feast of remembrance. Needless to say, he was not up to the task of organizing one.

If Didiala's pretense in stepping aside was as transparent to others as it was to his sons, he must have understood that he would remain a potential scapegoat for any misfortunes that befell the village. He could not claim to have abrogated responsibility for control of the crops and the climate simply by declaring rhetorically that he had taught his sons the magic and was now retired. By continuing to meddle in community affairs, by loudly voicing his opinions on every occasion, by allowing others to feel the weight of his influence, he was manifestly asserting his intention to retain his prestige and his power. In the sorry business of his recalcitrant daughter's wish to remain married, he responded in classic *unuwewe* style. Whether or not he invoked sun magic on that occasion no one now knows, but by behaving the way he did (leaving the village for several days) he clearly intended to convey the message that he had indeed "made the sun hot." The villagers were plunged into anxiety, and this was presumably the effect he wanted to create.

Didiala's dilemma was that he could not deny responsibility except by relinquishing his claim to authority. Yet, like the embattled King Lear, he frequently presented himself as a man unloved, falsely maligned, and sadly misunderstood. As an illustration of his

160

rhetorical use of these attitudes, I shall quote parts of his closing speech to a village gathering (held on 13 February 1968) which had been convened to debate the alarming appearance of new modes of sorcery attack. What had begun as an investigation into the cause of a sickness that had stricken several young men, and developed into a dialogue of recrimination between elders and their juniors, finally became a court of appeal at which Didiala protested his innocence of a malevolent act of rainmaking.

The deluge had occurred in October 1967. Eleven inches of rain falling in three days washed away a number of yam gardens and damaged many others, including Kimaola's. Didiala was immediately rumored to have been responsible, his motive suspected to have been anger at his failure to gain satisfaction in the interminable quarrel over his son's and daughter's brideprice, a quarrel that had meanwhile expanded to include Kimaola and some of his protégés. Yet on the day of the sorcery debate (some four months after the rainstorm), none of these issues were raised, and it was Didiala himself who seized the opportunity to pour out his resentment at being falsely accused. Lasting for almost an hour, it was by far the longest speech of the meeting. It is worth examining for the insights it gives into Didiala's view of his role in the community, and into the force and flavor of his sense of injury. We can also see how, by means of his oratory, he tried to manipulate his audience's understanding of past events, so that they might sympathize with him as a victim of their unjust persecution. My sense of the mood that prevailed at the end of the meeting suggested that he had gone too far. Didiala had protested too much. By revealing himself as one caught in the coils of *unuwewe* he had simply confirmed the general suspicion that he had been responsible for the deluge after all. But that scarcely mattered any more; the dry spell of weather which followed made the rain seem beneficial in retrospect.

DIDIALA: You have argued and finished, and now I would like to explain my thoughts to you, you who call me elder brother. My head is bald because I am old. I have seen many die. Iyahalina is old but he still has hair. Kumaibuwa is old, too, but he never speaks. I'm no longer young, so you can respect me only for what I did in the past.

161

But God knows me. I never performed sorcery. My knowledge consists only of stories [*neineya*]. My fathers prevented me from learning anything else; they taught me only the stories about food. You were all born after me, so I am ashamed when anyone dies. But I expect you to help me when I need it. I have helped you often with my stories. No, I'm not innocent of magic. God knows me, I am not a full Christian, a man of light. But who do you think makes this sun? Iyahalina has already told you: God. And who makes rain? God. And the earth we live upon, who made it? God. In the beginning we came out of Yauyaba mountain. Wailolo people too. And who else besides God knows how to bring rain? Yes, Kwabu [clan] of Wailolo. Now, who are Kwabu's friends in Kalauna?

IYAHALINA: Nouneya.

DIDIALA: Correct. And who are their other friends?

IYAHALINA: Malabuabua.

DIDIALA: There! And their third friends are Anuana II. And what of my side of Anuana? What do we call Kwabu men?

KIMAOLA: Your enemies.

DIDIALA: You see! Kwabu is my real enemy, by the hair of my ears. Who did they give a pig to recently? Keyayala, my son. And who did they give another pig to? Iyahalina, my *fofofo*. Truly, Kwabu are my enemies. Now, Kimaola, you tell us about rain.

KIMAOLA: He was a small weak bird, and his lower beak protruded. But he brought the earth its food to cover the seeds.

Kimaola answered one riddle with another. The solution to it is Kikifolu the bird-hero, who, in the myth of Oyatabu, brought soil to Goodenough Island (see chapter 8). The deluge that followed this heroic task was beneficial, for it washed down the soil from Yauyaba (where Kikifolu had deposited it) to cover the entire island. Didiala is suggesting that if Kwabu leaders know the secret of rainmaking, then their Kalauna friends might be suspected of having persuaded them to perform it; whereas he is their enemy and would never collaborate with them. In what follows Didiala uses heavy irony to discredit the simpleminded view that he might have been responsible for the deluge of October.

DIDIALA: You see, even a child can explain it. [Only fifteen years his junior, Kimaola must have bristled at this!] He said I cover the seeds

162

1. Modimodia hamlet, Malabuabua clan, looking inland to the mountain. These houses form one *unuma;* its sitting circle is far right. The old man is Kumaibuwa.

2. Anuana hamlet, at the center of Kalauna, during a village meeting. Didiala's house is behind the low sitting circle at the right.

3. Men laying out yams for *abutu* in Heloava, October 1966. Adiyaleyale's house is on the right, and behind it Kimaola's. The large tree (center) is the one planted by Malaveyoyo, and behind it to the left can be seen the top of Kalauna rock.

4. Didiala.

5. Didiala (right), Kimaola (center), and Wa'aula (left), Kimaola's wife.

6. Iyahalina orating outside
Didiala's house.

7. Iyahalina mixing a betel chew.

8. Iyahalina presiding over a food distribution in Heloava II during Kimaola's festival in 1968. The bowl in the foreground is stacked with taro.

9. Women carrying yams from *abutu* in Heloava, October 1966. They are crossing a corner of Anuana II. Behind the first line of stones is Aluwaita hamlet, with Wasimala's house (center) and his father Siboboya's house (left). Behind are the houses of Heloava II.

10. Kimaola.

11. Adiyaleyale on his new
   atuaha in Yabiliva.

12. The *etonita* design on a food bowl said to have been carved
by Malaveyoyo.

18. A newly-completed altar painting in the Catholic Church of Ulutuya, eastern Goodenough. The seated figure represents Jesus in the guise of Honoyeta. The panel to the left depicts a baptism. The caption to the right translates, 'Thank you, my Father, you give to me.'

with leaves for our prosperity. Did Kwabu give me this magic? No, my fathers did. [He is referring to the magic of yam planting.] You thought that Kwabu gave me rain secrets because they are my friends? You thought I experimented with their gift, and flattened your yam mounds? Well, I am ashamed if that is what you think. Shame has hit me hard and I have been unable to eat.

Didiala now suggests that far from trying to spoil their gardens with rain, he had been making magic to prosper them.

I wonder if someone saw me doing something that I was not trying to hide? I placed my taboo over there, where my coconuts are. Then my wife told me what people were saying. So I grew ashamed of your talking [i.e., his prospering magic]. I was not angry. But you stopped me and I bowed my head. I expected my group to support me but they turned away. So I thank you [sarcasm for misunderstanding his good intentions]. I brought benefit to Mulina; I aided Iwaoyana. So I thank you all. You should have waited, only waited. Kwavikwavi's mother suckled it in its bed of roots and stones. [In the myth of Oyatabu, Kwavikwavi is a yam, born of a human mother, which thrives on stony soil.] I began to tell this story [with its yam magic], but then I stopped that too. No, you don't know these secrets as I do. I can tell you about Ulefifiku and you would see the result. You would look at the trees and see those ripe clusters. You would see the fruits and say, "Oh, thank you, Didiala." Then I could die and still you would thank me. Or you could begin to thank my sons, for I gave the secrets to them and you could begin to forget about me.

Next Didiala reproaches everyone for taking credit for prosperity themselves, believing it to be the result of their own magic, yet blaming him whenever misfortune occurs.

You say you have secrets of your own. You say you are strong. But you have forgotten how I invoked Oyatabu and Kwavikwavi [the yams in the myth]. You have forgotten how I covered Yauyaba [another reference to the soil brought by Kikifolu]. You say you can turn the soil yourselves, chop down the trees yourselves, dig the yams yourselves. So why not also spoil the mounds with your magic? Yes, yourselves! Your own secrets making the earth turn, tremble, convulse and the rain gush down! I did nothing. I sang nothing. You blame me for nothing and I am ashamed. Yes, your gossip made me ashamed. You saw that I did not go to sing songs [at Kimaola's festival entertainments, which had begun in December]. I stayed in my house because I was ashamed. You know me, what a singer I am, and how well I beat the gourds. I guide everybody because I know the songs so well. But I did not come to lead because I was ashamed.

He then speaks of the song house, a shelter that Kimaola and his men had recently built over Kimaola's stone *atuaha* so that the entertainments could continue during inclement weather. He hints that although he was not consulted he approves of the idea. For his own contribution to the festival, he says, he will make special Oya-tabu magic later in the year ("so perhaps you will want to thank me then"). Everyone will see the abundant yams that will result, and Kimaola's festival will be a resounding success. Didiala tells the meeting that he has already asked Kiyodi (Kimaola's chosen heir, though an Anuana man) to assist him with the rites, which involve tying a pandanus streamer on an Oyatabu yam. Then he begins a complicated recital of the mythical and genealogical legitimations for this magic, concluding that it really belongs to Kiyodi's line, but that only he, Didiala, knows it. This digression appears to have been aimed at Kimaola, to put him firmly in his place as lastborn, *molu-mukumukana* (literally, "sperm-finished"), of the principal Lulau-vile I descent groups. But, Didiala says, he will divest himself of this magic and return it to its rightful line before he dies.

Didiala then elaborates colorfully on the benefits that will ensue, both for the community at large and for the success of Kimaola's festival, if he performs this magic. But, he warns, reverting to his theme of victimage, someone will surely suffer. At this point he makes a remarkable prophecy, intended to be rhetorical perhaps, but no less prescient in fact:

My friends [Kimaola and his group] are presenting their festival for your own good, to make your bones strong and your hearts light. I live, and I will see the party finish. Then I will die. Yes, that will be enough for me.

He continues, warning of the inevitable danger attendant upon an abundance of food.

> No, you cannot escape it. You cannot hide from it. No one can help you. Its rule is thus. It is the destiny of those who cry this magic. Our fathers died for Oyatabu, our mothers too. And your brothers, those born not long ago, they also died for it. The streamer we tie on Oyatabu will flutter, and big-men will sway with it and fall.

Didiala returns once more to his original plaint, to the rumor that he was responsible for the October rains. He weaves a new plan into his denial, evoking the memory of a previous deluge that had drowned a woman of Anuana in a flash flood. He proposes to commemorate her by inaugurating a large taro garden at the place where she died. He reminds his listeners that Kwabu people were believed to have been responsible for that flood, several years before, and he concludes:

> So I will cut the scrub when the feathery *hiyu* grass rises like smoke. And I will sing the magic for Eloelo, her bones smashed by the water. You will plant taro and her spirit will see it and say, "Oh, they are making a garden for the festival where Kwabu's rain carried me away. Thank you, my brother!"

These reflections on the tragic death of a sister lead him to lament anew his own mortality:

> I cannot urge myself to die. Only God can instruct us when to die, and then our breath may cease. My friends, our skin is alike, our food is the same, we chew betel together. Then why do you urge me to die?

He continues for several minutes in this vein, even swearing on the broken skulls of his ancestors that he is "empty-handed and innocent" of baneful magic.

I abbreviate his peroration. By invoking Ulefifiku (Tomoudi), it recalls the hero's anguished reproach to his wife, "Why do you want me to die?"

165

All you whom I have helped in the past, have you forgotten? Why do you urge me to die? You make me cry. You wrong me. Afterwards you will see the other side of the matter and you will say, "Oh, thank you, Didiala!" But when my sons grow up you will make them cry too. Men rot in the ground, become earth and rainwater. I could stop your prosperity then, stop it with my bones [become a maleficent spirit]. Or I could become like Ulefifiku and there would be seasons of plenty. My spirit would be benign and you would say, "Oh, thank you, Didiala!" I will die because of Ulefifiku, but you will still thank me for its benefit [i.e., they would kill him for the very reasons that they value him]. I will die but you will praise me. I will disintegrate and become soil, but you will thank me. So, my friends, you live. But you urge me to die soon and my heart cries.

Here Didiala poignantly reveals his perception of one of the most critical contradictions in Kalauna's scheme of values. As one elevated to the role of a miraculous provider, he feels the full force of an equal and opposite tendency to victimize him, not only when he fails but — more tragically — *especially* when he succeeds. This is the cruel lesson of Oyatabu. Society celebrates the abundance of food and those who would provide it, but it simultaneously derogates them by the devious means of institutionalized envy.

Didiala also pinpoints for us a mainspring of *unuwewe*. His resentment, like that of a long line of heroes, is an almost instinctive protest against the contradictory demands of the value system. Indeed, heroic resentment becomes enshrined as integral to the very achievement. The hero's double bind encompasses his victimage. "I told you so," he will say, and takes the revenge of being injured — even unto death.

∧∧∧∧∧

In the eyes of many Kalauna people Didiala had led a charmed life. They attributed his longevity (as did he) to his scrupulous caution in the casual exchanges of everyday life. *Abubuna* is among the simplest of sorcery techniques and one of the deadliest, if only because it is predicated upon the principle of trust among the unwary. It

166

involves no more than doctoring a piece of tobacco or a betel nut and handing it to the victim. It is a simulacrum of poisoning, though to my knowledge the only poison injected is a string of malevolent utterances. In a society where the give and take of tobacco and betel nut is the small change of all social intercourse, everyone is vulnerable to *abubuna*. But certain conventions have evolved to cope with the threat, or, in the outsider's view, to preserve trust. For example, a man will offer another his basket rather than a single betel nut, so the latter can rummage and select his own. Likewise, a man will pass the cigarette he is smoking himself instead of the one that is unlit. These points of etiquette are covert demonstrations of the absence of ill will. The sorcerer needs to circumvent them by deceptions: only pretending to offer a choice of betel nut, only pretending to smoke the cigarette he has bespelled. If the recipient should be in any doubt about poison in the gift, he makes in turn his own pretense of acceptance, putting the betel or tobacco aside "for later," then throwing it away.

By such artful tactics had Didiala survived the daily risks of greatness. His survival was proof, in the public view, that his defenses were strong and devious. Curiously, though, he had shown a cavalier disregard of other dangers, the widower's taboos which should have restricted his intercourse with Heloava (his dead wife's hamlet) and denied him all its food products. Such taboos, however, would have been particularly onerous for him to observe to the letter. Heloava men were his *fofofo* with whom he exchanged food in political partnership, and his second wife was also from Heloava so they remained perforce his affines. Accordingly, he had decided to take the taboos lightly and risk their sanction. The afflictions of age from which he suffered were attributed to his breaches of these taboos: his blindness, infections of the ear, and chronic stiffness of the legs were textbook demonstrations of the consequences. He accepted them gamely, and did not blame the malice of others.

His vigilance against sorcery was proverbial, and he warned constantly of its dangers, advising young men not to stick their necks out as he had done but to play safe with mediocrity. In the funeral oration of a young leader he declared:

167

If you want to climb a tall coconut [i.e., live to a ripe age] then do not plant too much or your food will kill you. If you plant too many bananas a bunch will kill you; if you dig too many yams then a big yam will kill you; if you rear a large pig then its tusks will pierce you.

It was neither a yam, nor a pig, nor a betel nut that killed Didiala in the end. According to those who said they knew, it was the center post of a food platform. There is an irony here of the kind that promotes the closure of myth and life, for Didiala himself was spoken of as a great *tolama* (support, platform) and *owola* (pillar, center post). According to one of the accounts given to me in 1973, the circumstances of Didiala's death were as follows.

Kimaola decided to end his Fakili festival. The *inuba* [sponsors, led by Kimaola] discussed who should perform the magic on the post of the food platform. [This is believed necessary to prevent it collapsing — not under the weight of pigs or yams, but from the malicious magic of enemies who would like to see the *inuba* lose face.] Kimaola invited Didiala to do it. He did not leave his house much at this time. He was being careful. But he agreed to come and do the magic on the post. First he made the helpers move it a little because he thought it was in the wrong place. This angered some of the men because they had already dug the hole. One man thought to himself, "Why does he tell us what to do? He is not the boss of this Fakili." That night, after the festival had finished and everyone had gone home, the same man walked past Didiala's house on the way to visit his sister in Ukevakeva. He spoke to Didiala as he went by, who answered from inside his house. As he spoke, another man caught his voice in a tin which he quickly snapped shut. Then he went home and heated the tin over a fire. The next day there was a portent: low clouds and a little rain. We thought it might have been for Yawaidiya, who was sick and ready to die. But Kwahihi wailed from her house step: "The big tree has fallen!" And we knew that Didiala had died.

Seven years later I asked Keyayala to tell me how his father had died. Perhaps inspired by the thought that his speech would be preserved on tape, he composed an impromptu elegy, full of simple pathos. It is worth translating here in its entirety, complete with the repetitions which gather the weight of a profound lament.

I will tell you how his breath ceased. We made a party in Kimaola's hamlet, and built a platform to tie the pigs beneath. Kimaola said, "Come and charm the post to secure it." Didiala said, "Good, I'll come and charm the post to secure it." Lavekeluna, his son, climbed up with him as he charmed the post to secure it. They descended and we slept in the evening.

Belebele came, Eweli came, Wailolo came. And we from Kalauna were there. We divided the pigs and they all went home and ate. And we slept in the evening. Didiala said, "Men, break up the platform!" So they broke up the platform. He said, "We won't wait much longer. You will eat your food and we will kill your pigs in the morning. The platform is broken and the party is over." So we slept in the evening. The big pig was for Monaiya, Kuyomanua, Aunamali, the helpers. We slept in the evening.

Two men appeared for evil. Two men went up to his house. They said, "Now the *lalava* tree blossoms, and the helpers chew raw food. We cannot wait." Didiala heard them and wondered and whispered to his wife, "It is them. They said, 'The *lalava* tree blossoms and we chew raw food.' They have come for my death." No one had told him what he knew. We slept in the evening. And he died.

Not years but days passed. I knew my father, a real man. A leader of men. His death happened and now you can see how bad things are. Our times are not good. Enough, for this is what I know, and I tell you it was thus.

The cryptic sentence the sorcerers uttered needs some interpretation. The *lalava* tree bears bright red flowers in the season when the gardens are being prepared for yams, when taro is the main staple, and when cooking fires are often extinguished by the wind. Hence, "people cannot wait to eat," though they may have to chew on half-cooked food. Didiala had asked the *fofofo* helpers to wait for their pigs; though strictly speaking it was not his decision, but Kimaola's, the chief of the festival sponsors. The two men who "came for evil" seem to be telling Didiala that his unwarranted interference has been resented. "It is them," he says, recognizing his executioners.

If I could summarize Didiala's biography with a single image, taking into account what I know of its outward form and his inward apprehension of it, I would choose the coil. The story is told of how the hamlet of Anuana was once called Unuwewe. A young coconut tree was growing there and one day a snake that had stolen a magician's package climbed the tree and hid in its fronds. From that time on the tree grew in a serpentine spiral. It was jestingly called Unuwewe and gave its name to the hamlet. That particular tree has long since gone, but a phenomenon one may see in any large coconut plantation is the occasional tree with a head cavorting on a few elegant twists of its trunk, gay and distinguished amid the marching monotony of the upright majority. The twists of fate in Didiala's life — the early death of his father and his rejection by scornful uncles; the envy of rivals; the deaths of those dear to him; the tragic double bind of his role as a great provider and guardian of the yams and coconuts; the scapegoating he endured in times of collective misfortune — all provoked the *unuwewe* response. Validated by the acts of his heroes, this drove him either to greater achievements or to the resentful writhing by which he sought to punish others by sorcery of sun and rain — even as he punished himself in doing so.

7
The Bones of Iyahalina

Numquam se minus otiosum esse, quam
cum otiosus, nec minus solum, quam
cum solus esset.

Never is he more active than when he is
idle, nor less solitary than when he is
alone.

—Cicero, *De Officiis*

∧∧∧∧

Iyahalina had a full mop of black hair and comported himself with
a lean and straight-backed dignity. He usually wore a red calico
around his waist and a unique black, not khaki, soldier's jacket, but-
toned almost to the neck. Sometimes he stuck a feather in his hair at
a rakish angle (a sign of mock aggressiveness), or a red hibiscus
flower over his ear (a sartorial hint of vanity). When away from his
house he carried an airline shoulder bag containing his comb and
betel-chewing kit. Withal, hardly an impressively dressed man, but
seen through the eyes of his generation (though not through those of
his more dandified juniors), he cut a figure of some elegance. His
face was narrow and pointed, and he had a habit of jutting his chin,
which accentuated an impression of keenness and guile. The most

171

conspicuous thing about his face, however, was his lopsided jaw, caused by the absence of a number of teeth. His smile was more accurately a leer, for the salient anterior teeth that remained hitched his lips sideways. But he smiled more than most men of his age, and this was welcome, though I came to understand that he smiled from wryness rather than mirth and to mock rather than ingratiate.

He smiled at me often in bafflement at my presence in the village, in irritation at my more absurd questions, and in contempt of my European habit of writing everything down. "Why does he write so much?" I once overheard him ask his son. To the reply that it helped me remember he shrugged and said, "All *dimdim* write too much. We remember with our minds, and what we forget is useless." His suspicion of literacy was probably well founded. Many of the elders deplored its effects in subverting their authority over youth, in facilitating adulterous liaisons, and in enabling a generation of young men to record the spells of foreign sorcerers.

It seemed appropriate that Iyahalina's superbly labile mouth should be his most impressive physical characteristic, for if any part of the human anatomy is celebrated in Nidula culture it is the mouth, *awa,* the source of the most exquisite pleasures and disastrous woes. The mouth, from which issues the magic that controls the world and into which goes the food the world is manipulated to produce, is the principal organ of man's social being, the supremely instrumental orifice and channel for the communication codes of language and food.

Iyahalina had a resonant voice to match his distinguished mouth, though even at the peak of my linguistic facility I found him frequently incomprehensible. Not only was his enunciation muffled by sparse teeth, but he was also a pedant in my presence and enjoyed tantalizing me with gnomic pronouncements, playing on my fumbling literal grasp of the tongue and my ignorance of its finer nuances. I was heartened by the fact that many of my contemporaries, including his own sons, did not fully understand him when he orated at meetings or otherwise spoke at length. Like other old men he used phrases and constructions from the old language of Nibita. This was neither an esoteric nor an honorific language, merely a dying dialect; for in the sixty years of missionary influence and forty years of missionary schooling, Nibita has been supplanted by the *lingua franca* of Bwaidoka. Enough of the old language remained to the elders, however, for them to talk over the heads of their juniors if they wished to befuddle or mystify. And it remains, after all, the language of magic.

Despite my difficulty in understanding his speech, Iyahalina was my favorite orator. I watched him perform in the arena of the fortnightly village meeting with keen pleasure. Taking up some contentious issue, he would work through a repertoire of rhetorical tricks, posturings, and histrionic gestures remarkable for one in a culture without theatrical art. In a startling resemblance to British parliamentary manner, he would clutch his lapels or fold his hands across his chest whenever he had something portentous to say. He assumed comic, tragic, and farcical roles with equal ease, taking two or three parts in turn, until one would wonder if this was the consummate actor, then who was the man behind the mask? Then he would reveal himself, a shoulder shrugging off the previous charade, an admonishing finger raised to eye level, and a mock-sour twist to those authoritative lips: here was the real Iyahalina, delivering his final homily before clamping shut his famous jaw and sitting down.

No one else in Kalauna could equal Iyahalina for dramatic skill. The source of this, perhaps, was his sense of irony. He presented himself as the most moral man in Kalauna. He took his duties seriously and was obsessively aware of his responsibility to the awesome tradition he had inherited. He was also one of the most vociferous Christians in the community. Yet in my presence he never made a statement—however grave or portentous—that was not accompanied by the flick of an eyebrow or (more characteristically) the twitch of a lip muscle. I observed this often enough to be fairly certain that it was the beginning, the inhibited birth pang, of his ironical smile. Iyahalina was what in our own civilization we would identify as an intellectual or a scholar. That he was also something of a genius I do not doubt, though comparisons are invidious across such cultural gulfs. He showed little innovative genius in his life's work, leaving the village much as he found it; but it is surely a bias of our own culture to extol innovation as the diacritical activity of genius, and in a society like Kalauna with its fragile back to the wall, we should ask whether genius is not better employed in the service of tradition and conservatism.

As an intellectual in his society (which yet lacked any tradition whereby he might recognize himself as such), he understood his culture as profoundly as anyone could without "anthropological" experience of other modes of existence. I credit his reflective intelligence with the paradox of committed conservatism and a capacity to take a distanced, ironical view of himself as an actor. He was, at least for the last decade of his life, a veritable pillar of his community. Yet he affected to bear this public cross with a knowing sense of the world's mischief. He knew he was playing a part, and that the drama was just a minor charade in a wider theater of relative values. Perhaps he could only come to terms with the colonial presence by demonstrating his sober integrity in the light of traditional values, while at the same time winking at their subversion by missionaries, magistrates, and now anthropologists.

/\/\/\/\/\

Few conventional biographical details are available for Iyahalina. He was born in Kalauna about the year 1910 and he died in Kalauna in May 1971. He claimed to remember Misibibi's visit in 1922, and showed me the place where this legendary Resident Magistrate ordered the first rest house to be built. Iyahalina's parents died when he was in his early twenties. During the Japanese war, when most Kalauna people were evacuated to Fergusson, Iyahalina went to live at Awaiya on the coast near Bolubolu, where his father's mother came from. After the war he spent eighteen months on a copra plantation near Dobu (for which he remembered being paid £9), and subsequently worked for a further eighteen months on Woodlark Island. The furthest journey he ever made from home was to Samarai, the administrative and commercial center of Eastern Division (Milne Bay District after 1950). He never saw Port Moresby, where his four sons were later to spend so many years.

Shortly before the war Iyahalina married a woman of Malabuabua clan. She bore him seven children (four boys and two girls have survived), but she died in 1958 while giving birth to his last daughter, a child whose custody he lost to an Awaiya man. Iyahalina's secondborn son Adiyaleyale was indignant about this, and in the late sixties he made repeated attempts to reclaim his young sister. There are many anecdotes I could relate to support the view that Iyahalina was a less-than-adequate father to his many children, hard pressed as he was to provide for them without the assistance of his subclan brothers. In Adiyaleyale's view he was also an unusually harsh and authoritarian parent.

When I was small he was always beating me and refusing me food. Once when I came home late from school he said: "Why does Bunaleya always arrive first? No food for you tonight!" And he told me to sit on the *atuaha*. I sat there waiting, getting hungry and expecting him to call me inside. But I waited for two hours and he still didn't call me, so I started to cry. I said: "You are treating me like someone else's son, as if I didn't come from my mother's womb." He got very angry and took a rope and tied me under the house. I stayed there until morning just like a dog. He did this many times to me, not just once. Sometimes he tied me upside down, sometimes by the arm, sometimes by the leg. Everyone in Kalauna knew what a cruel father he was. . . .

It went on like this until I was quite big, and I thought: "How can I improve my life and escape my father?" One day we were at Bolubolu at a Methodist Church meeting, and the Catholic missionary was also there with his boat from Wataluma. I got on the boat and asked if they could take me back with them to their school. They said I would have to wait and ask Fr. Abbott. Maika told my father that I'd gone aboard the "Pope's boat" and he came rushing down to take me off. [This was in 1959 when there was much hostility between the missions.] I ran to Fr. Abbott and begged him to take me to Wataluma. He talked with my father, and I joined in and talked angrily about how I was tired of being treated like a slave and not fed properly. . . . My father tried to take me off, but I hid on the boat and it left with me on it to start my new life. . . . My father tried to send Bunaleya to bring me back from Wataluma but my brother supported me. "You didn't treat him properly," he said, "that's why he ran away." I went to that school without food or anything, but at Christmas Fr. Abbott killed four pigs for the children to take home as presents. I brought

175

my piece home and gave it to my father. He was very pleased and said: "Oh, when you go back to that school you can take some food with you."

Adiyaleyale had other bitter memories of his father ("I wanted to pay him back for what he'd done to me, but when my mother died I became sorry for him"), but there was no mistaking the love, respect, and admiration he also felt. He wept and fasted for three days when Iyahalina died, behavior that is by no means required of a bereaved son. In his maturity, at least, Adiyaleyale trusted and confided in his father; he was genuinely proud of his wisdom and integrity, and believed, as I did, that Iyahalina was the most knowledgeable man in the community. On these grounds, he came to regard himself as fortunate to be his son.

Other views of Iyahalina emerged from those who linked his life and work with Didiala's, and I have already quoted Tabwaika's eulogistic account of their joint guardianship, when "the living in Kalauna was good and calm." Didiala's wife, Kwahihi, spoke of Iyahalina's brotherly solicitude for her. "I listened to his advice, and beneath my mind I can still hear his voice."

∧∧∨∧∧

Iyahalina succeeded late to the leadership of Heloava. He was not of the most senior line, and Malaveyoyo's direct descendants held the leadership until 1962. Although a somewhat younger man than Iyahalina, Kedeya (his father's father's brother's son's son's son) died in that year. Iyahalina immediately took over the hamlet's leadership and the quasi-office of *toitavealata* of Lulauvile II. His succession was almost by default, for by this time he was the oldest man in Heloava and the only one to possess its ritual lore. He had apparently been taught (along with Kedeya) by a previous leader, Malaveyoyo's grandson Kaweya, who died about 1950.

Iyahalina was never a gardener of particular merit, and being a widower incapable of feeding even his own offspring it is highly improbable that he would have achieved the hamlet's leadership in

176

competitive circumstances. The opportunity, however, had come late enough for him to have been released of the burden of caring for most of his children, and there were no other mature candidates for the position. The next leaders of Heloava would need to be taught by Iyahalina himself.

By 1966, then, Iyahalina was a man of public stature, though I should stress that this was not due to any conspicuous effort on his own part. Most Kalauna leaders must make considerable exertions to achieve community standing by demonstrable gardening prowess, followed by prominent participation in the organization and execution of food exchanges and festivals. Didiala, as we have seen, was the exemplar in his day of this type of big-man. Iyahalina never sponsored a festival nor prosecuted an *abutu* on his own behalf, though he acted as chief *fofofo* to Kimaola's Fakili festival in 1968. This was as high as he climbed in the glory stakes (and *fofofo,* after all, must be content with reflected glory). In the arena of competitive exchanging and munificent feasting, then, Iyahalina was scarcely a leader in the conventional view. His prominence in village politics after about 1960, and the authority he carried in hamlet, clan, and community affairs, he owed to talents and resources other than those of the super-gardener.

After living in Kalauna for almost a year I asked Iyahalina one day for "the story" of his life. He knew I had already recorded several other men talking about themselves, notably his brother-in-law Didiala, and he readily consented. He sat in front of the tape recorder and spoke without interruption for two hours. I denied him a live audience by keeping visitors away. On playing back his soliloquy a surprising fact emerged: there was scarcely a single autobiographical detail in the whole narrative. At first hearing it seemed to be a sequence of myths, already familiar to me in outline, followed by an impassioned assertion of the nature of his *toitavealata* duties. Being pressed by innumerable other problems at the time, I did not then consider the significance of this. When I needled Iyahalina one day for not having told me anything about his childhood, marriage, or work experience abroad, he gave me his lopsided grin and said *"Ika, anafaiwea,"* "Yes, like that," a conventional phrase of agreement. But if he had meant to say, "Yes, they are the same" (that is, the

177

stories he told and the events of his own life), he could well have uttered the same words. Iyahalina was teasing me again. Yet mature consideration of his text leads me to believe that Iyahalina did offer his myths as a kind of autobiography; at least, in his passion for asserting his own legitimacy, he wanted me to regard them as such.

In what follows I give a much abbreviated version of Iyahalina's narrative. Without preamble or distancing device ("Once upon a time"), he launched into a discursive rendering of his Kiwiwiole myth. This is another of the four myths that validate the ceremony of *manumanua*.

Neyalueya and her sister Kasifwaifwa lived at Awanake. They were planting across the river at Buluwaiya when a flood swept down Afuyana. Kasifwaifwa called to her elder sister: "Quickly, the river is rising!" She crossed safely. But Neyalueya was big with pregnancy and she hesitated and swayed, and hesitated again. The water gushed over her, knocking her down and sweeping her away. It took her away with a child in her belly, away to Muyuwa. She came upon the shore and there she recovered, and then gave birth to her child Kiwiwiole.

Now there was no food in Muyuwa, everyone simply licked stones. This wasn't enough for Neyalueya and she complained: "Oh, my real food! I left my real food behind when I was washed away. Here we eat only stones." Kikifolu, a small bird, heard her and said: "Ah, elder sister, I'm sorry for you. But stones are my real food. I enjoy licking them." "Not I," Neyalueya replied, "but you can help me by flying to my gardens at Awanake and bringing me my real food." Kikifolu agrees to try. "But because you eat only stones," she said, "you will not know how to recognize my food." She tells him to fetch leaves first and instructs him how to recognize the leaves by their size and shape, and where to find them in her gardens at Awanake.

Next day she urges him into the sky: "*Kikifolu-kikifolu-lakalaka-laka,*" and down again: "*Kikifolu-kikifolu-liliwaliliwaliliwa.*" The bird follows her instructions carefully and plucks leaves from all the different kinds of taro, yams, bananas, coconuts, betel nut, sugar cane and pitpit. He carries them back to Neyalueya in Muyuwa and collapses exhausted.

Next she explains to him what each of the leaves are and how to harvest the plants. He flies to her gardens again and digs up yams and taro, plucks coconuts and betel, and gathers all the other foods she mentioned. He puts them in a basket and flies back to Neyalueya. She

178

cooks some of her real food and gives it to Kikifolu. But he cries: "Ouch, sister, my stomach hurts! Those stones I lick are better for me than your food." "Ah, your stomach hurts because it is full; you never had enough to fill it before." Neyalueya then instructs her husband's kinsmen about real food [for she has married in Muyuwa, though Iyahalina neglects to mention it]. She directs them to cut the bush, burn the rubbish, turn the soil, plant the seeds, and lay boundary marks. They plant all of the various crops, which grow to make splendid harvests.

Meanwhile Kiwiwiole is growing up. While playing *o'o* with his young half-brother one day he accidentally spears him in the leg. [The game involves throwing sharpened sticks at a rolling section of banana-plant stem.] The boy runs to his mother [Neyalueya's cowife] and cries. His mother calls out angrily: "Who speared my child's leg? Kiwiwiole! Why did you hurt him? You are like the wafting water weeds. You are just a migratory bird who sits on driftwood. You were carried here by flood."

Kiwiwiole and his mother are sad and angry at these insults. She says to him: "They speak badly of us. You must return to our village, Awanake, where your grandmother lives. But I will stay here." She tells him to fetch sugar cane, coconut, and banana leaves and she fashions a boat from them. Then they gather crops of all the different kinds Kikifolu had brought. They load the boat with this food and Neyalueya teaches her son how to punt with a pole of pitpit. She tells him not to look back once he has begun his journey or the boat will break up and the food will be lost. She helps him launch his craft and sings:

> Heave, I heave
> Push, I push
> Ferment flies of *ulaiya*[1]
> Its aging hardness
> Its crow-blackness
> My pushing . . .

"You must learn this from me," she says, and continues:

> Heave, I heave
> Push, I push
> Taro tubers their mature swelling
> Yams their aging hardness
> Coconuts their sprouting
> Betel nuts their ripeness.

"You see," she explains, "I push cold food and I push bitter food, and

I push aside your appetite." So his mother taught him how to punt with the spell. "You must not turn around to look back," she reminds him. She tells him how to recognize Awanake on the mountain, and how to reach it by finding the river mouth of Afuyana at Yabalaveya, disembarking there and following the course upstream.

Kiwiwiole sets out. He poles across the sea until he reaches Yabala-veya. "This must be the mouth of the river," he thinks. He poles towards the shore, then turns around and cries: "Oh, sorry mother, I have arrived at Yabalaveya." But he has turned too soon. There are portents: thunder rolls, the wind rises, and waves smash his craft apart. All the food he has brought ("wealth like the cargo of white men") sinks into the water where it turns into stone — the large colored stones still to be seen in the narrow estuary of Yabalaveya.

Kiwiwiole wades ashore with his arm basket and fishing net. He begins to climb upstream, fishing as he goes. He moves from rock to rock, tying the fish through the gills as he catches them. Then he notices food peelings in his net and remembers his mother's teaching. He places the peelings to dry on the rocks and sings:

> I fish, I scoop with my net
> *Binamatu* fish I catch with my net[2]
> Ferment flies of *ulaiya*
> Its aging hardness
> Its crow-blackness
> Fishing, scooping making bitter
> Scooping, quelling appetite
> Taro tubers their mature moistness
> Yams their swelling hardness
> Coconuts their sprouting
> Betel nuts their ripeness
> Fishing, scooping making bitter
> Scooping, quelling appetite.

Kiwiwiole climbs up from the river to Awanake. There he sees his grandmother, Vineuma, who sits still like a rock. She has no eyes, no mouth, no anus, no vagina. He stares at her. "Oh, my mother told me she would be like this." Kasifwaifwa, his mother's sister, sees him and asks: "Whose child are you?" He tells her his story, then they cross the river for food from the gardens. While they are eating Kiwiwiole asks about his grandmother. "What about her? We are eating but she doesn't move." Kasifwaifwa answers: "Oh, my child, she has no eyes so how can she see food? She has no mouth so how can she swallow it? She has no anus so how can she excrete it? She is like this, her name is Vineuma. We can eat but she only sleeps."

The following day they go to the gardens again to plant and gather food. In the evening the woman cooks and they eat. Again Kiwiwiole feels sorry for his grandmother and asks about her, and again Kasifwaifwa answers in the same way. Finally Kiwiwiole decides to do something about her. One day, while they are planting taro, he searches for an *aikuya* snake, nicknamed "the lame one" because of its sluggish habit of remaining coiled in one place. He finds one and wraps it carefully in taro leaves. That evening, as Kasifwaifwa is removing the leaf platters after their meal, Kiwiwiole places the bundle of leaves with the snake inside on his grandmother's body. The snake stirs slowly. Vineuma feels it. She tries to see and her eyes pop open in fright; she tries to scream and her mouth bursts apart. All her orifices burst open. Then she swoons. Kasifwaifwa gasps: "What have you done? Perhaps you've killed her!" "No," says Kiwiwiole, "I played a trick on her because I felt sorry that she could not eat with us." They nurse her, and soon she awakens. "Ah, what happened to me? How do I speak and see?" Kiwiwiole tells her: "You stayed all the time without moving, without orifices in your body. So I played a trick to open them. Now you can talk and eat with us." "Ah, my grandchild," she says, "like that."

At this point in his narrative Iyahalina veered away from the conclusion of the myth. I recorded it from his son Adiyaleyale on another occasion. It ends as follows:

Now able to speak, Vineuma teaches Kiwiwiole all her food magic: *sisikwana, manumanua, yaleyale*. Then she goes to Oyaoya [in the south of the island] for baskets of shell valuables—armshells and necklaces—which she gives to Kiwiwiole. She also promises him sago from Waibula [in the north]. They make a feast, for Vineuma is about to leave Awanake forever. "You are going to take my place here," she tells him. "I am going to disappear at Waia'u'u" [literally, "head of the river"]. She teaches him the rest of her magic, good spells and bad, *tufo'a* hunger sorcery and *bolimana* wind magic. Then they travel to the north. She finds the river and tells Kiwiwiole to return to Awanake after she has disappeared. She sinks out of sight in a pool, and as she had warned him, a fierce hurricane ensues [her portent]. The river

181

rises and sweeps driftwood down. The wind rages and the rain batters Kiwiwiole. He is terrified. "How am I to get home? I will die on the way." But he tries the weather-stilling magic Vineuma had taught him and the elements are calmed. Kiwiwiole returns home safely, marries, and has a son called Adiyaleyale . . . [which introduces the next myth in the cycle].

I suspect Iyahalina omitted this ending in his narration to avoid the embarrassing implication that he possessed bad magic as well as good. Adiyaleyale made no bones about his father's knowledge of destructive magic such as *tufo'a* and *bolimana*, but Iyahalina consistently refused to admit to me that he knew any.

∧∧∧∧

A digression is necessary to analyze this myth in order to understand its significance in the *manumanua* rituals, and to give some intimation of its meaning for Iyahalina.[3] First, we should examine the names of the characters. Neyalueya and Kasifwaifwa are both praying mantis insects, the former with thick wings, the latter a more slender variety. Their generic name is *yakaiyaka,* and Iyahalina occasionally employs this in his narrative to refer to Neyalueya. The hesitant, to-and-froing gesture of these insects is described as *yakaiyakana,* and this is precisely what the pregnant Neyalueya does when she tries to cross the torrent. (The semantic field of *yaka* includes *yakayakai,* which means to feint or deceive; *yakai,* to dig up yams secretly; and *yakaikai,* which means pride, or hubris, and can be said of someone who carelessly allows food peelings to drift downstream — a crime in Iyahalina's view.) Kawanaba, whose version of the Kiwiwiole myth I refer to below, stressed the analogy between praying mantis behavior and his own *lokona* practice: "When I want to take food from my gardens, my storeroom or my pot, I pause and draw back my hands like *yakaiyaka.* I hesitate to take that food so that it may remain." Kiwiwiole, the hero, is a small black and white bird of the mangrove swamps, said to "fly around aimlessly, eating nothing but sea foam." Kikifolu, of whom I shall have more to say in another chapter, is a tiny bird that frequents the grasslands, "wanders aimlessly" and does not appear to eat. It has a long beak, however, and can fly very high, chirruping *kiki-kiki-kiki* as it ascends. Among the natural characteristics that fit these birds for the roles they play in the myth are evidently prodigious energy and frantic mobility (in contrast to the hesitant, almost immobile praying mantis insects). Finally, Vineuma appears to mean "silent woman" (*vine*, "female," *huma*, "deaf and dumb"). Her other name is Halihaliwanake, and this is sometimes offered as the title of the myth, stressing the importance of her role at the expense of Kiwiwiole's. *Halihali* is a tree that bears an extremely hard nut. Most unpalatable, it can nevertheless be eaten in times of famine, though it has to be soaked for three days and boiled interminably. *Awanake* means "no mouth."

The covert theme of the myth is the inadvertent loss and resolute regaining of food, counterpointed by the resolute loss and inadvertent regaining of the capacity or desire to *eat* food. Such, after all, are the principal concerns of the ritual of *manumanua*. I read the message of the Kiwiwiole myth as an attempt to resolve the notional contradiction between two fundamental Kalauna values: on the one hand "food is good to eat," but on the other "it is good *not* to eat food." The magic Kiwiwiole's mother teaches him are all *sisikwana* incantations; they invoke the abundance of food only to deny it to natural appetite by making it "bitter." All the characters in the myth exemplify in varying degrees these paradoxical propositions, as they are motivated to get food for themselves and for others, or motivated to enable others to eat or to deny themselves. There are reciprocal gains and losses, complementary movements and counter-movements (by land, water, and air), all of which have to do with the securing and relinquishing of food.

Consider, for instance, how Kiwiwiole deliberately reverses his mother's involuntary journey. With Kiwiwiole *in utero* she is swept downstream (like food peelings) and across the sea to foodless Muyuwa. Having been indirectly fostered by noneating Kikifolu, Kiwiwiole is sent back across the sea by his mother with food from Muyuwa (plus the secret of not eating it). He loses the food, however, and climbs upstream (saving food peelings on the way) to encounter his mother's mother, whom he transforms from an immobile "stone" into an active woman. He then accompanies her to the very source of food and water, where he leaves her to sink into her pool, having learned from her how to quell the waters that have brought him to this destiny.

At this point I must allude to a version of the myth Kawanaba told me, for it transposes Vineuma's portent from the time of her disappearance (as in Iyahalina's and Adiyaleyale's version) to the time of her bursting open. Although both versions have equal claim to "truth," it seems to me that Kawanaba's account of Vineuma's transformation is more apt and more consistent with the role of the myth in *manumanua*. Having tricked grandmother with the snake, Kiwiwiole watches in terror:

> Her eyes broke wide open. She tried to call out "Iyoi!" in fright and her mouth burst open. Her anus thundered. From her mouth and anus a southeast gale blew. Trees bent and broke, the earth shook and land slipped down the mountain sides. There was rain and thunder; floodwaters rose. All the food was released. "Broken-bottom" taro, hard yams, sprouting coconut, hard red betel nut, and all the other foods, all came scattering and spilling out. Kiwiwiole was very frightened and he fled. . . . Later everything calmed and Vineuma slept. A red ant entered her ear and she turned and awoke. "Ah, what happened? Kiwiwiole did this to me. He made me like all the others, and now I will have to come and go, move and eat. . . . He spoiled me and broke my house (*manua*)." Vineuma was *unuwewe*. [She leaves, taking Kiwiwiole with her. They pause and turn around at several places on the journey, but she can still see the distant trees of Awanake so they continue around the island until it is out of sight. Then she finds her pool at Waia'u'u and sinks into it. Kiwiwiole returns to "look after" Awanake.]

Kawanaba commented as follows on the "scattering" of food when Vineuma burst asunder:

> The food is released from her body. It means prosperity, not famine. She was heavy like *manumanua*. She could not walk about or steal, she could not eat or excrete. But she is not happy to be changed. She would rather remain heavy and still.

184

Water has motive power in the myth; it is an agent as well as an element. Stone symbolism is just as prominent. Stone is conceptually opposed to food as well as to water, but it is also a surrogate for food in stone-licking Muyuwa. (Other Kalauna myths that address the problem of food loss and discovery assert that stone-licking was man's natural condition; hence, food cultivation and food eating are preeminently cultural activities.) The relationship between stone and food in this myth undergoes several permutations. Neyalueya enjoys food but rejects stone, Kikifolu enjoys stone but rejects food; Kiwiwiole enjoys food but is taught to reject it, and he loses food when it sinks into the sea and is turned into stone, though (explicitly in Kawanaba's version) he regains food when he turns Vineuma (a stone) into a woman.

These concrete, substantive symbols of stone and food are linked to a more abstract, behavioral opposition that pervades the myth: between restlessness, activity, or movement on the one hand and quiescence, stillness, or stasis on the other. I have alluded to this symbolism elsewhere, for it is fundamental to *manumanua* ideology. While stone is clearly a multivalent symbol its essential properties are stillness, hardness, and durability. It is *bakibaki,* an anchor, and "keeps things in place," which is precisely one of the colloquial meanings of *manumanua.* Food, on the other hand, has a perverse habit of periodically disappearing in times of famine. It is distressingly and sometimes disastrously mobile. Hence, in Kalauna thinking, the supreme objective of *manumanua* ritual is to "bring it back" and anchor it. What *manumanua* is believed to achieve can be expressed in the form of a chiasmus, a complementary inversion of static stone and mobile food:

Thus, in order to be immobilized food must be imparted with the static attribute of stone. It must be petrified. In the process, however, stone becomes mobilized: hence Vineuma's activation by Kiwiwiole, not to mention all the disconcertingly active stones, rocks, and mountains of Kalauna mythology (see for example the myths of Hudiboyaboyaleta and Oyatabu below).

Mediating the opposite states of stillness and movement are acts of turning or revolving (*vilana,* which corresponds to several of the many colloquial meanings of the English "turning"). Kiwiwiole's food turns to stone when his canoe turns over, a result of disobeying his mother's instructions not to turn around. Later he selects a snake (which turns sluggishly upon itself) in order to turn his stone grand-mother into an active woman. Later still, when she has sunk into a pool (where the river turns sluggishly upon itself), the weather turns in fury and Kiwiwiole has to turn it back to stillness. *Manumanua* ritual, I was told, does indeed involve the physical turning of stones; but then, so do yam magic, pregnancy rites, and *bakibaki* sorcery to expel people from the village. "Turning," obviously, is the means of converting stasis into mobility and vice versa. More fancifully, one might observe that the turning point of the story occurs during the game of *o'o* (a splendidly ideographic utterance), when Kiwiwiole's fate is made to turn upon his own (and his mother's) *unuwewe.*

The object of *manumanua,* as we have seen, is not only to "turn" famine into prosperity by anchoring the food, but also to combat greed by persuading the human belly to abstain from food. Thus the stony property of nondesiring stillness must also be magically conferred on the belly. This problem is imaginatively conceived in the character of Vineuma: a cataleptic grandmother (once nurtur-ant and of proven fertility) who with her sealed orifices is stonelike in her self-containment and neither moves nor desires, though she is sentient and knows all the "secrets" of food. The myth makes her "release" her qualities for the general good, opening her orifices and showering the world with abundance. In verbally manipulating this complex symbol during the *manumanua* rites, the myth-teller would bring this state about, reinforcing it with *sisikwana* spells, which encourage the belly's restraint. So in the telling of the story, Kiwiwiole, the restless hero, fructifies and mobilizes his quiescent grandmother, while he learns to emulate her stillness:

These sets of relationships provide essential clues for an understanding of the remainder of Iyahalina's narrative, and especially
the conception he holds of his role as *toitavealata*.

∧∧∧∧

Iyahalina continued his story:

Kiwiwiole went hither and thither, backward and forward, to all the
gardens around Awanake and fetched food. He brought together
yams, taro, bananas, coconuts, pitpit, sugar cane, betel nut, and pigs.
He put them down and he said: "This is our real food." Then he
shared them out, saying, "You, that group, take this, it's your yam,
your taro . . . [etc.]" So in this way each clan got its pig, its yam, and its
other food. We Lulauvile had many things and we distributed them
thus. Then the others stood up and said, "These are our foods, our
pigs . . . [etc.]" But they are wrong, for "food" is Lulauvile's and "pig"
is Lulauvile's. *Our* pig is the real one, *yours* is the *kama* insect.[4] Again,
you cannot talk about your *lokona*, for I gave you that magic. You
cannot talk of having big pigs, for I led and you copied. I can tie my
pig to a pole, but you will find it hard to copy me and tie your *kama* to
a pole. I spear my pig and it will squeal, but you spear your *kama* and
it will not make a sound. Because I'm Lulauvile I can say "my pig,"
"my food," "my betel" [etc.] and you cannot contradict me. These
were mine and I shared them out. I gave them to you. You came from
the ground with empty hands[5] and carried nothing of value. But I
came from inside the ground with my possessions and my wealth. I
shared them out and now there is abundance for all. I am Lulauvile
Man: I feed large pigs, I preserve yams in my house, I hoard coconuts
and betel, I tie sugar cane. My customs adhere to me like the dirt of
my ancestors. The body dirt of my ancestors sticks to my comb and my
limepot. My possessions came from inside the ground, and I carried
them up. You came with empty hands over the surface of the ground.
You only found this wealth when Kiwiwiole gave it to you. He journeyed to and fro and brought them together and distributed them.
Then we lived at Kwabua, and after that we moved to Kwamalauta.
There we stayed until Kafateya called us to live here in Nibita.

In this passage, which I have translated quite literally, it becomes
clear that Iyahalina is using his mythology as a vehicle for his auto-

biography, defining his generalized identity as a corporation sole of Heloava. He not only identifies with Kiwiwiole and (as we shall see) his ancestors Adiyaleyale and Kedeya, but also reflexively represents himself as embodying Lulauvile clan as an entity. He declares that Lulauvile, as food-bringers personified by the culture hero Kiwiwiole, gave food to all the other Kalauna clans; but in the face of their arrogant claims to possess food themselves, he roundly asserts Lulauvile's primal claim to magical title. His sophistry bears the message that if it were not for him (*qua* Lulauvile) everyone would still be licking stones. People must remember this and respect him accordingly.

Iyahalina continues with the story of how Kafateya, the "chief" of Belebele people, invited the ancestors of Lulauvile II (Kedeya and Uyavaiyava) to occupy the site of Nibita/Kalauna following the murder of his son. I pass over Iyahalina's account of this legend since I have recounted and commented upon it elsewhere (see 1971: 30). The most conspicuous thing about Iyahalina's rendering on this occasion is the painstaking thoroughness with which he makes Kedeya (his own great-grandfather according to Iyahalina's reckoning) ascertain Kafateya's intentions, as if to be absolutely certain that his group will renounce all future claim to the site of Nibita. Iyahalina's fussy concern to establish legalities is once again evident.

Abruptly, Iyahalina embarks on the myth-legend of Adiyaleyale, whom he identifies as Kasifwaifwa's son (although as told to me by his namesake, Iyahalina's son, this hero is Kiwiwiole's own son).

Adiyaleyale makes fish nets while his wife gardens. But every plot she cultivates at Awanake yields poorly. So she moves from plot to plot in an ever-widening area in the search for *ulaiya*, bountiful tubers. [There is a structural parallel here with the preceding story in which Kafateya buries, exhumes, and then reburies several times over the body of his son in search of an auspicious grave. Likewise, both Kiwiwiole and Kikifolu had made journeys to and fro for the accumulation of food.] Adiyaleyale continues to spend his time fishing, seemingly indifferent to his wife's plight, for the people she borrows land from permit her to take only a portion of the crops she harvests. At length she crosses the ridge and finds herself on Nibita land. A Nibita man gives her several plots, each with gardens in different stages of growth. She tells her husband and they go to settle in Nibita. Adiyaleyale puts

aside his fish nets and decides to live up to his name [*yaleyale* is the
magic of tireless strength for gardening]. He takes an axe and cuts a
new taro garden, a communal one, and performs a sequence of rites
to prosper it. [This is the magic Iyahalina now performs, he says, com-
mencing with the cutting stage when he stands on a tree stump and
calls "KI . . . WI . . . WI . . . O . . . LE."] Adiyaleyale then carves wood-
en bowls, and when the taro is ready to be harvested he inaugurates
manumanua ritual so that the people will eat the taro sparingly,
allowing part of the harvest to rot. . . .

A second digression is necessary at this point to give the brief
myth of Hudiboyaboyaleta. This is also the name of the chain of
incantations that Adiyaleyale used for *manumanua* and which he
brought to Nibita from Awanake. They are cognate to, but not
identical with the Kiwiwiole spells. Both myths, it will be recalled,
provide Heloava's charter for the performance of *manumanua*. I
recorded only inconsequential fragments of Hudiboyaboyaleta from
Iyahalina, and the following version was given to me by Tabwaika
in 1977. He had learned it from Tobowa and narrated it (with many
apologies for telling a Heloava myth) at Kawanaba's request.

Hudiboyaboyaleta ("Ripe Bananas") is also called Ulewoka ("Bitter
Anus"). He had two granddaughters. He harvested taro, hard yams,
red betel nut, sprouting coconut, sugar cane, and pitpit, and he tied
them up in his hair. He hid them there and no one knew. His granddaughters liked to delouse him. But he always told them: "Do not untie the string in the middle of my hair. Search for lice only on the side,
back and front of my head." The girls did so and bit the lice they
found. "O grandfather," they said, "why are your lice so sweet, like
the juice of ripe bananas?" "That is the coconut juice I squeeze on my
hair," he told them. One day they were delousing him and his eyelids
flickered; he fell asleep on his granddaughter's thigh. The younger
girl said to her sister: "Perhaps his lice are sweet because his hair is tied
up with string. If we were to untie it we could see." "Ah, that is our
grandfather's secret. We are not supposed to know." Finally, the
younger sister prevailed. "All right, untie it and we'll see." They
pulled at the string until his hair fell down. Suddenly ripe bananas,
red betel nuts, sprouting coconuts, sugar cane, and plump tubers cas-
caded from his head and scattered plentifully. He woke up and cried:
"Ah, my granddaughters, you have found me out! You untied my hair

189

knot and the food burst forth. My name is Ulewoka. I do not need to plant. I harvest ripe foods and plump tubers, but I stay like this; my stomach turns and rejects food. But now you found me out, so you must learn this incantation, then I will depart and sink in my pool forever." He chanted:

> I am Ulewoka
> I am Hudiboyaboyaleta
> What pool will I go to
> Tubers will swell
> Betel nut will cluster
> Ferment flies of plump tubers
> Aging hardness of plump tubers.

"Sing like this," he said, "and food will increase; there will be no famine."

Kawanaba commented upon Ulewoka/Hudiboyaboyaleta: "He is like Vineuma. He keeps secrets inside his hair which are released by his grandchildren. He also vanishes in a pool." One might add, too, that like Honoyeta his secret is discovered by curiously intimate means, leading to his withdrawal in *unuwewe*. Hudiboyaboyaleta, I was told, is also a large stone. It was this stone that Adiyaleyale's wife brought from Awanake to Heloava, where it sometimes lives. But when I asked to be shown it, Heloava men said it had wandered off again. They declare that sometimes it can be seen in the bushes beneath Malaveyoyo's tree, with lights like fireflies dancing along its back. It can also transform itself into a snake or a large tailless lizard, which has been known to kill a pig by spitting at it. These alarming powers suggest that Hudiboyaboyaleta is not entirely subject to the control of the *manumanua* spells. (Kawanaba even suspected that Adiyaleyale's wife made a mistake and brought the wrong stone!)

∧∧∧∧∧

Now to resume Iyahalina's narrative. While describing Adiyaleyale's luxuriant gardens, Iyahalina gradually moves into another sustained address, concerning how his ancestors brought food from the ground. He stresses the importance of their origin *inside* the earth and summarizes cryptically: "So it is from inside the ground our customs came, for if only from the surface then our story would be pointless." For several minutes longer it is impossible to tell whether Iyahalina is referring to himself or to his ancestor Adiyaleyale as performing the ritual tasks of creating community prosperity. He chants spells. He describes with relish the practice of *lokona* and the bitter, unpalatable food that blunts appetite and banishes greed. He evokes shrivelled yams, white with mold spores, lying idle in the corner of the house; spongy taro rotting in the ground; overripe bananas swarming with ferment flies.

Then he tells of the sacred wooden bowls carved by Adiyaleyale (or by himself, though on another occasion Iyahalina confessed to being unable to make them). These bowls are called *nau'a* (the word for food is *au'a*). He refers to a recent event and revives his righteous fury at the stupidity of Ulaiya, a Heloava kinsman, who had smashed a named and unique *nau'a* in anguish at the death of his sister (see Young 1971:177-178). Then he recounts the legend of Kedeya's wife who is lewdly peeped at by her brothers-in-law while she is bathing, provoking the battle with coconut husks and the ensuing dispersal of the groups to Awaiya, Mataita, and Eweli. Kedeya parcels out their duties: one group is sent for salt and tree-cabbage, another for lime-gourds, and yet another for medicinal leaves. But Iyahalina is little concerned with this curious and archaic exchange system, and bends the story to validate his own priestly role: for it is he, a direct descendant of Kedeya, who must remain behind in Heloava. In another long passage he elaborates this hallowed task, and it now becomes evident that his *staying* is itself magically efficacious:

My father told me thus: I cannot leave Heloava. If I walk about without purpose other people will walk about without purpose. I must stay to anchor the people. I am their bones. If I walk about others will desert the village. If I climb trees and if I fish the rivers, bad things will happen. What I do, others do. This is my burden. But it is my promise to the ancestors. They made this their command, and I must follow. It is my duty to stay still for I am the bones of the village.

191

In what he says next, Iyahalina explicitly connects active wandering with the appearance of famine, *loka*. It is to counter the tendency of the food to disappear that he must stay still—like a rock.

> My big burden is *manumanua*. This is my *abutu*, my food-fame. And if it is good then the *abutu* of others will be good, with abundant food. But the people must obey me when I do my *abutu*. They cannot walk about, nor plant nor fish. If they do so then ancestor spirits will cause them to meet accidents for disobeying me. They will fall down trees, drown in rivers, or cut their legs with their knives like foolish Ulaiya [who had indeed recently sliced his kneecap when there was a taboo on planting].

Iyahalina sings more spells, sketches the central rites of *manumanua,* and adds that such incantations "make people good." A broader conception of his role now emerges as involving the instillation of virtue, particularly the virtue of restraint with regard to the temptations of food. It is not simply a matter of the magical power to make people's appetites shrink that constitutes his virtue, but also the moral force that emanates from his own exemplary behavior. And it is the mythological tradition — "true" by virtue of its ancestral origin — that provides the behavioral model:

> What I do, so will others do. That is why I must be still. It is the stories that tell me what to do; the stories that I tell you now. They tell me that my burden is thus; and they tell me that I and no one else can narrate them. So I cannot lie. I am not a big-man, but my name will live because my speech and my stories are true. They are the body dirt of my ancestors; they are my knowledge. The work of Heloava is food. Food is Heloava. So my stories about food tie together all other stories. My stories tie them like a bundle.

Next, he lists the ritual competences of other groups (Anuana's control of the yams, Ukevakeva's control of bananas, Valeutoli's control of betel nut, etc.), but restates his claim that they were originally Heloava's, and that *lokona* is the key to them all.

> I still rule taro and its prosperity. And I still rule *lokona* and *yaleyale*. These things are my fame. They live in me and my stories. I cannot

tell my stories for nothing. They are not for chatter but for work. And for them to work properly they must be true. So I cannot lie about them.

He begins to speak with some resentment about the frustrations of his duties:

My own group do not respect my orders. Some of them become *ya-kaikai* [too proud — a pride that implies squandering food]. If I do not do my work people blame me for other things. Whatever I do to prosper the people can be spoiled by someone who wants to ruin my name. I look after their fruit trees, their gardens, their pigs, and their houses; but if my enemy makes sorcery the people blame me and say: "Iyahalina hasn't looked after us properly. He is neglectful."

Moving into his peroration, Iyahalina recapitulates the roster of his principal duties: periodically to perform *manumanua,* to visit the gardens frequently singing his spells; otherwise to remain in Heloava, eating sparingly, telling the truth, and anchoring the people. If he does these things all will be well, and people will find large tubers in their gardens and abundant fruit on their trees. If he fails to perform these tasks, or if people disobey him when he tells them to sit still, the food will disappear and famine will come. He expatiates the horrors of famine: the drying, shriveling, and dying; the theft, killing, and cannibalism. To "turn" this state and to maintain prosperity so that people can be virtuous and lead good lives is what his work involves. This is what it means to be *toitavealata* — a man who looks after the people.

∧∧∧∧

What are we to make of Iyahalina's essay in autobiography? It is clear that Iyahalina dramatizes his life to a remarkable degree. One who did not know him personally might judge from his narrative that his self-dramatization was a symptom of megalomania. He speaks of himself as a veritable kingpin of Kalauna's universe, responsible for its health, virtue, and prosperity. Like a divine king, his very actions describe the fate of ordinary mortals; his own self-control imposes self-control on others. Such a grandiose conception of his own role is in part a function of the mythological interpretations he espouses, and in part an artifact of the rhetoric he employs. Both are rooted in a magical conception of omnipotent will, and both derive performative force from modes of speech that address the world as if — to use Kenneth Burke's heretical inversion — "things were the signs of words." ·

Thus, Iyahalina's whole narrative can be viewed as having performative force; he asserts this himself when he says that his stories cannot be told "for nothing," like chatter, but only to do work. The numerous spells he canted during the narration were further evidence that he was "working" on affecting the world even as he imparted knowledge about himself to me through the tape recorder. Finally, the "rubbed in" quality of his narration, which gives repetitiveness and density to his text (largely omitted in my transcription for reasons of space and the tedium it can breed), is wholly characteristic of magical spells in this area, as readers of Malinowski's Trobriand works will recall. As a mélange of myth, magic, and other performative assertions, Iyahalina's narrative does not lend itself to tests of truth or falsity, and must be, as Austin (1962) puts it, "normatively judged." It is helpful to recall the context of situation of his narrative, and to bear in mind Jean Guiart's observation:

> Myth contains at the very least two messages: the one the structuralist deciphers, studying his text as a vehicle of the culture as a whole, and the one the narrator impresses on it, which is the summary of his social position, affirming a disappointed ambition or one on the point of success, protesting against the wrong done him. [1972:113]

Iyahalina narrated in private to me, a cataloguing custom-hungry stranger, and to whatever limited audience might lie beyond the tape recorder (though he knew that one or two other Kalauna men might hear it as well). Some of the exaggerations of his account can be put down to his urge to persuade me of the grandeur of the "office" that now constituted his lifework. He knew that I was recording with bland impartiality (gullibility in his view no doubt) innumerable narratives from others, including men who were his traditional enemies. (He once discovered that an Ukevakeva man had claimed to me to possess taro magic, and came hurrying around to my house to put the record straight, hotly inveighing against "lies" people told me about their customs.) It was Iyahalina who sought me out when I first arrived to impress upon me the Lulauvile version of the history of Kalauna, and it was Iyahalina who, at the end of a lengthy session during the last week of my stay in 1968, asked me not to talk to anyone else about Lulauvile's myths, magic, and customs before I left. He thereby tried to ensure that his was the first and last truth that I should hear. The "appropriateness" of the content of his narrative, then, must be viewed in the light of his clear intention to propagate a social doctrine, an ideology.

Given that his bold self-dramatization was largely an advertising technique, it is still possible that Iyahalina had persuaded himself, at one level, that his identity merged with those of his ancestors, the mythical heroes, and the destiny of Heloava, Lulauvile, or even Kalauna as a whole. This would be difficult to substantiate, but it is a point I wish to return to after I have considered another facet of Iyahalina's biographical identity: his quest for legitimacy.

Being first a politician and only second a scholar of his traditions, Iyahalina chose to stress the theme of legitimacy in his story-telling. (His omissions are instructive here, as I have alluded to above and will elaborate upon below.) Never did a village meeting pass without a speech from Iyahalina about rights, duties, or prerogatives. I privately dubbed him the arch-conservative, and visualized him as the Kalauna analogue of a pedantic professor of law or a ponderous chief justice, such was his manifest concern with legalities. Yet he was professing law that is unwritten and adjudicating in a society that has formalized no such function. His mandates were from an oral, partial source, and his pronouncements had moral rather than legal force.

Iyahalina's concern with legalities in the public interest was, I suspect, the reflection (or projection) of his obsession with legitimacy in his private interests. His public life seemed to consist of a perpetual campaign waged, on the one hand, to legitimize his own position as leader of Heloava and, on the other, to impress upon the rest of the village the legitimate importance of that position.

His standing at home in Heloava was largely unassailable as long as he lived, for he could boast all the lawful credentials of hamlet leadership. There was some evidence of insecurity even here, however. His sons, real and classificatory, grumbled to me in private about his reluctance to teach them magic (the knowledge of which is latent power); and at times he seems to have been torn between encouraging his sons to compete in gardening feats for the greater glory of Heloava, and warning them to desist for fear of sorcery (see Young 1971:169). Could this have been the hint of an uneasy suspicion that one of them might usurp him?

But the ideological arena in which Iyahalina expended most of his political energies was the community at large, and here, like other leaders, he was embroiled in endless status battles. From an outsider's point of view, these resulted in little more than an ephemeral public acknowledgment of a transient dominance ungraciously tolerated. While comfortably at home in the free-for-all of a "manipulative, bargaining, transactional" milieu (Stanner 1959: 216), Iyahalina believed himself to be representative of a more authoritarian, indeed hierarchical tradition. Alas for his bids for rank were based upon the principle of primacy, however. The majority of Kalauna men (voicing a chorus of partial truths on behalf of the collocation of clans and hamlets) was not necessarily disposed to listen. At least one reason for this can be found in the significant *omissions* in Iyahalina's propagandized narrative.

To me the most notable lacuna in his personalized history of Kalauna is any mention of Malaveyoyo, the Heloava despot. Iyahalina was bitterly ambivalent about this ancestor (his father's father's brother) partly because he was a Christian, and Malaveyoyo has come to typify the evil excesses of the pagan culture. Yet Malaveyoyo was also in the noble line of Kiwiwiole, Adiyaleyale, and Kedeya, and he did, after all, awesomely glorify Heloava. Iyahalina would not speak to me about him outside the closed caucus of Heloava men, and even when he did so a quick glance over his shoulder attested to his unease. For, through his wanton cannibalism, Malaveyoyo had sown seeds of enmity which Iyahalina was reaping two or three generations later. (Or so he firmly believed. It is another complication of his story that others—descendants of the victims of Malaveyoyo and therefore Iyahalina's traditional enemies—bore

196

him less personal malice than he seemed to imagine. So here was some slight evidence of a paranoid projection devolving from "the sins of the fathers": a syndrome that his son Adiyaleyale was to manifest also, though that is another story.)

At all events, Malaveyoyo's name bears an aura of positive renown in Lulauvile; but it is a name that is anathema to almost every other clan. Iyahalina could not escape the fact that Malaveyoyo constituted a significant link in his tradition, that he too had been a *toitavealata,* but one who had succumbed to the temptations of tyranny and "sent all the food away" with the most disastrous consequences in Kalauna's folk-history. Acutely sensitive to this lesson, and to others' possible reading of it, Iyahalina was publicly circumspect about his ritual powers to a far greater degree than either Didiala or Kimaola, the other *toitavealata.* From this viewpoint, his Christian mien, his moralizing, and his concern with legitimacy may be seen as an attempt, if not to redress Malaveyoyo's wrongs, then to rehabilitate the noble Heloava tradition which this ancestor had perverted.

In a society where words speak as loud as actions, Iyahalina never once (to my knowledge) admitted to the possession of antisocial magic. Despite this, there was not a person in Kalauna who did not believe that if Iyahalina knew how to prosper the crops then he must also know how to ruin them. Man's nature is as double-sided as his magic. An admission that he did know the *kwauna* or negative side of all his beneficial magic would have surprised me in Iyahalina's narrative; but what I could not have foreseen was his suppression of any hint that there might be any such thing. The entire dimension of the potential for evil of the powers legitimated by his stories is conspicuously absent from his account. This suggests that Iyahalina was probably unaware of the amount of gossip I had heard about him, and he did not wish to sully his self-advertisement with denials of hypothetical allegations. In his narrative, he employed the oratorical principle that it is better to ignore your opponents until they shout you down better, that is, not to concede the existence of an alternative viewpoint until it is unavoidable.

Yet it is material to this analysis that, in the popular Kalauna view, Iyahalina held title to the most heinous sorcery in their universe. This magic, *tufo'a,* which is applicable on an individual or collective scale, is the *kwauna* (the obverse) of the hunger-depressing, appetite-spoiling magic of which Iyahalina so proudly boasts. *Tufo'a,* the magic of voracious greed, is the shortest cut to *loka,* the doomsday state of total foodlessness. One should note, too, that man himself is the agent in this terrible process; for the conception of this magic touches the culture's profoundest anxiety: that men, driven to unrestrained oral excess, will destroy themselves. An evocation of cultural suicide by cannibalism, the eating of children, logically follows. This very sequence, from *tufo'a* through famine to the cannibalization of children, is encapsulated in the Malaveyoyo legend. Small wonder, then, that Iyahalina wished to avoid being identified with this particular ancestor.

To my knowledge he was never accused of employing *tufo'a,* though he was (during my relatively brief stay) widely suspected in 1968 of spoiling part of the yam crop by invoking a plague of scarab beetles, and in late 1967 of causing a hurricane that damaged several houses (see Young 1971:178-180). Trivial as these powers may seem when compared to the sorcery of gluttony, they were a source of irritation and resentment to those persuaded of Iyahalina's culpability. We must take such attitudes into account when judging Iyahalina's claim that he lived to prosper the people. The "validity" or "appropriateness" of his narrative (since "truth" is ruled out) or of his rhetoric in a village forum, is of an expedient kind — like the sincere radio commercial, which betrays reality by what it does *not* say.

Iyahalina's quest for legitimacy, then, can be understood in the light of the fact that other Kalauna groups did not accept his own evaluation of his role. One might fancy him a king who had lost his scepter. His particular political battle, nicely exemplified in his text, was a perpetual harangue against the hostile, resentful, skeptical, or simply indifferent attitudes of other leaders. This, perhaps more than anything, shaped his personal political style and obliged him to be an ideologue. Like Kiwiwiole and his mother in Muyuwa, he was insulted and bitter when others forgot that it was "he" who brought the food, and when they claimed to be able to make their gardens grow without his help. Even when they did acknowledge some benefit from his work, it was not without complaint at the cost. I cite one example.

198

In 1966, Iyahalina was arraigned at a couple of village meetings by several (notably Ukevakeva) men, who complained that his magic had spoiled their manioc crop. Others joined the chorus, saying they were afraid to feed sweet potatoes to their children lest they "spoil" them. Iyahalina had put a taboo on half the village's coconuts to regenerate them following a poor season the previous year. People assumed that the magic to protect and prosper the coconuts had somehow contaminated other crops (by falling dew and spiders' webs, according to one imaginative theory). Iyahalina protested that he had done it for everyone's good, that he had certainly not put his taboo on other crops, and that if they wanted to "chase" him away he was happy to go and live in Awaiya. The councillor, convenor of the meeting, had to respond to this display of *unuwewe* by imploring him to stay and smoothing his ruffled dignity.

It was characteristic of Iyahalina as a Kalauna man that he should threaten to leave the community following an insult. But as a *toitavealata* it was more than a display of *unuwewe*; it was also a punitive sanction. Whether or not people subscribed to the doctrine that he "looked after them" in the manner he claims in his narrative, they did believe that if he left the community in anger and resentment he would "take away" the food with him. As far as Iyahalina was concerned, such behavior is sanctioned by his Kiwiwiole story.

∧∧∧∧∧

There is little need here for further elaboration of the symbolism of the myths Iyahalina recounted. But in the context of a discussion of his quest for legitimacy (and the apparent attempts of other political interests to deny it to him), I cannot avoid drawing attention to the symbolic behavior Iyahalina himself stresses. Each one of his stories has a plot that involves a search for secure legitimacy. This is not merely an artifact of Iyahalina's narrative style, for it is evident in the other versions I collected. At an overt thematic level, the tales are populated by characters in search of rightful niches: Kiwiwiole seeks his "place" in Awanake, succeeding Vineuma, who seeks hers in a pool; Adiyaleyale and his wife find their destiny in Kwama-

199

lauta; Kafateya finds a new site at Belebele, inviting Kedeya to occupy Nibita, from whence he sends several groups to new homes. The movements of these characters from place to place—over the sea, up and down rivers, across the landscape—are provoked by insults, death, discovered secrets, or the denial of rights. Their quest for legitimate status, being an impulsion of *unuwewe,* is at another level a quest to rehabilitate spoiled identity (just as Honoyeta's bitter quest was to avenge it). And having found what they seek, they stay put like anchoring *bakibaki.* The quest constitutes the heroic task, but true virtue consists in sitting still. One is reminded of Pascal's observation that the evil in the world derives from men's inability to sit quietly at home. But for Iyahalina it is a magical efficacy which he imputes to quiescence; hence his duty to be still in order to anchor the people and make them good.

If we visualize the various behavioral symbolisms of movement and stillness along two axes in the form of a cross, such that the vertical one represents stasis and the horizontal one mobility, then a number of things become clear in Iyahalina's narrative. The vertical axis stands for legitimate status, held or regained; in Iyahalina's conception it might be said to represent Heloava's ascent from "inside the ground," bringing the secrets of food and thereby establishing a hierarchical principle. In contrast, the horizontal axis stands for quest, competition, and the "empty-handed" wandering over the land: it connotes "fighting with food" and the principle of egalitarianism.

HIERARCHY
(stasis, restraint)

EGALITARIANISM
(competition,
mobility)

ABUTU
(threat of
loka)

MANUMANUA
(guarantee of *malia*)

Relating these things to the dominant concern of all Kalauna people, it might be added that the vertical, anchored axis posits *manumanua* and the state of plenty (*malia*), whereas the horizontal, shifting axis describes the state of famine (*loka*), when communities do indeed disperse. In the same figurative mode I might mention Malaveyoyo's (and Iyahalina's) sorcery of dispersal. While his incantation is being broadcast by the smoke of a fire, the sorcerer removes the vertical stone backrest of his sitting platform (beneath which the *bakibaki* stone lies), turns it to and fro, then lays it horizontally on the ground. The people of the village, it is said, are impelled by this magic to abandon their homes and disperse, "wandering aimlessly."

Iyahalina's autobiographical narrative exemplifies two principal contradictions. The first is conveyed in his Kiwiwiole myth with its theme of the loss and regaining of food, and its paradox that while food is good to eat, it is even better to abstain from it. With regard to the magic to which the myth gives charter, the antimonies are posed between food-prospering magic (*sisikwana,* etc.) and food-destroying magic (*tufo'a,* etc.). Iyahalina's dilemma is that he cannot be esteemed and exalted for "bringing" or "anchoring" the food without also risking odium and ignominy for "sending it away." If this is his moral and philosophical conundrum, it has a social corollary (his second contradiction) in that he represents a principle of hierarchy in a community where the egalitarian principle is predominant. Caught at the intersection of the two axes, as it were, his only practical recourse is to follow the injunction of his ancestors and sit still. He referred to this as his burden, his "heavy thing." He might just as well have called it his cross.

What I have called the self-dramatization of Iyahalina's narrative (the two-way identification of his self with his ancestors and with the wider group he represents) should now make better sense, and we can intuitively reconcile it with his quest for legitimacy. Both are expressions of a single impulse to solve the conflicts of his social identity through the intellectual resources of his culture: namely, the mythical paradigms of his heritage. Only *these* myths can answer his predicament, for they are as truly his own as the clothes he wears. No one else can relate them, he says, and therefore he cannot lie. But the contradictions within and between the stories are also the contradictions that his heritage obliges him to live, and no amount of sophistry and legerdemain will bring them comfortably into line with Kalauna's current social reality, for they speak of a tradition at variance with it. On the one hand they assert his title to dominance through his ownership of a means of production (food magic); on the other hand, they deny him effective authority by patenting the distribution of powers among the clans, not to mention the other subclans of Lulauvile.

Pagan priest or Christian sorcerer, dispossessed chief or privileged commoner? The merging of Iyahalina's own biography with those of his ancestral heroes suggests at one and the same time an "identification" with them and a "distancing" from himself—an erasure of his personal history in his generalizing of it. This is his way of grappling with the contradictions of his social identity. Moreover, self-dramatization is a psychological expedient which in itself can be effective in reconciling contradictions (witness his irony and developed sense of theater). Though to take Iyahalina's view, it would be another way of working upon the world through symbolic action. For in the metonymic device of substituting part for whole there is a clear homology between taro magic, for example, and the dramatized, performative utterances of Iyahalina's text. In the former he selects a single taro for concentrated ritual attention, nursing it to a splendid fructification which inspires by its example all other taro in the garden. So, too, in his personification of his lineage he views himself as the single part which fructifies the whole: "What I do, so will others do. That is why I must be still."

The end of Iyahalina's story would take long to tell in full. His struggle with the conflicting aspects of his role and with the contradictory expectations of his myths led him to the familiar solution of victimage. In a radical version of Kiwiwiole, which Iyahalina did not tell, the hero is hunted and slain by villagers. Iyahalina, like other Kalauna leaders, was disposed to view his fate in similar terms as the price of any kind of achievement. He lived to serve the village through the special competences of his heritage, and to protect men

202

from themselves (from their greed particularly), and he would die at their hands through their sorcery of envy or malice.

In the circumstances of his own death there was a dramatic irony that could not have been contrived more tragically by fiction. During his management of Kimaola's festival (the task that was to be the pinnacle of his public career), he was offered, and he accepted, Kimaola's widowed sister in marriage. He died a few years later believing that Kimaola had ensorcelled him through the treachery of his wife. This is how his son Adiyaleyale told it to me, each detail corroborated by Kawanaba:

My father was a great smoker. But he knew his enemies and was careful whom he asked for tobacco. Then he married Kimaola's sister and she learned his habits. One day my father had no tobacco and he asked his wife. "Yes," she said, "I have a piece." She gave him some which Kimaola had prepared. When my father had smoked part of the cigarette, she took it back and gave it secretly to her brother. . . .

My father was sick for three months. He guessed the cause of his suffering for he told Kawanaba a Bible story. "Do you remember Samson?" he asked. "He was a very strong man. His enemies wanted to kill him but they couldn't find the secret of his strength. So they sent their sister to marry him, and she discovered the source of his power. She weakened him so that her brothers could kill him. That is why I am dying from this sickness now."

Early one morning I woke up and heard my father calling me from his bed. My stepmother had brought a piece of ginger from her brother and put it between his lips. He had chewed a little, then slept. Then he called out to me: "Adiyaleyale, look quickly! See that dog!" I saw a large black dog with a white neck jump from the house and disappear. I asked him if he had seen anyone. "No, only that dog. But it came to bite me. I'm going to leave you this afternoon. I want you to go to Yaueda and clear the coconuts there, and when you come back I shall be ready to die."

I went to Yaueda with my wife. I was working when a black *bulowoi* bird alighted on a branch above my head. I threw a stone at it and it flew away. Then it cried and wheeled back again to the same tree. "Your father-in-law is dead," I said to my wife. "The dog took his spirit away when it bit him, and now that bird has come to tell me his life had ended."

I hurried back to the village. "He's waiting for you," said my mother Kwahihi [Didiala's widow]. "His breath lingers but his spirit is gone." I went to his side and talked to him, but he didn't answer. Kawanaba and Kuyomanua came and talked to him too. "We are all here, your children," they said. "Don't worry about us. Don't keep coming and going this way. Go now, forever." I went down to the *atuaha* and wept all night. And I decided to name two pigs for him: Kanulove ["Abandoned"] and Awaniya ["All talk"—what gossips had said of Iyahalina, meaning that he talked a lot about food but did not plant any].

The next day we buried him, eight of us, and that night he gave me a picture of how he died. He had always told me: "Don't search for sorcerers; I will show you after you plant me in my grave." We had placed spiked branches over the grave to protect it from dogs and pigs. I was sleeping on my house step with my back to the door when it seemed to burn me. It was my father's spirit. I stood up and looked at the grave. I could hear leaves rustling. I went down and saw that my father had moved the spiked branches to form a circle around his grave. It was like a fence: the shape of a widow's fence. [A recently bereaved widow dwells under her brother's house in a space enclosed by a wall, or "fence," of woven coconut leaves.] I remembered how his widow walked away from the grave when we buried my father. [According to custom she should allow herself to be carried away, prostrate, by her brother.]

A few days later I had to go to Bolubolu for a council meeting [he was village councillor at the time], and I saw her there, his widow, with a fine hibiscus in her hair. I boiled inside. I went to the government office and I spoke to the European A.D.O. "Can I kill that woman who killed my father?" "No," he said, "you must only speak to her." I went back to Kalauna, still angry. I got my bushknife and fishing spear; Kawanaba carried a spear and Awadava [his youngest brother] held a stone. I confronted that woman. "O my son..." she said. "I am not your son!" I shouted. "You killed my father with your brother's tricks. I saw that *yafuna* [i.e., the sorcerer's dog, which had taken Iyahalina's spirit]; I saw my father's message from the grave, your widow's fence; and I saw your disrespect for him...." I was going to kill her, truly, but my brothers held me back, so I just broke part of her house....

Iyahalina had told his sons something else before he died. "I know many magical secrets," he said. "I have suffered, and my spirit will feel resentment and seek its revenge." They implored him not to bring them harm. "We have already taken your place," they said. "We have learned your secrets. But if you do anything it will harm us too." "All right," he assured them. "But Kawanaba and Kuyomanua must look to my head and my feet when you put me in the grave. You must bury me properly." They understood what he meant, for the special burial rite of *kemo ana baluveda,* "marking out the path of the grave," had been done for Didiala and Awakili recently, and Kawanaba had performed it when he helped to bury Tobowa. It should be done for all those known to possess powerful food sorcery.

Accordingly, Kawanaba and Kuyomanua scratched the outline of the grave in the hard ground at the side of Adiyaleyale's house. They removed the topsoil and carefully laid it aside. The other gravediggers then dug the hole with its side chamber. They wedged Iyahalina's body, wrapped in a new pandanus mat, into the chamber and prepared a wall of black palm planks to seal it. Kawanaba stood at the end where the dead man's feet lay (*waiaiye*) and Kuyomanua at the head end (*waia'u'u*). First one, then the other drove a sharpened stick of iron-hard black palm into the floor of the grave, securing the retaining pole that held the wall in place. They sang the incantations, then fetched the topsoil and pressed it down firmly around the two sticks. Finally, they called the other buriers to hurry and fill the grave with the rest of the earth. The rite was completed.

To explicate this simple prophylactic ritual, we need only observe that Iyahalina's body was laid with his head pointing "upstream" to the mountains and the source of food (*waia'u'u* means head of the river), and with his feet pointing "downstream" to the sea to which food peelings drift (*waiaiye* means foot of the river). The spells sing of closing the dead man's mouth and anus, and of stopping their malevolent, dying expirations. They also invoke the holding power of well-trodden hamlet topsoil and bid the people stay and not have need of wandering.

Kawanaba and Kuyomanua did all this for Iyahalina and "nothing happened—no crops were ruined and there was no hunger." They had buried him properly, anchoring him in death in Heloava's stony soil as he had anchored himself there in life, "the bones of the village."

8
The Belly of Kimaola

A man's worst enemies are those
Of his own house and family;
And he who makes his law a curse
By his own law shall surely die.

—William Blake, *Jerusalem,*
Plate 27

There was a time when all the body's
  members
Rebelled against the belly.

—*Coriolanus,* I, i

∧∧∧∧∧

After the deaths of Didiala and Iyahalina, the most powerful man in Lulauvile and the most prominent figure in the village was unquestionably Kimaola. He might have been set for the career of despotism which I had predicted for him in 1968.[1] Others, too, were inclined to read his motives in the light of a simple dominance theory of ambitious big-manship. They pointed out that his hamlet, dominated by a beetling rock called Kalauna, gave its name to the whole village: Kimaola would emulate its solid eminence. But we were wrong. Kalauna did not tolerate another monolithic regime. A new

206

generation of leaders was in the wings and would gradually prevail. Kimaola overreached himself, and by 1972, persecuted by Iyahalina's vengeful son, he seemed to have lost his nerve. In 1977, when he was nearing sixty years of age, I found him quietly retired in a sunny new hamlet, surrounded by his beloved yam gardens.

The deaths of Didiala, Iyahalina, and old Siboboya of Aluwaita found a younger generation of Lulauvile men—their "sons"—with new responsibilities and an awakening sense of their own importance. In Anuana, Keyayala could not hope to fill his father's grand role, but he coped adequately for a few years. It was Kaniniku, a pushy man with square shoulders and a powerful voice, who began to emerge as Anuana's leader. Hitherto he had dwelt in his mother's hamlet, Kwakwaiboka, where the master-gardener Yaneku was leader. Then in 1971 Yaneku died, and Kaniniku leaped into prominence by forcing an *abutu* contest upon an Ukevakeva man who had willfully violated the mourning period by beating a drum. About the same time, Kaniniku was appointed *komiti,* the village councillor's offsider, a job that required much energy and some officiousness. While he would never be heir to Anuana's magic (being of a junior line), he showed promise as an efficient organizer with sound initiative, those very qualities Didiala's sons appeared to lack.

In Heloava, three men in their early thirties were each of an age and inclination to take over from Iyahalina. These were Kuyomanua, Kawanaba, and Adiyaleyale, two of them sons of leaders. Kuyomanua and Adiyaleyale had both been taught Iyahalina's magic; Kawanaba had received from his mother all that his father, Kaweya, had known. Their respective magical inheritances were similar but not identical, and there was a good deal of muted antagonism between Adiyaleyale and Kawanaba, especially over what each believed the other knew. In the year before his father's death, Adiyaleyale had been elected local government councillor for the village.

In Aluwaita, Siboboya's son Wasimala had long been its effective leader, a position he confirmed by provisioning a spectacular memorial feast a year after his father's death in 1972. Wasimala was comparatively wealthy by Kalauna standards, having a regular job as an assistant agricultural officer at Bolubolu Patrol Post, one of the few

207

men able to draw a local cash income. Finally, in Kimaola's own amorphous group, his chosen heir Kiyodi was showing signs of independence. A sturdy if somewhat sullen young man, Kiyodi enjoyed widespread respect for what he was believed to know of Honoyeta and Oyatabu, among other powerful magical systems. These, then, were some of Lulauvile's emerging leaders, young Turks of the 1970s who would challenge, individually or concertedly, defiantly or subversively, Kimaola's dominance of the clan.

On the fourth day of mourning Iyahalina, after bathing in the sea with the other buriers, Adiyaleyale hung his father's basket upon a coconut tree on the bank of the river at Dayaya. This signified that the river was taboo for fishing as long as the basket remained. Kaniniku announced that when the prohibition was lifted and the buriers had gorged themselves on fish, he would light a fire on Heloava's *atuaha* and thereby inaugurate the Fakili festival which would honour Iyahalina's memory. Accordingly, a year later, when all the mourners had been released from their taboos and had begun to eat normally again, the young men of Heloava began their commemorative Fakili. Kaniniku, acting as principal *fofofo,* called out after lighting the fire:

> My friends, people of Kalauna! You must not be afraid. This festival is not to shame you by giving you *ketowai* gifts. We merely want to pay our debts. So you can come and sing with us and be happy.

For the first month no one came. Heloava and Anuana sang alone night after night. Then they organized a feast of cooked food to attract the others. But no one else attended that either. So Heloava and Anuana were obliged to exchange and eat one another's pots. The young men of Heloava believed the cause of the boycott to be Kimaola. He had told them scathingly, "You are small boys and don't know what you are doing." He instructed his own *fofofo* (Anuana II) to keep away, and presumably dissuaded the rest of the village also. For their part, the other clans were suspicious of Heloava's intentions, despite Kaniniku's assurance that no *ketowai* gifts would be given to shame them. Gradually, however, attendances at the nightly entertainments picked up. Men and women from the other

208

Kalauna hamlets, and even some from neighboring villages, regularly appeared to be given betel nut, tobacco, and a breakfast of cooked taro after singing the night away.

Heloava kept the festival warm for several months. It had been a poor yam harvest in 1972 (some spoke of *loka*), but Heloava owed no debts of yams and was content to amass taro for the grand distribution at the climax of the festival. Kaniniku was good as his word: save for two or three *ketowai* gifts given to traditional enemies (who expected to receive them anyway), the pigs and the huge cylindrical containers stuffed with taro were largely used to repay existing debts.

Kimaola had consistently withheld his support from the festival. He offered no pigs and forbade the men of Anuana II and Aluwaita to provide stands of taro. He still spoke disparagingly of the presumptuous young men. So although it was their prerogative as "chiefs of the festival" to mount a platform during the climactic giveaway and perform the proud role of *kaiwabu,* they ostentatiously refrained. Instead of dressing in shell finery and resplendent face paint, they donned their most ragged clothes, neither washed nor combed their hair, eschewed all shell ornaments and even refused to chew betel nut. They squatted in the dirt on the edge of the hamlet, quietly stirring the dust at their feet. Visitors from other villages came and stared in wonder. "Where are the *kaiwabu?*" "There are no *kaiwabu,*" Kaniniku told them. "Look, over there! Only poor men, rubbish men." The visitors were impressed. Iyahalina's sons had repaid Kimaola's jealous spite with a fine display of mock humility. Their behavior attests yet another political possibility of *unuwewe.*

A full year later wisps of rumors still circulated concerning who was responsible for the *loka* of 1972, when the yams had shriveled and for a time, late in the year, all food was in short supply and many adults ate no more than a single coconut each day. Some said the men of Heloava, in collaboration with those of Didiala's heirs who knew sun magic, had done *tufo'a,* the sorcery of famine, which brings to everyone the pinch of hunger. Nouneya's leader, Kafataudi, declared at one village meeting: "I feel it myself. When I cook and eat, then converse for a while, I want to eat again too soon."

209

Heloava and Anuana were thought to have had at least two good reasons. Their beloved fathers had recently died, and, more immediately, their Fakili festival was being scorned. Those who exculpated Kimaola believed Heloava men were directing their vengeance against him. Ironically, they said it was Kimaola's own heir, Kiyodi, who had inadvertently blown the conch shell that Kuyomanua had bespelled with *tufo'a,* broadcasting the malevolent magic on the wind while they carried a pig to Kalauna. But another rumor had it that Kimaola had performed the sun magic from anger at Siboboya's death. Yet another, inspired by Adiyaleyale, had it that Kimaola's sun sorcery was a spiteful attempt to sabotage Heloava's Fakili. "Do you remember when we were fishing?" Adiyaleyale asked rhetorically, at the same meeting where Kafataudi complained of his hunger. "And a man with a pipe went to a tree and drew a ring around it with his firestick? And do you remember how he then left the village for many weeks?" There were also those who believed that Kimaola was punishing Heloava for Adiyaleyale's persecution of him.

Whichever way the rumors drifted they seemed somehow to implicate Kimaola. The dearth of food had been a fact, but who was punishing whom for what was never clear. From this confusion of rumors I could only deduce an unwillingness to let the blame settle, such that the most fanciful theories could float in an atmosphere thick with mistrust. But all of this, in 1973, was a sign that Kimaola had already lost some ground. I observed that the membership of his hamlet had declined from twenty-eight to twenty in five years, due to the defection of two of his protégés.

∧∧∧∧

Throughout *Fighting With Food* I referred to Kimaola as a bigman. During 1968, with his Fakili underway, he was the biggest man in the community. With his piping voice he called the tune to village activities; he directed the resources of the largest clan toward the aggrandizement of his festival; and he was surrounded constantly by a company of young henchmen. It was the summit of his

210

career, though I had no way of knowing whether he would rest content with the renown of his Fakili, and I echoed the misgivings of others that Kimaola was "treading Tobowa's path to local despotism by the coercive use of sorcery" (ibid.:92). He had created a thriving hamlet from scratch by attracting to himself all manner of kinfolk and affines in the classic managerial style of the Melanesian big-man (ibid.:98-101), and by June of 1968 his hamlet seemed full to bursting with its twenty-eight persons crowded into six small houses. In those days, then, with his opportunism and his thickskinned invincibility, Kimaola impressed me as a big-man who transcended customary constraints and manipulated social rules to his personal advantage. Two characteristics were evident: he was ambitious and he was unscrupulous.

I admit that I never knew Kimaola well, though we were acquainted over a period of ten years. I rarely spoke to him alone, for when he visited me it was usually in the company of others, and when I visited him others were present to absorb whatever might have become personal in our relationship. He tacitly refused to enter any contractual relationship with me over the exchange of goods or favors for information. Although I often urged myself to push him further my courage failed me in the end, and I was left to fantasize what it might have been like to apprentice myself to a sorcerer. I recall a few occasions when he looked me in the eye and seemed to wonder; most times his bland indifference was galling. Unlike Didiala he never asked who I was, and unlike Iyahalina he never asked why and what I wrote in my notebooks. One occasion of illuminating eye contact was sparked by a "familiar" of my own. A white dog I had facetiously named Dimdim (the term for whites in the Massim) stole a chicken of Kimaola's one day, and I visited him apologetically with compensatory gifts of money and tobacco. But as we joked about Dimdim's theft I realized that the intended irony of the name had misfired. Instead of appreciating that I was mocking my own European status, Kimaola chose to see only that my privileged and relatively well-fed dog was aptly named, the envy of all the other village mongrels. "If dogs could do sorcery," he said, "Dimdim would die."

Kimaola had a childlike delicacy of frame. His nickname Kafama

211

(Skinny) alluded particularly to an abnormally collapsed stomach; it was as if his abdominal region had been excavated. As a child he was allegedly small and sickly, and "did not grow well." There may be something in the theory that he rejected his mother's milk (to which he refers in his autobiographical narrative). But his stomach was remarkable in the same way as Iyahalina's distinguished mouth: they were bodily expressions of notable preoccupations of the culture. Kimaola's small belly and birdlike appetite were apposite for a food magician, one of the *toitavealata,* who, like *kaiwabu* on permanent display, should not be seen to eat in public in order to advertise the virtue of restraint.

Kimaola's fondness for betel had almost emptied his mouth of teeth by middle age. The blackened, salient incisors that remained gave his speech a hissing quality. Added to the thin production from his throat, this rendered him an unimpressive orator. He had mastered the gestures and rhetorical forms, but the pitch and weakness of his voice contradicted the authority he sought to convey. His sad, almost cherubic face was framed by a halo of curly hair. His punctured earlobes dangled, only recently bereft of the ginger root he used to wear as a sorcery prophylaxis. Invariably he held a stubby pipe or a crimson limestick. His alarming taste in T-shirts could be explained by his build, which obliged him to wear children's sizes; but there was something faintly sinister about the cartoon characters who adorned his chest.

Kimaola was evasive and as opaque as a stone. He deflected most questions. When I coaxed him to tell me his Oyatabu myth (omitting, if he wished, the secret incantations it contained) he did so reluctantly, only after Iyahalina and Didiala had told me their own stories. But even when he did record Oyatabu before a tiny, handpicked audience, he obfuscated the tale so much that it had to be lengthily unraveled with the help of more intimate informants. With some revealing exceptions (which I reproduce below), his autobiographical fragments were also deceptive — offhanded and obtuse, as if, in his wariness of others, he was afraid to admit to any emotion that was not calculated. It was not only I, the outsider, who found him opaque and elusive. One good reason so many villagers feared him was their uncertainty of his moods and intentions. Yet, paradoxically, he also had a reputation for bluntness and a bluff honesty when it suited him. He was not to be trusted, however, for he was known to be devious, guileful, and manipulative. Time and again he admitted to acts of injurious sorcery. To my knowledge no one else in the village since Tobowa had done so, and he clearly savored the power it gave him.

∧∧∨∨∧∧

Taught by his father and a succession of casual mentors on his many travels, Kimaola accumulated a repertoire of curing techniques which became his stock-in-trade. He was first introduced to me as a curer of local fame with a reputation of many years' standing. There were several other curers in the village with their own specialties, but only two could claim a professionalism equal to Kimaola's. He treated almost the entire spectrum of illnesses and disorders, from flu epidemics (when he administered doses of hot water in which crushed ginger had been boiled) to chronic hysteria in women and violent *amok* in men. Many of the other curers "extracted" an intrusive object — a stick, stone, piece of rubber or witch's tooth — from their patients' bodies. But Kimaola did not practice this particular deception; the agents of sickness he dealt with remained unseen. Although induced trance states are alien to the Nidula healer's art, Kimaola relied heavily upon dreams to assist him with diagnosis. In Kalauna belief, a person's spirit becomes detached from the body during sleep, and dreams are held to be the spirit's nocturnal experiences. But only Kimaola and one or two other men of knowledge could control their spirits' movements and hence their dream experience.

It is well known how he acquired this faculty. Before his father died he instructed Kimaola to break his coconut-shell drinking cup and bury half with his body; the other half Kimaola was to keep by his pillow while he slept. His father promised to guide his dream travel and show him secrets hidden from mortal eyes. Subsequently, any ailing person, on the payment of a fee, could request Kimaola to dream why he or she was sick and what course of action to take to restore health. Kimaola also made private and gratuitous prognoses, often in the form of warnings. One doesn't need to be cynical to imagine the political potential of this means of influencing another's behavior. Indeed, few people regarded Kimaola's curing expertise unequivocally. It is a truism in Kalauna that most curative magic is but the obverse of injurious sorcery, though amateur curers usually managed to remain blameless of causing the ills they cured.

A case I observed closely involved Adiyaleyale, whose first wife suffered an obstructed childbirth. Since she was a woman of his own clan segment, Kimaola offered his services immediately the complications became apparent. The anxious husband promised him money, clothes, and pots of cooked food, while Kimaola tended the woman for a day and night, singing soothing *tomoduwe* spells, massaging her abdomen and back with doctored leaves, and generally supporting her throughout her travail. Eventually she gave birth to a dead infant. Kimaola had already hinted that Adiyaleyale was at fault for disregarding his advice that the couple should practice contraception for a few years (certain roots are chewed to this end, roots whose actual pharmacological efficacy is unknown). Adiyaleyale was penitent and accepted the misfortune as "a punishment from God." But a few days later Kimaola also intimated to him that Iyahalina might have left some *sisikwana*-contaminated betel nut lying around the house (*sisikwana* magic is held to be inimical to processes of growth and it wreaks havoc with a woman's reproductive system). Adiyaleyale refused to believe this (and Iyahalina also protested when he heard the imputation), whereupon Kimaola implanted yet another suggestion. He claimed to have seen a certain woman (whom Adiyaleyale had good reason to believe held a grudge against him) tamper magically with the doorpost when the labor pains began. For several months afterwards Adiyaleyale's and his afflicted wife's suspicions rested there, though they took no action against the suspected sorceress.

About a year later, however, Adiyaleyale suddenly declared to me that Kimaola had been responsible all along. He presented an elaborate argument to support his conviction: how Kimaola had been angered by an insult to his sister and was avenging himself on Adiyaleyale by ensorcelling his wife; how Kimaola had sought to disguise his act by ostensibly curing her and directing the blame elsewhere; how he had extorted money and gifts for his bogus services; and how, Adiyaleyale concluded, it was only a matter of time before Kimaola admitted what he had done. "This is his custom; he tricks you for a while, then he tells you the truth."

While this case might tell us as much about Adiyaleyale's search for a scapegoat as it does about Kimaola's mode of operation, it does not stand alone. Kimaola did appear repeatedly to play upon equivocation. Mystification and legerdemain were the essence of his personal style. Within the village at large he did not inspire great confidence as a trustworthy curer, reputedly good though he was. While the ambivalence toward his profession is a special instance of the general anxiety concerning the double-edged instrument of magic, Kimaola exacerbated it by refusing to cultivate a reassuring bedside manner.

As for Kimaola's unabashed deployment of sorcery (or rather, his manipulation of sorcery fears), several examples appear throughout the book (see also Young 1971:136-137). I will confine myself here to a single additional example as an illustration of his cool political opportunism.

On 12 February 1968, Wasimala told me of a terrible dream he had "seen" the night before. A *balauma* spirit with a ghastly face, long ears, and huge teeth had appeared to him and offered him a pig's leg. A second *balauma* had tugged him by the arm, urging him to come into the bush. Wasimala jabbered at them fearfully until he woke up. He was feeling weak and slightly feverish. (Without much conviction Kawanaba suggested he was having this trouble because his two wives were quarreling; it is a "mission idea" that polygyny makes one's "head go round.")

That night Wasimala dreamed again. He thrashed around in distress, crying "Akoi! Akoi!" Several neighbors rushed to pacify him, holding him down and saying "No, no, no!" while stroking his chest. Kimaola stuffed some ginger between Wasimala's teeth and he woke up sweating. He described his dream as similar to the previous one, except that this time the *balauma* held a child, whom they offered to him.

On 13 February, Wasimala dozed fitfully throughout the day with a light fever. From 7 P.M. about a dozen Lulauvile people gathered in and around his house. Wasimala was hallucinating again, though it was difficult to tell whether he was asleep or awake. Kimaola put ginger between his lips and the people outside sang curing songs. At about 9 P.M. Wasimala sat bolt upright and gazed around, crying "Akoi!" The people near him stroked his chest soothingly, saying "No, no!" Kimaola sent for Enowei and asked him to help. So that everyone could hear, Enowei said: "I will try to make him better, but if I succeed you must not say it was I who sorcerized him." Enowei climbed into the house and took a root and some leaves from his basket. He lay the root on Wasimala's head and shook some lime onto the leaves, which he then rubbed together between his palms. Then he clapped his hands loudly over Wasimala's head. Wasimala gradually settled down and appeared to sleep peacefully.

Later that night Kimaola said he had been standing under the house while Enowei performed his rite. He saw two *balauma,* a male and a female, leave the house. They were empty-handed. Kimaola said he spat his ginger at them and they vanished into the dark. Enowei and Kimaola then discussed where they might have come from. Kimaola thought they lived in Wailolo, where there is a tall, decorated Sagali post from the last festival. Wasimala passes it every day on his way to work at Bolubolu, and Kimaola surmised that the *balauma* had become enamored of him. "He is a handsome young man. They wanted to take him away for themselves." Wasimala had recovered by the next day.

Five days later, Enowei went to visit Wasimala and was given a dollar and a tableknife. Kimaola and Siboboya, Wasimala's father, were in the house. Enowei told me later that Kimaola had suddenly said to them, "Now perhaps you will come to my Fakili, or you will get more bad dreams." Siboboya had protested that they had no pigs, and were therefore ashamed to sing at his festival. "The *balauma* do not care about that," said Kimaola. Enowei asked, "My brother, if you brought the *balauma,* why did you ask me to send them away?" "Because you know better than I how to banish them," Kimaola replied.

It is interesting to note how Kimaola manipulated the symbolism of Wasimala's nightmares. Retrospectively, the pig's leg in his first dream could be seen to stand for the pigs he and his father were ashamed to lack. Likewise, the child (*kwamana*) which the *balauma* offered to him in his second dream represented the *fofofo* (also idiomatically called *kwamana*) whom Wasimala spurned in avoiding the festival. As for the *balauma,* Kimaola had only to remind people of what they were quite ready to believe: that terrifying demons are summoned by sorcerers to protect the support post of the pig platform at the climax of a festival.

∧∧∧∧

I suggest there were three facts about Kimaola that provide some clue to understanding him. The first of these was his diminutive size; the second his lack of brothers and cousins; and the third was the status of his descent line as the most junior of Lulauvile I. Given also that he was unusually ambitious and endowed with a sharp intelligence, one can surmise the compensatory nature of the battling stance he adopted toward his fellows. He identified strongly with his father (himself an only son) and acknowledged no other protector and mentor. Stigmatized almost at birth as one physically and socially weak, he matured precariously with the idea that magical intimidation was the best means to secure and advance his position. From the safe standpoint of one who has lived through the worst, he could, in 1977, view his survival with complacency, while declaring that he owed everything to his father:

> I was fed by my father. He looked after me and taught me everything. Only he fed me. I grew up and he told me, "Don't walk over a man's new coconuts, or his sorcery will find you and you'll live a short life." I kept his advice all my life. I was wary of men. I did not break their taboos. I respected their property. That is why I am still alive, and no sickness cripples me.

As a young man he endured the harsh conditions of indentured labor several times: gold mining in Misima, plantation work at Giligili and Mogubu, stevedoring in Port Moresby. He was working on a rubber plantation near Sogeri when the Japanese invaded New Guinea. He and his companions walked to Port Moresby to find the town in turmoil.

> There was no government. We carried off calico which the whites had left when they fled. We drank bad water [alcohol] and nearly died. We fell on the grass and slept anyhow, and the sun awoke us with its heat. They gave us medicine, but we only licked the spoon.

Then, recruited by the military to carry munitions:

> They put machine-gun legs on our shoulders. We were strong but could only carry them a little way. Some men couldn't move at all. They just trembled, so we took the guns off their shoulders and the *taubada* [white officer] sent them home to their villages. But he said to us: "You can help the soldiers. You can lead the way into the bush." So they found us uniforms and gave us guns. "Don't shoot anyone," they said, "but if Kwaiyale [a bush people] try to attack you, you can shoot at them." We led the way, and the men who carried rice followed. We walked and walked over the mountains until we reached the Japanese, then we came back and carried again.

Such was his view of the notorious Kokoda Trail in 1943. He detailed some experiences of the marches and his glimpses of the violence of the war. Two or three incidents will suffice:

> One Japanese climbed to the top of a sago tree. We were walking in file and he shot at us. He killed a Kiwai man and the *taubada* asked us, "Hey, Gosiagu, is this man your friend?" We said, "No, he's Kiwai." We stood around the tree and they shot the Japanese. He fell to the ground and we took the money from his trousers and put it in our pockets.... We went to find a cement box which the Japanese had built. They were inside and we tried to smash it, but it was too strong. So the soldiers sent a message to their American friends and they appeared with diving glasses, swimming in the sea with their rifles. We just watched, but the Americans in the sea were shooting at each other, at their own friends. Then someone took a small hand bomb and pulled the pin out and threw it at the box. Then we took the red flag of the Japanese. A native of Buna was trying to save it, but we

218

shot him dead.... There was a Japanese soldier entangled in some lawyer cane, still alive. A *taubada* asked us: "Are any of you local men?" "No," we said. So the Americans made the local Tufi men fall into line and gave them bayonets. Ten of them. They said, "You can kill this Japanese because he shot your friends." So the Tufi men rushed in and speared him with bayonets while we clapped our hands.

Later, at Higaturu in the Northern District, when the Japanese had been routed and congratulations were in order, a senior officer reviewed them.

He told us to fall in. Then the *tabauda* told him, "Go and shake Kimaola's hand." And he made a speech in Motu to all the men there. "Kiwai, Mailu, Kokodara, Gosiagu," he said, "all of you look at this man. Kimaola is only a small boy. Perhaps he didn't like his mother's milk. But he wanted to help, and with men like him we have beaten the enemy."

Kimaola returned to Port Moresby and eventually found his way home to Goodenough Island.

We might have died. My father wept and said: "I heard news that you must be dead." "No," I said, "I have returned safely." And my father showed me the valuables he had broken in his grief: a nosebone snapped in two, a cassowary headdress cut into pieces, a crushed belt and necklace. He spoiled all these things for nothing because I was still alive. And Wakaluma, my father's kinsman, had hit the other youngsters in his anger. He praised me and scolded them for laughing in the village while I was dying with the soldiers far away.

Kimaola proved to everyone, including himself, that his diminutive size need be no obstacle to heroism and renown.

∧∧∧∧∧

Lacking the personal and political support of brothers or other close male agnates, Kimaola made the most of his three sisters. More than any other Kalauna leader that I know, he exploited his sisters' potential as wives in bestowing them strategically. As "wife-giver" he could expect a steady flow of goods and services from their husbands, the almost unqualified assistance of his sisters' sons, and the promise of a substantial portion of their daughters' bride-wealth. He could have demanded these things whoever his sisters married, but he made his own calculations for maximizing them. Nor was he reluctant to persuade them to break their marriages if he was convinced a fresh union would be to his advantage. Between them, his three sisters had had, by 1973, a total of eight husbands.

His elder sister, Newela, was a commanding person in her own right, the owner of powerful pig magic and *kaneala,* a spell for bringing green parrots to ravage the banana crop of anyone who might cross her. Her first marriage was to an Ukevakeva man, by whom she had one daughter. (Kimaola later disposed of this daughter by marrying her to someone of his own choice, overriding his sister's protest that the man was too old for her.) Newela left her first husband, and, with Kimaola's encouragement, married another Ukevakeva man, leader of his subclan and the possessor by primogeniture of Iwaoyana's important banana-growing magic. Some say it was because of this magic that he died in 1967, leaving his widow with six young children. Another, probably malicious, rumor blamed Kimaola himself, by suggesting that he wanted to "pull back" his sister and her children to stock his own hamlet. They did indeed return to live under his wing for several years.

As I have mentioned already, at the height of his festival Kimaola offered Newela in marriage to Iyahalina, seemingly as a reward for the efforts on his behalf which Iyahalina was making as principal *fofofo* partner. But it was also to Kimaola's advantage to place Iyahalina under his obligation as a wife-receiver. Moreover, it changed his sister's status to *fofofo* also, so that she took on an increasingly important role as hostess during the nightly entertainments. While Kimaola slept some evenings, she cooked and directed the activities of the other *fofofo* womenfolk, and she was almost as prominent in this regard as Tayaune, Kimaola's second wife. Widowed again when Iyahalina died, Newela did not remarry.

Kimaola's second sister, Ivinuya, was a few years his junior. After a brief marriage to an Ukevakeva man of little account, Kimaola married her to Kafataudi, leader of Valeutoli hamlet and Nouneya clan. This marriage was arranged as a reciprocal favour. Kafatuadi had "fed" and "looked after" Kimaola while they were in Port Moresby and the latter had been unable to find work. "When we return," Kimaola promised him, "you can marry my sister." Although several years younger than Kafataudi, Ivinuya was apparently willing. There were some tragic complications, however, for a Malabuabua suitor had tried to win her by love magic, and several years later he succeeded in seducing her. The acrimony between this man and Kafataudi was exacerbated by their status as traditional enemies, and they fought with food over the woman on several occasions. Kimaola took a particular liking to this sister's eldest son, Kafataudi's heir, and he used some extraordinarily subtle ploys to prize him away from his parents and to shame Kafataudi into acquiescence (Young 1971:238). Kafataudi died in 1975, and his widow and six children moved to Kimaola's hamlet.

With Mialaba, his youngest sister, Kimaola had a warm and affectionate relationship. He was indulgent and protective, something she spoke of herself.

> I always obeyed him and did whatever he advised. I looked after him when he was sick. He killed a pig for me once, and gave me many things when he returned from working abroad. I shared them out among my sisters.

Just as Kimaola kept their dead father's broken coconut bowl, Mialaba kept their mother's.

> Once when I was a young girl I was sleeping in a garden house with the cup by my head. My mother spoke to me in a dream and told me Kimaola was very sick. So I left at once in the dark, and I came to the village to nurse him.

Their solicitude was mutual:

221

Kimaola knew whenever I courted with too many boys. He would dream, then next day he would scold me and warn me of the boys he didn't trust. Our dead father has always protected us from sorcery by watching over us in this way.

Mialaba fell in love with a Fatavi man from Fergusson Island who dazzled her with his dancing at a festival. Kimaola permitted them to marry, but insisted they live for part of the first year in Kalauna.

When I went to Fatavi for the first time Kimaola was so said he didn't eat for a month, and when I returned he waited for me at the beach and cried to hear my voice. I also remembered him in my heart while I was away.

Her young husband died within the year, stricken by sorcery at another dance—a common fate, it is said, of skillful dancers, who evoke a jealousy as intense as that inspired by superb gardeners.

Kimaola permitted Mialaba a second choice and a few years later she married Matayuwa, an Ukevakeva man by whom she had five children. In 1971, however, her brother persuaded her to leave him and marry Iyahalina's son, who was persecuting him over the death of his father. This union lasted less than two years; then, with her brother's tacit approval, Mialaba divorced Adiyaleyale and returned to Matayuwa. (With what malicious glee Kimaola must have watched the antagonism flare between these two men—traditional enemies as their groups were, one the descendant of Malaveyoyo, the other descended from Tomonauyama—as several times they fought with fists in rivalry over Mialaba!)

The network of alliances Kimaola provided for himself through his own marriages, and those of his sisters and sisters' daughters, was unusually comprehensive. Although I cannot credit him with a master plan (simply with an astute talent for expedient matchmaking), he was remarkably successful in shaping the refractory and amorphous marriage system to meet various and immediate purposes of his own. There was scarcely an important descent group in Kalauna in which he did not at some time wield indirect influence as a brother-in-law or father-in-law, and in which he did not have some access to an obliging ear for their secrets. As one born without brothers, he amply compensated himself by acquiring influential affines, complaisant sisters' sons, and deferential classificatory sons-in-law.

Kimaola married three times. His first marriage to Makaleta of Ukevakeva amounted to nothing more than the common trial-marriage of shy youthful partners. The couple never cohabited, for Kimaola went to the Misima gold field to work for a year and he divorced her immediately on his return. He claimed to have "dreamed" about her adultery with a Malabuabua man, and took his revenge by shriveling his rival's yams with sorcery—an apt symbolic assault on the adulterer's potency. Kimaola next married Wa'aula, Tabwaika's widowed sister, who was a few years is senior. About 1960 he married another widow, Tayaune of Anuana II, a member of his *fofofo* group, who had lost two husbands in five years. She brought a son and two daughters to the marriage, all of whom were married themselves by 1973.

Both wives, Kimaola claimed, looked after him well, and their joint cohabitation (usually in separate rooms of the same house) was harmonious. He took some credit for this himself, declaring that it was always his policy to be impartial, gardening with them strictly in turn. He drolly admitted a failing, however:

I have one fault. I never carry firewood. I do not chop my wives' firewood either—just as if I were a *dimdim*. When we plant and my wife carries food home, she also has to bring the firewood. She chops it and scrapes coconut for our meal. But I do nothing. I just sit and chew betel nut. She cooks the food and then calls me, "Come and we'll eat."

To my knowledge, no shadow of scandal ever touched these marriages of Kimaola, and he valued both women highly for their productive efforts on his behalf. He was also grateful for the "respect" they had shown him—by which he meant that they never afflicted him with *doke,* the cuckold's debilitating disease (see Young 1971: 212).

Kimaola had no children of his own, a fact that others attributed to his wives' infertility and he to his own celibacy. In popular belief a woman's infertility is due to contraceptive magic, administered by her father or (far less often) by the husband himself. But in a society where concupiscence is held to be more damaging to one's manhood than celibacy, Kimaola could boast of his abstinence with good faith. For several months of the year at least, while he was performing the role of ritual guardian of the yams, his celibacy had the sanction of taboo: the yam crop would fail if he slept with his wives. But he went further than duty demanded in declaring that he never slept with them, and few people believed him. The reason he gave to me for not wanting children seemed specious: that he had no brothers and there would be no one to care for them if and when he died. He had fostered a number of young men (various sisters' sons, the sons of Tayaune and even Tobowa, and the sons of several Anuana men including his favorite, Kiyodi), so he was well provided with heirs and he had insured himself for old age. As for personal continuity, Kimaola sought, like the immortal Honoyeta (childless despite his two wives), to be remembered by other means.

∧∧∧∧

The roster of duties that Kimaola performed annually over a period of years in prospering the community's yam crop I have described elsewhere (1971:147-155). Some points need to be made here, however. Kimaola's rites and incantations, forming the great cycle of magic derived from the Oyatabu myth, are directed principally at his own yam plot but they are supposedly efficacious for the whole area of the community's plantings. They inaugurate the three main phases: planting, "killing," and harvesting the yams. By deciding when these phases shall begin, Kimaola imposes his own timing on the village's year. He is said to "make the sun right," as if the sun also obeys his behest.

As a consequence of his ritual involvement with the yam crop he is responsible for its general success or failure, though this is a politically negotiable matter. In practice it is not difficult for him to deny responsibility for failures caused by drought or crop pests. In Febru-

224

ary, 1968, for instance, a plague of scarab beetle grubs ravaged the yams. After announcing that someone was spoiling his efforts (he privately suspected Iyahalina or his son), Kimaola declared that he would perform no further magic that year. With more than a hint of resentment he called upon the villagers to harvest their yams whenever they chose, as he was washing his hands of the business (Young 1971:179).

It is easy to take the credit for a good crop, and some three out of every four are fair to good. (In any season, of course, some individuals' gardens suffer for one reason or another, but such personal misfortunes are explained by personal enmities.) As I have mentioned, however, the principle that a successful crop be credited to the garden magician is one that is open to challenge by sceptics and iconoclasts such as Tabwaika, who assert that the individual yam grower with his armory of personal magic can do just as well for himself without the help of Lulauvile's communal magic. An interesting point about the drought of 1965, supposedly caused by Didiala's sun magic, was that Didiala and Kimaola (who supported him) were apparently prepared to risk the yam crop in order to teach Tabwaika the folly of his anti-Lulauvile heresy. They were clearly depending upon there being a sufficient number of Lulauvile-supporting traditionalists (or "royalists," as Iyahalina seemed to think of them) who would revile Tabwaika as the cause of their misfortune rather than the men who were believed to have actually brought the drought.

At all events, for both "republicans" who deny Lulauvile's claim to preeminence and "royalists" who champion it, the penultimate phase of the yam gardening cycle is the crucial one for deciding the disposition of village power-politics in the year to come. This is the phase (after the yams have been "killed" and their leaves are withering) during which individual magic comes into its own. So in the last analysis, the reputations of individual yam gardeners and of the groups they belong to (as these reputations are challenged in *abutu* contests) ultimately depend not upon Lulauvile magic but upon the ritual resources and technical skills of each gardener. Thus does egalitarian ideology subvert Lulauvile aspirations to dominance.

The phase of "stealing the yams," as I have glossed it (1971:153-

154), is a month or so of furtive visits to the gardens when no communal magic whatsoever is performed, when each gardener sings his own spells to increase the size of his tubers at the expense of his neighbors'. Up to this point in the gardening cycle, Kimaola's magic has been performed to ensure and promote the "natural" growth of yams and to provide, as it were, a uniform prosperity of large, healthy tubers for everyone. (This is understood to be commensurate, of course, with well-known horticultural constraints such as soil types, slope and aspect of plots, quality of seed yams, and all the technical skills of planting and careful tending, skills that are distributed throughout the community no more evenly than is magical knowledge.)

By and large, much is thought to depend upon what happens during the "stealing" phase for the ultimate size of one's tubers, though what is or is not "stolen" is a mystical entity. The vexed question of the status of yam spirits (*maiyau*, "image, shadow, spirit"), and whether they have individual volition or whether they are transported from place to place by ancestral spirits invoked by incantations, is perhaps not one for logic to solve. My informants seemed to regard it as an improper question. In analogical thought, however, there seems to be little problem. The yams are quasi-human since, according to myth, they were born of human parents. They are said to have the faculty of hearing (although they cannot speak or see). They are responsive to the human voice, or any kind of noise for that matter (they can be disturbed by stamping on the ground or chopping firewood). They can also smell after a fashion, for they are able to detect the scent of cooked food or sexual secretions on a gardener's hands. Consequently, the yam gardener prohibits noise in the vicinity of his plot and avoids eating and sexual contact when he is about to plant or tend his yams. Finally, any kind of vocal disagreement (even gentle bickering between spouses) must be avoided in the gardens. If a man is planting a plot and someone comes by and questions his right to plant there, the man might as well replant his seeds elsewhere, for the yams would have heard and will probably refuse to grow.

So like humans! Yams are sensitive to slight, anxious about their rights, easily saddened and alienated. They respond with *unuwewe*

226

to the disrespectful gardener who does not treat them considerately. They can be said to "abandon" or "flee" their plots; though if it is due to the compulsion of magic, they are "chased away." It is because "yams are the children of a woman" that they are so susceptible to insult and *unuwewe*.

But how do yams prevent themselves from growing against the magical persuasion to do so? The magic calls upon ancestral spirits (not necessarily the singer's own, but the spirits of any famed yam growers of the past) to fetch or restrain the yam's *maiyau*. The conception, therefore, is of detachable yam spirits which can be induced to inhabit other gardens, leaving behind the shrunken appearances of yams with reduced food content. It would seem, then, that although the yams (or their spirits) are attributed with faculties and feelings, it is their spiritual guardians, the ancestors who, acting as agents for the humans who invoke them in magic, perform the invisible manipulations that result in big tubers. Between the human owner and his yam, therefore, Kalauna thought has interposed not one but two imaginary mediators: the removable spirit of the yam, and the independent ancestor spirit in service to the correct human incantation.

To no other plant or food crop in Kalauna is attributed so many human qualities. No other crop is so regularly spoken of as possessing *maiyau;* though coconuts, taro, bananas, and other crops are said to "flee" or "return" in periods of drought or prosperity, but these are ellipses that presume the unseen agency of ancestral spirits. Coconuts cannot hear or smell as yams are said to be able to do.[2] Although taro can be "stolen" magically, they do not shrivel with *unuwewe* to punish the planter. In short, only yams are humanized as metaphor for their central importance in Nidula economic and political life. Their fickleness also may be understood as a statement of men's fetishistic dependence on them to court fame and win reputation.

In presiding over every stage of the yam gardening cycle except the one that is crucial for individual reputations, the Lulauvile magician could reap prestige without incurring obloquy for uneven success or suspicion of favoritism. Despite his doubtful integrity in many matters, Kimaola was never once suspected of wielding the ritual powers of his public office for his own or Lulauvile's particular advantage. Moreover, should he ever have needed an escape clause, the doctrine that yams are sentient, sensitive, and humanly fickle provided one. Thus the adaptive closure of the belief system could support, at one and the same time, a self-contradictory social ideology of privileged access to ritual powers and a countervailing, individualistic milieu of egalitarianism.

∧∧∧∧

Kimaola's father taught him the great cycle of spells and accompanying rites that constitute the magic of Oyatabu, the name of the most famous of the class of large yams (*kuvi*). Kimaola rhetorically claimed descent from the parents of Oyatabu, a way of saying that the magic has always been associated with his line notwithstanding its junior status in Lulauvile I. For reasons I could never fathom, Didiala also claimed the same magic, or a very close variant of it. Both systems (if indeed they are different) go under the name of Yauyaba Kaviyuwana (the "brains" of Yauyaba, the sacred hill). I do not know if these two men ever quarreled over their claims, though Didiala's presentiment of death at the end of the sorcery debate (see chapter 6) followed his assertion that men die "because of Oyatabu." As we shall see, the principal taboo of Oyatabu is *vekwageya*, "fighting with words," especially between those who call one another "brother."

The following account of the myth is essentially Kimaola's, with some additions to make the story self-explanatory.

Ninialawata and her husband, Yaloyaloaiwau, lived near Yauyaba. She gave birth to Kawafolafola, but when she saw him she said: "What a black, ugly boy!" And she pierced his throat; hence his name [*kawa,* "throat"; *fola,* "pierce"]. Next she gave birth to Wameya [also the name of one of the Amphlett Islands], whom she washed and carefully put down. Then she became pregnant again and gave birth to Oyatabu, whom she washed and put down. Finally, she bore Kwavikwavi [another type of *kuvi* yam]. She fed her children milk and they grew well. When they were grown she said to the two boys: "Go and cut

Oyatabu's bed . . ." [At this early point in the story Ninialawata instructs her human children on the entire yam gardening cycle, from cutting the scrub to harvesting and preserving the tubers with *sisikwana* magic.]

Kawafolafola and Wameya carried their brother yams down to Bolubolu and loaded them onto a canoe. They paddled away, seeking a new home at Galuwata, stopping at various places along the coast to ask if they had reached it. Finally, they struck inland and found Galuwata high under the peak of Mount Madawa'a. They built their houses there, planted gardens, and their wives gave birth to sons.

Then the two brothers quarreled bitterly over their gardening prowess. They argued interminably about food and who was the better gardener. One night Wameya fastened up his house firmly and made rain. He was angry with his elder brother and had decided to leave. A flood rose and carried away his house to Luamata [an island to the north of Goodenough], then to Imulakaka [an island in Moresby Strait just north of Fergusson], and finally to Duduwe [beneath Taboo Mountain — Oyatabu — in the northeast corner of Fergusson Island]. At each place he urged his house to float further, for he could still see Galuwata. In the tidal mouth of a river beneath Oyatabu he said: "Here, this is far enough. We have come to Duduwe bringing our brother Oyatabu with us."

At Galuwata, Kawafolafola found that his crops would not grow, and when he tried to dig the ground he found only stones. His wife chided him: "Your younger brother has taken all the food away, and all the soil too." They spent days digging for food, but only managed to fill one pot. His wife complained. "You shouldn't have fought with your brother. Before there was plenty, now there is nothing." Kawafolafola didn't answer. They stayed hungry for a long time.

One day Kawafolafola announced a Modawa festival, although there was nothing to eat. He called all the birds to come and dance, and promised them a pig if they would do something for him. "I want you to fly to Oyatabu," he said. Binama [hornbill] said he would try. He started but did not get very far. He returned, and Bunebune [pigeon] tried. He set off but soon came back. All the birds tried in turn, but they all gave up and came back. Then Kawafolafola saw a small bird sitting on a stalk of grass. "Who's that?" he asked the other birds. "That's Kikifolu." "Can you go to Oyatabu and bring soil from my younger brother?" Kawafolafola asked him. "Ah, I'm only a small bird," said Kikifolu. "All these big ones have tried and failed. I'm just

229

a poor, aimless wanderer." But he tried while Kawafolafola chanted his name: "Kiki-kikifolu!"

He flew up and up, higher and higher, then he came down, down on the platform near Wameya's house at Oyatabu. He collapsed exhausted. Wameya's children ran up and saw him. "Hey, look what we've found!" An ant entered Kikifolu's ear and he woke up. "Who are you?" he asked the children. "We are Wameya's children." "Where is your father?" "You can hear him cutting trees in the bush. He is making a garden." "Go and tell him that Kikifolu has come to see him," said Kikifolu. They hurried off to find their father. "Come, father, a stranger has arrived." "What is his name?" asked Wameya. "We've forgotten." "Then go back and ask him," said their father. They ran back and asked the bird his name. "Kikifolu," he said. They went back to their father. "Father, a visitor has come." "What is his name?" "Er . . . ?" "Go back and tell him to give his name, for we are making new gardens." They returned once more for Kikifolu's name. "Are there any fallen logs on the road?" he asked them. "Yes, there is one." "Well, when you go back to your father repeat, 'Kikifolu-Kikifolu-Kikifolu' and walk around the log. Do not jump over it or you will forget my name." The children hurried back and went around the log. "Well, what's his name?" asked their father. "Kikifolu," they told him. "Go back and tell him that we are pulling his food up, and then go to the beach and spear some fish."

As Kikifolu waited he heard a conch shell blow. "What is that for?" he asked the children. "Oh, that's just for breakfast; they are bringing the food now." They dragged up a tuber as big as a canoe. They cooked, ate, and rested. Then Wameya asked Kikifolu: "What did my elder brother say to you?" "He said we should parcel up some soil." So Wameya took some black soil and wrapped it up in a banana leaf and put it in a basket. Then he took some sandy soil, clay soil, fine stony soil, red soil, brown soil and many other kinds, and wrapped each one and put it in the basket. "Now," he said to Kikifolu, "You fly up from my platform and I will call your name."

Up and up flew Kikifolu with the basket of soil on his neck, and he landed on the summit of Yauyaba. He slept for a while. When he awoke he emptied all the soils from their packages, singing the spell that Wameya had taught him. It began to rain and thunder and the soil was spread by the rain all over Goodenough Island.

Kikifolu returned empty-handed to Kawafolafola. "Did you ask my brother to come back?" said Kawafolafola. "Yes, but he said he didn't want to." Soon Kawafolafola saw that the soil had spread. He planted and grew big tubers, so he was happy and said, "Ah, Kikifolu really did bring back the soil."

Some time later Kawafolafola's wife said to him, "We should go and visit my brother-in-law." So they went down to the coast and cut two canoes, then they paddled to Duduwe where they landed on the beach. They went up a little way until they reached Wameya's house. Kawafolafola sent his son to find him in his gardens. When Wameya appeared he said: "How did you arrive without my knowing? I should have heard the rain and thunder [the portents of magicians]. That's what I would do to announce myself."

Wameya's wife cooked food, and there were tubers and fish piled high in dishes. Wameya did not let his brother finish one dish before giving him another. Kawafolafola began to cut one of the tubers in half, but it was very soft and his shell knife slipped, cutting his hand. Blood flowed profusely. "See, you have cut your hand; I warned you that the food was soft," said Wameya. Kawafolafola let the blood drip onto a small yam, wiped his bloody hand on it, then threw the food away. "Tomorrow we will go back home," he told Wameya.

Next day Wameya helped them load the canoes. He brought Oya-tabu and other *kuvi* yams and heaped so many on one canoe that it began to sink. He instructed Kawafolafola's son to get off the canoe and cut some sugar cane for poles, then he transferred all the *kuvi* to Kawafolafola's canoe, putting only small yams on his son's canoe. He told them to paddle home quickly, Kawafolafola with the big yams, his son with the small ones. "When you get close to Galuwata," he said, "you must paddle hard, or the thunder will break your vessels." They reached the shore of Goodenough. Kawafolafola landed safely with the *kuvi*, but the rain and thunder broke up his son's canoe and the small yams were lost.

They lived at Galuwata for a while, then Wameya and his family came to repay their visit. When they approached Galuwata, Wameya announced himself with rain, thunder, and lightning. The rain lulled Kawafolafola and his family to sleep, so when Wameya arrived he surprised them. "Ha, didn't you recognize my portent? I caught you asleep in your house." Kawafolafola protested that he didn't usually stay indoors all day long. "Soon your sister-in-law will bring food and we'll eat," he said. His wife appeared and cooked for the visitors. While he was eating, Wameya tried to cut a tuber with his shell knife, but it was so hard he broke the edge. "Ah, look, I've broken my knife

231

on your food," he said to Kawafolafola. "I warned you my food was hard," he replied. "We cut only small pieces, very gently."

When they had finished, Wameya sat back and chewed betel nut. Then he said to his elder brother: "Here at Galuwata you will plant your yams in big mounds with the top of the seed poking out. And you will need a stick to support it or it will break off, like the edge of my knife. Over there beneath Oyatabu I shall plant my small soft yams, red as your blood, without mounds or sticks to support them. I have made things fair and square with you. Now I will go back to Duduwe and never return to Galuwata."

On the etiological level this myth explains a number of cultural givens, notably, that yams are of human ancestry and that control of them is vested in men; that yam cultivation on Goodenough and Fergusson differs in practice, as do the types and quality of their respective crops. The most dramatic theme of the story, however, concerns the enduring quarrel between two brothers, for it is their mutual antagonism that establishes critical and permanent differences. It is interesting that a permutation of this myth describes the quarrel as occurring between Oya Madawa'a (one of the three main Goodenough peaks) and Oyatabu, which abandons his "brother" and settles in its present location on Fergusson Island.[3] (It might be added that this identification of men with their respective mountains is echoed, in yet other stories, in a manner that links their "moving" and "sitting still" to the *manumanua* ceremony. Mountains, after all, are the most weighty symbols of "anchoring" imaginable.)

In Kimaola's version, however, human interest is paramount, and the myth is addressed to the problem of the quasi-human status of yams and the distribution of control over them. The elder brother is stigmatized at birth by his mother. He is repeatedly shamed and insulted by his younger brother, and quite literally deprived of the things that matter most: food and the means to grow it. His nagging wife makes it clear, however, that he is to blame for their misfortune by being so quarrelsome. Only with the aid of a tiny bird does he restore to Nidula the soils that the younger brother, in *unuwewe*, took away with him to Fergusson. Again, it is the generous second-born who, having clearly demonstrated his superiority as a gardener

232

and weather magician, returns the *kuvi* yams to his elder brother. The distribution of customs and powers that the myth establishes results from their reciprocal visiting, events that are precise inversions of one another. (Arriving unannounced by portents, Kawafolafola finds his younger brother working; he is fed sumptuously and cuts his hand with a knife on soft food, and reddens the small yams which will become Fergusson's specialty. Announced by portents, Wameya arrives to find his elder brother sleeping; he is fed meagerly and breaks his knife on hard food, which forever will be Goodenough's specialty.)

These later sequences expound differences between brothers notwithstanding their natural similarity; whereas the first, magic-laden part of the myth (most of which I omitted), expounds similarities between men and yams notwithstanding their natural differences. Thus, the magic that derives from this myth establishes a man/yam homology and argues anthropomorphically from the first to the second. Similarities are maximized and differences minimized as a means of metaphoric control. (We may note, though, that this very control generates the human tragedy of the myth: a fierce fraternal competition, such that differences between brothers are maximized and similarities minimized.)

In his rites of Oyatabu, Kimaola brings to bear his own similarity to the mythical characters. He invokes Kawafolafola and Wameya as ancestors; he reenacts Kawafolafola's plea for the Oyatabu yam spirits to return from Duduwe; and he enjoins Kikifolu to replenish the soil of Nidula.

/\\/\\/\\

Kawafolafola, the enigmatic antihero, is a far more significant figure in Nidula lore than Kimaola's version indicates. He appears in many myths told elsewhere on the island, though insofar as these are known in Kalauna they are scorned as incorrect. In one set of such myths Kawafolafola is *unuwewe* because his grandchildren laugh at his comic and futile attempts to eat: the food falls through the hole in his throat. He makes rain and creates a flood that scatters food and people, resulting in diverse customs and the babel of tongues. In another set of stories he takes a different revenge, carrying off his disrespectful grandchildren on a canoe voyage and marooning them on an atoll. These stories borrow the theme of Manukubuku or Kuyokwokula, and in one version the grandsons avenge themselves by cutting off Kawafolafola's head. In another, they turn the tables and maroon their grandfather, who is then consumed by demonic *balauma*.[4]

To survey the whole corpus of myths in which Kawafolafola appears as culture-hero would take me well beyond the task in hand. I mention his other guises, however, to substantiate a point Kimaola made in a cryptic comment: "Kawafolafola invented festivals and was the first *kaiwabu*." At first I took this to be the specious claim of one who was eager to legitimize his ambition to dominate Kalauna, and who thus fondly fancied himself to be of a preeminent line. But this was no literal charter; rather, as other commentators confirmed, it was a metaphorical exegesis of Kawafolafola's mythical status. Although Kimaola's version makes no mention of it, other myths attribute him with the discovery of taro, even though he was unable to eat it himself.[5]

Let us consider more closely Kawafolafola's curious disability: a pierced throat, such that it is difficult if not impossible for him to ingest food. This feature is pure invention, and does not occur in nature as does Honoyeta's sloughed skin, Kiwiwiole's feathers, and the clamped beak of the *manukubuku* bird. We might ask what sort of riddle has to be posed to produce an answer like "the hero has a hole in his neck"? Putting the question to Kimaola, it was Kiyodi who answered first: "A man who eats to no purpose." That is, a glutton, like one afflicted with the terrible magic of *tufo'a*. As such, Kawafolafola would be an antihero, one who wasted food in the vain attempt to quell an insatiable appetite. But Kimaola averred that Kawafolafola had surmounted his handicap and made, in effect, a virtue of it. He was a *tolokona*, a man who finds it necessary to eat only sparingly, if at all, thereby conserving his food. (Just like, I need hardly point out, Kimaola himself.)

Thus does Kawafolafola epitomize the *kaiwabu*. Whether or not he made a virtue of necessity in becoming a *lokona* man, content

with small gardens and hard food, practiced in hunger by the deprivation caused by his brother Wameya, Kawafolafola is by his very
name and deformity a food-conserver who restricts ingestion. And
whether or not he was the first to plant and harvest taro, and the
first to sponsor a festival, his behavior conforms to the definition of
kaiwabu as one who conspicuously does not eat in order to bestow
food munificently upon others. Significantly, too, Kawafolafola is
unable to laugh (Young 1977*b*:86).

∧∧∧∧

On one occasion I asked Kimaola what lesson he derived from his
Oyatabu story. He took me quite literally to mean the injunctions or
"rules" imposed upon him by the myth, but he also took the opportunity to moralize about the hard work he expected of his helpers.

> Ninialawata gave this advice to Kawafolafola. She told him to sing the
> magic for his brothers, the *kuvi* yams. "But you cannot quarrel and
> you cannot eat them yourself. Nor can you eat eels, coconuts, *iloloke*
> or *laiwai* [foods which pierce or are pierced?], lest the leaves of the
> yams get holes. And if you break these taboos your eyes will swell as if
> you had been poisoned." Oyatabu's mother taught us these rules. And
> another thing about our yam story: it means hard work. I told my
> "sons" [two of the Anuana men he fostered, but who no longer lived
> with him in 1973], "Hey, you work hard and we can live well. I'm get-
> ting old, but if you garden properly then I won't need to." But they
> didn't listen to me. They planted only for themselves and their chil-
> dren; they walked about aimlessly. I told them our yam story many
> times, but they didn't listen. Only Kiyodi listened. When I die he can
> become boss. The others don't test their blood by trying. I never got
> angry with them. I didn't chase them away. I only gave my advice and
> they rejected it. I told them the lesson of Oyatabu, but they didn't
> heed.

Of the characters in his myth with whom Kimaola might have
chosen to identify, I suspect the one that appealed to him most was
Kikifolu, the brave and busy little bird who mediates between the

estranged brothers, flies far and high, and delivers salvation for the island by replenishing its very soil. I recall how Kimaola was incensed at Iyahalina's "borrowing" this theme for his version of Kiwiwiole (and I confess that for a long time I confused the two bird-heroes, as Iyahalina may have intended me to). I had been puzzled by the sequence where Kikifolu's name is repeatedly forgotten by Wameya's children, though I could see that it was an analogous expression of the difficulty of communication that irked the two brothers and that led them to ignore one another's warnings. Kimaola tried to enlighten me by saying, "It was an insult to Kikifolu to forget his name, but he was patient; and when they did call his name it rose up high."

We have seen repeatedly the power of insult to provoke *unuwewe* in both myths and reality. We know that Kalauna people often behave as if words uttered by the human voice had some purchase on the invisible, as if qualities were actually transferred by means of metaphor and metonymy. The performance of naming not only states the case of what is desired, but also helps to bring it about. Hence the insult, an exemplar of the hostile speech-act, is a potent political weapon.

The ultimate payoff in *abutu,* after one has defeated a rival by giving him more food than he can repay, is the ability to insult him with impunity (and with evident accuracy): "You are a useless gardener who grows tiny yams." Again, there are the more esoteric flights of abuse such as the one uttered to Kiwiwiole: "You are a bird who drifts on flotsam." Political ascendancy in Kalauna is attested by calculated insult of this kind, and it evokes complementary gestures of humiliation: submissive silence or the *unuwewe* of withdrawal.

Insult, then, is the antithesis of the name-calling that occurs at a public distribution of food, when the named recipients are thereby acknowledged as holders of legitimate statuses. Many insults are intended to negate legitimacy (like the one directed at Kiwiwiole), while the insult of forgetting humble Kikifolu's name seemed to deny him any importance whatsoever. Yet when Kikifolu's name *was* called he flew high. As it is said of the man frequently called to receive pork or food at distributions, "his name ascends" in fame.

But there can also be ironic connotations to some of the names

236

called at distributions (Young 1971:237). In the case of *ketowai* gifts bestowed upon enemies and rivals at the climax of a festival, the names called by the *fofofo* are linked to delicts, so that the "legitimizing" act is a denigrating and unwelcome one. "Abela, my enemy, come to receive your pig and do not sleep with my brother's wife any more!" Publicly pronounced an adulterer, Abela's name flies low with ignominy.

The confined, face-to-face polity of Kalauna is acutely sensitive to the nuances of name-calling and veiled insult. It could not be otherwise given that Lulauvile's status as food-bringers and food-guardians implicitly derogates the other clans. As a corollary, Lulauvile claims are constantly put to the test. The following incident, which occurred in early 1967, nicely illustrates the Lulauvile conundrum as well as Kimaola's studied use of insult as a political weapon.

The agricultural officer at Bolubolu Patrol Post asked Iyahalina to report to him the number of Kalauna coconut trees damaged by a locust plague. Taking his son, who could count and write, Iyahalina visited every corner of the village lands. One expedition involved the inspection of Ukevakeva hamlet's coconuts on a parcel of land given over to the cultivation of bananas. While threading his way through the plantation Iyahalina was seen by Awalovai, younger brother of Tomoadikuyau, one of Ukevakeva's leaders. Later that day, his task completed, Iyahalina was relaxing in the garden house of his son-in-law on land adjacent to Ukevakeva's. Suddenly, Awalovai appeared with a huge bunch of bananas.

"Iyahalina!" he called, trembling with the passion of one who gives food coercively. "You are Lulauvile, enemy of my group! I saw you inspecting our gardens, counting our food. Maybe you were also spoiling our crop with your spells. You can call your *fofofo* to take these bananas, and we can make *abutu*."

Iyahalina was silent, though another Lulauvile man who was present protested that he had only been counting coconuts for the government. "Be quiet," Iyahalina told him. "They are our traditional enemies, and if they want to make *abutu* we cannot stop them."

They returned to the village and sought out Didiala and Kimaola. Didiala was unwell, so Kimaola took charge as *fofofo* spokesman.

He decided immediately to call Awalovai's bluff, and sent word to all Lulauvile men to be ready before dawn next day. They bathed in the river, smeared their faces with ochre and charcoal and put hornbill feathers in their hair. Kalauna is a compact village, peopled with light sleepers avid for intrigue. The Lulauvile men's passage through the hamlets to Ukevakeva was marked by ripples of movement in the houses as curious eyes peered through coconut-leaf doors. In the dim grey light the men of Ukevakeva were already climbing down from their houses as the Lulauvile party arrived. Iyahalina began to orate at once.

"Forgive me, my friends, coming like this in the night. I stay uselessly in my house. I have no food in my gardens. I am, as you know, like a bird. I drift aimlessly. I flutter around in the bush. I steal bananas like the green parrot. So, truly, you were very kind to give me food yesterday. I have talked to my *fofofo,* and they agreed that we should come to you for more food [the first prestation in an *abutu* contest]."

He went on in this vein for several minutes, stressing his humility and poverty, gushing feigned gratitude. Tomoadikuyau, to whom the speech was principally addressed, hung his head in silence, an icon of embarrassment. Then it was Kimaola's turn. His irony joined to a rising rage.

"You are all wealthy men in Ukevakeva. You have many big gardens and many kinds of food. Do you use your hands or do you use machines? The rest of us only use our hands to plant, so *abutu* is an important matter. Its meaning is this: we show the strength of our hands and test one another. Why do you take it lightly, as if you grew food with machines like Europeans?"

To save some face, Tomoadikuyau turned on his brother Awalovai and berated him for his impetuosity. Then he spoke to Iyahalina and Kimaola.

"I am truly sorry, my friends. You will remember we made *abutu* last year [in October 1966, when a contest was provoked by Adiyaleyale's affair with the wife of an Ukevakeva man]. How can we make *abutu* again so soon? We do not want to cause more enmity."

Kimaola replied with another show of anger: "Then why did Awalovai say to himself, 'Ah, this is our enemy in my gardens. Caught him! Now we can challenge im to *abutu*'? He must know you have plenty of food, more than the rest of us, or how could he have been so silly? No, we have come for your food and we are waiting to be given it. Or should we go home and get our food ready for you?"

Neither Tomoadikuyau nor Awalovai answered, the former an unwilling party to the empty challenge of the latter. The sun was beginning to touch the sago-thatch of the roofs. As if waiting for its blessing, Kimaola said: "All right. There is no food for us here, so we must laugh. You are afraid of us, and of the amount of food we could give you, so we are going to make fun of you. You invited us, we came, but we go away empty-handed." And Kimaola led a Lulauvile chorus of "Aha... ye!" followed by an insulting ditty:

> *Dududu manua*
> *Abilovena*
> *Wana bawe aitoya*
>
> Dududu house
> Let it go
> Be like wild pigs.[6]

Having chanted this a couple of times at their hapless enemies, the Lulauvile men departed, delighted to see that the rest of the village had heard their taunts. To have insulted them so loudly in their own hamlet was a considerable achievement. Nor did the matter end there. Kimaola told Lulauvile men to miss no opportunity to rub in their advantage during the following weeks. Like a schoolmaster giving license to his boys to stone members of a rival school, Kimaola exhorted: "Every time you see them, whether in their gardens or fishing at the beach, you must cry 'A...ha...ye!' And if they get angry you must tell me, and I'll talk to them again."

∧∧∧∧

Kimaola's blunt and passionate public style was revealed on another occasion, when, responding to an insult to Lulauvile and failing to avenge it, he indulged in a display of resentment to save his own face. It was just before I left Kalauna in July 1968, when his festival had only run half its course and his ambition seemed vaunting. The event he precipitated dismayed his *fofofo* and baffled his enemies.

Biale of Aluwaita overheard malicious gossip in Wailolo concerning a Kalauna woman and her Wailolo husband, who, following some quarrel with the latter's kin, had earlier sought refuge with Kimaola. The gossips went further, and maligned Lulauvile people for their "*kaiwabu* behavior" and other affectations, "always walking through our village, carrying food to the market along the road we look after." Even worse, Kimaola's Wailolo enemy (who had given him a large *ketowai* pig the previous year at the conclusion of their Sagali festival) was heard to say, "We need take no notice of Lulauvile people. Their yams have been spoiled by grubs." On being told this by Biale, Kimaola alerted his *fofofo*. "Very well," he said, "we shall fight them with taro." He announced his intention of paying back the pig he owed Wailolo, using it as a lure to challenge *abutu*.

Iyahalina was dispatched to Wailolo to invite them to collect the pig. The rest of Lulauvile was sent to the gardens for taro and bananas, which Kimaola instructed should be placed out of sight on the edge of the village, so that he could spring the surprise *abutu* on his enemies when they came to collect their debt. But there was a disappointment in store for him. A Wailolo man returned with Iyahalina to explain that they did not want the debt to be repaid just yet: they would wait until the conclusion of Kimaola's Fakili, when custom decreed that such debts should be paid.

In trying to settle his festival debts out of turn Kimaola was violating the rules, but having done it before and succeeded he would try it again. His creditors were usually too intimidated to refuse. To understand this point it is necessary to appreciate that there are times when it is as inconvenient to receive a pig as it is to have to give one; and much political strategy hinges upon timing: when to give, when to receive, and when to pay back. Men strive to become unindebted, but, generally speaking, the more ambitious they are the more debts they incur. It was an easy temptation for Kimaola to try to coerce people into accepting his returns when it suited him, rather than when they wanted him to pay back. The festival system provides a predictable and regulated context, a kind of moving feast for the repayment of debts. To force repayments on "enemies" outside that context is to undermine the system.

Custom was, then, on the side of Kimaola's Wailolo enemies. They could be assured of their repayment in time, but meanwhile they preferred to retain the ascendancy of creditors. Kimaola cajoled and insulted provocatively, but in vain, for the Wailolo representative adamantly refused. Everyone knew that unless he could be persuaded to accept the repayment (the "bait," as Kimaola saw it) any *abutu* challenge would be redundant.

When he had gone home, a disgruntled group of Lulauvile men sat on Kimaola's *atuaha,* consoling themselves with expressions of frustrated bravado. Suddenly Kimaola leaped to his feet and snapped the order to Kiyodi to kill his pig, the pig which would have been given to Wailolo. Kiyodi obeyed, spearing it as it slept. A kind of bloodlust seized Kimaola as the anger of his rejection took full hold. He called to two young men who had promised pigs for his Fakili to slaughter them also. Iyahalina, who was chief *fofofo* to Kimaola at the time, was visiting another hamlet, but someone went running to tell him that Kimaola was killing the festival pigs and Iyahalina scurried back to Heloava as fast as his legs would carry him. He protested, but it was too late; the pigs were already dead and Kimaola was threatening (verbally at least) to kill even more. Kimaola explained that he was "ashamed." He had promised Lulauvile and the rest of Kalauna *abutu,* with sumptuous feasting to follow. Well, there would be no *abutu,* since Wailolo men were "afraid." But Kalauna could still eat pork, plus the food Lulauvile had brought from the gardens in readiness for the abortive contest. He instructed his *fofofo* to lay out six piles, the largest for themselves and the other five for the remaining clans. The pork was distributed similarly. Kimaola and his hamlet, of course, could eat none of it.

The controlled and spiteful fury with which Kimaola set about massacring the pigs earmarked for his Fakili distribution (still many months hence) was an impressive display of *veumaiyiyi.* He seemed to be saying to the villagers, "See, our enemies have evaded combat and deprived us of the spoils of victory, but I, your leader, will indulge you with the rewards I promised. Go ahead, and enjoy this

241

feast at my expense." So Kimaola, too, was susceptible to the temptation of *unuwewe*. Though as it proved, his Fakili was not seriously disadvantaged and he found other pigs to replace those he had so recklessly killed.

Although he failed to pressure Wailolo in this instance, it was acknowledged to be one of his special talents to force others to engage in *abutu*. Secure in his reputation as a sorcerer, he could press further than most men in provoking anger by invective. He made such moves whenever *abutu* was in the offing and he wanted to see some action. He often made them mischievously, careless of the consequences for those he affected to support. "I want to see what you can do," he would say. "I want you to test one another, to see who digs the biggest yams nowadays." On several occasions I watched him exacerbate quarrels in this fashion. The antagonists might have mentioned *abutu* in the heat of the moment, playing at brinkmanship in the knowledge that there would be no enthusiasm for *abutu* among their respective kin and *fofofo*. Then Kimaola would goad them, stir the quarrel, and tell them to "show" their pigs and their yams. "I am boss of yams," he would say. "You have my permission to fight with them." They found it harder to back down once Kimaola had prodded them to test their mettle.

His favorite role in *abutu* (when he was not challenging it himself) was to play the double game of assisting both sides. Like any other Kalauna man his primary allegiance was to his agnates: at the widest span the whole of Lulauvile, which included his *fofofo*. But thanks to the widespread network of affines he had created, he could rationalize the deployment of his resources in support of almost any other clan he chose. When Adiyaleyale made *abutu* with Sikomu of Ukevakeva, Kimaola urged the protagonists to the point of no return, though more conciliatory voices in the village would have favored a settlement of the quarrel by some other means. Kimaola also encouraged Adiyaleyale to believe that he would support him to the utmost in the *abutu;* albeit on the rather dubious grounds that Kimaola's grandfather had assisted Malaveyoyo kill an Ukevakeva girl, and that he was therefore a traditional enemy of Ukevakeva as much as any man in Heloava (see chapter 4). But during the contest Kimaola contrived to send his biggest yams to Ukevakeva under cover of darkness, so that the next day they could be given to embarrass Adiyaleyale. His excuse, when this defection came to light, was that his sister Mialaba had married into Ukevakeva and he was helping her to avenge a personal insult by Adiyaleyale.

$$\wedge\wedge\wedge\wedge\wedge$$

Such deceptions were typical of Kimaola's political style. He appears to have feigned and feinted through life, using the confounding artifices of one who grows up beset by handicaps. Initially, with less to lose than most, he seemed prepared to risk obloquy, deprivation and even death in the pursuit of his ambitions. The tension between the impulse to achieve and fear of the consequences which had so troubled Didiala troubled Kimaola, too, but not until he had clambered to the top and found nowhere else to go. And although, like Iyahalina, he was concerned to legitimize his position, he scorned legal niceties and was impatient of the pedantic moralizing Iyahalina relished.

Kimaola's myths, Oyatabu and Honoyeta, were as pertinent to his life as he chose to make them. Oyatabu, perhaps, spoke to his sense of solitude and deprivation; Honoyeta to his devious and sometimes suicidal anger. But *unuwewe,* the emotional stock-in-trade of most heroes, was less befitting a man like Kimaola who had, as it were, conferred a heroic status upon himself and spent a lifetime forcing others to acknowledge it. For Didiala and Iyahalina, and for the ordinary man whose name is maligned or whose status is impugned, *unuwewe* is the recourse that elicits the balm of contrition and restores dignity. For Kimaola, whose hold on public sympathy was insecure (thanks to his inflated vision of personal destiny and the means he adopted to attain it), *unuwewe* was a technique of uncertain efficacy. He surrendered himself to the sympathies of the community with neither the frequency nor the confidence of Didiala or Iyahalina.

Kimaola did not publicly claim the Honoyeta myth in the way that he proudly claimed Oyatabu. More than once I asked him to tell it to me, but he always refused, even though he knew I had vis-

243

ited Honoyeta's grave in Galuwata. He was afraid, he said, that if he were to tell me the sun would "spoil everything," for the sun was Honoyeta's portent and the story should not lightly be told. But I suspect a more personal reason for his refusal: he would have exposed himself to an uncomfortable degree in the telling.

More than once Kimaola spoke cryptically of Honoyeta as the "cause," the "origin" of cannibalism, as if the hero signified for him oral conquest or glorified achievement by oral means. With this clue, we can see that Kimaola's identity and personal style are indeed characterized by modes of oral rebellion: his purported rejection of his mother's milk; his anoretic disposition to eat as little as possible, by preference as well as in the service of his ambition. There was also his aptitude for oral aggression by insult, invective, and incantations; his favorite sorcery technique was said to be "stealing the voice" of his victim. Had cannibalism persisted during his lifetime, one might imagine Kimaola as its most enthusiastic advocate.

∧∧∧∧

Kimaola's own persecution was real. Unlike the fancied ones of Iyahalina and Didiala, which were the fabrications of rumors, Kimaola's persecution was as earnest as the exposure of Honoyeta's duplicity and as awesome as the shredding of his skin. The collusion between the deceiver and his public had reached the intolerable point where he was tempted to own to acts of sorcery and mystical threat in order to enhance his notoriety. These were not confessions. Kimaola was not being victimized or scapegoated; rather, he willfully seized blame the better to intimidate. But the more he did so the more inclined people were to attribute random woes to him, including deaths. It was a dangerous and spiraling game of deception within deception that Kimaola played during the years of his Fakili. He did not, like Honoyeta, seek death for himself, though he spoke of it frequently and expectantly. "Enjoy yourselves, do not fight, and go home happy with the food," he declaimed at the grand climax of his festival. "And when I die, as soon I must, you will remember my Fakili."

It was Didiala who died instead. Inevitably, Kimaola was suspected, even by those who were closest to him. The community read
his ambition and surmised his motive: "Why does this old man's
name still fly higher than mine?" There was no immediate retribution, though some people attributed the following year's drought to
Anuana's revenge. Yet others suspected Kimaola himself of bringing
the *loka,* invoking Honoyeta's wrath to punish the community for
Siboboya's death the same year. Then it was Iyahalina's turn to die,
with the consequences I described at the beginning of the chapter.
It needs only to take up the story of his son's vengeance.

Adiyaleyale was in no doubt that Kimaola had killed his father
through the perfidy of his new wife, Kimaola's elder sister. Moved
by grief and outrage — a Hamlet troubled by his father's spirit — Adiyaleyale threatened his stepmother with violence and embarked on a
veritable rampage. With the courage of righteous anger he confronted Kimaola directly. In his capacity as village councillor he
wrote to the government officer at Bolubolu, forewarning him that
he was about to bring in a sorcerer to be charged. Then he ran-
sacked Kimaola's house for evidence, tearing up ginger plants, forcing Kimaola to eat the leaves he found in his basket, tossing out
stones, bones, knives, and killing (so he claimed) two flying foxes.[7]
Adiyaleyale could not stop ("Watch out," he warned. "I have no
brakes"), and riding the wave of his fury he tackled several other
men too. They denied sorcery but somehow incriminated one another and Kimaola, passing blame like betel nut.

By now Kimaola was frightened. Adiyaleyale took three suspects
to Bolubolu, and on the way they pleaded with him. Kimaola
begged him to pity "a sick old man" and drop the charges, promising to swear on the Bible that he would never make sorcery again.
Adiyaleyale was scornful: "You are no Christian. You told everyone
you were a follower of Saint Lucifer." Kimaola tried bribery, and
offered Adiyaleyale his youngest sister, Mialaba. With his weakness
for spirited and pretty women, Adiyaleyale was sorely tempted. "She
is married already! But would I be such a fool? My father married
your sister and died!" Nevertheless, faced with the alternative reality
of the European officer's court, Adiyaleyale watered down the
charges and relaxed his demands. (He had intended to ask that
Kimaola be marooned like Kawafolafola on Imulakaka, an unin-

habited islet that can be seen from Kalauna.) The government officer lectured them, warning that the law punished sorcerers and instructing Adiyaleyale to keep an eye on them and to report them again if he heard of their practicing it. There were no charges.

They returned to the village and Adiyaleyale suspended his witch-hunt. A few weeks later he amiably agreed to take Mialaba as his second wife. He felt relatively secure so long as he remained councillor.[8]

For a time people obeyed Adiyaleyale's instruction that no one should consort with Kimaola or any of the other named sorcerers, but during the bustle and easy sociability of Lulauvile's new Fakili the rule was forgotten. Kimaola began to play his own game of undermining Adiyaleyale's support by calling his festival into contempt. He took to curing again in neighboring villages. By 1973, when I visited Kalauna, he had reclothed himself with the shreds of dignity. He seemed quieter, saner than I remembered him five years earlier. "He's a nice man now that he's discarded his sorcery," remarked one Mulina man. "Yes, but he can't throw away what's in his heart," said another. I observed that he was still a force in local politics, provoking *abutu* when he could, stirring the quarrels of others, orating deviously—a Melanesian Machiavelli. But it was true that no recent deaths had been attributed to him, and no delayed childbirths had occurred since Adiyaleyale denounced him at those reportedly electric village meetings of 1971. His flagrant intimidations had ceased.

Kimaola had not died at the peak of realizing his ambitions, when, aspiring to be the very rock of Kalauna he held the village in fear of him. The anticlimax of his persecution came when he had virtually exhausted his possibilities for achievement. There was nothing left for him to do but survive. When I saw him again, in 1977, he seemed mellow, relaxed and almost jovial. His wizened yet cherubic face had lost some of its guardedness. He had founded a spacious new hamlet with two or three of his old supporters. A bright and airy site amid the gardens, its view extended to the Amphlett Islands, and but for the northern shoulder of Fergusson one could have seen Oyatabu.

It was the old custom for the leader of a hamlet to build his eldest son and heir a house for the unmarried youths of the place. They decorated it with the unique designs of their lineage and bespelled its main post with powerful *sisikwana* magic, so that the best yams of the hamlet could be kept there securely, to harden and finally to rot. Any visitor to the hamlet could deduce the status of its leader by the size and splendor of his son's house, though the leader himself might dwell in a hovel. Likewise, at the climax of a festival, the sons and daughters of the sponsors mount a platform and conspicuously play the role of *kaiwabu,* deflecting attention by their haughty and theatrical demeanor from the real "chiefs of the feast," their elders, who sit modestly in the shade of their houses. Having at last learned Honoyeta's lesson, it seemed, Kimaola now affected retirement. He sported a Mickey Mouse T-shirt, a curiously apt expression of the political philosophy of disguise and dissimulation bequeathed by Honoyeta. Kimaola would practice penury for a while, sending his wives to the gardens while he sat quietly, pigless, by his hearth, consoled, perhaps, by Honoyeta's secret that reality is more than skin deep.

9
Revelations

The myth does not exist that is not the
ever-renewed revelation of a reality which
so imbues the being that he makes his
behaviour conform to it. Short of this, it
slowly hardens into a story which will
become cold one day.

—Maurice Leenhardt, *Do Kamo*

/\/\/\/\

If there were brick walls on Nidula one might expect to see them
daubed with the slogan "Honoyeta Lives." It was Adimakaiya, an
elder of Iwaoyana clan, who gave me the most profound formulation of Honoyeta's "secret." He had spent the best part of twenty
years dwelling in his gardens, seeking refuge from real or imagined
persecutions. But long before that he had been taught, almost un-
willingly, fragments of Honoyeta's magic by his mother's brother,
Nawakelukelu of Anuana. When the latter died, Adimakaiya
wanted to bury the sun stones (called *vidona*, Honoyeta's flesh) in
the same grave "because they are evil." The dead man's son, Taukwadu, forbade it, and now Ewahaluna (Taukwadu's son) had inherited them.

Before telling me Honoyeta's secret, Adimakaiya narrated the story in elliptical phrases, quickened by gestures of hand and head. He concluded by telling of the deaths of all those who had touched or tasted the hero's body. Then he whispered the cryptic formula. Honoyeta's message was *domudomuna kwakwahana,* "destruction unto death." I asked him to elaborate. "Everything withers and dies," he said. "Leaves fall off the trees, bark peels, plants droop, the ground goes hard like stone, men and animals die from hunger." Then he offered a second, familiar key: *unuwewe.* And in his explanation of this he mentioned two motives, *miwa* and *ulo,* revenge and suicide. "Honoyeta gave himself to be killed," he added, "like Jesus Christ."

Unuwewe, then, is the cause that precipitates vengeful self-sacrifice and an apocalypse of death and destruction. With remarkable perspicuity Adimakaiya said, "Honoyeta did it for himself, but we do it for others." By this he meant that the self-contained hero, aloof and asocial, avenged his own death even as he sought it. His double-skinned duplicity effected a kind of circularity (the now-familiar serpentine resentment) of provocation and revenge. Men cannot accomplish this by themselves, for they are in and of society, bound by reciprocity, sustained in mutual dependence. Therefore, "we do it for others"; we seek the vengeful punishment of those we believe to be responsible for our injuries and the deaths of our close ones. When this vengeance is pursued in Honoyeta's mode we devastate blindly in rage, grief, and resentment, conjuring the bones of Honoyeta to turn. And because our own gardens will suffer and because our neighbor's loss is also our own, we sacrifice something of ourselves too.

Thus does Honoyeta's tragic model cleverly conjoin the two principal modes of victimage. These, as we have seen throughout the book, are projective ("we need our enemies," as Kalauna people admit), and introjective ("I'll make you sorry"). In the first mode Honoyeta provokes the very behavior he punishes; in the second he abnegates himself to abnegate others. Because he is singular in his duplicity they are twin aspects of his acts of abandonment and self-sacrifice. In Honoyeta the two modes (in their extreme forms of homicidal revenge and suicide) are exemplified, apotheosized, by the same mortifying hero. And in every other hero, from Malave-

249

yoyo to Kimaola, we have heard plangent echoes of the same *unu-wewe* principle. They are men who poison their bodies or scorch the crops to bring down the sky.[1]

In Adimakaiya's mind the link between Honoyeta's curse and the death of a loved one—his daughter—was palpable. The black grief of loss hardens into an *unuwewe* that would condemn the world to conflagration—or rather to cannibalism, for Honoyeta's terrible curse was the power to make men kill and eat one another. How, then, could Honoyeta be likened to Jesus Christ? Adimakaiya was not the only man in Kalauna to draw the parallel. His sister's son's son, Ewahaluna, who had inherited the sun stones, did so too. Claiming to be of Honoyeta's line, Ewahaluna observed taboos on eating "yellow" coconuts and—his own imposition—working on Fridays, since this was the day of the week Jesus died.

In other villages the notion that Honoyeta was Nidula's Christ had the force of doctrine. When a young guide from Iwabu pointed out to me the abandoned site of Yabiliva, his words were: "That is where they killed Jesus." The Catholic mission, whose headquarters are in northern Goodenough, has unwittingly abetted the identification. In 1974 it approved the enactment of Honoyeta's myth at a church celebration. The villagers of Iwabu performed their ancestors' roles, "sacrificing" a complaisant young man splendidly adorned as the hero, tearing coconut "flesh" off him and trying vainly to cook it, then staggering under its burden to the top of a nearby hillock to represent Galuwata, where they buried the "flesh" and promptly "died" themselves. It was a passion play, but the missionaries had no inkling that it might have had a more profound significance for the actors, one that obscurely encompassed the Imitation of Christ.[2]

But beyond the similar configurations of sacrificial death, transformation, and immortality, what parallels could there possibly be between two religious heroes whose ethics were so antithetical? In the mind of the syncretist there must be some point at which the meanings of their messages overlapped to suggest identity. The cultist had to discount the promise of love instead of dread, overlook the discrepancy between Christ's body as a sacrament and Honoyeta's body as a curse, and ignore the ethic of forgiveness as against the duty of revenge. Also to be discounted were the doctrines that Christ was a savior while Honoyeta was a destroyer. But the messages were one in that the world was somehow deprived by these heroes' deaths, and rebirth was the key: a millenarian solution of a Second Coming.

/\\/\\/\\/\\

The millenarian ambience on Nidula (as in so many other parts of Melanesia) is pervasive and persistent. Cargo cults, those peculiarly Melanesian experiments with ritual means to achieve secular ends, are ever-nascent. For reasons I have suggested elsewhere (1971a), there had been no fully fledged cults on the island since 1960. But in 1976 a new set of circumstances stimulated a recrudescence, and in that year four local cults emerged. They were centered upon Wagifa and Kilia in the south, Mataita in the east, and Iwabu in the north of the island, each with its catchment area of membership. The background circumstances were concomitants of political change at the national level: Papua New Guinea's self-government in 1973 and its independence from Australia in 1975. Both events had been played down by the new government; quiet, sober, dignified celebrations were the order of the day. Yet on both occasions a ground-swell of anxiety surged through Goodenough communities, evoking those traditional intimations of calamity.

On the first of December, 1973, I sponsored a feast in Kalauna to celebrate self-government day, and men flocked from neighboring villages to hear me speak. What will happen, I was asked, when the whites abandon the country? When the Queen's army is disbanded and the Highland peoples invade Papua? When the trade stores close? When there are no more jobs to earn money for taxes? I was not on Goodenough when independence struck even more gently less than two years later, but I am reliably informed that similar anxieties surfaced then.[3] By 1976 economic discontents were widespread. The price of tobacco, rice, tinned meat and fish had risen steeply, along with the cost of those other "staple" luxuries such as tea, sugar, and kerosene. Having weathered almost eighty years of colonial rule (notable for its neglect rather than its impositions),

251

Goodenough Islanders were as bewildered by the disappearance of the wealthy whites as they had been by their first appearance. What was there to show for their coming and their going? Why were people still impoverished and wealth as elusive as ever? What was the secret of Goodenough's name?

Few could have known that the island was named by Captain John Moresby in memory of a British Navy commodore who had died in another archipelago from a stray poisoned arrow; but it was a name that signified to many people of the Massim a place of hidden wealth *good enough* for any who might learn the secret of retrieving it. There are folk on the mainland whose myths tell how *their* wealth was taken to Goodenough by a disgruntled mythical hero, even as Matabawe took Goodenough's wealth to Muyuwa or the Louisiades; while an educated pastor from Sudest confided quite seriously to me that the secret of Goodenough's wealth lay in tablets of gold hidden on the peak of Madawa'a. Obviously, such currents of belief have no geographical center; they drift inconsequentially from mind to mind. But the Goodenough cultists of 1976 revived the allure of a Millennium in which the people of the island would annul history and at last repossess their rightful wealth.

A detailed account of these cults would be superfluous here, and I shall simply offer an outline. They took the form of business stock enterprises. Speaking with the authority of myths and dreams, the leaders offered shares in the movements, attracting buyers with displays of fetishized "money": foreign coins, Monopoly money, and Australian lottery tickets. They entered members' names in a book and issued receipts, which were cherished as "tickets" for the vast dividends the leaders promised. Some of the money collected in this way was expended on feasts of European food, and some of it was salted away by the leaders. The leaders held regular seances at gravesides or in specially constructed "offices," and transmitted messages from the ancestors or cult deities. They exhorted others to pray and to tend graves; they emptied coins into graves or affixed banknotes on the crosses that marked them. They prophesied various dates for the Millennium, when the ancestors would return to life and the cult deities would cross the sea with money and cargo. Such ritualized business meetings constituted the main activity of

252

the cults, though there were also rules to be observed regarding restrictions on gardening and domestic activities, and rules demanding curtailed cooperation with the missions, the local government council, and the administration.

The accession to wealth was a matter of waiting for the vaults to be unlocked, the graves to open. For many months members spent their days in idleness, suspended, bored and expectant by turn, waiting for news. And the leaders, traveling and conferring with one another, delivered pronouncements from the gravesides, and were driven to elaborate fresh fantasies of hope and invent new deceptions to bolster faith. They placed torches in the graves; they feigned the voices of saints and ancestors and announced new dates for the Millennium. As each date came and went they explained the hitch: recent deaths had "blocked" the way of the cargo; one of the heroes had visited Port Moresby to confer with the governor-general; inclement weather had delayed another.

The heroes were Dodogesa, Matabawe or Matabikwa, and, of course, Honoyeta. Dodogesa, an autochthonous deity of Wagifa, took his wealth to Australia long ago, but, according to the prophet's dream, he had promised to return it after independence and settle in his true home. Matabawe, as we saw in chapter 3, was the serpent who abandoned his home in Bwaidoka, taking the island's wealth to Muyuwa or the Louisiades. He, too, had promised to return. The prophet, needless to say, appropriated these myths as his own, and even fabricated his life story to solicit their pity: he became the hungry orphan on the seashore who is succored by a father-figure.[4] Another minor prophet challenged people to kill him when the cargo did not come, offering his own life as sacrificial atonement for the original sin of killing Christ/Honoyeta.

But the most remarkable of these imitations concerned Mwakeba, a man from the southwest of the island, who claimed to be an incarnation of Honoyeta. He had disappeared into the forest for several days, and when he was found he pursuaded his followers he had died, gone to heaven, and returned again. His outer skin was Mwakeba's, but he could unzip himself to reveal—to true believers—a white, inner body which was Honoyeta. To unbelievers Mwakeba suffered merely from *molobe* or *sipoma,* the greyish, flaky skin disease (*tinea imbricata*) colloquially known as "double-skin." Following his second birth, Mwakeba visited Yabiliva (where Honoyeta was slain) for a sign, and to collect money from gullible cultists in the area.

Another cult had already been founded at Yabiliva by an Iwabu man, Yadiyubu, who had dreamed of Honoyeta and obeyed his instructions to clean up the old village site and build a cult house there. Adiyaleyale of Kalauna was a member of the local government council tax committee, and he visited Yabiliva in September 1976, just a few weeks after Mwakeba had collected 200 kina ($A200) from Wataluma people. The council's tax patrol collected a mere 75 kina in this ward. Adiyaleyale described his observations in Yabiliva.

> People came regularly to receive messages from Honoyeta. When I visited Yadiyubu his policeman and housegirl served me tea. I asked Yadiyubu, "Can I see this spirit of Honoyeta? I want to know if he is really like a man." Yadiyubu replied, "My rule is that no one may enter the house, but you can stay outside and Honoyeta will speak to you." I stood by the wall. Then Yadiyubu went into the house and a muffled voice came through the wall. I made a hole and peeped inside. I saw Yadiyubu speaking into a cup so that it altered his voice. I got angry and told all the people, "Don't listen to this man! He is telling lies and you'll waste your money if you give it to him."

⋀⋁⋀⋁⋀

One other Kalauna man went to Yabiliva, though with a greater investment of faith than Adiyaleyale. This was Ewahaluna of Anuana, one of the few men in Kalauna who did expect an imminent day of judgment. My own relations with him were always uneasy, for I suspected he thought I was an ancestor. My questions invariably met bland evasion. I could be an ancestor and hence might know Honoyeta personally, in which case my questions would have another significance: a guileful testing that could be of immense importance to him. It was Adimakaiya, however, who told me what Ewahaluna had done when he heard about the cult of Honoyeta.

"If he has risen then I must see if he has a message for me," he told Adimakaiya. "For I am an owner of his story, one of his own lineage." So he journeyed to Yabiliva dressed in betel-palm fiber instead of shorts, fiercely painted in black, wearing armshells and a boar's tusk pendant around his neck. But he was disappointed. When he returned he reported to Adimakaiya. "I am still waiting for a message. Honoyeta did not speak to me properly." He went south to visit Mwakeba also, but again in vain. "They were pretending," he said, just as Adiyaleyale had discovered.

But Honoyeta sat heavily on Ewahaluna's shoulders. One of the messages he so urgently sought was some word from his sister, a young woman who had died in 1974, ensorcelled, he believed, by her husband's brothers who had been angered by her interference in their trade store enterprise. It had been a quarrel over money that had caused her death. Before she was lowered into the grave, Ewahaluna had placed a seed yam in her cold hand and whispered into the sleeping mat they wrapped her in. Then, as they laid the bent body in the earth, he sang quietly:

> Land of the dead
> Its distant wailing
> Take our yams to that place.

"He spoke to her thus," said Adimakaiya, "and she took all the yams with her. Our harvest that year was truly spoiled." After ruining the crop with this yam sorcery Ewahaluna left the village. He boarded a boat for Esa'ala on Normanby Island and worked on an isolated plantation for almost a year. His *unuwewe* over the death of his sister survived this bitter exile, and when he returned to Kalauna he proceeded to bespell the yams a second time. It was on this occasion that he visited Yabiliva for a message from Honoyeta, a message he hoped would endorse his plan of spitting at the sun to bring a drought. But Honoyeta was silent, the cult leaders were charlatans who "pretended," and Adimakaiya and Kimaola prevailed upon Ewahaluna to make things right. The yam crop of 1976 was saved, a deed for which Kimaola took most of the credit. It was in March of that year that Kimaola abandoned the village to retire in his new garden-hamlet.

∧∧∧∧∧

When I returned to Kalauna for a month's visit in May 1977, I was dismayed to find that this hitherto consolidated community had all but broken apart. It was as if an explosion had occurred in the center of the village, and in slow motion the blast had flung family groups and even entire hamlets outward and downward, scattering them over the gardenlands that slope toward the sea. The old village had a sad and desolate air; far more people now lived outside than within it. Yet the diaspora had not been as dramatic as it first seemed. Indeed, had I been more percipient I might have recognized the beginning of the trend as early as 1968, when over a one-year period I had observed a trickle of people leaving to set up hamlets outside the village. *Fighting with Food* was partly addressed to the problem of how such a large and quarrelsome community could cohere without unified leadership. It was clear that there must be a social as well as physical limit to the expansion of the community, and my earlier monograph is strewn with unwitting hints that this limit might already have been reached by the late sixties.[5] But anthropologists are as blinkered by time as the people they study, and I did not articulate the notion that Kalauna might have been starting to break up during my very presence.

In 1973 I could no longer fail to see what was happening. My census in that year showed that a quarter of the people now lived outside the village, though the population had increased by only eleven percent since 1966. Yet the community seemed as busy, as quarrelsome, and as vital as it had been five years previously, and I was reluctant to predict that it would continue to disintegrate. I witnessed a particularly acrimonious *abutu* contest in that year,[6] though I interpreted it as a positive sign that the competitive focus of the clans was still community-centered, and that the fraternal rivalry within each clan was still subordinate to the competition between them. But as it happened, this was to be the last *abutu* of the Kalauna I had known. The population continued to expand (to 550, a 7 percent increase in four and a half years) and the drift away from the village continued.

On my return in 1977 I had to face the fact that Kalauna had broken under its own weight. With the wisdom of hindsight, I could see how the *abutu* competition of December 1973 had been a blueprint for the dispersals that occurred in the following years. Cracks in the hitherto solid alliances between certain clans had appeared; fissures within the major clans themselves were revealed. One of the remarkable facts about the pattern of resettlement in 1977 was that the clans had fragmented unevenly, and not always along predictable lines of structural stress. Even true brothers now lived apart. In the reasons people gave for abandoning Kalauna for the spacious slopes, the only coherent theme was that of individual motivation itself, borne by undercurrents of *unuwewe*. Many of those who moved glossed their motives as "to seek a better life," or its reciprocal, "to escape Kalauna." Clearly, something at the center had failed to hold, for it was those who remained who were among the most resentful and who bemoaned the present "bad times."

Lulauvile itself became fragmented over the course of six years. Kimaola's new hamlet was, in 1977, numerically the largest coresidential group of Lulauvile people. Anuana had split in two; Heloava and Anuana II into three or four family groups. It was as if one half of Lulauvile had abandoned the other half in *unuwewe*. The explanation of Lulauvile's conservatives must be given some weight, though it cannot stand alone. They look back nostalgically to the sixties as a golden age, a climax-period of florescence in their tiny civilization. I have already cited a number of people to the effect that when Didiala and Iyahalina were alive and working together, things were harmonious and "all lived well." The views of Adiyaleyale and Kwahihi (Didiala's widow) could hardly be more partisan; for them, as for most other Lulauvile people, there was no doubt at all why Kalauna had broken apart. "Those big-men were our *bakibaki*, our achorage," said Adiyaleyale simply, "and when they died the people began to separate." Kwahihi agreed and lamented:

Our guardians of the house posts died; that's why men wander with their houses now. Those big-men kept us warm while they were alive, and people stayed still. Now their fires are dead and the village grows cold, the grass invades. The pillars of the village have gone, that is why the house of Kalauna is falling down.

257

The big-man theory of history is here given its due. A few others went further, suggesting that not only did these men hold the village together during those halcyon days, but that their deaths engendered vengeance sorcery which broke the *bakibaki* and disordered the magic in the sitting circles. One or two believed that Kimaola had actually performed magic to impel people to abandon the village—not by turning the *bakibaki* stone in his hamlet, but by another technique of rolling up a bespelled sleeping mat and carrying it to his new abode. Such views of the diaspora saw Lulauvile as an exhausted and demoralized rabble after the heroic voices of its leaders had been silenced.

There is certainly some truth in a demographic argument which would see the support systems of a community weakened by the dying off of the strong leaders, leaving an as yet untested generation of men of uncertain capacities. This view complements another which would see in the trade store craze of the mid-seventies (when no fewer than nine store licenses were held by Kalauna men) further evidence of the trend towards individualism. It was the younger generation of leaders who became obsessed with "business," and in some cases at least this encouraged them to move in the hope that they might find a "good place" to earn profits.

So between the pragmatic and the mystical, the causal-rational and the acausal-magical, there were enough explanations to allow most Kalauna people to accept with equanimity their communal fragmentation. For many, life was comfortable this way; the sunny slopes seemed healthy and peaceful. It was a phase of social and spiritual diastole, for many also declared their intention of returning in the future. It was, however, a sad experience for me, the uncasual visitor whose own life was obscurely entwined with Kalauna's multiple destinies, to see the dilapidated houses and the unweeded hamlets empty of laughing children and squealing pigs, and to see the pathetic huddle of people who remained, lonely in a village suddenly too large for their numbers. But Kalauna had come together from the ridges, clung together for a while, dispersed, and come together yet again, and was now dispersed once more. It could come together in the future too.

258

∧∧∧∧

Standing on the rocky rim of Anuana (which once was called Unuwewe), at the point where it abutted Aluwaita and Anuana II, within a yard or so of where Tobowa's house once stood and with my
back to the site of old Siboboya's house, I could see Didiala's grave,
and by turning my head to the left, Kimaola's abandoned house just
ten paces away; while a few paces beyond that, in the shade of the
great tree planted by Malaveyoyo, were the posts of Iyahalina's last
house. In the single sweep of a gaze one could thus encompass the
tiny rock-strewn stage of the heroes of this book: the still center of
Lulauvile.

I am reluctant to summarize their lives into even tighter patterns
than I have been tempted to do already (pattern in lives, perhaps,
being largely an artifact of ignorance of detail). But it is necessary to
invoke them once more and suggest how a few last fragments might
illuminate design. It is evident that even a society as "simple" and
homogeneous as Kalauna can harbor the most diverse personalities;
and I have argued that the distinctive identities and political styles
of these men were greatly influenced by the various myths they
inherited and claimed as their own. These men were born into a traditional and preliterate milieu; each did his bit to transform it, but
for the most part they cleaved to traditional values and pursued traditional aims in traditional ways. Their generation came to an end,
more or less, about the time that Papua New Guinea achieved
nationhood.

But their children are likely to see at least as much change as they
ever saw, notwithstanding the trauma of the Second World War.
Their sons' story, indeed, would need another book. I have suggested that these younger men, too, fell under the influence of their
myths; though somewhat more readily than their fathers, perhaps,
they appreciate the essential relativity of the myths and the possibility of disengaging themselves from them. The life patterns of their
fathers are no longer the only exemplary models. Awareness of
enactment of a mythical pattern transforms the event, both for the
actor and for his audience. The choice of modifying it or of opting

out altogether is thus a possibility. So too is irony as a self-conscious mode of playing with fate. I suggested that Iyahalina possessed this capacity in great degree, though in the last analysis he believed in his role and identified with his mission. His son, Adiyaleyale, is more liberated (or alienated, depending upon one's viewpoint) by his education and his years of travel abroad; he knows that he has the choice of rejecting his myths in favor of others, or of trying to live without any at all. Captivated by Honoyeta in a personal crisis, Adiyaleyale fled the village and named his new hamlet Yabiliva ("because they are trying to kill me"). But he could also say: "I do not want to anchor myself here with *bakibaki,* for I may want to return to the village later."

Malaveyoyo, as we saw, exemplified the negative possibilities of Honoyeta's archetype and primal drama, precipitating Kalauna's "oral" guilt in a manner that still affects the lives of his descendants. Tobowa was a "modern" leader who made heroic but misunderstood attempts to break from the past, only to become stereotyped by his contemporaries as yet another "oral" tyrant. To Iyahalina at least, he seemed set upon the destruction of Lulauvile.

In the political relationship between the three "guardians" of the sixties, there was a permanent alliance between Didiala and Iyahalina (brothers-in-law and *fofofo* partners), and something of mutual hostility toward the maverick Kimaola. Didiala, the prepotent provider, exemplified the success story of the big-man. This story, although implicit in his mythical charters, was less constrained by mythical protocol than Iyahalina's. It was to a great extent improvisatory; for to be a big-man one must struggle against whatever odds are given, risk what one has to get more, and shake up the comfortable routines of the household economy to create a surplus. Myths only hint at how this might be done, for circumstances change and ways of seizing the main chance cannot be prescribed. Opportunism characterized Didiala's life almost as much as Kimaola's. Yet Didiala was particularly concerned to stress how he fulfilled his obligations to those who raised him, just as Iyahalina stressed his identification with his forbears in their responsibility for community wellbeing. These were two sides of a moral coin; Didiala exemplifying the reciprocal, intergenerational mode of social order, Iyahalina exemplifying the hierarchical mode of a public duty that assumed almost cosmic proportions, like a philosopher king wedded to *lokona,* the queen of the Kalauna sciences. Their myths, too, interlocked and mutually informed one another: Tomoudi and Kuyakwokula complement Kiwiwiole and Hudiboyaboyaleta. Against the complementary relationships of these two men, Kimaola set himself as a lone rebel, an "orphan" and deprived younger brother, fighting with his wits, cunningly disguising himself in order to prevail. And his myths were tales of men at odds with their brothers.

These were the three principal characters, each of whom in his own way used his myths for self-glorification. We have perceived a discrepancy between what they thought of themselves and what others thought of them. Through their myths, however, not only did they legitimize their roles and personal identities, they also attempted to enforce a consensus of their qualities and powers.

∧∧∧∧∧

To see Kimaola's role in its widest perspective we must review Lulauvile's place in Kalauna; this will also suggest another way of understanding Kalauna's disintegration in the seventies. At one level, this book records the decline and fall of Lulauvile, the "ruling house" that seemed to be forever disappointed in its expectations. The social conflict I have alluded to throughout is not merely a structural one of Lulauvile versus the other clans, but more fundamentally an ideological one. On the ground, Kalauna was roughly divided into two blocs of clans, one led by Lulauvile, the other by Iwaoyana. This arrangement was largely contingent upon the clustering of institutionalized *fofofo* partnerships and countervailing "enemy" relationships (Young 1971:72-74). What emerged as the balance of power in Kalauna was two opposed sets of clan alliances, which were ratified or renegotiated during every confrontation of the two major powers. Hence, the main cleavage in the community was in practice determined by the statistical outcome of decisions made by individual gardeners, decisions as to which group they were going to support with their food resources. In addition to a variety of moral and

261

pragmatic considerations, what influenced a man's choice was an ideological disposition. Although this tended to be a concomitant of clan membership, it was not invariably so.

The competing ideologies came down to this: whether or not (good) food can be grown and safeguarded without Lulauvile's help. On the one hand, the conservative or "royalist" view espoused by Lulauvile and most of its allies is that its magical guidance and guardianship is essential, and they predict dire consequences for a community bereft of Lulauvile support. The progressive or "republican" view, on the other hand, asserts that Lulauvile's ritual is not essential to village prosperity, that each man's unaided effort and private magic are enough. Clearly, this latter view runs with the grain of egalitarian assumptions that constitute the bedrock social philosophy of Kalauna. Hence the paradox of Lulauvile's position. For in the last analysis egalitarianism is saved by the choice of food as the idiom of contention. Being ephemeral, perishable wealth, food cannot underwrite nor provide any security for permanent rank. Its investment permits no more than temporary increments in status.

Lulauvile's claim, however, is to exercise control at a precedent level: to secure conditions for the successful production of food-wealth. It thereby presumes to provide the very circumstances that make the claims of egalitarianism possible. Iyahalina argued precisely along these lines in his narrative; it was casuistry, but from the viewpoint of hierarchy his logic was impeccable. "Your *abutu*," he said, referring to the equality-adjusting game of the republicans, "cannot take place without my *abutu*," by which he meant the *manumanua* ceremony over which he presided. As we have seen, the recurrent plots of political confrontation in Kalauna frequently involved a clash of these ideologies which disputed the locus of true authority.

Let me harden the antinomies by depicting them as competing visions of Kalauna society. Lulauvile represents the very model of the ordered domain of hierarchy, its rich and regal traditions entitling it to be the master clan, its duties both paternal and punitive in guiding and guarding the others, symbolized in its ritual functions as well as expressed in the terms associated with hierarchy: authority

262

(*vemeiya*), restraint and containment (*lokona*), fixity, durability, and permanence (*bakibaki*). Its weighty symbols are bones and stones, the house post and the house (*manua*). Visually and behaviorally, all these qualities are imitated and exemplified by the *kaiwabu*, "the chief of the feast," as he sits immobile on his platform (Young 1971:248-253).

Opposed to this ordered, almost bourgeois domain of solid virtues is the alternative vision of society as a fluid realm of reciprocity in which status is forever negotiable, legitimacy in question, and identity at risk. The terms of egalitarianism are those of exchange and competition, of squandering, unrestraint, and mobility. Its fluid symbols are water and blood, "feminine" symbols that seek their own level through the lateral spread of ties of cognation, leveling hubris and pretensions to fame. The solid symbols of hierarchical stasis, with its vertical imagery of agnatic descent and autochthonous ascent, are thus antithetical to the symbols of flux and the lateral imagery of egalitarian mobility.

The antinomies could be pushed even further to incorporate male and female domains, oral values, and the ceremonial moiety division; but at this stretch the opposition loses its precise definition and becomes a rather empty catalogue of dualisms without practical consequences or ideological weight. The main point is clear, however. If Lulauvile stands for centralizing order, continuity and stasis, then the dispersal of Lulauvile in the seventies betokened an unequivocal defeat. Conversely, Kalauna's new era of "wandering" betokened a victory for the principle of egalitarianism and its impulse toward individualism.

Now we are in a position to take the disaffected Lulauvile view, and see that the principle of order succumbed to disorder through *unuwewe*—a self-inflicted victimage—in the protean figure of Kimaola. From the assemblage of pieces I have presented we can discern at last the fatal twist: for if any person was responsible for the fall of Lulauvile and the disintegration of Kalauna it was Kimaola. The irony, of course, is that it was a Lulauvile man who traitorously destroyed its leadership in his very pursuit of it. This was *unuwewe* on a heroic and potlatching scale. For of all the Lulauvile leaders who conformed to the hierarchic, order-figure ideal, Kimaola was least fitted by birth and personal disposition. People feared his "oral" aggression and were suspicious of his restlessness. Unlike a true *toitavealata,* he could not sit still. Lulauvile men were even more afraid of him than were the men of other clans, for he was a threat to their most cherished values. Whether or not he actually attempted to kill Tobowa, Didiala, and Iyahalina (not to mention other Lulauvile men whose stories I have not told), Lulauvile believed that he did—and that he succeeded. Perhaps it was the case that Lulauvile men projected their anxieties onto him because he was the one most different from themselves; but it was also the case that he deliberately encouraged them to do so. This provocative and precarious stance was also Honoyeta's. Kimaola came to be identified as the enemy within, and hence a true scapegoat. But he was the one who survived to "continue his death by some other means": an individualist responsible to no one, beckoning a kind of lonely sainthood like Honoyeta's metamorphosis into the sun.[7]

∧∧∧∧

Honoyeta's myth can be seen as but one episode in a great cycle of transformations, though one must look beyond Kalauna to find the various metamorphoses of the wandering hero. Matabawe, the secluded serpent whose home was Bwaidoka, becomes Honoyeta the young/old man whose home was Galuwata. After transforming into a spirit of the sun (Tomokauwana), he is killed yet again at Ebadidi on Fergusson Island, where he becomes Manukubuku, the "grandfather bird." He returns to southern Nidula as Ulekufuyo, a sentient clay pot, and founds a cult of the rain and sun. Finally, he changes into a rock, which sinks underground, whence he emerges as a serpent again.[8]

This cycle of myths of a hero whose subterranean identity is best defined as serpentine has no more specific ethnographic locus than the western D'Entrecasteaux. There were old men in Bwaidoka (where the cycle might, from their point of view, be said to begin and end) who joined some of these myths from head to tail. They were emancipated by the Methodist mission from the view that

264

regards myths as secret and discrete items of property, and hence they were not averse to joining myths in series according to the metamorphoses of the hero. But if, as seems to be the case elsewhere, the cycle has no identifiable social locus, then everything militates against it being perceived as a cycle at all. It cannot be located in any mind save that of the distanced ethnographer, who is in the privileged position of knowing something about every domain and who, moreover, is not bound by the doctrine that certain kinds of knowledge are the exclusive property of certain social groups.

One day, with what I thought to be an inspired image, I tested my theory of the Honoyeta cycle of myths on a small group of Kalauna men, using the Ouroborus figure of a serpent biting its tail to describe its circularity. My audience was bemused and skeptical. They shook their heads. "It cannot be thus because those stories of Tomokwauwana and Ulekufuyo do not belong to anyone in Kalauna. Our Manukubuku and Matabawe heroes are also different." Precisely. They were forced to deny the sequential metamorphoses of the hero because the snakelike tale had been chopped up by their clannish sociology of knowledge and its pieces geographically dispersed. These pieces are separately owned and jealously guarded against the possibility of reintegration (which would represent a denigration of the unique importance of each piece), thereby effectively occluding any vision of the whole. To the extent that they were unable to construct for themselves a transformational series or cycle, Kalauna men were denied a relativizing perspective which would help—by the creation of a second-order myth—to release them from the snare of literalism. The grip of myth, then, might be said to be largely a function of a distribution of esoteric knowledge in which the secretive mode of transmission encourages deceptions, hardens dogmatisms, and generates discontinuities.

Yet my fanciful image of the timeless serpent swallowing its own tail has analogues in the Nidula design motifs traditionally painted on house boards. "A very common pattern," according to Jenness and Ballantyne, is "a number of rough concentric circles alternately red and black, which they said represented the sun" (1920:198). Few of these can be seen today, for house styles have changed and new ones are rarely, if ever, decorated. "One of the commonest patterns consists of rows of triangles painted in red and black, with the interstices filled in with white" (ibid.: 197). These can be seen today on a large decorative mural behind the altar of the new Catholic church at Ulutuya (see note 2). The triangles are called *buibui*, cumulus clouds. In color symbolism, red connotes wealth, youth, fertility and life; black connotes war, age, sorcery and death. The alternation of these colors, both in the rings of the sun and in the triangles of the clouds, recalls the cycles of drought and prosperity that inform Goodenough Islanders' conceptualization of historical time as an alternating sequence of plenty and famine, associated with the systole and diastole of community life — the "sitting still" or "wandering" of the people.

Other than alternating colors, the simplest way to express these temporal fluctuations visually is by means of a zigzag (for those conceived of as abrupt), or by a wavy line (for those conceived of as undulating phases). Jenness and Ballantyne write:

Either the chevron,  , or the continuous curve, the latter usually double, appears in most of the

carving, whether on the canoe, the drum, the club or the bowl; they are frequently used to separate two patterns. [Ibid.:199-200]

Lulauvile's mythicized history (which as we have seen is also the paradigm for Kalauna's) is replete with the coming and going of groups on and beneath the earth's surface: from the original emergence at the summit of Yauyaba and the return underground during the phase of Nibita's crablike existence in the shadow of Manubutu, to the new emergence, congregation, and fresh dispersals. *Manumanua*, Lulauvile's constitutive ritual of community and cosmic maintenance, encapsulates the same vertical and lateral movements, aiming as it does to procure anchored wealth by summoning the symbolisms of dearth and wandering and submitting them to the symbolisms of abundance and stasis. The alternating cycle of abundance and famine is brought under human magical control during *manumanua*. It ties a knot and effects a timeless closure by imitating the heroes.

266

It should not surprise us, therefore, to learn that Lulauvile, the guardian of Kalauna history and of *manumanua,* should have as its emblem the zigzag, Jenness and Ballantyne's chevron sequence. This rigidified version of the wavy line is called *etonita,* and is known as Lulauvile's "sign" or "marker," which non-Lulauvile people copy on pain of mystical death. *Etonita* literally means "to enable one to see." Seeing is a magical act associated with the "eye" (*mata*) of the all-seeing sun (and we can recall that to protect mankind from his gaze Honoyeta had his grave hermetically sealed). Lexically, *mata* (eye) puns on *mota* (snake); though it puns even better in the nearby language of Dobu in which snake is *mwata.* The sine-wave motif, Jenness and Ballantyne's double continuous curve, is identified as *mota* in Kalauna. Appropriately, then, the Lulauvile design motif points to both the sun and the serpent. These represent, after all, a fair though somewhat esoteric summation of Lulauvile's cosmic powers. The best exemplification of the *etonita* motif I have seen was on one of the wooden food bowls said to have been carved by Malaveyoyo. The *etonita* was not inscribed (which would have been the easier task), but carved in relief around the rim, so that it forms a continuous circle. Likewise do *mota* incisions undulate around the rims of the clay pots made in northern Goodenough. [9]

To extrapolate the fancy even further, it will be obvious that much—perhaps too much—can be subsumed under the graphic representation of this sinuous motif. It describes not only Honoyeta's own metamorphoses and wanderings (up and down as well as across the surface of the land), but also the temporal and spatial transformations of Nidula communities like Kalauna. The dialectics of this kind of history have been sufficiently well documented throughout the book; here I would simply try to effect my own closure on the theme by recapitulating the serpentine structure of *unuwewe* at the level of irreversible event and individual biography.

The serpent's progress in a spiral form is an image of the *unuwewe* double bind: the masochistic revenge of self-mortification, motivated by the impulse to make others suffer by suffering oneself. The undulations involve the projective mode of victimage, which typically produces a reactive, resentful, and self-pitying mode of introjective victimage. This is the suicidal *unuwewe,* which is the hallmark of Honoyeta. For the sake of illustration, let me dissect the drama of Didiala's sorcery of the sun following the death of his daughter (see chapter 6). If we view the events as starkly as they were presented to me, their dialectical progression takes on the jagged outline of *etonita*:

1. An enemy was angered and shamed because Didiala had defeated him with his yams in *abutu*. (Didiala performed a heroic deception; his enemy suffered victimage.)
2. The enemy killed Didiala's daughter by sorcery; ironically, with a coconut, Didiala's mythical "child." (This was an act of counter-deception and subrogation; Didiala suffered vicarious victimage.)
3. Didiala's response was *unuwewe,* which he expressed by making sun magic. (This was a heroic revenge, which broadened the quarrel to implicate the world.)
4. Didiala left the village for a year to let it suffer and "feel sorry." (This was heroic abandonment and exile to stress the double-edged victimage.)
5. After the drought had caused hunger and community dispersal, Didiala returned to set things right. (Not all heroes can be relied upon to do this.)

The sequence of abundance-famine-abundance is here made correlative with a drama of death and vengeance involving two modes of victimage. And by this means is Kalauna people's affective theory of social action coordinated with their patterned view of history. The cause, consequence, and resolution of Didiala's *unuwewe* (with the possible exception of (5) above) imitates the cosmic *unuwewe* of the heroes, most notably Honoyeta's. This conjunction precipitates the palpable sense of fatedness for the actors, for the heroes' *unuwewe* is a transcendant form that reflects an ineluctable course.

∿∿∿

The design of my chapters created dramatic presentations concluded by the deaths of leaders, their biographies sealed by the grave. But this was expository artifice, for the life of the community pulsed on beyond the rise and fall of leaders which described the parabolic form or the rigid triangle of *etonita*. Plot and subplot are likewise a matter of selective focus. The succession of the generations, the killing of the fathers and the vengeance of the sons, constitute innumerable plots and subplots played out simultaneously on different scales, twining and conjoining messily in the business of life, and only rarely coinciding in their peaking in a cathartic resolution which enables people to breathe deeply and start afresh. The death of a leader can give this illusion of a meshing of the cycles, a coincidence of plots, which brings an "era" to an end and evokes a readiness in the community to embark upon the next upswing of an undulation.

More frequently, it seems, a death carries the seeds of further tragedy, for the revenge cycle is never completed: *unuwewe* flows relentlessly on. The burial ceremony, at which the community attempts to purify and purge itself by making a scapegoat of the corpse, is also the occasion on which embittered kinsmen inflict the punishment of crop or weather sorcery, thereby inciting a new round of victimage. Hence, a death need not conclude a tragedy, but in the acts of *unuwewe* it provokes may provide the nudge toward yet another one. The nemesis of the sons (Siusiu, Adiyale-yale) in avenging the deaths of their fathers (Tobowa, Iyahalina) were subplots that generated new plots. A more accurate visual depiction of the multiple trajectories of intertwined *unuwewe,* then, would resemble those complex curvilinear figures (like scrolls, interlocking birds' beaks, or breaking waves) such as Malaveyoyo incised on another wooden food bowl that survives in Kalauna.

The largest cycle into which all these fluctuations fit is intimated by the shape of the food bowl or by the serpent completing its own circle. But whether or not Kalauna people conceive of their historical destiny — their Platonic Year — as an eternal serpent, the idea is familiar to them that in their end is also their beginning. The deprivation which the resentful heroes inflicted can only be annulled by their return to set things right. The colonial era underscored this theme in their world view by presenting the people of Nidula with an invidious comparison, forcing the recognition of an accursed and predestined poverty. The cargo cult, then, becomes the means to complete the cycle and bring home the wandering heroes. Thanks to its unusual leadership, however, Kalauna has trafficked little in such cults and resisted the appeal of their literalism. Iyahalina for one, I like to think, would have preferred to agree with Lévi-Strauss that "mythical heroes can truly be said to return, but their only reality lies in their personification" (1966:237); or, better still, with Yeats:

> That they, time overthrown,
> Were dead, yet flesh and bone.

Epilogue

Whereof what's past is prologue.

— *The Tempest,* II, i

Books have an irksome tendency to go on writing themselves long after their authors wish to have done with them. Having dealt with convergent destinies, timeless plots that nudge people into recurring patterns of fate, it should have been easy for me to discount recent news from Kalauna as redundant, superfluous to any scriptural lessons of this book. Having heard of fresh sorcery deaths and a renewed persecution of Kimaola, I might have been excused for thinking, "What is there left to say?" But I cannot pretend so to the myth of my own book that I could imagine my Kalauna to disappear the moment I ceased to recreate it; just as I cannot pretend to the security and the terror of those who submerge their biographies in myths. In short, I could only have written this book by standing to one side of the arguments it adopts and the views of Kalauna's world that it offers. This gives me warrant, then, to tell of how the House of Lulauvile succumbed once again to Honoyeta's curse.

I left Kimaola by his hearth, ruminating on his hero, after he had all but accomplished the physical collapse of his clan, the "belly" of Kalauna. Ostensibly retired and the only one of my five leaders still surviving, I fancied Kimaola to be wisely seeking his death by means

271

other than the sacrificial *unuwewe* of Honoyeta. It was with shock and dismay, therefore, that I learned of the events of July 1979, almost a year after completing the manuscript for this book, and two full years after I had seen him last. I was informed of these events by Fr. John Fallon, the Catholic missionary at Bolubolu, who sent me several pages of notes and commentaries. I am indebted to him for allowing me to use them, and also for soliciting tape-recorded testimonies from a number of Kalauna men. What follows is constructed from these sources.

In June 1979, Tabwaika's eldest daughter died in childbirth. Her husband was a Lulauvile man of Anuana II. At the postburial meeting Kimaola was covertly accused of her death, and his wife Wa'aula (Tabwaika's sister) admitted that Kimaola had given ginger to her "daughter" just before she died.

For several weeks rumors thickened. On 24 July, Tabwaika prevailed upon the village councillor to summon a meeting to discuss the death of his daughter. Tabwaika was sad and angry. "She was too young to die for nothing; I want to know why." Neailena, the councillor, took the precaution of inviting a policeman from Bolubolu to attend the meeting. Kimaola did not make an appearance. The first speaker demanded to know where he was, and if anyone had advised him not to come. An uproar ensued. A group of a dozen Lulauvile men, including the husband and a brother of the dead girl, snatched up spears and bushknives and ran down the path to Bouloula, Kimaola's hamlet in the yam gardens.

> His wife Wa'aula was cooking pumpkin for his breakfast. "He's not here," she lied. But men of Anuana II climbed into his house and found him in a corner. They hit him with their hands until blood ran from his nose and mouth. We others also set about him, and someone threw a stone which gashed his head. "Oh, my children are killing me!" he cried.

The Bolubolu policeman and Neailena arrived in time to prevent further violence. They escorted him to the road, where the police truck took him to the patrol post for his own safety. Meanwhile, the enraged Lulauvile men had begun to tear apart Kimaola's house. Adiyaleyale hunted for the notorious white stones by which Kimaola controlled *kwahala* and *yafuna,* the ravening fanged spirits which were his familiars. Having emptied his yam store and wrecked the house, they set fire to it.

> We pulled up ginger plants and threw them on the burning house. And one of those white stones shot out and over our heads like a rocket. Then we slashed two of his gardens with our bushknives, and we cut down all his bananas. We chopped his yams into pieces. Then we speared his pig and carried it back to Kalauna. We butchered it, cooked it, and ate it, together with some of his big yams. We also chased his two wives back to the village. We told them they must divorce him because he is a wicked man.

A few days later the officer-in-charge at Bolubolu heard the charges against Kimaola and his persecutors. There was insufficient evidence to convict Kimaola of practicing sorcery, and the charge of riotous behavior against the Lulauvile men was also dismissed. An assault charge against two of the men who had beaten Kimaola was sustained, and they served a month's hard labor cutting grass on the station. Kimaola took refuge with Tabuona, a distant kinsman in Belebele village.

Two months later, a meeting was called by the Bolubolu officer in charge at the request of the Kalauna councillor. It was convened to confront Kimaola with some new charges that he had buried sorcery beneath the houses of his Lulauvile "family" in Bouboula. At this meeting Adiyaleyale complained again to the officer in charge: "We handed this sorcery business over to the government — but it is not settled yet. We want to go back to the law of Moses. Give us this man and let us kill him now!" The officer refused and told them they must make peace. Whereupon a succession of men stood up and arraigned Kimaola for causing the deaths of newborn children, of women in childbirth, and of countless others, men and women. Kawanaba spoke of his own father, and of Didiala and Iyahalina: "Our fathers died because of Malaveyoyo, and Kimaola does not forget nor forgive him." Even Mialaba's husband, Kimaola's brother-in-law, accused him of trying to kill his own sister's children.

Tabuona of Belebele told how he was trying to reform Kimaola:

I am sheltering him until your troubles are over. I speak to him about the Bible night and day. "You are a big-man," I tell him, "but you have spoiled your life. Now you live like a child or a rubbish man, and it is your own fault."

Bunaleya, Iyahalina's eldest son and the Catholic Church leader in Kalauna, addressed the old man directly:

We cannot let you kill or be killed, but you must think which way you are going to go. If you go God's way you will love your neighbors and yourself. But if you go Satan's way you will kill yourself and destroy your family and your village.

The United Church pastor urged all Kimaola's accusers to forgive him, and to promise on the Bible not to harm him again. They refused, though Kimaola agreed to swear on the Bible that he would renounce sorcery. Adiyaleyale and others were sceptical: "We remember how he promised to give up sorcery when I was councillor in 1972. But it goes on and on; young people and old continue to die."

Finally, Kimaola defended himself: "Some people die themselves from sickness. Others die from forgotten quarrels with old enemies. But now you blame only me." He denied putting sorcery under the house of his kinsmen at Bouboula, or under the houses of those Anuana men who had succeeded him as guardian of the yams. He concluded, resentfully:

I will come up to Kalauna again for you to cut off my head. But you can take your time; I will live at Belebele for a while. Then I will return and you can begin to kill me.

In November of 1979 a detailed tape-recorded report arrived from Adiyaleyale on the state of Kalauna. He spoke of drought, of shriveled gardens and dry creek beds:

274

Kwabu people of Wailolo are trying hard to make rain. But Kimaola
spits at the sun as it rises and chases the clouds away. For five months
now this sun has burned. It is Honoyeta's sun.

In December I received word that the drought had eased, but a full
year later Kimaola had still not returned to live in Kalauna.

In these events and in Kalauna men's commentaries on them
might be found as many themes of Honoyeta's primal drama as one
may care to seek. My own astonishment upon hearing of them was
not that my "theory" of mythical mimesis should enjoy such patent
demonstration, but rather that the myth should be played out in
such stultifying fashion, enacted with such banal violence. I was dismayed by the failure of the men of Lulauvile — the "sons" of this
book — to find for their problems a better solution than that of making Kimaola the perfect scapegoat: one who is heaped with evil and
banished, and who can only return under threat of sacrificial death.

From the "sons'" point of view, of course, Kimaola is unquestionably and irredeemably guilty; and they are terrified of his destructive powers. They perceive his threat in the Honoyeta mode. He
insults young fathers by killing babies or striking at parturient wives.
By conflating the sequence of generations, as Honoyeta's riddle
sought to do, he confounds time itself. Indeed, some of the Lulauvile men now accused Kimaola of lewdly molesting their wives, of
coercing them to accept his advances under threat of a stillbirth or a
lodged placenta. This was a disconcerting revelation, for it contradicted my reading of his character as one unmotivated by sexual
appetite. But it might still be the case that these charges are the fanciful projections of the anxious "sons," alarmed at his notoriety for
stopping births and hence preventing succession.

But what could have possessed them to tear apart and burn his
house like the skin he hid inside, to slay their "father" symbolically
by chopping up his yams and butchering his pig? Did they wonder as
they feasted on his sacrificial pieces whether they soon might die,
like those who tried to eat the body of Honoyeta?

From Kimaola's point of view, his resentment could not match
the monstrous *unuwewe* of his hero. But I was dismayed, too, that
he should provoke his "sons" thus, offer himself to be killed, and
punish them in the meantime with threats of Honoyeta's sun. The

double-victimage of Honoyeta's drama is also evident in the fears that Kimaola had sown sorcery beneath the houses of his heirs and closest kinsmen. If he really did so, was it in resentment at their failure to protect him? Or was it done from his abiding resentment at being alone and virtually kinless, forever excluded from the amity of true brotherhood? In a fundamentally insecure society, Kimaola is the most insecure of men. And it is also fitting and tragic that his mythical hero should be one who personified solitariness.

If his public denial was honest, however, and if the sorcery beneath Lulauvile houses was some figment of the minds of those who fear him, then his isolation is all the more profound. His banishment is his dismemberment from the body of Lulauvile. It is certain, though, that while he remains bereft in exile his persecutors will fear his terrible vengeance, and his resentment will feed ceaselessly upon itself. The pity is that, by his own conduct, he confirmed the expectations of those who watched him so suspiciously. Therein lies the tragic closure by which Honoyeta's curse finds its purchase on human lives.

Appendix I

The Myth of Vatako: An Interrupted Narration

WASIKENI: *Iya'eku Vatako. Yana-ifufu yaka-custom faina.*
I am Vatako. Its story my custom because of it.
Vavineku yadi-veumaiyiyi faina ya-na-luifufuyena Iya
My wife her resentment because of it I will tell story about it. I
Sinayeta Yayila. Vavineku hi-veumaiyiyi. Wada tova matatabuna
Fishnet Weaver. My wife she is resentful. That time all of it
ya-yiyayila yaku dewa faina. Tova matatabuna
I weave and weave my custom because of it. Time all of it
vavineku vitonouna hi-ala'alahidi. Natukweyao vitonouna
my wife hunger she constantly. My children hunger
hi-ala'alahidi. Ada hi-veumaiyiyiyeku ada nikoko hi-dabadabana
they constantly. So she is resentful to me and black palm she cuts up
ada kwatauta lakaina aiya'aine hi-vetahovina. Vavineku
and pot big in it she cooks it. My wife
hi-obu melala hi-luluyiliyili. Iya ya-yiyayila. Vavineku
she descends hamlet she sweeps. I I weave My wife
kwaudi hi-ulolo. Hi-ya'eyo: "Vatako, au'a u-na-itana
her back it hurts. She says: "Vatako, food you can watch it
ai-tu a-na-na nimama a-na-kolana yada-lokoloko a-na-kolana.
fire and I will go my hands I will wash our things I will wash.
U-na-laka au'a u-na-itana." Vavineku hi-nau lokoloko
You can go up food you can watch it." My wife she goes things
hi-kolakola atu ya-laka'e yaku-manuweya. Ya-laka'e ya-luyahina
she washes but I go up my house to. I go up I uncover it

ya-itana.   *Taka ya-luyahina*   *lubu*   *ya-itana analoi maniutu.*
I see it.   Pot   I remove it   leaf lid   I see it   only   black palm.

Maniutu   *yayana hi-vetahovina vavineku.*   *Keke ya-da-ifuifufu*   *atu*
Black palm   only   she cooks it   my wife.   Not   I would speak   but

ya-obu   *yaku-metana ya-vaina ya-hututaina yaku-alevatu ya-yiyayila.*
I go down   my shuttle   I take it   I thread   my fishnet   I weave.

Vavineku   *hi-na'e*   *daudeya hi-ela'e*   *hi-laka'e*   *hi-itana.*
My wife   she went   river to   she came   she climbed up   she saw it.

Ada hi-yaheyo: *"Ahene*   *u-lakava*   *u-itana?"*   *Keke*
And she said: "Already   you went up   you saw it?"   Not

ya-da-venua'atadi   *hi-laba'ahi*   *faina.*   *Taka hi-fewana*   *ada*
I would answer her   she furious   because of it.   Pot   she lifts   and

hi-heyebuyena   *melaleya.*   *Hi-biyavayavalina.*   *Yaiyawona*   *ada*
she throws it   ground on to.   It breaks into pieces.   Pot (type)   and

nikoko   *hi-beleyeyena. Ada iya*   *ya-unuwewe.*   *Ya-laka*
black palm   it spills out.   And I   I am resentful.   I climb

atuaheya.   *ya-yiyayila aiyeta luwei*   *boyi*   *luwei.*   *Ya-ulobe*
sitting platform.   I weave   days   two   nights   two.   I am suicidal

ya-miyemi'e   *ya-yiyayila. Eh,*   *hinayeku*   *hi-didi....*
I remain   I weave.   Eh,   my inside   it cold....

TODAIYANA: *Medema*   *yava'adi*   *u-luhifufuye?*   *Yava'adi*
              That   what   you tell story?   What

ya-noiyayali? Kabala aiya'aine   *wa-nuwanuwahuya o*   *ai*   *aiya'aine?*
I am hearing? Stone   from it   you get learning   or   tree   from it?

O natu,   *meda*   *ahene Yawalele*   *hi-nuwahuya? Hadeni Yawalele*
Your son,   that one   already Yawalele   he learned?   Where   Yawalele

meda   *kalivamoena? Ahene*   *hi-nuwahuya?*
that   man himself?   Already   he learned?

YAWALELE: *Ika,*   *hid'e'i.*   *Ahene*   *ya-toledadana Tony*   *ama*
            Yes,   here.   Already   I questioned   Tony   but

hi-woneku ada keke ya-da-hawata.
he told me   and   not   I would stop (them).

WASIKENI: *Talavefofo!*   *Bana'*   *aiya'aine*   *keke*
            Answer back! (= Forget it!)   He   to him   not

ya-da-vele.   *Yava'adiyo*   *ya-da-vele*   *hidema custom ya-kudu*
I would give.   Whatever   I would give   this one   custom   I shut

vaiyahina   *ada*   *hi-miyamiya'e*   *keke ya-da-vele*   *Yawalele.*
forever   and   it remains   not   I would give   Yawalele.

YAWALELE: *Yada-custom   yada-ifufu atu   iya   tauku   tamaku*
              Our custom   our story   but   I   myself   my father
ya-ve'etobodana   ada   keke   hi-da-veleveleku.
I make to wait   and   not   he is giving me.

WASIKENI: *Ka-kolosi vaiyahina ada   bana'e   keke hi-na-alamanena.*
              We close   forever   and   he   not   he will know it.

TODAIYANA: *Yada   custom hi-alialikena.   Meda   bana'e*
               Our   custom it killed him.   That one   he (John)
small boy   oye   keke a-size   keke Nimakoyo
small boy   you   not   your age   not   "Bad Hand" (= Nadeweya)
ana-size. Bana'   muliliya hi-alika   custom faina.   Ahene
his age. He   after   he died   custom because of it.   Already
u-ya'e-be: "Ya-woneni   custom   hi-alialikena."
you said so: "I tell you   custom   it killed him."

WASIKENI: *Hi-na'e   hinafanine.   Vita   lakaina*
              He went   in the middle. Heavy   big (= weighty matter)
ama   keke ka-na-luhifufuye.   Etoveyaba   luwei   ada   keke
so   not   we can talk about. Support posts two   and   not
ka-na-luhifufuye.   Atu   hida   bana'   ahene   kaliva   hi-alamenena
we can talk about.   But   this one he   already people   they know it
Nimana Avilana.   Hida   faina
"Hand Turn" (= "Lazy Gardener").   This one   because of it
ka-luhifufuyena.   Atu   bana'   meda   hademi etoveyaba   ama
we tell the story.   But   he   that one   about   support posts   our
law   hi-miyami'e ada   keke ka-na-hifuifuye.   Hida   yayana
law   it remains   and   not   we can tell story. This one   only
Nimana Avilana.   Awe,   Michael....
"Lazy Gardener."   Enough,   Michael....

Appendix II

The Myth of Honoyeta:
Kafatoudi's Version

Anafaiweya *Honoyeta* *vavineneyao*   *luyei.*   *Hi-miyamiyana*
Thus   Honoyeta   his wives   two.   They living
anafaiweya *Yauyaba*   *ada*   *vavineneyao*   *luyei hi-fwafwayadi.*
like this   Yauyaba   and   his wives   two he deceives them.
Ada *waihinaona*   *hi-wowona:*   *"Kwa-nana*   *ada-leyaya*
And first   he says: "You will go our saltwater bottles
kwa-na-kibolu-tu *Iya* *kaliva* *lakaiku. Ya-na-eno."*   *Ada*   *kaliyao*
you will fill but I   man   old.   I will sleep."   And   ashes
wayaine   *hi-fifina*   *hi-enoeno.*   *Vavineneyao*   *luyei*   *hi-vavaina*
in it   he curls up he sleeps.   His wives   two   they take it
fuwama.   *Feyewa*   *hi-vavaina*   *ada*   *leyaya*   *hi-dodona.*
basket.   Basket   they take it   and   bottles   they put inside it.
Hi-tatauya   *hi-nana* *leyaya*   *wayaine*   *hi-ohobu*   *adi-leyaya*
They start   they go sea   to it   they go down   their bottles
hi-kikibolu.   *Bana'e*   *hi-a'a'e* *hi-luluku*   *hi-viviyau*
they fill.   He (Honoyeta)   he eats   he enters   he dresses up
hi-wakadi. *Hi-fafalasi*   *ana-bunadoka*   *hi-yoyowodi*   *ana-la'ila'i*
well.   He decorates   his headdress   he ties them   his armshells
hi-veveyayedi   *ana-dakula*   *hi-dodonedi.*   *Hi-viviyau*   *hi-yavaina.*
he wears them   his feathers   he puts in them. He dresses up   he finishes.
Hi-ohobu   *yana-udila*   *hi-siwakawakana*   *hi-ohobu*
He goes down   his fish-spear   he pulls it out   he goes down
Laue'e.   *Hi-vevetuyaya*   *hi-balabala*
Laue'e (beach near Bolubolu).   He throws often he follows the beach

280

ada hi-yeyemouna   vavineneyao   hi-i'itadi.   Vavineneyao   matadi
and he appears   his wives   he sees them. His wives   their eyes
hi-da-sena-ma   hi-wonayo: "Ah biya,   wada   kaliva
they would put and   they say: "Ah friend,   that   man
hi-ela'ela   wada   kaliva   dewadewana.   Kaliva   ana-ita
he is coming   that   man   good.   Man   his looks
dewadewana. Hi-ela-be   ka-na-itana."   Hi-yeyemouna   hiyana
handsome.   He comes so   let us see him." He approaches   fish
hi-o'onadi-ma   hi-uhuyadi   hi-balabaledi
he spears them and   he guts them   he brings them along the beach
hi-yemouna. "Eh, o   ha'ami   u-tauya?" Hi-wona: "Keke, Iya
he arrived. "Eh, you   where   you go?" He said: "No,   I
ya-veuveudila."   "Ah, nouma,   tamo kevakeva   u-da-velavela'e?"
I spear-fishing." "Ah, our brother, some   fish   you would give?"
"Ah,   ya-da-velavela'e-tu   wadeya   moyanemi?   Wade   iyana
"Ah,   I would give but   what about   your husband? That   fish
wa-na-vaidi-tu   moyanemi   hi-na-ela'e-be   hi-na-itaku?"
you can take them but your husband he will come and   he will see me?"
Hiyana   hi-babakalidi   vavineneyao   hi-veveledi.
Fish   he tears them (off string) his wives   he gives them.
Hi-yavaina   bana'e   hi-yeyewa. Badi vavineneyao
It finishes (= then) he (Honoyeta)   he returns. They his wives
hi-aiboboula-tu   bana'e hi-yeyewa manuweya.   Hi-nana
they stoop (to fill bottles) but   he   he returns house to.   He goes
manuweya   ana-lokoloko moya'aina hi-seselukulukuwedi.   Hi-yavaina
house to   his valuables many   he hides them inside.   Then
hi-vetoyana   kaliyao   wayaine   hi-totowana   kaliyao   wayaine.
he sits down   ashes   in it   he washes   ashes   with it.
Hi-enoeno.   Hi-lalakayemouna.   Hi-wowonayo:
He sleeps.   They (his wives) climb up and appear. He says:
"Eh, ahene   ada-leyaya   kwa-kiboluna?" Hi-wonayo: "Eh,
"Eh, already   our bottles   you filled?"   They said: "Eh,
ahene a-na   ada-leyaya   a-kiboluna-be a-ela'e."   Kevakeva
already we went   our bottles   we filled and we come." Fish
hi-veledi   tauna-ma   hiyana hi-akabukabu. Hi-wona: "Ah, hima
he gave them   himself and   fish   they roast.   He said: "Ah, this
ada-hiyana?" Hi-wona: "Ah,   tawala hi-taine-be   atuwada
our fish?"   They said: "Ah,   tide   it ebbed and   far
nidiya   wade   a-toyataotaona-be   a-yaudi-be
exposed shoal there we sat on them and we caught them and

a-aliya'e   *kevakeva*   *ka-na-a'e."*   *Hi-a'e.*   *Hi-nuwedi hi-nuwedi*
we brought   fish   we can eat."   They ate.   It carried on and on

hi-nuwedi. Hi-yavaina   *vavine*   *sa'eyana*   *tova hi-luku*   *ada*
and on.   Then   woman   one   time   she entered   and

hi-itana vaiyau   *sa'eyana*   *la'ila'i*   *sa'eyana*   *la'ila'i*   *hi-itana.*
she saw shell   one   armshell   one   armshell   she saw it.

Hi-itana   *anafaiweya*   *wowona*   *bunabunamina*   *nila.*
She saw it   like   his body   fresh oil   coconut.

Hi-itana   *hi-wona:*   *"O, taidei*   *anafaiweya*   *kaliva*   *ime*
She saw it   she said: "O, this   like   man   we

hi-fwayafwayama. Taumeyao moyanema   *ada*
he is deceiving us.   Our own   our husband   and

hi-vekavekauneyema.   *Kaduwe*
he is chewing betel (courting) with us.   Again

hi-vekavekauneyema   *ada*   *taidei*   *moyanema*   *aku*
he is chewing betel with us   and   this one   our husband   but

hi-fwayafwayama   *vaita mali*   *kaliva.*   *A-obuobu*   *leyaya*
he is deceiving us   as if another   man.   We going down   sea

wayaine   *waianahona*   *ada*   *bana'e*   *waihimulimulina*   *hi-ela'ela'e,*   *eh,*
to it   going first   and   he   going last   he coming,   eh,

a-kaukauneya'e."   *Ada tova*   *moya'aina*   *tauna vavineneyao*
we chew together again."   And times   many   his own wives

hi-fwayafwayadi   *anafaiweya*   *kauboi.*   *Hi-kaukauboyedi*
he deceives them   like   cowboy.   He tricks them like a cowboy

Ada tova moya'aina   *vavineneyao*   *tauna*   *hi-vekavekaudi.*   *Ada*
And times many   his wives   himself   he courts them.   And

vavine   *sa'eyadi*   *vineainahona*   *ada*   *lokoloko*   *ana-eyana*   *la'ila'i*
woman   one of them   first wife   and   valuable   its name   armshell

wayaine   *hi-itanuwayana*   *hi-itana*   *ana-ita*   *anafaiweya*
on it   she discovered it   she saw it   its appearance   like

bunabunamina   *nila*   *wayaine.*   *Ada vavine*   *vineainahona*
grease   coconut   of it.   And woman   first wife

hi-wonayo: *"Tubuiyaku,*   *siule*   *taidei*   *kwa-na-sinafuna*
she said: "My friend,   please   this one   you can spy on him

anafaiweya   *kaliva*   *ime*   *waianahona*   *ka-nana'e*
like   man   we   go first   we can go

ka-na-lowoya   *umi*   *kwa-na-yewami*   *wa-na-vealafama*   *ada*
we can go to the forest   you   you can return   you can hide   and

kaliva   *wa-na-itaveabina*   *taidei."*   *Ada adiseluya*
man   you can look after him   this one."   And two of them

malabutuya   *eita koloki*   *adiseluya*   *leyaya*   *hi-dododi.*
in the morning   eight o'clock   two of them   bottles   they put them inside.
Hi-yavaina   *hi-nanau*   *leyaya*   *wayaine ada hi-itadi.*   *Vavine*
Then   they go   sea   to it   and he sees them (go).   Woman
vineaimuli   *hi-yewadi eda*   *wayaine*   *hi-vealafama*   *ada hi-bodaboda.*
second wife   she returns   road   by it   she hides   and she waits.
Vavine   *vineainahona*   *hi-nau*   *leyaya*   *wayaine.*   *Bana'e*
Woman   first wife   she went   sea   to it.   He (Honoyeta)
hi-luku   *vaiyau*   *hi-sedima*   *hi-towa*   *hi-viyau*
he entered   valuables   he put them out   he washed   he dressed up
hi-falasi   *hi-yavaina.*   *Hi-wakana*   *ada udila*   *hi-vaina*
he decorated   he finished.   He good   and fish-spear   he took it
kaduwe hi-yewana   *leyaya*   *wayaine.*   *Hi-na-fwaya*   *faina.*
again   he returned   sea   to it.   He will deceive   because.
Hi-tauya   *hi-na*   *hi-obu*   *hi-veudila*
He started   he went   he went down   he threw fish-spear
hi-balabala.   *Vavine sa'eyadi*   *hi-itadi*   *adikaibe.*
he followed the beach.   Woman   one of them   he saw her   alone.
Ada bana'e   *hi-obu*   *hi-towa.*   *Hi-yavaina*   *nuyana*
And he   he went down   he washed.   Then   his skin
hi-kiuwauwana   *he-vaina*   *vilaya*   *wekawekane*   *hi-sena.*
he folded it   he took it   Alocasia plant   on its shriveled leaf   he put it.
Nuyana   *anafaiwea*   *mota*   *hi-sivealilina.*   *Hi-sena*   *vilaya*
His skin   like   snake   he shed it.   He put it   Alocasia
wayaine   *hi-luhayahayana hi-senitu*   *hi-viyau.*   *Hi-yavaina*
on it   he hung it   he put it and   he dressed up.   Then
kadu   *hi-nau.*   *Hi-nana*   *hi-bayabayauma hi-veuveudila*
again   he went.   He goes   he fishes and   he throws fish-spear
hi-balabala.   *Vavinena*   *sa'eyadi*   *hi-nuwayadi*
he follows the beach.   His wife   one of them   he finds her
vineainahona. *Aku*   *vineaimuli*   *ahena*   *hi-nau*   *anafaiweya kauboi*
first wife.   But   second wife   already   she went   like   cowboy
hi-vealafama   *wola'a*   *wayaine*   *hi-lubodaboda.*   *Ada*   *badi*
she hid   forest   in it   she is waiting.   And   she (first wife)
taudi   *hiyana*   *hi-veledi*   *Ada badi vavine*   *vineitaliya*
herself   fish   he gives her.   And she   woman   wife who watches
hi-yewadi nuyana anafaiweya   *vilaya*   *wayaine*   *hi-sena*
she returns his skin   thus   Alocasia   on it   he put it
hi-vaina   *ada*   *nuyana hi-kelilina.*   *Hi-kelilina*   *hi-yavaina*
she took it   and   his skin   she tore it up.   She tore it up   then

hi-seyena.   *Tuvavine*   *hi-yewadi*   *hi-yemouna*   *melala*
she threw it away.   That woman   she returned   she arrived   village

wayaine   *hi-bodaboda. Bana'e*   *hi-na*   *hi-yewana*   *hi-yemouna*
at it   she waits.   He   he went   he returned   he arrived

hi-itana.   *"Oh, Honoyeta!"*   *"Siule*   *vavineku.*   *Bademo*
she saw him. "Oh, Honoyeta!"   "Thank you   my wife.   Already

nuyaku   *wa-nuwayana atu*   *nuyaku*   *hi-da-miyana*   *ada*   *aimo*
my skin   you found it   but   my skin   it would stay   and   soon

ka-da-itana.   *Anafaiweya*   *yavaiyami ka-da-itana*   *iya*
we would see it.   Like this   how   we would see it   I (am)

kaliva.   *Ama nuyaku*   *bademo*   *wa-kelilina."*   *Ada hi-nuwakoyo.*
a man.   But my skin   already   you tore it up."   And he angry.

Vavinena   *vineainahona.*   *hi-ela'e-da*   *hi-miyamiyana*   *melala*   *wayaine.*
His wife   first wife   she came and   he is staying   village   in it.

Au'a   *hi-vetahova*   *keke*   *nuwanuwana*   *hi-na'a*
Food   they cooked   not   want   he will eat

hi-miyamiyana.   *Hi-miyamiyana*   *ada*   *kalimu*   *hi-laka*
he remains (without eating).   He remains   and   betel tree   he climbs

hi-atuna   *ana laibida*   *hi-koluna.*   *Ada*   *hi-miyana-eeeeeeh.*
he plucks it   his mustard leaf   he picks it.   And   he stays and stays.

Malahiboyi   *mala*   *hi-itana*   *hi-obu*   *hi-viyau.*   *Hi-yavaina*
Evening   time   he saw it   he went down   he dressed up.   Then

hi-towamididi   *melala*   *sa'eyana sa'eyana hi-lakava.*   *Tauna*
he stood up to go   village   one after another he climbs up to.   Himself

nuwanuwana   *hi-na-mununa*   *faina.*   *Sa'eyana*   *melala*
wants   they can kill him   because.   One   village

hi-yeyemouna   *hi-lalakava*   *hi-nunuwakoyo*   *hi-sisiweya.*
he arrives   he climbs up   he gets angry   he swears.

Hi-wowonayo: *"Iya yaku-nuwanuwa aimodi*   *wa-na-munuku."*   *Atu*
He says: "I   my thought   now   you will kill me."   But

badi kaliva   *keke*   *yadi-nuwanuwa hi-na-mununa.*   *Kaliva*
they people   not   their thought   they will kill him.   People

hi-alamanena   *ana-eyana*   *yiduwa.*   *Bana'e*   *hi-na-mununa*
they know him   his name   god.   He   (if) they will kill him

kaliva   *moya'aidi*   *hi-na-akwaha.*   *Ada hi-venuwadadanena*
people   many of them   they will die out.   And he wandered about

melala   *sa'eyana sa'eyana hi-fatana.*   *Hi-nuwena hi-nuwena.*   *Hi-na*
village   one after another he visited all.   He went on and on.   He went

melala   *ana-eyana Iwabuya.*   *Ada*   *atuaha*   *ana-eyana*
village   its name   Iwabu to it.   And   sitting platform   its name

284

Kwasedamaneku   *tabone*   *hi-laka*   *ada*   *kaliva*
You-Wrong-Me   on top   he climbed   and   people
hi-fahana.   *Eh,*   *kaliva*   *sa'eyana*   *natuna*
they were gardening.   Eh,   man   one   his son
hi-miyamiyanena.   *Ada bana'e*   *hi-wonenayo:*   *"Eh,*
he was minding him.   And   he (Honoyeta)   he said to him: "Eh,
taidei   *taini*   *u-miyamiyanena."*   *Hi-wona:*   *"Keke,*
this one   your younger brother   you are minding."   He said: "No,
idaiya natuku."   *"Keke,*   *ya-itani taini."*   *Hi-wona:*
this my son."   "No,   I see you your younger brother."   He said:
"Keke, iya natuku."   *Hi-sena*   *hi-wonawona he-sena.*   *Kaliva*
"No,   I my son."   He put it   he replied   he put it.   Man
hi-nuwakoyo ada   *hiyo*   *hi-kakilina*   *hi-obu*
he angry   and   spear   he took down   he went down
hi-onana.   *Hiyo*   *bubuna*   *wayaine*   *hi-lakava.*   *Hiyo*
he speared him.   Spear   his body   in it   it went up.   Spears
moya'aidi   *hi-laka*   *keke anafata hi-na-alika.*
many of them   they went up   not   enough   he can die.
Ada hi-obu   *hi-wona:*   *"Keke, taidei*   *iya*   *Honoyeta.*
And he came down   he said: "No,   this one I   Honoyeta.
Aku-fuluma   *ana-ita*   *anafaiweya.*   *U-nana*   *ai*
My taboo-stick   its appearance   thus.   You can go   tree
ana-eyana   *ilumwadaleta u-na-talana*   *ada*   *u-na-ela'e.*
its name   *ilumwadaleta* you can chop it   and   you can come.
Anafaiweya   *anafata-be awakukauliku u-na-launa*   *ada*   *ya-na-alika.*
Thus   enough and my throat   you can hit it   and   I will die.
Keke   *meyameyanina*   *ya-na-alika.*   *Iya*   *aku-eyana Honoyeta.*
Not   easy   I can die.   I   my name   Honoyeta.
Aku-eyana yiduwa. Anafaiweya   *keke vaita anafaiweya iya kaliva."*
My name god.   Thus   not   as if   like   I   man."
Hi-na   *ai*   *ilumwadaleta hi-talana*   *ada*   *hi-aliyena.*
He went   tree   *ilumwadaleta* he chopped it   and   he brought it.
Hi-yavaina awakukaulina wayaine   *hi-launa.*   *Hi-launa-da*   *hi-na*
Then   his throat   on it   he hit him. He hit him and   he went
hi-vetoyana babi   *wayaine.*   *Atuaha*   *wayaine*   *hi-vetoyana.*
he sat down ground   on it.   Sitting platform   on it   he sat.
Hi-yavaina aiyila   *hi-vaina*   *talayina*   *moya'aidi*
Then   knife   they took it   his limbs   many of them
hi-dabana.   *Ada*   *hi-fuifufu-tu*   *Wela*   *wayaine*   *hi-fulumafuna.*
they cut off.   And   he speaking still.   Pot   in it   they filled up.

Wela   hi-mididelina.   Hi-yavaina atu   keke hi-da-kwau.
Pots   they stood in a line. It finished but   not   he would cook.
Awana   hi-fuifufu   hi-bonabonaluya   anafaiweya   wela wayaine
His mouth it is speaking he is talking weakly thus   pot   in it
hi-taotahova.   Wela   wayaine   hi-da-vevetalakai.   Keke anafata
he is cooking. Pot   in it   they would stir up. Not enough
hi-na-kwau.   Babi   hi-ala'owodi   keke   anafata.   "Oh,   taidei
he will cook. Earth   it burned   not   enough.   "Oh,   this one
keke kaliva.   Hida   yiduwa.   Ka-munufanina   ada   keke   anafata
not   man.   This   a god.   We killed in error   and   not   enough
vidona   mata'ina.   Keke   kevakeva   hi-da-kwau.   Kai
his flesh   raw.   Not   meat   it would cook.   If
hi-da-kwau   ka-da-ana   atu   taidei   keke yava'adi.   Hida
it would cook   we would eat it but   this one   not   what.   This
bana'e   yiduwa."   Ada   nila   hi-dabadi   hi-yavaina
he   a god."   And   coconut leaves   they cut them   then
hi-foyana.   Hi-foyana   hi-yavaina   moya'aidi
they wove baskets. They wove baskets then   many of them
hi-wahina.   Huleya   hi-wahidi   dabadaba
they carried. Conch shell   they carried them   coconut branches
hi-wahidi   giyo.   Hi-tuwa   hi-vagilili   hi-wahina
they carried them   spears. They shouted   they rioted   they carried
hi-nuwedi hi-nuwedi hi-nuwedi.   Hi-tuwavagilili   hi-na
they went on and on and on.   They shouted riotously   they went
hi-nuwena hi-nuwena hi-nuwena.   Kabu   hi-etowolota   hi-bala
it went on and on and on.   Ridge   they crossed   they traversed
hi-aliyena hi-aliyena   hi-aliyena.   Hi-na   Yaluwata.
they brought him brought him   brought him. They went Galuwata.
Hi-lukuwena   ana-eyana   Awa'awana Kaliyata.   Kaliyata
They took him inside   its name   Mouth of Kaliyata.   Kaliyata
hi-lukuwena   ada   babi   hi-folena   hi-yavaina.
they took him inside   and   ground they dug   it finished.
Oya Tuwaka   dobone.   Eh,   hi-yavaina luluna
Mount Tuwaka   halfway up.   Eh,   then   his bones
hi-foyana   talayina   hi-foyena   hi-luku
they put in basket   his limbs   they put in basket they entered
hi-bauna.   Eh,   anafaiweya   simenti kabala lakaina
they made a pile. Eh,   like   cement stones   big
lalafadi   hi-vaidi   hi-sedi   hi-yavaidi.
flat and wide   they got them   they placed them   they finished them.

Hi-mididi   *babi*   *hi-vaina*   *hi-vetauna*   *hi-yavaina.*
They stood up   earth   they got it   they buried him   they finished it.
Tauna   *nafone*   *hi-fuifufuyedi.*   *Vaita*   *kalivamoena*   *keke*
Himself   inside   he is speaking to them.   As if   man real   not
hi-da-alika.   *Nomada*   *bubunaya*   *atu*   *kuluwana*   *wayaine*
he would die.   No matter   his body only   but   his head   from it
hi-fuifufu.   *Bana'e*   *ana-eyana*   *yiduwa*   *kuluwana*   *wayaine*   *hi-fuifufu.*
he speaks.   He   his name   god   his head   from it   he speaks.
Hi wona: *"Keke*   *wa-itana*   *taidei*   *hi-mamahalina*   *mataku*
He said: "Not   you see it   this one   it lets light in   my eye
wa-na-kibodana.   *Meme'i*   *ya-itaitana."*   *Ada*   *babi*   *nafone*
you can close it.   There   I am seeing (still)."   And   earth   inside
hi-miyana   *hi-vevehawaledi*   *ada*   *hi-kikibodaboda-tu*   *hi-na*
he remains   he shows them   and   they seal it and   they go
hi-luyabuna.   *Hi-wona:*   *"Oh,*   *ahene*   *wa-luyabuna*   *ada*
they complete it.   He said: "Oh,   now   you complete it   and
anafaiweya   *ahene*   *wa-kidaliku-da*   *ahene*   *wa-luyabuku.*   *Iya*
thus   already   you cover me and   already   you finish me.   I
aku-eyana   *Honoyeta.*   *Anafaiweya*   *wa-na-ifufu*
my name   Honoyeta.   Thus   you can speak (spell)
wa-na-luivauku   *babi*   *wayaine*   *ya-na-enovilavilaku*   *Kawana*
you can waken me   earth   in it   I will turn myself over.   Sun
lakaina   *hi-na-kabuna. Au'a*   *keke.*   *Anafaiweya*   *wa-na-ifufu*
big   it will burn.   Food   none.   Thus   you can speak (spell)
luluku   *matatabuna*   *hi-na-eno*   *dewadewa*   *babi*   *wayaine.*
my bones   all   they will sleep   well   earth   in it.
Eh,   *au'a*   *moya'aina-be*   *lokoloko*   *moya'aina*   *wa-faha-be*
Eh,   food   plentiful and   valuables   many   you plant and
yaitoma   *moya'aina.*   *Amiya-be*   *ami-nila*   *yaitoma*
things   many.   Your food and   your coconut   things
moya'aina.   *Yo*   *wa-na-ana.*   *O wa-na-ifufu*   *anafaiweya*
many.   All   you can eat.   Or you can speak (spell)   like this
iya   *ya-na-enovilaku*   *kaduwe*   *yaitoma keke*   *moya'aina keke.*
I   I will turn myself over   again   things   not   many   not.
Iya   *aku-eyana*   *yiduwa.*   *Bademo*   *wa-munuku-da*
I   my name   god.   Already   you killed me and
wa-munufaniku.   *Iya*   *aku-eyana*   *Honoyeta."*   *Ada*   *ana-tomunuya*
you killed me in error.   I   my name   Honoyeta."   And   his killers
boyi   *hi-au'a'e*   *hi-enoeno*   *kaliva*   *moya'aidi*
that night   they eat food   they sleep   people   many of them

biyabiyama-be   *kaliva-be*   *yaluketa-be*   *bawe*   *hi-enovayata.*
children and   adults and   dogs and   pigs   they slept forever.
Awe   *yiduwa*   *hi-enoeno*   *babi*   *wayaine.*   *Melala*   *sa'eyana*
So   the god   he sleeps   earth   inside.   Village   one
hi-ela   *hi-foyana-da*   *hi-kidewedewena-da*
they came   they put him in basket and   they prepared him and
hi-sena   *oya*   *Yaluwata*   *wayaine*   *hi-kumulina*
they put him   mountain   Galuwata   at   they entombed him
ada hi-miyamiyana.   *Kaliva*   *ana-eyana*   *Honoyeta.*   *Yiduwa.*
and he is staying.   Man   his name   Honoyeta.   A god.
Hi-mununa   *atuaha*   *tabone*   *ana-eyana*   *Kwasedamaneku.*
They killed him   sitting platform   on top   its name   "You Wrong Me."
Melala   *ana-eyana*   *Yabiliva.*   *Melala*   *kaliva*   *adi-eyana*   *Iwabuya.*
Hamlet   its name   Yabiliva.   Village   people   their name   Iwabu.
Honoyeta   *hi-mununa.*   *Bana'e*   *keke*   *kaliva.*   *Bana'e*   *anafaiweya*
Honoyeta   they killed him.   He   not   man.   He   like
Yaubada   *anafaiweya*   *viviluwa.*   *Honoyeta*   *ana-tubuya*
God   like   spirit.   Honoyeta (his story)   its ending
anafaiwea.
thus.

Notes

1: OF MYTHS AND MEN

1. A brilliant extrapolation of this notion can be found in Jorge Luis Borges's parable of Pierre Menard, a twentieth-century author who began to rewrite *Don Quixote* word for word, and whose version—by virtue of the centuries that had elapsed and the different meanings that such a project must entail—was "almost infinitely richer" than Cervantes's original.

2. The principal published sources for Goodenough Island oral literature are Jenness and Ballantyne (1928), Maribelle Young (1979), and several booklets in the Iduna language published by the Summer Institute of Linguistics (Huckett and Lucht 1975, 1976*a, b, c*). A number of my own writings examine myths and legends (1971*a*, 1977*a*, 1982*b*), oratory (1974), and jokes (1977*b*).

3. Leenhardt's professional academic career at the College de France was overshadowed by his predecessor Marcel Mauss and his successor Claude Lévi-Strauss. *Do Kamo* has suffered undue neglect by anglophone anthropologists too, a neglect recently rectified by B. M. Gulati's English translation (1979). My own belated reading of *Do Kamo,* in December 1980, brought me both delight and dismay, for although it corroborated many of my own insights into lived myth, I realized that I had neither attempted nor risked so much as Leenhardt. I am most grateful to Donald Tuzin for insisting that I read, at the eleventh hour, James Clifford's authoritative intellectual biography of Leenhardt (1982), a study worthy of its subject.

4. The potential for identification is therefore greater than in traditions where mythical characters are "free-floating" and not attached as putative ancestors to particular lines or groups. For example, heroes of the *wayang* mythology of Java "were the consciously approved models by which a child

grew up.... Precisely because the moral and physical models are enshrined in a universally accepted mythology...the young Javanese is presented with a wide choice of models for his own personality, which he can be sure will win approval anywhere in Javanese society" (Anderson 1965: 24-25). This latitude is far from being the case in Kalauna.

5. Some illustration of this is presented in chapter 7, where I comment on different renderings of the same myth by two of its owners, Iyahalina and Kawanaba. These men were separated by thirty or more years and by marked personality differences; their narrations of the myth disagree fundamentally on a number of thematic issues. There were so many possible reasons for this, however, that I have been unable to discuss them in this book.

6. It is probably true to say that all biographical traditions involve some interweaving of mythical elements (just as the inspirational uses of myth for literature and other art forms is to be found almost everywhere). Eliade writes of "the very general human tendency to hold up one life-history as a paradigm and turn a historical personage into an archetype" (1968:32). Otto Rank (1959) isolated an exemplary biographical pattern in the lives of many mythical and historical persons, which he surmised to be a universal pattern rooted in the human psyche. Other psychoanalysts, notably Ernst Kris (1952) and Erik Erikson (1958, 1969), have explored the role of myths as exemplary patterns in the lives of artists and religious leaders. Religious traditions in particular are commonly mediated by myths and based on sacred biographies that mythicize the founders — the case of the historical Christ being but one example, though the "imitation of Christ" has clearly been differently construed at different periods of Christianity's historical development (cf. Campbell 1972:319-320). To cite a final example of the dialectic, Cardinal Newman's biographical writings, according to Capps, selected "aspects of the lives of individual saints which especially illumined his own experiences [and] *his* life thereby assumed the mythical cast which identification with the saints inevitably accorded it" (Capps 1976:216).

7. The phrase is James Clifford's (1978:43). The success of biography in our own culture, he suggests, is due to our "myth of personal coherence." See also Clifford (1982:7).

8. Cf. Olney (1972:34): "The self expresses itself by the metaphors it creates and projects, and we know it by those metaphors."

9. Many of the issues touched upon in this section are dealt with by Langness and Frank (1981), an updated and expanded version of Langness (1965). This concise but remarkably comprehensive work on the current state of the art of life history studies came to my notice after the present work had been submitted for publication.

10. The phenomenological perspective on life history materials has been discussed in two recent papers by Watson (1976) and Frank (1979). Watson

presents a kind of checklist of descriptive categories for understanding a life history (ibid.: 101-107). Those relevant to hermeneutical issues are: (1) the socio-cultural context; (2) the individual life in this context; (3) the immediate context of life history elicitation; (4) preunderstanding or preconceptions of the investigator; (5) the dialectical relationship between the investigator and the subject or the text. Those categories relevant to understanding the phenomenological attitude of the subject are: (1) the lifeworld; (2) cognitive organization; (3) self-identity (or self-image); (4) conflicts (or contradictions); (5) decisions (or "turnings"); (6) the unity of the subject's consciousness. While I have not employed the language of phenomenology nor attempted to apply these categories rigorously to my data, my own text is informed by a general awareness of them.

11. "Dramatism" is Kenneth Burke's term, but the dramaturgical perspective on human social interaction has a venerable usage in Mead, Goffman, Duncan, and other American sociologists of communication (see Burke 1966, 1968; Duncan 1962, 1969; and for an overview of the place of "dramatism" in the sociology of symbolic interactionism, see Brittan 1973).

12. It is difficult to find a succinct statement of this idea in Burke's rambling and terminologically untidy system, though the following will also serve to show the link he perceives between victimage and hierarchy: "The principle of drama is implicit in the idea of action, and the principle of victimage is implicit in the nature of drama. The negative helps radically to define the elements to be victimized. And inasmuch as substitution is a prime resource of symbol systems, the conditions are set for catharsis by scapegoat (including the 'natural' invitation to 'project' upon the enemy any troublesome traits of our own that we would negate). And the unresolved problems of 'pride' that are intrinsic to privilege also bring the motive of hierarchy to bear here; for many kinds of guilt, resentment, and fear tend to cluster about the hierarchical psychosis, with its corresponding search for a sacrificial principle such as can be embodied in a political scapegoat" (1966:18-19).

13. Northrop Frye identifies the tragic mode of the fall of a leader as "high mimetic tragedy" which is "balanced midway between godlike heroism and all-too-human irony" (1957:37).

14. Alfred Gell writes: "In synchronicity, the subjective process of establishing meaningful relations between events in the world is reflected back in quasi-objective form as an organizing principle revealed in events themselves. . . . And by invoking synchronicity relations, by weaving them into patterns of symbolic action, magical thought seeks both access to, and control over, the hidden contingencies which govern human life" (1974:26).

15. The original text of Wasikeni's narrative together with the argument which interrupted it are presented as appendix I.

16. Resentful heroes are ubiquitous not only in the mythology of Nidula

291

(Young 1982*b*) but in that of the Massim at large. The curious recurrence of the type, however, has hitherto gone unremarked. The most accessible general collection of Massim folktales (in Seligman 1910) contains several resentful heroes, as does a collection of northeast Normanby Island narratives analysed by Carl Thune in a valuable, but as yet unpublished, doctoral dissertation (1980). A recently published epic tale from the Trobriands (Leach 1981) features a typical resentful hero, whose quest for the beautiful Imdeduya is an analogue of a Kula expedition.

2: HOUSE OF LULAUVILE

1. I have described the environment and social structure of Kalauna, as well as many other topics which this chapter touches upon, in an earlier work, *Fighting With Food* (1971). Fuller details can be found there, though I have refrained from cluttering the present text with more reference to it than seemed necessary. The ethnographic present to which I refer, unless otherwise indicated, is the late 1960s.

2. In *Fighting With Food* I unequivocally labeled the segments I and II without making this important caveat. In 1977, a Heloava man suggested to me that when Kimoala died "Lulauvile Number Two" would revert to calling itself "Lulauvile Number One"!

3. On the power or efficacy of magical paraphernalia one Kalauna man explained: "The betel pepper leaf does not turn red when I chew it alone. Its redness only appears when I mix the juice with lime in my mouth. The lime is like a spell."

3: TIME'S SERPENT HONOYETA

1. The twelve versions were recorded in the following villages: Abolu, Bwaidoka (2), Galuwata, Goiyala, Ibawana, Imuleya, Kalimatabutabu, Kalauna (2), Utalo, Wakonai.

2. See Jenness and Ballantyne (1928:26-27) for two published versions of this tale.

3. In Iyeya's view, Honoyeta's son is none other than the Biblical Noah.

4. This narrator called the sitting circle Lakavagata, which means "Climb-up-forever" (i.e., and die there).

5. These pendants used to circulate in the *kula* and are still to be found throughout the Massim, though nowhere in such numbers as on Goodenough Island. The persistent confusion between mythical serpents' teeth and real boars' tusks was first attested by Captain Monckton (1897), who was himself deceived.

6. The one version that attributes Honoyeta with fatherhood makes it the excuse for him to tell his child that the desecration of the father's skin means the loss of immortality for the son.

7. This is also the fate, in another Nidula tale, of a man's long and unruly penis that seduces women during their husbands' absences.

8. See Adiyaleyale's complaints against his father Iyahalina in chapter 7.

9. See Young (1971:43-46) for some illustration of this point.

4: BLOOD OF MALAVEYOYO

1. Elsewhere I have given a historical sketch of Kalauna based on oral traditions and documentary references (1971:29-32). See also my account of the myths of origin of Kalauna clans (ibid.:62-66), and a compressed folk-history in which an abbreviated version of Malaveyoyo's legend is given (ibid.:186-187).

2. See Young (1971: ch. 11) for an account of festivals in Kalauna.

3. Moiye means cuscus or possum, and his clan, Lalauneya, is said to have been a group of landless hunters who crossed the island from the west.

4. The weight I have given to the details of this atrocity follows the original narrative. The blunt final sentence, for instance, contrasts starkly with the circumstantial details of the struggle.

5. See Jenness and Ballantyne (1920:85).

6. I have shown elsewhere (Young 1977a) how Bwaidokans firmly believe that the Wesleyan mission appeared in response to news of a cannibal death, and how Dr. Bromilow was acclaimed a "savior" who brought them peace.

7. See Young (1971:31-32; 1977a) for legendary accounts of Misibibi and Bromilow respectively.

5: JAW OF TOBOWA

1. The main reason given for burying a kinsman under or beside one's house is to guard the grave. Certain old women were suspected of necrophagy, too, though not necessarily of having magical command of *kwahala* (see also Jenness and Ballantyne 1920:118).

2. See Young (1971:130-131). As a microcosm of the total sample, these attacks attributed to Tobowa are sociologically instructive, for they illustrate essentially the same distribution pattern of accusations characteristic of the whole sample. "Thus, nine of Tobowa's victims were men, and four were women; eight were agnates, one was an affine (his wife) and four were unrelated; six of the attacks were attributed to his grievances over food,

three were thought to be motivated by vengeance, two by his competition with other leaders, one by the adultery of his wife, and the motive for one was not known" (ibid.:131).

3. For accounts of such meetings in recent years, see Young (1971:144-145; 1974).

4. I have presented the details of this nightmarish sequence of sorcery deaths elsewhere (see Young 1971:90-91).

5. But see Young (1971:91), where an alternative interpretation of Towakaita's death is given.

6. I have described the quarrels of these two men (1971:78-79).

7. I asked Tabwaika many times to tell me the story of Auyoke (it being understood that he would omit the magic anyway), but he was reluctant. Finally, he gave me a very abbreviated version, having made all due acknowledgments to Nikuya, the story's "true" owner. I was astonished when the tale turned out to be almost identical to the last part of Iyaha-lina's Kiwiwiole myth (see ch. 7), though this fact provides a clue to Iyaha-lina's dismay over its alienation. Tabwaika could not, or would not, tell me whether the story really started at the point where he began to narrate it.

Auyoke is the name of a "grandfather" with sealed orifices (cf. the "stone" grandmother Vineuma in Iyahalina's myth), who lives with his granddaughter Wayakolu (cf. Vineuma's grandson Kiwiwiole). Wayakolu frightens Auyoke with a snake, causing his mouth and anus to burst open. The pair then load a canoe and paddle around the coast to the north of the island where Miyavaina people live. On the journey they stop at every point and look back until they can no longer see Yauyaba (the hill that marks the position of their village). Finally out of sight of Yauyaba, they enter the river and Auyoke declares he will "disappear" at Waia'u'u, its source. His granddaughter returns home alone. Tabwaika concluded: "Auyoke stayed there at Miyavaina's place, and there was no famine. With abundant sago they have prosperity forever."

8. For an account of Tabwaika's challenge to Lulauvile, see Young (1971:82-85).

6: HEAD OF DIDIALA

1. I recorded an extended autobiographical narrative from Kwahihi in 1977. An earlier draft of this book included a chapter devoted to her, one designed to complement those on Didiala and Iyahalina. I abandoned this plan, however, since it raised too many issues irrelevant to the themes of the overall work. Rich though her narrative was, it revealed none of her menfolk's concern with personalized myth, and my analysis of it will be published elsewhere (Young 1983).

2. This version was recorded by Kawanaba, who, though not himself an owner, told it to me with Keyayala's approval. I had neglected to get more than an outline of the story from Didiala while he was alive.

3. Note the convergence of this tale with Vatako's, as given in chapter 1.

4. In 1966 Didiala's extended family of wife, sons, sons' wives, and their children numbered eleven. Adding to this the families of his father's brother's sons' sons, his *unuma* numbered nineteen all told. The remaining *unuma* in Anuana (comprising the families of three men) had a strength of only thirteen. There were in addition five other Anuana men who at this time had chosen to join Kimaola in his hamlet of Heloava II (see Young 1971:100).

5. Didiala never explained how he came to acquire so much money when the standard wage in Misima in the twenties was only £6 a year.

6. Yaneku was to die only a few months after Didiala, "killed" (it was said) by his obsessive compulsion to plant large gardens. This was in spite of the intimations he had already had of the envy of sorcerers (see Young 1971:168-169).

7: BONES OF IYAHALINA

1. *Ulaiya* is the Nibita word for taro, but in incantations it refers to plump and heavy tubers of any kind. The imagery of these three lines, however, evokes their unpalatability when they are old, hard, black, or rotten. Like the bird heroes of the myth, ferment flies are said to "fly aimlessly to and fro without eating."

2. *Binamatu* is a sucker fish that "sits still" by anchoring itself to stones.

3. I was given two other versions of the Kiwiwiole myth, one by Kawanaba of Heloava and one by Dakwakeke, an old woman of Anuana II. Both are as long as Iyahalina's version, and I cannot review them here. However, neither of them contradicts the interpretation I offer for Iyahalina's version, though they do invite different readings of Kiwiwiole's role and character. Thus, for Kawanaba, Kiwiwiole is fathered by a Muyuwa man and feathered like a bird by his mother for the task of flying back to Goodenough; Kikifolu is therefore unnecessary to his version. (Indeed, Kawanaba argued that Iyahalina had improperly appropriated Kikifolu from Kimaola's myth of Oyatabu.) For Dakwakeke, whose version almost amounts to a different myth since it gives charter to *yaleyale* magic rather than to the hunger-quelling magic of *manumanua*, Kiwiwiole is indubitably a bird; he is insulted by his human brothers and absconds to Muyuwa with his mother, later to return and be killed. I hope to explore the structural relationship of these versions to one another (and to other myths in the corpus) in another context. For my purpose here it is enough to note

that Iyahalina's version "humanizes" Kiwiwiole and sharpens the fatherless hero's quest for legitimacy.

4. *Kama* is a large phasmid insect (*Eurycantha latro*), which grows up to fifteen centimeters in length and is remarkable for its immobility.

5. The origin myths of the Kalauna clans agree with one another in many fundamental respects (see Young 1971:62-66), though there is some dissension as to who brought what customs from the ground and in which order. Iyahalina exaggerates when he claims that the other clans emerged "empty-handed," and he would not have said this in a public forum.

8: BELLY OF KIMAOLA

1. See Young (1971:92).

2. Coconuts grew out of Tomoudi's body, however, and in this sense they too have a mythical human ancestry.

3. See the version collected by J. Huckett in Wakonai, a village peopled by Galuwata migrants (McElhanon 1974:116-118).

4. In a long published version of this myth collected at Bwaidoka, Kawa-folafola is brought back to life by his daughter; but in his *unuwewe* at having been abandoned, he banishes the food and betel nut, leaving Good-enough destitute (Jenness and Ballantyne 1928:83-104). See also Young (1982b).

5. See Jenness and Ballantyne's version (ibid.).

6. Dududu is an Eweli hamlet, reputed to have been settled from the other side of the island by people who were hunters rather than gardeners. An expanded gloss of the verse would be: "Why bother to pretend to plant food? Release your tenuous hold on a gardener's life, and go back to your hunter's piglike habits."

7. The flying fox (*manukiki*) is classified as a bird in Kalauna and it is the most likely natural model for the imaginary *kwahala,* or sorcerer's familiar (see chap. 5). Kimaola was believed to control *kwahala,* as we have seen in the account of Tobowa's persecution. Another incident in which Kimaola owned to terrorizing Kalauna with these creatures is described in Young (1971:136-137).

8. After Adiyaleyale lost office the following year he divorced Mialaba. He felt vulnerable again and was astonished at his past audacity. He eventually abandoned Heloava for a haven in the gardens, calling his new hamlet Yabiliva in memory of Honoyeta's suicidal self-sacrifice. But his is another—and longer—story.

9: REVELATIONS

1. A. E. Housman mocks the mood of grandiose self-pity in one of his short poems. The poet purchases a cheap knife and threatens:

> I need but stick it in my heart
> And down will come the sky,
> And earth's foundations will depart
> And all you folks will die.

I am indebted to Judith Wilson for bringing this poem to my attention, and also for recalling a snakes-and-ladders board upon which the largest snake was tagged "from resentment to ruin."

2. See also plate 13, a photograph of the almost completed altar painting in the new Catholic church which was being built at Ulutuya in eastern Goodenough in 1977. The seated figure is a *kaiwabu;* in front of him is a pot of food and a circle of awed men. There is a basket beside him and a croton plant growing out of the sitting circle. The triangular panel above his head is composed of rows of *buibui* (clouds), alternately painted in red and black. Lawrence Iaubihi, who conceived the design, explained: "We used to believe that Jesus came only for the whites, but now we know that there is a Jesus for every people. This is a picture of ours, like Honoyeta at Yabiliva before they killed him."

3. For many details of the events of 1976, including data on the various cargo cults of that year, I am greatly indebted to Fr. John Fallon who kindly made his written observations available to me. He is not, of course, responsible for the interpretations I have placed upon them.

4. Fr. John Fallon independently noted in 1976 that Isekele, the Wagifan prophet, had appropriated the biographical "fiction" I attributed to a youth called Gimaula in my article (1971a:47). The myth of the hungry orphan who is succored by a bird is presented in chapter 3.

5. See for example, Young (1971:34-35), on the ambivalence generated by "the bittersweet life of intensive sociality." In an article on settlement size in New Guinea, Anthony Forge (1972) cogently argues that under the "egalitarian specification" community size cannot rise much above 350 to 400, to eighty or ninety adult males. Kalauna is somewhat complicated by Lulauvile's aspiration to provide what Forge would call "classification by ascription of status in some hierarchical scheme" (ibid.:375). But the present book is, in a sense, a history of Lulauvile's failures, just as *Fighting with Food* illustrates Forge's ominous dictum: "Egalitarian societies can only be maintained at the cost of continuous vigilance by their members" (ibid.: 374).

Kalauna reached Forge's maximum optimal size of 400 in the year 1962. Some idea of the problem of handling face-to-face relationships can be given by the number of dyadic relations involved at increasing population levels [as given by the formula $\frac{1}{2}(n^2 - n)$]:

Year	Population	Dyads
1962	400	79,800
1967	470	110,215
1973	508	127,778
1977	547	149,331

Thus, a 36 percent increase in Kalauna's population over fifteen years produced an 87 percent increase in the number of dyadic relationships.

6. This contest, between Mifoloyai and Iwaoyana clans, was an intricate political affair in which Lulauvile sided with Iwaoyana, its erstwhile "enemy," against its ally Mifoloyai. I have described it briefly elsewhere (Young forthcoming).

7. Cf. Sartre's depiction of the saint:

In consenting to be no longer in the world, he places himself above all goods, they are all given to him, nothing is good enough for him. If some inner difficulty leads him away from war, he cannot come to life again: he must continue his death by some other means. Thus he sometimes chooses Saintliness. The Saint, too, is a dead man: though he is in this world he is no longer of it. He does not produce, he does not consume; he began by offering up his wealth to God, but that is not enough. It is the entire world that he wants to offer: to offer, that is, to destroy in a magnificent potlatch. [1963:200-201]

8. I cannot adduce all the evidence for this interpretation here. A full-scale study of Nidula mythology (which shades indeterminately into other areas of the Massim) is still in progress. Jenness and Ballantyne (1920:129-131; 1928:166-167) give some details of the cult of Ulekufuyo (or Ulekofuyo), the pot that "ruled the rain and sunshine," and whose owners "extorted" tribute from half the island. Interestingly, these authors refer to the pot as *manumanua,* "because of its influence on the crops" (1928: 131n), but this is the only reference to the term in either of their two works. The Rev. A. Ballantyne destroyed the cult by confiscating, and accidentally breaking, the sacred pot: an act that Malinowski condemned scathingly as an example of "dangerous and heedless tampering" with tribal traditions by missionaries (1922:467n).

9. The snake motif is, of course, ubiquitous in the Massim and far

beyond. The association of serpents with pots on Goodenough occurs throughout the mythology (e.g., see Matabawe's myth in ch. 3). Regarding the serpent's association with the sun, I might add that it is common Nidula belief that eclipses of the moon are caused by Matabawe "swallowing" it.

Glossary of Kalauna Terms

abutu	competitive food exchange
atuaha	sitting circle or platform made of stone slabs
au'a	vegetable subsistence food; root crops
bakibaki	anchoring magic placed in sitting circle or beneath house post
balauma	malicious, fearsome spirit; demon
bolimana	southeast wind or monsoon; wind magic
dewa	custom, habit; hence, characteristic behavior, distinctive way of life
dimdim	European; whites
etonita	zigzag design motif belonging to Lulauvile clan
Fakili	"Comb" ceremonial moiety; type of festival complementary to Modawa
fofofo	hereditary food exchange partner
giduwa	see *yiduwa*
ifufu	speech, story, tale
inuba	initiator; sponsor of feast or exchange
kaiwabu	ceremonial "chief" of a feast or festival; one who gives *niune* (q.v.)
ketowai	shaming gift of pork given at the end of a festival
kuvi	large yam (*Dioscorea alata*)
kwahala	birdlike agent of mystical attack; sorcerer's "familiar"; witch
loka	famine, dearth, state of foodlessness

301

lokona	practice of food conservation by abstemious eating habits
maiyau	spirit or image of person, animal, yam, etc.
malia	prosperity, plenty, state of abundance
manua	house, home
manumanua	ceremony of "staying at home" to anchor food and banish famine
manuamadumadu	ceremonial group-visiting to solicit food-gifts from other villages
miwa	vengeance, blood revenge
Modawa	"Drum" ceremonial moiety; type of festival complementary to Fakili
mota	snake, serpent
nau'a	wooden food bowl
neineya	heritable myth giving charter to a magical system
nibai	hereditary traditional enemy
niune	gift (usually food) that cannot be eaten by owner or recipient, but must be transferred to exchange partner
sisikwana	magic of appetite suppression and food conservation
toitavealata	"man who looks after" the community; ritual guardian of the crops
towava	climatic portent accompanying a magical act or a death
tufo'a	sorcery of greed and insatiable hunger
ulaiya	large desirable tubers, especially taro; "rich food"
ulo	suicide, suicidal state
unuma	patrilineage; descent group within a hamlet
unuwewe	suicidal resentment leading to withdrawal
veumaiyiyi	angry resentment leading to confrontation
vilaya	tarolike plant, *Alocasia macrorhiza*
yafuna	devouring spirit taking the form of an animal; agent of a sorcerer
yaleyale	magic of tireless strength for gardening activities
yiduwa	god, culture hero, "dema"

Bibliography

Anderson, Benedict R. O'G.
  1965. *Mythology and the Tolerance of the Javanese.* Monograph series, Modern Indonesian Project. Ithaca: Cornell University.
Austin, J. L.
  1962. *How To Do Things with Words.* London: Oxford University Press.
Barth, Fredrik.
  1975. *Ritual and Knowledge among the Baktaman of New Guinea.* New Haven: Yale University Press.
Borges, Jorge Luis.
  1975. *A Universal History of Infamy.* Harmondsworth, England: Penguin Books.
Brittan, Arthur.
  1973. *Meanings and Situations.* London: Routledge and Kegan Paul.
Burke, Kenneth.
  1966. *Language as Symbolic Action.* Berkeley and Los Angeles: University of California Press.
  1968. "Interaction: Dramatism." In *International Encyclopedia of the Social Sciences,* 7:445-452.
Burridge, Kenelm.
  1969. *Tangu Traditions.* Oxford: Clarendon Press.
Campbell, Joseph.
  1972. *The Hero with a Thousand Faces.* Princeton, N.J.: Princeton University Press.
Capps, Donald.
  1976. "Newman's Illness in Sicily: The Reformer as Biographer." In *The Biographical Process,* edited by F. Reynolds and D. Capps. The Hague: Mouton.

Champion, F. A.
 1940. Patrol Report: 9/9/40-13/9/40 (C.R.S. G91. #493). Canberra,
 Australia: Commonwealth Archives.
Clifford, James.
 1978. "Hanging Up Looking Glasses at Odd Corners: Ethnobiographi-
 cal Prospects." In *Studies in Biography,* edited by Daniel Aaron,
 Harvard English Studies, 8. Cambridge, Mass.: Harvard University Press.
 1982. *Person and Myth: Maurice Leenhardt in the Melanesian World.*
 Berkeley, Los Angeles, London: University of California Press.
Crapanzano, Vincent.
 1979. Preface to Maurice Leenhardt, *Do Kamo: Person and Myth in
 the Melanesian World,* translated by Basia Miller Gulati. Chicago: Chicago University Press.
 1980. *Tuhami: Portrait of a Moroccan.* Chicago: Chicago University
 Press.
Duncan, Hugh Dalziel.
 1962. *Communication and Social Order.* London: Oxford University
 Press.
 1969. *Symbols and Social Theory.* New York: Oxford University Press.
Egloff, Brian.
 1972. "The Sepulchral Pottery of Nuamata Island, Papua." *Archaeol-
 ogy and Physical Anthropology in Oceania,* 7:145-163.
Eliade, Mircea.
 1959. *Cosmos and History: The Myth of the Eternal Return.* New
 York: Harper Torchbooks, Harper and Row.
 1968. *Myths Dreams and Mysteries.* London: Fontana Library, Col-
 [1957]. lins.
Erikson, Erik.
 1958. *Young Man Luther.* New York: W. W. Norton.
 1969. *Gandhi's Truth: On the Origins of Militant Nonviolence.* New
 York: W. W. Norton.
Forge, Anthony.
 1972. "Normative Factors in the Settlement Size of Neolithic Cultiva-
 tors (New Guinea)." In *Man, Settlement and Urbanism,* edited
 by P. J. Ucko, R. Tringham and G. W. Dimbleby. London:
 Duckworth.
Frank, Gelya.
 1979. "Finding the Common Denominator: A Phenomenological Crit-
 ique of Life History Method." *Ethos,* 7:68-94.
Frye, Northrop.
 1957. *Anatomy of Criticism: Four Essays.* Princeton, N. J.: Princeton
 University Press.

Gell, Alfred.
    1974. "Understanding the Occult." *Radical Philosophy* (Winter), pp. 17-26.
Guiart, Jean.
    1972. "Multiple Levels of Meaning in Myth." In *Mythology,* edited by P. Maranda. Harmondsworth, England: Penguin.
Hallowell, A. Irving.
    1955. "The Self and its Behavioral Environment." In *Culture and Experience.* Philadelphia: University of Pennsylvania Press.
Holland, Norman.
    1968. *The Dynamics of Literary Response.* London: Oxford University Press.
    1975. *Five Readers Reading.* New Haven, Conn.: Yale University Press.
Huckett, Joyce, and Lucht, Ramona, eds.
    1975. *Laugiyo Kahihina.* Ukarumpa, Papua New Guinea: Summer Institute of Linguistics.
    1976a. *Manuga Kahihidi.* Ukarumpa, Papua New Guinea: Summer Institute of Linguistics.
    1976b. *Hida Nainaiya.* Ukarumpa, Papua New Guinea: Summer Institute of Linguistics.
    1976c. *Dewa Kahihina.* Ukarumpa, Papua New Guinea: Summer Institute of Linguistics.
Jenness, D., and Ballantyne, A.
    1920. *The Northern D'Entrecasteaux.* Oxford: Clarendon Press.
    1928. *Language, Mythology and Songs of Bwaidoga.* New Plymouth, New Zealand: Avery and Sons.
Kantorowicz, E. H.
    1957. *The King's Two Bodies.* Princeton, N. J.: Princeton University Press.
Keesing, Roger.
    1978. *'Elota's Story: the Life and Times of a Solomon Islands Big Man.* St. Lucia, Australia: University of Queensland Press.
Korzybski, Alfred.
    1941. *Science and Sanity.* New York: Science Press.
Kris, Ernst.
    1952. *Psychoanalytic Explorations in Art.* New York: International Universities Press.
Langness, L. L.
    1965. *The Life History in Anthropological Science.* New York: Holt, Rinehart and Winston.
Langness, L. L., and Frank, Gelya.
    1981. *Lives: An Anthropological Approach to Biography.* Novato, Calif.: Chandler and Sharp.

Leach, Jerry W.
1981. "Imdeduya: A Kula Folktale from Kiriwina." *Bikmaus,* 2, 1:50-92.

Leenhardt, Maurice.
1979. *Do Kamo: Person and Myth in the Melanesian World,* translated
[1947]. by Basia Miller Gulati. Chicago: Chicago University Press.

Lévi-Strauss, Claude.
1966. *The Savage Mind.* London: Weidenfeld and Nicolson.
1970. *The Raw and the Cooked.* London: Jonathan Cape.
1981. *The Naked Man.* London: Jonathan Cape.

Lithgow, David R.
1976. "Austronesian Languages: Milne Bay and Adjacent Islands
(Milne Bay Province)." In *New Guinea Area Languages and
Language Study,* vol. 2, edited by S. A. Wurm. Pacific Linguis-
tics, Series C, no. 39. Research School of Pacific Studies, The
Australian National University.

McElhanon, K. A.
1974. *Legends from Papua New Guinea.* Ukarumpa, Papua New
Guinea: Summer Institute of Linguistics.

Malinowski, Bronislaw.
1922. *Argonauts of the Western Pacific.* London: Routledge and
Kegan Paul.
1935. *Coral Gardens and their Magic,* vol. 1. London: Allen and Unwin.
1936. *The Foundations of Faith and Morals.* London: Oxford University Press.
1954. "Myth in Primitive Psychology." In *Magic, Science and Religion*
[1926]. *and other Essays.* New York: Anchor Books, Doubleday.

Massal, E., and Barrau, J.
1956. *Food Plants of the South Sea Islands.* Technical Paper no. 94.
Noumea, New Caledonia: South Pacific Commission.

Monckton, Whitmore.
1897. "Goodenough Island, New Guinea." *Journal of the Polynesian
Society,* 6:89-90.

Munn, Nancy.
1977. "The Spatiotemporal Transformations of Gawa Canoes." *Journal de la Société des Océanistes,* 33:39-51.

Olney, James.
1972. *Metaphors of Self: The Meaning of Autobiography.* Princeton,
N. J.: Princeton University Press.

Peacock, James.
1969. "Society as Narrative." In *Forms of Symbolic Action,* edited by
Robert F. Spencer. Seattle: University of Washington Press.

Rank, Otto.
  1959. *The Myth of the Birth of the Hero.* New York: Vintage Books.
  [1909].
Read, Kenneth E.
  1965. *The High Valley.* London: George Allen and Unwin.
Sartre, Jean-Paul.
  1963. *Saint Genet.* New York: George Braziller.
Schieffelin, Edward L.
  1976. *The Sorrow of the Lonely and the Burning of the Dancers.* New
  York: St. Martin's Press.
Schwimmer, Erik.
  1973. *Exchange in the Social Structure of the Orokaiva.* London:
  C. Hurst.
Seligman, C. G.
  1910. *Melanesians of British New Guinea.* Cambridge: Cambridge
  University Press.
Stanner, W. E. H.
  1959. "Continuity and Schism in an African Tribe: A Review."
  Oceania, 29:1-25.
Strathern, Andrew.
  1979. *Ongka: A Self-Account by a New Guinea Big-Man.* London:
  Duckworth.
Strathern, Marilyn.
  1981. "Subject or Object? Women and the Circulation of Valuables in
  Highlands New Guinea." Paper presented at Australian Anthro-
  pological Society conference, August, Canberra, Australia.
Thune, Carl E.
  1980. *The Rhetoric of Remembrance: Collective Life and Personal
  Tragedy in Luboda Village.* Ph.D. dissertation, Princeton Uni-
  versity. University Microfilms International, Ann Arbor, Mich.
Timperley, A. T.
  1941. Patrol Report: 7/5/41-27/5/41 (C.R.S. G91. #493). Canberra,
  Australia: Commonwealth Archives.
Tolhurst, N. M.
  1949. Patrol Report: 8/2/49-30/3/49. Port Moresby, Papua New
  Guinea: Samarai Station Papers, National Archives.
Turner, Victor.
  1957. *Schism and Continuity in an African Society.* Manchester: Man-
  chester University Press.
  1974. *Dramas, Fields and Metaphors.* New York: Cornell University
  Press.
Tuzin, Donald.
  1972. "Yam Symbolism in the Sepik: An Interpretative Account."
  Southwestern Journal of Anthropology, 28:230-254.

Wagner, Roy.
  1972. *Habu: The Innovation of Meaning in Daribi Religion.* Chicago:
        University of Chicago Press.
  1978. *Lethal Speech: Daribi Myth as Symbolic Obviation.* Ithaca,
        N. Y.: Cornell University Press.
Watson, Lawrence C.
  1976. "Understanding a Life History as a Subjective Document."
        Ethos, 4:95-131.
Williams, F. E.
  1932- "Trading Voyages from the Gulf of Papua." *Oceania,* 3:139-
  1933. 166.
  1940. *Drama of Orokolo.* Oxford: Clarendon Press.
Wilson, Peter.
  1974. *Oscar: An Inquiry into the Nature of Sanity.* New York: Ran-
        dom House.
Woodhill, R. K.
  1950. Patrol Report: 17/1/50-18/2/50. Port Moresby, Papua New
        Guinea: Samarai Station Papers, National Archives.
Young, Maribelle.
  1979. *Bwaidoka Tales.* Pacific Linguistics, Series D, no. 16. Research
        School of Pacific Studies, The Australian National University.
Young, Michael W.
  1971. *Fighting with Food: Leadership, Values and Social Control in a
        Massim Society.* Cambridge: Cambridge University Press.
  1971a. "Goodenough Island Cargo Cults." *Oceania,* 42:42-57.
  1974. "Private Sanctions and Public Ideology: Some Aspects of Self-
        help in Kalauna, Goodenough Island." In *Contention and Dis-
        pute,* edited by A. L. Epstein. Canberra: Australian National
        University Press.
  1977a. "Doctor Bromilow and the Bwaidoka Wars." *Journal of Pacific
        History,* 12:130-153.
  1977b. "Bursting with Laughter: Obscenity, Values and Sexual Control
        in a Massim Society." *Canberra Anthropology,* 1, 1:75-87.
  1982a. "Ceremonial Visiting in Goodenough Island." In *The Kula: New
        Perspectives on Massim Exchange,* edited by E. R. Leach and
        J. W. Leach. Cambridge: Cambridge University Press.
  1982b. "The Theme of the Resentful Hero: Stasis and Mobility in Good-
        enough Mythology." In *The Kula: New Perspectives on Massim
        Exchange,* edited by E. R. Leach and J. W. Leach. Cambridge:
        Cambridge University Press.
  (forth- "On Refusing Gifts: Aspects of Ceremonial Exchange in Kala-
  coming) una." In *Metaphors of Interpretation: Essays in Honour of
        W. E. H. Stanner,* edited by D. Barwick, J. Beckett, and M.
        Reay.

308

1983.   "'Our Name is Women; We are Bought with Limesticks and Limepots': An Analysis of the Autobiographical Narrative of a Kalauna Woman." *Man,* 18 (in press).

Young, Michael W., and de Vera, Maribelle.

1980.   "Secondary Burial on Goodenough Island, Papua: Some Archaeological and Ethnographic Observations." *Occasional Papers in Anthropology,* no. 10. Anthropology Museum, University of Queensland.

Index

Abstention. See *Lokona*

Abutu. See Competitive food exchange

Adiyaleyale, 182, 190, 191, 196, 199; myth of, 188-189

Amphlett Islands, 74, 92, 138-139, 145, 228, 229, 246

Bakibaki, 44, 51, 200, 201, 257, 258, 260, 263. *See also* Sitting circle; Stasis

Biography, 4-5, chap. 1 passim; anthropological, 26-28, 290n, 291n; autobiography, 24-26; and myth, 4-5, 10, 18-20, 26-28, 111, 146-147, 153, 170, 178, 187-188, 259-261, 268-270, 271-276 passim, 290n; and *unuwewe,* 267-269

Birds: in mythology, 139-140, 162, 182-183, 186, 229-231, 235-236, 295n. *See also* Kikifolu; Kiwiwiole; Manubutu; Manukubuku

Bolubolu, 138-139, 146, 149; patrol post, 45, 245, 272

Bones: burial of, 79, 96-97, 100, 101; of Honoyeta, 64-65, 79, 80-81, 82, 86; of Iyahalina, 191, 205; of Malaveyoyo, 100, 107. *See also* Burial

Borges, J. L., 25, 26, 289n

Brothers: hostility between, 38-39, 86, 90-91, 108, 139, 141, 207, 228-233 passim, 242, 255, 261

Burial: of Didiala, 135, 160; of Ewahaluna's sister, 255; of Honoyeta, 64-65, 78-79; of Iyahalina, 204-205; of Ma-

laveyoyo, 100; premature, 82-83; secondary, 79; sorcery at, 255, 269; symbolism, 57, 70, 87, 205, 269; of Tobowa, 127-128; of Tomoudi, 144-145. *See also* Death

Burke, K., 29, 47, 194, 291n

Burridge, K., 10, 34, 66

Bwaidoka, 83, 94, 123, 143, 146, 149-150, 173, 253, 264, 293n

Cannibalism, 6, 48, 88, 91, chap. 4 passim, 244, 250; and *abutu,* 107-108; of Honoyeta, 64, 76-78, 86-87; Malaveyoyo's, 93-96, 101-103, 104-105, 196-198 passim; Tobowa's, 113

Cargo cult, 7, 46; and Honoyeta, 72, 81-82, 250, 253-255; millenarian expectations, 133-134; on Nidula in 1976, 251-254, 297n; and return of heroes, 269-270; Tobowa's response to, 118, 123

Christianity: Bible, 114, 203, 274, 292n; Dr. Bromilow, 109, 293n; Jesus victimized, 34, 82, 250-251; missionaries, 33, 93, 114, 175, 250, 274, 298n; mission influence, 46, 106, 130, 162, 172-173, 196, 197, 215, 245, 264-265, 273, 274

Clans. *See* Kalauna

Clifford, J., 14, 15, 289n, 290n

Colonialism. *See* European

Competitive food exchange: challenge, 237-239, 240-242; Didiala's, 148,

149, 153, 156, 268; ideology of, 200, 238, 262-263; Iyahalina's, 192; Kimaola's provocation of, 103, 240-243; Malaveyoyo's invention of, 93, 98, 101-102, 107-108; political significance of, 45, 46, 125, 207, 236, 256-257, 261-262; response to adultery, 89

Death: of Honoyeta's killers, 65, 80-81; and immortality, 82-83, 85, 108; of Malaveyoyo's killers, 99-100, 107, 108; origin of, 72, 80-81. *See also* Burial; Didiala; Iyahalina; Malaveyoyo; Tobowa
Didiala, 7, 14, 20, 50, 55, 115, 118, chap. 6 passim, 176, 177, 197, 205, 206, 207, 212, 225, 228, 237, 243, 257-258, 259, 260-261, 264, 268, 273, 295n; achievements of, 147-153; biographical sketch of, 134-137; death of, 135, 160, 168-169, 245, 257-258; death of daughter of, 156-157, 268; as "great provider," 153, 260; *manumanua* of, 137-138; myths of, 138-147, 261; oratory of, 161-166 passim; response to anthropologist, 133-134; sun magic of, 153-159, 268; *unuwewe* of, 138, 147, 151, 156-157, 160-161, 166, 268
Dream, 213, 215-217, 221, 222, 223, 252, 254
Drought. *See* Famine

Eliade, M., 16-17, 290n
Enemy, 45, 261; and competitive food exchange, 107-108, 209, 221; Didiala's, 162; Iyahalina's, 237-239; Kimaola's, 240-241; Malaveyoyo's victims, 98-99, 101, 102-103, 196-197, 242
Esa'ala, 118, 119, 120, 122, 124, 255
European, as ancestor, 133-134, 254; contact, 8, 11, 33-34, 46, 47-48, 92-93, 109, 122, 134, 174, 251-252; flight in World War II, 156, 218; and Papuan, 132-133, 172; wealth, 81-82, 132-133, 152-153, 252-253. *See*

also Christianity; Government; Wage labor
Exchange partnership, 44-45, 49-50, 141, 261; of Didiala, 135, 149, 167; of Iyahalina, 177, 220, 237-238; of Kimaola, 208, 217, 220, 240-242; of Lulauvile, 102-103, 169; in *manumanua,* 56, 146; of Tobowa, 125-126. *See also* Festival; Gift

Fakili. See Festival
Famine, 47, 53, 68, 137, 139; cycles of, 266, 268, 274-275; Didiala's, 154-155 passim, 268; Honoyeta's, 80-81, 87, 249-250; Malaveyoyo's, 94-98, 102-103, 104; and *manumanua,* 185-186, 192, 193, 201; of 1958, 148; of 1972, 209-210, 245; sanction of *toitavealata,* 53, 59-60, 91, 198; Wameya's, 229. See also *Manumanua; Tufo'a*
Father and son: ambivalence, 28, 31, 38, 88-91; Didiala's sons, 148-149, 151, 158, 159-160, 168-169; and Honoyeta's negations, 85-87, 88-91, 107, 293n; Iyahalina's sons, 1, 175-176, 188, 196, 197, 203-205, 245; Kimaola's father, 213, 217, 219; Kimaola's "sons," 224, 235, 272; Lulauvile sons, 207-210 passim, 247, 259-260, 269, 272-276 passim; Malaveyoyo's son, 99, 107; Tobowa's sons, 116, 127-129, 130; Tomoudi's sons, 144-146
Fergusson Island, 74, 92, 118, 135, 145, 154, 172, 222; and Honoyeta myth cycle, 264; and Oyatabu muth, 229-232
Festival, 44, 45, 102, 125, 148, 150; Heloava's, 208-210, 217, 246; Kawafolafola's, 229, 234; Kimaola's, 159, 164, 168-169, 177, 203, 210-211, 216, 220, 240-241, 244-245; Malaveyoyo's, 96, 101
Fighting with Food, 47, 210, 256, 297n
Fishing, 44; of Adiyaleyale, 188-189; of Bwaidoka for Kalauna, 149; of Honoyeta, 62, 63, 68-69; of Kiwiwiole, 180; poison, 76; of Tomoudi, 143-

144, 147; of Vatako, 36-37, 39

Fofofo. See Exchange partnership

Food, 22, 53, 178-180, 183-193 passim; ambivalence regarding, 48, 87, 89, 108, 183, 201; in ideology, 262-263; origin of, 50, 60, 187-188; symbolic uses of, 47-48. *See also* Competitive food exchange; Famine; Ideology; Taro; Yam

Freud, S., 28, 85-87, 107-108. *See also* Father and son; Orality

Galuwata, 64-65, 71, 78-79, 229, 231-232, 244, 250, 264

Gardening, 42-44, 45, 89, 148-149, 225-226, 261-262; cycle, 54; for fame, 148-153, 177, 179, 189, 225, 230; lazy, 38-40; market, 45, 119, 121; sex inimical to, 87, 89, 226; taboos during *manumanua,* 55-56, 58. *See also* Competitive food exchange; Food; Taro; Yam

Gift: and concept of person, 22-23; debts, 240-241; *ketowai,* 125, 208, 209, 237, 240; *niune,* 45, 140-141; repudiation of, 87; and sorcery, 167. *See also* Competitive food exchange; Festival; *Manuamadumadu*

Goodenough Island. *See* Nidula

Government: court, 124, 245-246, 273; encouragement of Tobowa, 118-122 passim; first census of, 134; and Papua New Guinea self-government, 251-252, 259; suppression by of cargo cult, 123; village constables, 111, 117, 124-125. *See also* European; Misibibi

Hoarding. See *Lokona*

Honoyeta, 6, 7, 12, 14, 28, 60, chap. 3 passim, 100, 126, 133, 138, 140, 142, 190, 200, 208, 224, 234, 243-244, 245, 247, 260, 264, 267-268, 271-272, 275-276; cult of, 82, 250, 253-255; and Jesus Christ, 82, 249-251, 297n; and Malaveyoyo, 100, 106-109 passim; names of, 82; narrative versions of, 62-66 passim, 292n, 293n;

secret of, 82, 248-250; transformations of, 264-265

Hudiboyaboyaleta (Ulewoka), 56, 138, 189-190

Hunger: and greed, 59, 91; in myth, 138, 141-142; *tufo'a,* 12, 39, 54, 59, 91, 98, 182, 198, 201, 209, 210, 234. *See also* Famine

Hunting, 44, Didiala's, 148, 152; pig, 125; shotgun, 119

Ideology: of "feeding," 88-89; of Malaveyoyo legend, 100-103; of *manumanua,* 56-60, 185-186, 200-201; political, 5-6, 29-32, 45, 49, 53-55, 73, 195, 196-198, 200-202, 225-228, 261-264

Insult: of Didiala, 151; Honoyeta's, 64, 76, 85-86, 275; of Kikofolu, 236; Kimaola's, 239, 240, 244, 275; of Kiwiwiole, 179, 198; of Tobowa, 125, 128. *See also* Name

Iwaoyana, 52, 101-103, 261; customs and myths, 35-41; enemy of Lulauvile, 35, 97, 101-103, 237-239, 298n; version of Malaveyoyo legend, 97, 98. *See also* Kalauna

Iyahalina, 2-5, 7, 14, 19, 20, 25, 28, 50, 55, 93, 101, 102, 103, 115-116, 129-130, 133, 134, 135, 137, 138, 146, 156, 162, chap. 7 passim, 206, 207, 212, 214, 220, 225, 236, 237-238, 240-241, 243, 244, 245, 257-258, 259, 260-261, 262, 264, 269, 270, 273, 290n, 295n, 296n; autobiography and myths of, 177-202 passim, 260-261; contradictions of, 201-202; death of, 176, 202-205, 208, 257-258; as father, 175-176; as orator, 173; personality of, 171-174, 193-194; quest of for legitimacy, 195-202 passim

Jenness, D. & Ballantyne, A., 265-266, 292n, 293n, 296n, 298n

Jung, C. G., 18, 33, 85

Kafataudi, 62, 80, 81, 209, 221

Kaiwabu, 45, 70-71, 141, 209, 234-235, 240, 247, 263, 297n. *See also* Festival; Leadership; Stasis

Kalauna: biographical idioms, 27-28; concept of person, 20-24; description of, 1-2, 6, 42-44, 258-259; dispersal of, 256-258; dramatistic perspective on, 28-34; and economic development, 45, 119-121; ethos of, 32-34, 64-68, 72-73, 106-109, 132-133, 174, 196, 262-263; evacuation in wartime of, 118, 135; folk history, 51-53, 93-100 passim, 109, 188, 191, 195, 196, 293n, 296n; language, 7-8, 21-22, 172-173; oral literature, 11-12; political dramas, 28-34, 97-98, 130-131, 262; population size, 256, 297n, 298n; social structure, 44-46, 256-257, 261-262, 292n

Kawafolafola, 12, 228-235, 245, 296n. *See also* Oyatabu

Ketowai. See Gift

Kikifolu, 162-163, 178-179, 182-183, 185, 188, 229-231, 233, 295n. *See also* Oyatabu

Kimaola, 7, 20, 31, 50, 62, 102-103, 159, 161, 162, 164, 168-169, 177, 197, 203, chap. 8 passim, 255, 259, 260-261, 295n; ambitions of, 206-207, 210-211, 243, 246; challenges *abutu,* 237-243; as curer and sorcerer, 115, 127, 150, 213-217, 223, 244-246, 264, 272-276, 296n; marriages of, 223-224; mythical heroes of, 234-237, 243-244, 247, 264; persecution of, 244-246, 271-276; personality of, 211-213, 217, 243-244, 246-247, 264; retirement of, 246-247, 271; *unuwewe* of, 242-243, 263-264, 274-276; wartime experiences of, 218-219. *See also* Festival

Kiwiwiole, 56, 138, 178-187, 188, 189, 196, 198, 199, 201, 202, 236, 294n, 295n. *See also* Vineuma

Kula, 140, 292n

Kuyakwokula. *See* Manukubuku

Kwahala. See Sorcery

Kwahihi, 135, 156, 168, 176, 204, 257, 294n

Leadership, 2-3, 6-7, 28-29, 31, 125, 247, 256-258 passim; and despotism, 31, chap. 4 passim, chap. 5 passim, 196-197, 206, 210-211; dramas of, 28-32, 97-98, 198-199, 202-203, 263-264. See also *Kaiwabu;* Lulauvile; *Toitavealata*

Leenhardt, M., 13-16, 61, 289n

Legitimacy, 29, 31, 141, 142, 147, 150-151, 164, 178, 188, 195-202 passim, 236-237, 243, 263

Lévi-Strauss, C., 10, 47, 270, 289n

Lévy-Bruhl, L., 14, 17

Local government council, 44, 122, 254; Kalauna councillor, 207, 245, 246, 272

Lokona, 48, 87, 95, 139-142, 148, 153, 157, 180, 182-193 passim, 212, 234-235, 247, 261, 263

Lulauvile, 5, 6, 7, chap. 2 passim; *abutu* challenge, 238-239; "body" of, 271-276; dispersal of, 257-258, 263; *etonita* design, 266-267, 268, 269; leadership, 32, 53-55, 94, 97, 111, 129, 135, 151, 159-160, 176-177, 187, 192-194, 206-210 passim, 257-264 passim; *neineya* myths, 12, 62, 129, 187, 191; origin myths, 51-53, 188, 266; rank of, 45-46, 52-53, 54-55, 129, 187, 196, 225, 237, 262-263, 297n; structure of, 49-51; subclans, 141, 164, 257

Madawa'a, 75, 79, 229, 232, 252

Magic: coconut, 56, 100, 143-146, 163, 199; and fame, 24; garden, 48-49, 53, 54, 179; Honoyeta's, 80, 82; or impersonation, 17; incantations, 12-13, 57-58, 154-155, 179, 180, 190, 192, 194, 205, 292n; inheritance of, 94, 129-130, 135, 139, 141, 144-145, 146, 176, 181, 182, 183, 187, 205, 207, 208, 248; and *neineya,* 12, 62; of pig platform, 168-169, 217; rain, 157, 161-163, 165, 229, 233, 275; *sisikwana,* 39, 56-57, 179-180, 181, 198, 201, 214, 247; sun, 65, 80, 140, 153-159, 160, 210, 225, 268, 274-275; taro, 189, 192, 202, 227; Trobriand,

17; wind, 95, 128, 146, 181-182; war, 21, 105-106; yam, 89, 162-166, 224-235 passim; *yaleyale,* 35-39 passim; 119, 181, 189, 192. See also *Bakibaki;* Hunger; *Manumanua;* Sorcery

Malaveyoyo, 6, 31, 52, chap. 4 passim, 110, 111, 138, 176, 201, 259, 267, 269, 273; death of, 99-100, 107, 108; legacy of, 93-94, 100-103, 106-109, 196-197, 222, 242, 260, 273; legend of, 94-97, 98-100

Malinowski, B., 13, 15-16, 84, 194, 298n

Manuamadumadu, 74, 140; Didiala's, 149, 150; Honoyeta's, 74-75; Manukubuku's, 140-141; Tobowa's, 126

Manubutu, 51, 88, 266

Manukubuku, 138-139, 234, 264, 265

Manumanua, 3, 6, 12, 53, 100, 111, 141-142, 181, 183-202 passim, 232, 262, 266-267, 298n; ceremony of, 54-59; Didiala's, 135, 137-138, 146; Malaveyoyo's, 97-97; Tobowa's, 116, 129-130, 146, 294n. See also *Bakibaki;* Famine; Gardening; Ideology; *Lokona;* Myth; Stasis; *Toitavealata;* Wandering

Marriage, 44, 48, 49, 220-224 passim; Didiala's, 135; exchange, 158; Honoyeta's, 62-63, 66-72, 85-86; Iyahalina's, 203, 220, 245; Kimaola's, 223-224; Kimaola's sisters', 220-223, 245, 246; payments, 152, 158; Tobowa's, 113, 125, 128; Vatako's, 36-37, 39-40

Massim, 42, 140, 252, 292n, 298n

Matabawe, 83, 87-88, 252, 253, 264, 265, 292n, 299n

Matabikwa. *See* Matabawe

Misibibi, 109, 134, 174, 293n

Mount Madawa'a. *See* Madawa'a

Mourning, 128, 176, 208, 219. *See also* Burial; Death

Muyuwa, 42, 83, 145, 178-179, 183, 185, 252, 253. *See also* Massim; Trobriand Islands

Myth, chap. 1 passim; Auyoke, 146, 294n; cycle, 264-265, 270; *ifufu,* 11, 12, 18, 29, 100; Kelukeketa, 88; lived, 13, 14-20 passim, 32-34, 34-41

passim, 61, 250, 253, 259-261, 264, 265, 267-268, 270, 275-276; narration of, 10-12, 13, 34-39, 62-66 passim, 94-97, 99-100, 138-139, 143-145, 178-182, 188-190, 192-194 passim, 248-249, 277-279, 280-288; *neineya,* 11-12, 34-35, 100, 162; Oedipal, 28, 85-87, 88, 107, 275; origin of sun and moon, 68; ownership of, 4, 12, 18-20, 34, 35-41, 132-133, 138-139, 146-147, 189, 201-202, 228, 265, 289n, 290n; sociology of knowledge of, 265; *Totem and Taboo,* 86; Trobriand, 13. *See also* Adiyaleyale; Biography; Birds; Cargo cult; Honoyeta; Hudiboyaboyaleta; Kawafolafola; Kikifolu; Kiwiwiole; Lulauvile; Manubutu; *Manumanua;* Manukubuku; Matabawe; Oyatabu; Tomoudi; Vatako; Vineuma

Name: fame, 21, 24, 29, 88-89, 236-237, 245; of Honoyeta, 82; of Kikifolu, 230, 236; nicknames, 21, 211. *See also* Insult

Nibai. See Enemy

Nibita. *See* Kalauna

Nidula, 42, 46; cosmology, 265-267; design motif, 265-267, 297n; Honoyeta's wanderings in, 74-75; mythology, 39, 65, 83, 84, 88, 90, 264-265, 289n, 291-292n, 298n, 299n; name of, 8, 92; as name of Goodenough, 252

Orality, 47-48, 85, 172, 198, 212, 260; denial of, 87; of Kimaola, 244; in kinship and politics, 88-91; oral aggression, 107-108, 244, 264; of Tobowa, 112-113

Oyatabu, 162-165 passim, 212, 228-236 passim, 243, 295n. *See also* Kawafolafola; Kikifolu

Portent, 12, 79, 139, 141, 164, 168, 180, 181-182, 184, 230, 231, 233, 244

Port Moresby, 150, 217, 218, 219, 221, 253

Prosperity. See *Manumanua*

Resentment. See *Unuwewe*

Sacrificial: acts, 253, 275; heroes, 84, 249-250
Samarai, 119, 123, 156, 174
Sartre, J-P., 20, 298n
Schwimmer, E., 11, 17
Serpent: Honoyeta as snake-man, 63, 67, 81-82, 85-87, 264-268; in myth, 88, 181, 184, 186, 190, 299n; Ouroborus figure, 265, 267, 269; tattoo, 114; of Unuwewe hamlet, 170. *See also* Matabawe
Sexuality, 86-87, 89, 223-224, 275
Siboboya, 50, 207, 210, 216, 245, 259
Sickness, 115, 116; and curing, 213-216; Didiala's, 167; Iyahalina's, 203; Kimaola's, 127; Tobowa's, 126-129
Sitting circle, 44; of Galuwata, 79; Kimaola's, 164; Malaveyoyo's, 97, 104; of Mataita, 126; sorcery of, 98, 201, 258; of Wifala in Bwaidoka, 106; of Yabiliva, 64, 75-76, 292n
Sitting still. *See* Stasis
Sorcery, 18, 29, 31, 33, 34, 39, 53, 80, 103, 135, 155, 156-157, 160, 161-163, 166-169, 197, 198, 203-204, 210, 211, 220, 222, 268, 269; battle of Malaveyoyo, 95, 97-98; battle of Tobowa, 127, 129; of dispersal and wandering, 98, 201, 258; fear of, 46, 48, 127, 196, 215; Kimaola's, 127, 150, 213-217, 223, 244-246, 264, 272-276, 296n; of *kwahala*, 112, 127, 273, 293n, 296n; of prevented birth, 214-215, 272, 273, 275; Tobowa's, 112, 113, 115-116, 125, 127, 293n; of weather, 53, 91, 95, 98, 128, 181, 198. *See also* Hunger; Magic; Yam
Spirits: ancestor, 191-192, 226-227, 252-253; *balauma*, 215-217, 234; of the dead, 165, 166, 204; yam, 226-227
Stasis, 4, 51, 55-59, 138, 183-186, 191-193, 200-202, 205, 257, 264, 266. See also *Bakibaki; Manumanua;* Wandering
Stone: Honoyeta's, 82, 248, 250; Hudi-

boyaboyaleta's, 190; licking of, 58, 60, 178-179, 185, 188; sorcerer's, 122, 154, 273; symbolism of, 139-140, 180, 184-186, 192, 263. See also *Bakibaki;* Sitting circle
Sun: design motif, 265-266, 267; god (Honoyeta), 62, 67-68, 77-78, 85-87, 90, 109, 244, 248-249, 264, 299n; and yam planting, 155, 224. *See also* Magic
Synchronicity, 33, 291n

Taboos: Honoyeta's, 250; during *manumanua*, 55-56, 58, 192; mourning, 208; Oyatabu's, 235; widow's, 128, 204; widower's, 167; on yam planting, 224, 226, 228
Tabwaika, 114, 117, 118, 121, 129-130, 137, 157, 176, 189, 223, 225, 272, 294n
Taro, 42, 51, 54, 56, 143, 209, 234, 240, 295n. *See also* Magic
Tobowa, 7, 31, 109, chap. 5 passim, 135, 138, 146, 189, 205, 211, 224, 259, 260, 264, 269; as big-man, 125-126; death of, 110-111, 127-129, 130; as entrepreneur, 118-122; oral excesses of, 112-113, 260; as prophet, 122-123; as sorcerer, 112, 115-116, 124, 125, 127; as village constable, 117-125; violence of, 114-115; in wartime, 118; widow's disrespect, 128-129
Toitavealata, 45, 53-59, 91, 111, 115, 118, 135, 137, 176, 187, 191-193, 197, 199, 202, 212, 257-258, 260-261, 264, 274. See also *Manumanua*
Tomoadikuyau, 36, 38-39, 237-239
Tomoudi, 56, 100, 138, 140, 143-147, 149, 153, 157, 163, 165-166, 296n
Towava. See Portent
Trade store, 251, 255, 258; Tobowa's, 119, 120
Trobriand Islands, 13, 17, 92, 292n. *See also* Muyuwa
Turner, V., 28-29, 30

Ulefifiku. *See* Tomoudi

Unuwewe, 47, 80, 85, 90-91, 142, 170, 200, 209, 236, 249-250, 257, 263, 267-268, 269, 297n; defined, 72-74; Didiala's, 138, 147, 151, 156-157, 160-161, 166, 268; Ewahaluna's, 255; Honoyeta's, 70-74, 107, 249, 272, 275-276; Hudiboyaboyaleta's, 190; Iyahalina's, 193, 198-199; Kawafolafola's, 233, 296n; Kimaola's, 242-243, 263-264, 274-276; Kiwiwiole's, 186, 198; Malaveyoyo's, 98, 99, 107, 108; Matabawe's, 83; Ulefifiku's, 147; Vatako's, 37-40; Vineuma's, 184; Wameya's, 232; of yams, 226-227

Vatako, 35-40, 295n

Vengeance, 29, 48, 249, 250; of Didiala, 155, 157, 268; of Iyahalina's son, 245-246, 269; of Kimaola, 210, 274, 276; of Malaveyoyo's era, 99-100, 103, 105, 107, 108; of Tobowa's, 129, 269. *See also* Victimage

Veumaiyiyi, 37, 47, 73, 126, 241

Victimage, 29-33 passim, 91, 98, 157, 249-250, 263, 264, 267, 268, 269; Burke on, 291n; Didiala's, 160-166 passim, 268; Iyahalina's, 202; Kimaola's, 244-246, 271-276 passim. See also *Unuwewe;* Vengeance

Vineuma, 180-186, 190, 199. *See also* Kiwiwiole

Vivian, R. A. *See* Misibibi

Wage labor, 34, 45, 119, 134, 135, 152-153, 174, 217

Wagner, R., 10-11, 84

Wailolo, 115, 117, 157, 162-163, 216, 240-242

Wandering: eras of, 51-52, 137, 257-258, 263, 266; of Honoyeta, 74-75; theme in myth and ritual, 57-58, 59, 95, 98, 107, 183, 184-186, 191-193, 200-201

Warfare, 44, 99-100, 104-106

Wealth, 21-24 passim; food and pig, 126, 187, 240-241, 262; shell valuables, 99, 145, 181. *See also* European

Wooden bowl, 96-97, 101, 189, 191, 267, 269. See also *Manumanua*

World War II, 115, 117-118, 135, 156, 174, 218-219, 259

Yabiliva, 64-65, 75-76, 81-82, 85, 250, 254-255, 260, 296n

Yaleyale. See Magic

Yam, 42, 45, 54, 56, 95, 96, 148, 149, 156, 242, 247, 273; gardening cycle, 119, 155, 224-228, 229; inheritance of seeds, 88-89; male pride in, 88-89, 108; origin of, 228-233 passim. See also *Lokona;* Magic; Oyatabu; Spirits

Yauyaba, 51, 62, 93, 162, 228, 230, 266

Designer:	UC Press Staff
Compositor:	Janet Sheila Brown
Printer:	Braun-Brumfield
Binder:	Braun-Brumfield
Text:	11/13 Baskerville, Compuwriter II
Display:	Cooper Black